DATA ENTRY:

CONCEPTS AND EXERCISES

1807 1982
175 YEARS OF JW PUBLISHING

IVA HELEN LEE
MCLENNAN COMMUNITY COLLEGE

DATA ENTRY:

CONCEPTS AND EXERCISES

JOHN WILEY & SONS   NEW YORK   •   CHICHESTER   •   BRISBANE   •   TORONTO   •   SINGAPORE

Text Design: Judith Fletcher Getman
Cover: Yasuo Kubota

**TO MY PARENTS
WHO MADE MY EDUCATION
POSSIBLE**

Copyright © 1982, by John Wiley & Sons, Inc.

All rights reserved. Published simultaneously in Canada.

Reproduction or translation of any part of this work beyond that permitted by Sections 107 and 108 of the 1976 United States Copyright Act without the permission of the copyright owner is unlawful. Requests for permission or further information should be addressed to the Permissions Department, John Wiley & Sons.

Library of Congress Cataloging in Publication Data:

Lee, Iva Helen.
Data entry concepts and exercises.
Includes index.
1. Electronic data processing—Data entry.
I. Title.
QA76.9.D337L43 001.64'2 81-11403
ISBN 0-471-08605-3 AACR2

Printed in United States of America

10

PREFACE

During the past decade there has been a growing recognition by industry of the importance of data entry. Increasingly sophisticated data entry equipment and software has been introduced. Remote data entry is now possible as a result of the proliferation of terminals.

Textbooks devoted completely to keypunches are outmoded. This textbook presents modern data entry concepts and laboratory exercises that can be used on any equipment. Study guide questions in the text are generalized for any equipment type. The most commonly used kinds of industrial equipment are described as examples. However, if different equipment exists in the institution, this textbook can be used along with manufacturer manuals.

This book is written in modular form so that only those units appropriate to the local community can be covered. However, it is recommended that Parts 1, 3, and 4 be assigned as a common core. The nine units of the book can be briefly summarized as follows:

Unit 1, "Computers and Computer Centers," provides a simple explanation of what a computer is and how computer centers are usually organized.

Unit 2, "Data Entry Operations," discusses the importance of data entry, the abilities needed to be a successful data entry operator, the typical duties of the data entry operator, the job prospects, job environment, and possible career paths.

Unit 3, "History of Data Entry," discusses the development of punched card codes, data entry equipment, and the elements of record design.

Unit 4, "Buffered Keypunches," describes the most common equipment still found in industry. (Unbuffered keypunches are covered in Appendix H.)

Unit 5, "Key-to-Diskette Devices," covers equipment using the floppy disk as a recording medium.

Unit 6, "Key-to-Disk Devices," describes the recent equipment developments using the hard disk, with data later being transferred to tape or via communications lines. This equipment has software providing sophisticated data validation techniques and specification of formats and checks peculiar to that company. Key-to-tape only is not discussed, except in a historical sense, since its use is disappearing.

Unit 7, "Terminals," describes and examines the relation of terminals to distributed/decentralized data entry.

Unit 8, "Word Processing and Data Entry" discusses these two merging technologies.

Unit 9, "The Future," examines the problems of data control, new equipment developments, data security and privacy, the need for an operator code of ethics, the upgrading of the data entry profession, and reviews career development paths and the need for continuing education.

Part 4, "Laboratory Exercises," consists of keying exercises that can be used on whatever institutional equipment is available. Many of these exercises contain source documents with handwritten data to be keyed. These typify what the student will find in industry.

The Appendices contain additional helpful information, including the standard abbreviations recommended by the U.S. Postal Service, a modulus 10 and 11 explanation, a unit on the IBM 029 for those institutions still using this equipment, the 96-column-card code, advice for students on employment preparation, and operations job descriptions.

The Instructor's Guide provides the following aids for teaching:

1. Performance objectives for each unit.
2. Answers to study guide questions in the text.
3. Unit tests that can be photocopied and answers.
4. Suggested outside reading material on data entry.

5. Suggested library and departmental reading material for both instructors and students.
6. Suggested clubs.
7. Information on data entry tests and instructional material that can be purchased from outside sources.
8. A unit on the IBM 5280 Distributed Data System that may be substituted for one of the three systems discussed in Unit 6 "Key-to-Disk."
9. A grading program written in COBOL, which can be used to grade the keying exercises.
10. Program formats and answers for the keying exercises.

Iva Helen Lee

ACKNOWLEDGMENTS

I am grateful to many people for their help, time, and suggestions.

I particularly thank Marjorie Leeson of Delta College, Michigan who encouraged me to write and did a wonderful job of reviewing the first draft.

My thanks go also to reviewers Charles E. Paddock of Houston's North Harris County College; Victor P. Maiorana of Dear Park, New York; Dominick Orefice, County College of Morris, Randolph, New Jersey; Donna Kimble, James Ramsey Vocational Technical Center, Martinsburg, West Virginia; Janet C. Dowdy of DRILCO, Houston, Texas, and Nancy Britton, part-time instructor at McLennan Community College (MCC), Waco, Texas.

A special thanks goes to the following persons in industry for all their kindness and time: Larry Zeske and John Caruth of SPERRY-UNIVAC in Dallas, Texas; Jim Nordstrom and Dave Mount of NIXDORF in Dallas, Texas; Tommylu Groth of FOUR-PHASE in Dallas, Texas; A.W. White, Mike Glaspie, and Gene Autry of IBM; John Culverhouse and Anita Blake of the State Comptroller's Office, Austin, Texas; Linda Roberts of Commercial Computer Services, Waco, Texas; and to my brother, Rodney Lee, and others of Naman, Howell, Smith, Lee and Muldrow, Waco, Texas.

Linda Compton and Jo Holley helped convert my rough draft into a fine manuscript. Their work was done on a MICOM 2001 word processing system.

Assistance on exercises was provided by my niece, Rebecca Lee and McLennan Community College students, Jean Phillips and Debra Sanford, with keying and verifying being done by Nancy Britton and Beverly Wright of MCC and Paddy Scardina of El Centro College, Dallas, TX.

Programming work was done by Don Hurst of MCC.

Photography work was done by Alecia Bateman of Waco and Tommy Turner and Eric Gay of MCC.

Editorial advice for the Instructor's Guide was given by Jeannette McGinnes of MCC.

Finally, I thank my editor Leonard Kruk and his fine editors for their advice, help, and patience.

Many individuals at McLennan Community College gave a great deal of encouragement during this project. The administration, under the leadership of Dr. Wilbur Ball, has created an atmosphere that encourages creativity, participation in professional organizations, dedication to teaching excellence, and efforts to remain current in one's field of instruction.

It is my hope that this book will assist McLennan Community College and other institutions in modernizing their data entry courses.

I. H. L.

Copyright 1982, John Wiley & Sons, Inc.

CONTENTS

PART 1 INTRODUCTION TO DATA ENTRY 1

    UNIT 1 Computers and Computer Centers 3
                What Is Data Processing? 4
                What Is a Computer? 4
                How Is the Computer Center Organized? 6
                Study Guide 7

    UNIT 2 Data Entry Operations 9
                Duties of the Data Entry Operator 10
                Job Prospects and Career Paths 10
                Abilities Needed 11
                Work Environment 11
                Study Guide 12

    UNIT 3 History of Data Entry 15
                Section A The Hollerith Punched Card 16
                Section B The 96-Column Punched Card 19
                Section C Data Entry Equipment 22
                Section D Record Design 25
                            Study Guide 29

PART 2 DATA ENTRY EQUIPMENT 35

    UNIT 4 Buffered Keypunches 37
                Section A Introduction 38
                Section B The IBM 129 Data Recorder (Model 3—Prints, Punches, and Verifies) 40
                Section C The UNIVAC 1710 VIP 51
                Section D Other Equipment 60
                    The UNIVAC 1810 VIP 60
                    The IBM 5496 Data Recorder 61
                    The TAB 501 Punch/Verifier 63
                            Study Guide 64

    UNIT 5 Key-to-Diskette Devices 69
                Section A The Diskette 70
                Section B Key-to-Diskette Device Characteristics 73
                Section C The IBM 3740 Series and the IBM 3742 75
                Section D The TAB 700 Series 102
                Section E Other Diskette Devices 123
                            Study Guide 125

    UNIT 6 Key-to-Disk Devices 133
                Section A Introduction 134
                Section B Key-to-Disk Hardware and Procedures 137
                    The Magnetic Tape 137

		The Magnetic Disk	140
		The Central Processing Unit	142
		The Communications Controller	142
		Programming	142
		Passwords	143
		Verifying	143
		The Keyboard	143
		The Display or Video Screen	150
		The Installation Supervisor	153
		Section C The UNIVAC 1900/10	153
		Section D The FOUR PHASE IV System	169
		Section E The NIXDORF 80 Series	183
		Section F Additional Types of Equipment	192
		Study Guide	194
	UNIT 7	Terminals	199
		Section A Introduction	200
		Section B The IBM 3270 Information Display System	202
		Section C Other Terminal Devices	212
		Study Guide	212

PART 3 FUTURE APPLICATIONS 219

	UNIT 8	Word Processing and Data Entry	221
		Introduction	222
		Recent Equipment Developments	224
		Software	224
		Comparison of Data Entry and Word Processing	226
		Study Guide	227
	UNIT 9	The Future	229
		Introduction	230
		New Data Entry Methods	231
		Verification	232
		Security and Control	232
		Privacy	233
		Conclusion	234
		Study Guide	234

PART 4 LABORATORY EXERCISES 237

	Section A Numeric Keying Exercises	238
	Section B Alphabetic Keying Exercises	241
	Section C Keying Exercises Under Program Control	244

APPENDIX A	Glossary of Data Entry Terms	313
APPENDIX B	Standard Abbreviations	319
APPENDIX C	The Hexadecimal and Octal Number Systems	323
APPENDIX D	Methods of Data Validation	327
APPENDIX E	The 96-Column Card Code	329
APPENDIX F	Employment Preparation	331
APPENDIX G	Job Descriptions	335
APPENDIX H	The IBM 029 Unbuffered Keypunch	337
INDEX		351

PART 1

Introduction to Data Entry

AFTER READING THIS UNIT YOU WILL KNOW:

What data processing is.
What a computer is and its main parts.
The functions of the main parts
of the computer.
How you and the computer are alike.
How business and scientific
data processing differ.
The most common computer center
job positions.

What the following terms mean:

Acronym	I/O
CPU	Input
Data entry	Output
Data processing	Secondary
Encode	Storage device

UNIT 1

COMPUTERS AND COMPUTER CENTERS

WHAT IS DATA PROCESSING?

Modern data processing is the processing of facts, using the computer and other associated equipment, to achieve a desired result.

There are two main types of data processing: business and scientific. Business data processing usually produces statements or reports for activities such as payroll, inventory control, accounting, and sales. These activities usually involve few computations and many pages of printed material. In contrast, scientific data processing deals with mathematical, engineering, scientific, and research material. These activities usually involve many computations but very little printed material.

You will probably be working in the business data processing area. Therefore, this textbook and its exercises will deal with business data processing.

WHAT IS A COMPUTER?

A computer is a piece of machinery that can process data by performing arithmetic operations and making logical decisions. When we speak of *data*, we mean a collection of characters that have some meaning such as your name, your social security number, your age, or your address.

A computer is really quite similar to you. For example, suppose someone gave you the following problem:

Given the numbers A, B, and C. If A × B is greater than 20, add C to the product. What is the answer if A = 4, B = 6, and C = 10? Write the answer in the space to the right. _____

You reason 4 × 6 = 24; 24 is greater than 20. Therefore the answer is 24 + 10 or 34. You write 34 in the blank.

Now let's compare you to the computer. First you received the instructions for the problem by reading them. Therefore your *input* device was your eyes. Information is received through input devices. Computers also have input devices. In the old days these input devices were usually card readers.

You also received some data (numbers) by reading them. Therefore your input device read *two* kinds of things: instructions and data. Where did all these instructions and data go? Into your brain, of course, which has a memory! Computers also have a brain or storage device called a memory. This is sometimes referred to as *main storage*. It holds instructions and data and is in a part of the computer called the *central processing unit*. The acronym for central processing unit is *CPU*. An acronym is a word that is usually formed by the first letters of several words. The acronym for the United States of America is USA.

Returning to our number problem, suppose we have the same set of instructions but different data. A = 483, B = 6842, and C = 5421. Now quickly, what is the answer? _____ Why does it take so much longer for you to write the answer now? Perhaps you have multiplication and addition tables, stored in your head only for smaller numbers. Therefore you must do written computations for larger numbers. A computer does not have a stored table of arithmetic facts. It multiplies 4 by 6 by adding 6 + 6 + 6 + 6 very quickly with its arithmetic unit.

Using the first set of data you made a logical decision that 24 was greater than 20. A computer also has a *logical unit* that can make simple comparisons. So the CPU shown in Figure 1.1 contains an arithmetic unit, logical unit, and a memory.[1] It also has a unit that controls the order in which operations are performed.

Returning to our problem again, how did you give the answer? By writing the answer in the blank as instructed. Your handwriting was your *output*

---

[1] In some books the memory is shown outside the CPU.

PART 1 INTRODUCTION TO DATA ENTRY

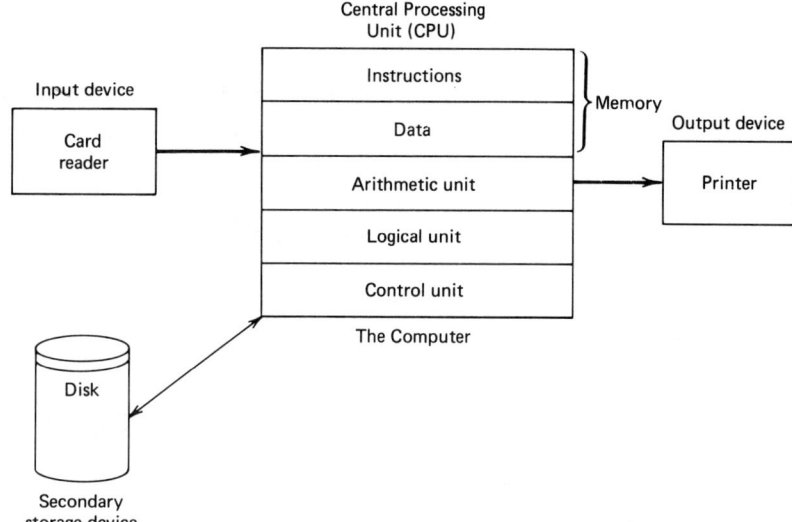

FIGURE 1.1
A comparison of the human being and the computer.

device. Information is given out through output devices. A computer also has output devices; the most common one is a printer.

Sometimes large amounts of information are calculated and need to be saved. When you go to sleep, you don't forget your name, your address, or your phone number. But when some computers are turned off, all the information that they have read or calculated is erased or lost. Therefore secondary storage devices exist to store large amounts of data for later use. You will see some examples, such as disk and tape drives, in computer centers.

Devices that can read data or have data written on them are called *input/output* devices. The acronym for this is I/O.

Summary

Data processing is the processing of facts, using computer equipment, to achieve a desired result such as a report. There are two kinds of data processing: business and scientific.

Computers are similar to humans. Each computer has an input device, a central processing unit, an output device, and secondary storage devices which can act as input or output devices.

1. An *input device* reads or transfers data into a computer.
2. An *output device* writes or records data from a computer on some outside material or media (such as paper).
3. The *central processing unit* has a memory (main storage), an arithmetic unit, a logical unit, and a control unit.
4. *Secondary storage devices* are used to keep or store large amounts of data. They can act as input or output devices. The devices in the input-processing-output cycle are shown in Figure 1.2.

HOW IS THE COMPUTER CENTER ORGANIZED?

You will probably be working in a computer center and will need to know how it is organized. The organization of a computer center depends upon its size. In very large centers there may be a systems manager, a programming manager, and an operations manager. But the most common organization is shown in Figure 1.3.

The duties of the areas shown are:

1. The *manager* directs and controls all activities in the center.
2. The *systems analyst* plans new projects under the direction of the manager, and the analyst works closely with the user. Users are those persons requesting that a project be done on the computer.
3. The *programmer* writes instructions to the computer in a form that the computer understands. Different languages are used to write these instructions depending on the type of problem and the type of computer. Just as we have English, German, Spanish, and many other languages

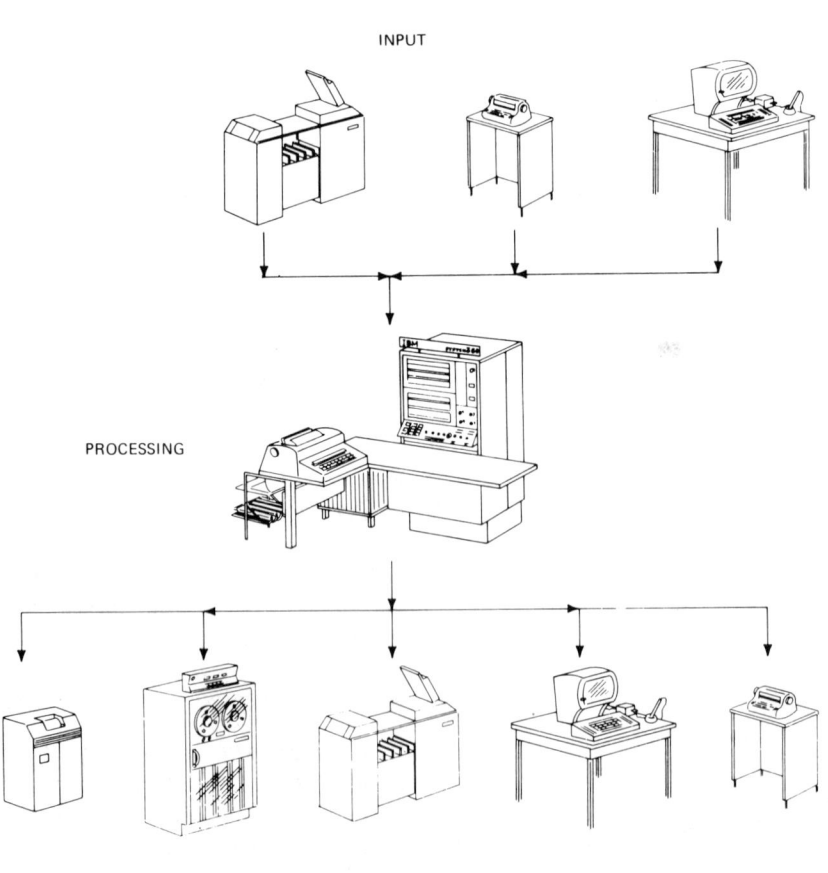

FIGURE 1.2
All data processing systems have input, processing, and output (Courtesy of IBM Corporation).

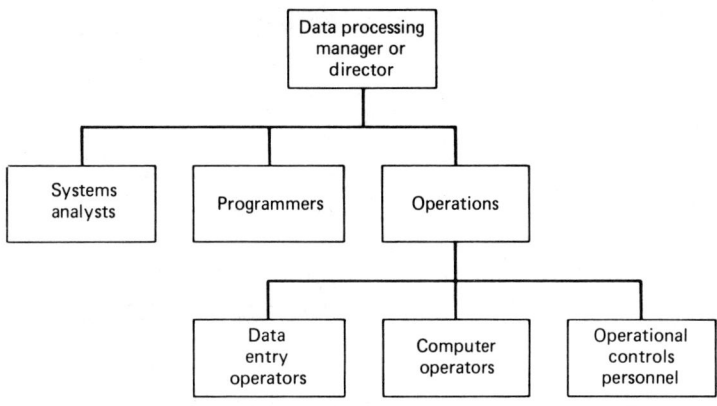

FIGURE 1.3
Computer center organization.

in the world, computers use different languages such as COBOL, RPG, FORTRAN, PL/1, and BASIC.

4. *Computer operators* operate or run the computer.
5. *Operational controls personnel* consist of data controllers, librarians, and schedulers. Data controllers see that all data entering a computer center is processed completely, accurately, and in a timely manner. Librarians keep records and keep track of materials used. Schedulers plan the times that certain jobs will be run on the computer.
6. *Data entry personnel* operate *data entry* devices that convert human readable data into a form that the computer can understand. This is called *encoding* data. *Decoding* is changing codes back into human readable form.

This textbook will be concerned mainly with *data entry* operations; although, more will be said in later chapters about the other computer center positions that might affect your work.

STUDY GUIDE

Answer these questions in your book. If asked to do so, tear out the pages and hand them in to your instructor.

1. Define:
   a. Data _a collection of characters that have some meaning such as name, SS# age, address_
   b. Data processing _processing of facts using computer equipment to achieve a result as a report_
   c. Input device _transfer data in computer_
   d. Output device _records the data on some outside media ex. paper_
   e. Acronym _a word that is usually formed by the 1st letter of sev. words. So in USA_
   f. Secondary storage device _store a very large amt of data_

UNIT 1 COMPUTERS AND COMPUTER CENTERS

g. Encode _____

h. Decode _____

i. Main storage _____

j. User office _____

2. State the meaning of:

   a. CPU _____

   b. I/O _____

3. State the two types of data processing.

   (1) _____

   (2) _____

4. List the four parts of the CPU.

   (1) _____

   (2) _____

   (3) _____

   (4) _____

5. Matching: Choose the answer that best defines the items at the left.

   You   **The Computer**
   ____ (1) Your brain   a. Input device
   ____ (2) Multiplication tables   b. Arithmetic unit
   ____ (3) Ears receiving instructions   c. Memory
   ____ (4) Your sense of smell   d. Output device
   ____ (5) Your eyes—reading   e. Logical unit
   ____ (6) Your sense of touch
   ____ (7) Writing answers
   ____ (8) Comparing the size of two numbers
   ____ (9) Your voice giving answers

6. Answer true or false by circling the correct answer.

   T or F (1) Business data processing often deals with payroll.

   T or F (2) Business data processing commonly involves calculating the path of a rocket to Mars.

   T or F (3) Data is often stored outside the computer's CPU.

   T or F (4) An example of a piece of data would be your phone number.

   T or F (5) A data entry operator writes programs or instructions for the computer.

   T or F (6) An operations control person might schedule when computer runs are to be made.

   T or F (7) Computers use different languages.

UNIT 2
DATA ENTRY OPERATIONS

AFTER READING THIS UNIT YOU WILL KNOW:

What a data entry device is.
The duties of the data entry operator.
The qualities needed to be a successful data entry operator.
Operations positions available and the main duty of each position.
A possible career path in data entry operations.

What the following terms mean:

Batch processing
Centralized data entry
Data entry device
Data validation
Distributed/De-centralized data entry
GIGO
On-line; off-line
Peripheral equipment
Record format
Recording media
Source document
Verify

DUTIES OF THE DATA ENTRY OPERATOR

A *data entry device* converts (or encodes) source data from human readable form into a code that can be understood by the computer.

The main duty of a data entry operator is to operate data entry equipment. This equipment changes source data into a coded machine readable form that may exist on punched cards, diskettes, magnetic tape, magnetic disk or drum, and, more rarely now, paper tape. These materials on which data is recorded (or written) are called *recording media.* They will be discussed in later chapters.

Data entry operators often have other duties such as:

1. *Verifying* (or checking) the accuracy of data that have already been converted into a code.
2. Determining that the data entry machine is in proper working order and correcting minor problems.
3. Operating *peripheral equipment* related to, but not necessarily directly connected to, the data entry device. Examples of peripheral equipment are printers, card readers, disk drives, and tape drives.
4. Reviewing, organizing, and identifying inaccurate or incomplete *source documents*. Source documents consist of unprocessed data in handwritten or typed form.
5. Performing general clerical duties.
6. Preparing *record formats.* These are plans for recording data on the media used and are usually done on special forms.
7. Following all installation procedures or rules regarding the privacy and security of data.

The data entry operator has one of the most important and responsible positions in a computer center. This has not always been understood in industry. With the increased use of the computer and the development of many new data entry devices, the importance of the data entry personnel is being increasingly recognized.

We have a saying in the computer field:

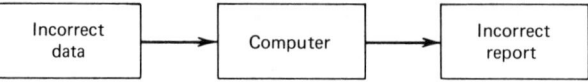

FIGURE 2.1
GIGO, GARBAGE IN, GARBAGE OUT!

A computer can be compared to a dumb beast that does exactly what it is told. Assume that the computer has been told to read a name on a card and print it.

If you record MICKY incorrectly as DICKY, and it is used as input to the computer, DICKY will be printed. Thus the expression *GIGO:* Garbage in, garbage out.

There are three main causes of incorrect output by the computer.

1. Incorrect input data (due to incorrect source data or incorrect data entry).
2. Incorrect instructions to the computer.
3. Machine malfunction (the computer is not operating properly).

Incorrect output usually occurs because incorrect data has been entered into the computer. Therefore, your main duty as a data entry operator is a *most* important one.

JOB PROSPECTS AND CAREER PATHS

If you acquire the necessary skills in this course, you should be able to obtain a data entry operator position. As a trainee you may be required to work on the night shift; however, if your work is satisfactory and you prefer the day shift you will probably be able to arrange a transfer at a later date.

Recent studies made by the Data Entry Management Association (DEMA)[1] show that the demand for data entry operators is expected to grow faster than the average for all occupations through 1985. Job descriptions for data entry and related operational positions can be found in the Appendix G of this text.

In the past, data entry operations jobs have been rather restrictive with very little opportunity for advancement possible above the data entry supervisor position. This is no longer true. Today a data entry person may write computer programs for data entry devices or progress into management positions. Doing the report at the end of this chapter after studying current job position and salary articles will help you determine a possible career path.

ABILITIES NEEDED

To be a successful operator you need to be able:[2]

1. To perform under the pressure of critical deadlines.
2. To follow written and oral instructions.
3. To enjoy activities that involve routine, concrete, organized procedures.
4. To respond quickly and accurately.
5. To be absent or late very little, to be loyal and willing to do more than just carry your load, and to seek additional tasks.
6. To participate in team work.
7. To give attention to detail.

WORK ENVIRONMENT

There are currently two types of data entry conditions that you may be working under: *centralized* and *decentralized* (distributed) data entry.

Centralized data entry takes place at one central location, usually near the computer. The advantages of such organization are:

1. Common standards for data entry and *data validation* procedures are easier to control.
2. Fewer management and support personnel are needed.
3. Equipment and staff are used to maximum capacity.
4. Salaries are generally better; thus better personnel can be obtained.
5. The quality of work is easier to control.

Centralized data entry seems to be more prevalent and remains batch oriented. *Processing in batches* means collecting data for different jobs over a period of time and entering it all at one time.

Distributed or *decentralized data entry* takes place at a site remote from the computer, and its use is increasing. It may be done:

1. *On-line* (connected directly to the computer) using remote terminals.
2. *Off-line* (not connected to the main computer) using keypunches, or key-to-diskette or key-to-disk systems. These systems are discussed in later chapters.

Advantages of decentralized data entry are:

1. Data validation (checking the correctness of the data entered) is done by the user's personnel. Since they know the office data better, they are more likely to catch errors.

---

[1] "Data Entry Management Association 1979 Member Equipment Survey," *DEMA Newsletter,* Vol. 29, No. 5 (May 1979).

[2] Mildred F. Johnson, *Job Specifications for the Computer Production Operations and Skill-Related Data Processing Job Cluster,* Ann Arbor, MI: University Microfilm International, 1976.

2. Certain types of off-line data entry equipment are very cheap. Therefore, each remote site can have this equipment.

In the key-to-disk chapter, the advantages of the use of key-to-disk or off-line equipment and the associated minicomputers is discussed. The typical data entry devices covered are:

1. Unbuffered keypunches (Appendix H).
2. Buffered keypunches or data recorders.
3. Key-to-diskette.
4. Key-to-disk.
5. Terminals.
6. Special devices not involving actual keying, such as voice recognition, optical readers, light pens and wands.

STUDY GUIDE

Report: Locate a recent salary survey in the magazines *Datamation* or *Infosystems.* Make a written or oral report (as instructed by your teacher) as follows:

a. Give information on salaries for data entry operators for all classifications including supervisors.

b. Examine job descriptions from the lowest paid job up through computer operations. If there are job descriptions that do not appear in Appendix H of this book, give information on these job descriptions.

c. Compare these salaries and job descriptions, and draw a chart showing a possible career path.

Questions: Answer these questions in your book. If asked to do so, tear out the pages and hand them in to your instructor.

1. Define:

   a. Data entry device _____

   b. Encode _____

   c. Verify _____

   d. Validate _____

   e. Source document _____

   f. Recording media (medium) _____

   g. Peripheral equipment _____

h. Record format _____
_____

i. Centralized data entry _____
_____

j. Decentralized/distributed data entry _____
_____

k. On-line _____
_____

l. Off-line _____
_____

m. GIGO _____
_____

2. State the significance of GIGO to data entry and computer output.
_____
_____

3. List at least five abilities needed by the successful data entry operator.
   (1) _____
   (2) _____
   (3) _____
   (4) _____
   (5) _____

4. State two advantages of centralized data entry.
   (1) _____
   _____
   (2) _____
   _____

5. State two advantages of decentralized data entry.
   (1) _____
   _____
   (2) _____
   _____

UNIT 3
HISTORY OF DATA ENTRY

AFTER READING THIS UNIT YOU WILL KNOW:

Past types of data entry devices.
The oldest type of data entry device.
The types of recording media codes used.
Who Herman Hollerith was.
The terms associated with the Hollerith code.
The advantages and disadvantages of noncard data entry devices.
What is meant by a base two number system.
The factors to be considered in record design.
How negative numbers are keyed.
The rules for the proper care and handling of cards.

What the following terms mean:

BCD
BIT
Control punch
EBCDIC
Field
File
High order position; low order position
Record
Right justify; left justify
Row; column
Zero fill; blank fill;
Zone punch; digit punch

SECTION A
THE HOLLERITH PUNCHED CARD

Dr. Herman Hollerith, a statistician employed by the United States Census Bureau, developed a code that could be used to represent data on a card. This card is often mistakenly called an IBM card, perhaps because Dr. Hollerith later left the Census Bureau and established the Tabulating Machine Company, which eventually became the IBM Corporation. IBM is an acronym for International Business Machines. The correct term for the card is the *Hollerith* card. Since many types of computers use this card for input, it is also called the standard punched card. Later chapters show that other types of *media* are replacing the punched card.

Pictures of the punched card are shown in Figures 3.1, 3.2, and 3.3.

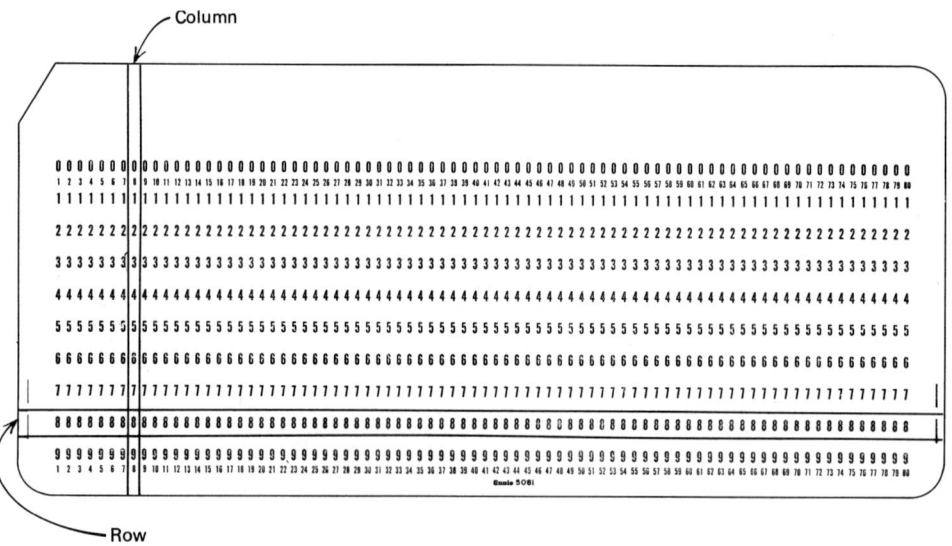

FIGURE 3.1
Hollerith card, column and row.

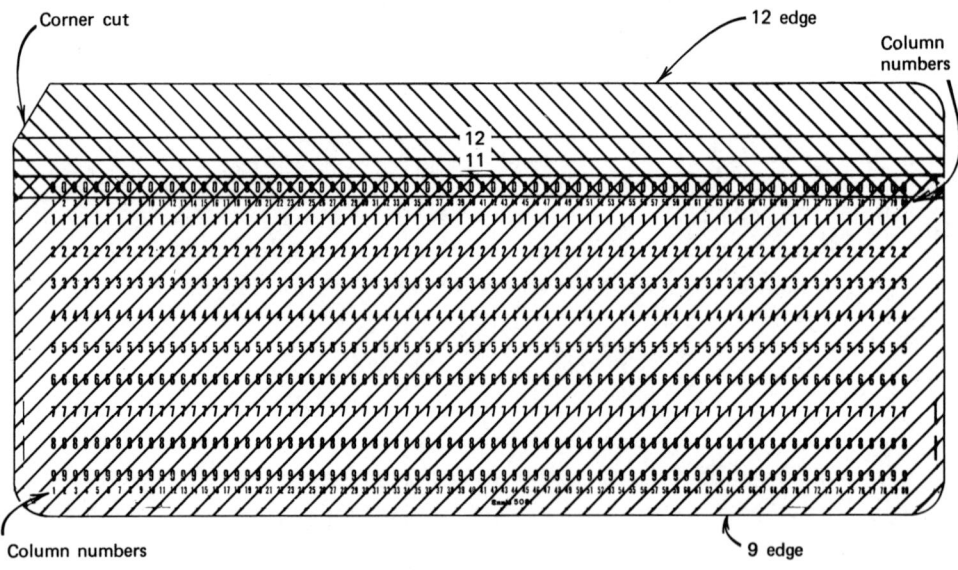

FIGURE 3.2
Hollerith card features.

16   PART 1 INTRODUCTION TO DATA ENTRY

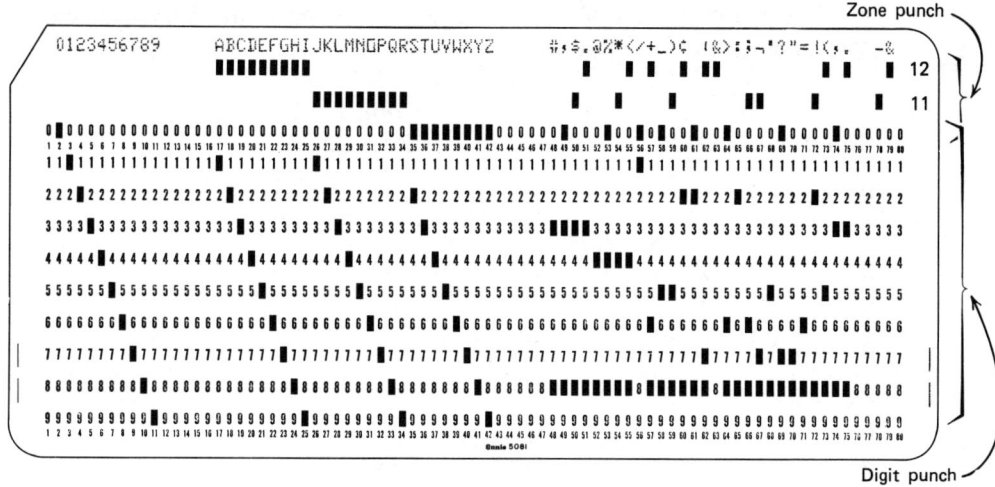

FIGURE 3.3
Hollerith card codes.

Figure 3.1 shows that:

1. A *row* is a horizontal line going from left to right.
2. A *column* is a vertical line going up and down.

Figure 3.2 shows that a Hollerith card has:

1. Eighty columns numbered 1 through 80.
2. Twelve rows, two unmarked rows at the top of the card called 11 and 12, and ten other rows numbered 0 through 9.

The *12 edge* of a card is the top edge next to the twelfth row. The *9 edge* of a card is the bottom edge next to the ninth row. The *face* of a card is the printed side of the card.

Often cards are manila color. However, more expensive cards in solid colors or with colored stripes for identification purposes may be purchased. For example, a gray stripe might indicate payroll cards and a red stripe might be an inventory card. Information loaded into the computer from cards is now kept on other storage devices. The cards are then thrown away. Therefore, card colors are no longer of major importance. However, colored cards are sometimes used to show the beginning of a new job in a batch of control cards in a job.

The cut corner in the card shown in Figure 3.2 is used to show if cards in a group (deck) are upside down or backwards. When cards are ordered from a supplier, a left cut (left corner) or right cut (right corner) can be specified.

The punches in the card in Figure 3.3 are rectangular punches. If a punch falls on row 9, it is said to be a 9 punch; on row 12, a 12 punch; and so forth.

1. The zone rows are shown at the top of the card by stripes going from left to right. A *zone punch* is a punch in rows 0, 11, or 12.
2. The digit rows are shown in the bottom portion of the card by stripes going from right to left. A *digit punch* is a punch in rows 0 through 9.

A punch in row 0 can be either a zone or a digit punch. If there is only one punch in the column, it is a digit punch. If there are two punches, it is a zone punch.

A *character* is defined as a digit, a letter of the alphabet, or a special symbol that is used to represent data.

UNIT 3   HISTORY OF DATA ENTRY

The Hollerith code for our 10 digits, 26 letters of the alphabet, and 26 special characters is shown below.

Character	Code	Character	Code Zone Digit
0	0	A	12-1
1	1	B	12-2
2	2	C	12-3
3	3	D	12-4
4	4	E	12-5
5	5	F	12-6
6	6	G	12-7
7	7	H	12-8
8	8	I	12-9
9	9	J	11-1
& _____	12	K	11-2
¢ _____	12-8-2	L	11-3
. _____	12-8-3	M	11-4
< _____	12-8-4	N	11-5
(_____	12-8-5	O	11-6
+ _____	12-8-6	P	11-7
| _____	12-8-7	Q	11-8
- _____	11	R	11-9
! _____	11-8-2	/	0-1
$ _____	11-8-3	S	0-2
* _____	11-8-4	T	0-3
) _____	11-8-5	U	0-4
; _____	11-8-6	V	0-5
¬ _____	11-8-7	W	0-6
, _____	0-8-3	X	0-7
% _____	0-8-4	Y	0-8
_ _____	0-8-5	Z	0-9
> _____	0-8-6		
? _____	0-8-7		
: _____	8-2		
# _____	8-3		
@ _____	8-4		
' _____	8-5		
= _____	8-6		
" _____	8-7		

Your data entry device may have fewer special characters and/or different codes for the special characters. If your institution uses Hollerith cards and has a different character set, your instructor will help you:

1. Mark any that you do not have in the appropriate blank.

2. Record any special symbols that are different in the blanks by your codes.

Studying Figure 3.3 and the chart on page 18, note that:

RULE 1   Digits have only one punch.

Example   The number 0 in column 2 of the card has a 0 punch or a punch in row 0.

RULE 2   Letters of the alphabet have two punches, a zone punch and a digit punch.

For example, the letters

A to I have a 12 zone punch and a digit punch.

J to R have an 11 zone punch and a digit punch.

S to Z have a 0 zone punch and a digit punch.

Each of these three groups has digit punches ranging from 1 through 9 except for the third set S through Z. This set begins with a 2. The special symbol (/) a slash, is represented by the code 0-1.

RULE 3   Special symbols are represented by one, two, or three punches; but in all cases, there will be at least one zone punch.

Since the following special characters are used frequently, the punches used to represent the characters should be memorized. The characters are:

0-1, the slash.

11, the minus sign or hyphen.

12, the ampersand (or on some devices the plus sign).

SECTION B
THE 96 COLUMN PUNCHED CARD

Another kind of punched card that has been very common in the past is the 96-column card which was widely used by the IBM System/3 computer. This card uses a modification of the BCD code. *BCD* is an acronym for *binary coded decimal*. This is sometimes called a six-*bit* code. BIT is an acronym for *binary digit*. (This is an unusual acronym in that the BI in BInary and the T at the end of digiT were used to form BIT.)

Binary digits are the digits 0 and 1 and are used in the base-2 number system. In our number system (base 10), the number 1111 or

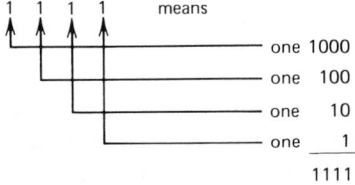

UNIT 3   HISTORY OF DATA ENTRY

In base 2,

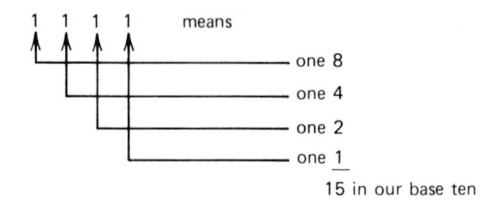

```
1 1 1 1   means
↑ ↑ ↑ ↑
        └──── one 8
      └────── one 4
    └──────── one 2
  └────────── one 1
             ─────
             15 in our base ten
```

So we have:

Base 10	Base 2
0	0000
1	0001
2	0010 (one 2)
3	0011 (one 2 + one 1)
4	0100 (one 4)
5	0101 (one 4 + one 1)
6	0110 (one 4 + one 2)
7	0111 (one 4 + one 2 + one 1)
8	1000 (one 8)
9	1001 (one 8 + one 1)

Because of the definition of a base-2 number and the powers of 2, these digits or bits are called the 8 4 2 1 bits. Both the BCD character code and the 96-column card code have a zone and digit portion as the Hollerith code had. The digit portion is the 8 4 2 1 bits and the zone portion has two bits called the B and A bits. The zone portion of the two codes follows:

Hollerith Zone	96-Column Card Code
12	11 or BA
11	10 or B
0	01 A
None	00 None

A comparison between the two codes for numbers and letters (special characters have some exceptions) is:

Character	Hollerith		96-Column Card Code			
	Zone	Digit	Zone BA	Digit 8421		
A	12	1	11	0001	or	BA 1
K	11	2	10	0010	or	B 2
Z	0	9	01	1001	or	A 8 1
6		6	00	0110	or	4 2

A complete list of the 96-column card codes appears in Appendix E.

The System/3 card shown in Figure 3.4 shows that there are four print areas with column numbers 1 to 32, 33 to 64, 65 to 96, and 97 to 128. The fourth print area is not normally used because printing is column for column.

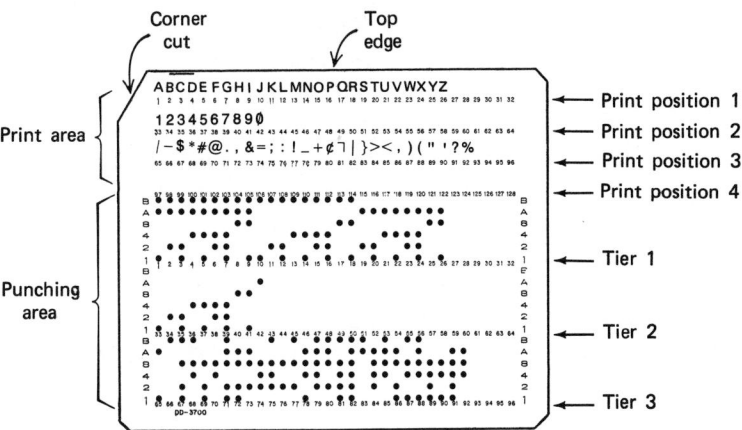

FIGURE 3.4
The 96-column card.

The punching area is divided into three tiers (a series of rows placed one above the other). The first tier contains columns 1 to 32, the second tier columns 33 to 64, and the third tier columns 65 to 96. The six bits discussed above correspond to the punching positions BA 8421.

Notice that punched holes may be circular or rectangular. Looking at the letter A in column 1 of print position 1 and then in the first column of tier 1, circular punched holes can be seen in punching positions B, A, and 1 (corresponding to the six-bit code 11 0001).

In the same way, K in column 11 appears with B and 2 punches; Z in column 26 appears with B, 8, and 1 punches; and 6 in column 38 appears with 4 and 2 punches.

The advantages of the System/3 card over the Hollerith card are:

1. Ninety-six characters can be punched on it but only 80 can be punched on the Hollerith card.
2. The 96-column card is smaller and takes up less storage space.

However, the Hollerith card has remained the most popular with users still using cards as recording media.

Advantages of using cards as recording media are:

1. The data recorded on cards can easily be seen.
2. Corrections are easily made by pulling the card from a deck and changing it.
3. Cards can easily be added or removed from a file.

Disadvantages are:

1. Storage cabinets are expensive and take up lots of space.
2. Cards are easily lost.
3. Paper is becoming increasingly expensive.
4. Cards are easily torn or dented by rubber bands.
5. Trays of cards are inconvenient to carry around.

The rules for proper care and handling of cards are:

1. Do not bend, fold, or mutilate the cards.
2. If damaged, cards should not be stapled or taped. Make a new card.
3. Store in a cool, dry place. A deck of cards should not be left in a car and exposed to heat and humidity. Such treatment warps the cards and can cause terrible card jams in computer input devices.

UNIT 3   HISTORY OF DATA ENTRY

4. Keep cards away from dust and ashes. You should not smoke while handling cards. Ashes and dust contaminate I/O devices. Most computer centers will not allow smoking in the computer center area.
5. Keep rubber bands off-center around card decks. This prevents nicking cards in the center. Nicked cards can cause card jams on computer input devices.

SECTION C
DATA ENTRY EQUIPMENT

Machines that first converted *source data* from human readable form into the Hollerith code were called *keypunches*. They have keyboards similar to typewriters. When a key is depressed, a character is printed at the top of a card column and a Hollerith code for that character is punched in that column. Examples of these keypunches are the IBM 024, the IBM 026, and the IBM 029. If your institution still uses the IBM 029, then your instructor may refer you to a discussion of the IBM 029 in Appendix H. A picture of the IBM 029 is shown in Figure 3.5.

Until about 1970, IBM (International Business Machines) was the main supplier of 80-column card data entry equipment. Then a large number of companies entered the data entry equipment market. These other companies also produce good equipment. Some of the most widely used equipment will be discussed in this book in the order of historical development.

In 1970, IBM introduced the IBM 129 *buffered* keypunch or data recorder. The advantage of a buffered keypunch is that it has a memory similar to the computer discussed in Unit 1. Therefore, the card is not punched until the entire card has been keyed. Thus errors can be corrected before the card is punched. The buffered keypunch is also faster than the old unbuffered keypunch. A skilled operator's speed may increase by as much as 28 percent on a buffered keypunch.

FIGURE 3.5
The IBM 029 keypunch (Courtesy of IBM Corporation).

FIGURE 3.6
A magnetic tape character.

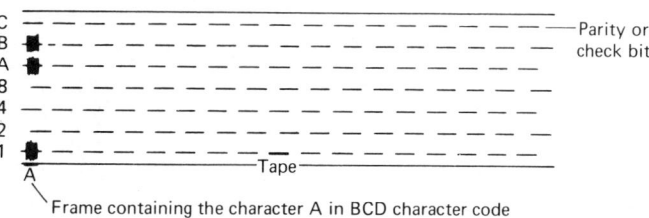

Actually, buffered keypunches were preceded by magnetic tape recorders. In 1964, Mohawk Data Sciences introduced a data entry device using magnetic tape as a recording media. A magnetic tape is a long strip of material on which codes can be recorded as a series of magnetized spots, as shown in Figure 3.6. These key-to-tape devices have a memory. Errors can be corrected before the data is written on tape. Like the IBM 129 data recorder, this machine can also be used to verify the correctness of data; whereas a separate machine, the IBM 059 verifier, is needed for the old unbuffered keypunches. Some companies that produced key-to-tape equipment are:

Mohawk 1100, 6400, 9201

Burroughs Series N

Singer Keytape

Tally 620

NCR 735/736

Data Action 150

Machines of the type listed above were called computer compatible key-to-tape devices because the tapes produced by them could be used to input data into the computer. There were other types of key-to-tape (cartridge) equipment produced, such as the IBM 50 data inscriber. Nevertheless, key-to-tape devices are rapidly becoming obsolete because they are being replaced by terminals or key-to-disk equipment. Therefore, although they are still found in some places in industry, they will not be examined in detail in this book. Figure 3.7 shows one of the Mohawk 6400 Series key-to-tape devices.

In the 1970s data entry devices were introduced that use floppy disks that look like small 45 RPM phonograph records. Characters are recorded on these floppy disks or diskettes as magnetized spots. Today, disks (nonflexible platters) are being used in combination with magnetic tapes. Some of this key-to-disk data entry equipment is connected directly to the computer. These devices will be discussed in later chapters.

Key-to-disk devices use the third and last code that will be discussed. This is the eight-bit EBCDIC code. *EBCDIC* is an acronym for *Extended Binary Coded Decimal Interchange Code.*

Examine the following table.

Character	Hollerith Code		BCD Code		EBCDIC Code	
	Zone	Digit	Zone BA	Digit 8421	Zone 8421	Digit 8421
A	12	1	11	0001	1100	0001
K	11	2	10	0010	1101	0010
Z	0	9	01	1001	1110	1001
6		6	00	0110	1111	0110

The EBCDIC code is similar to the BCD code if you extend the BCD

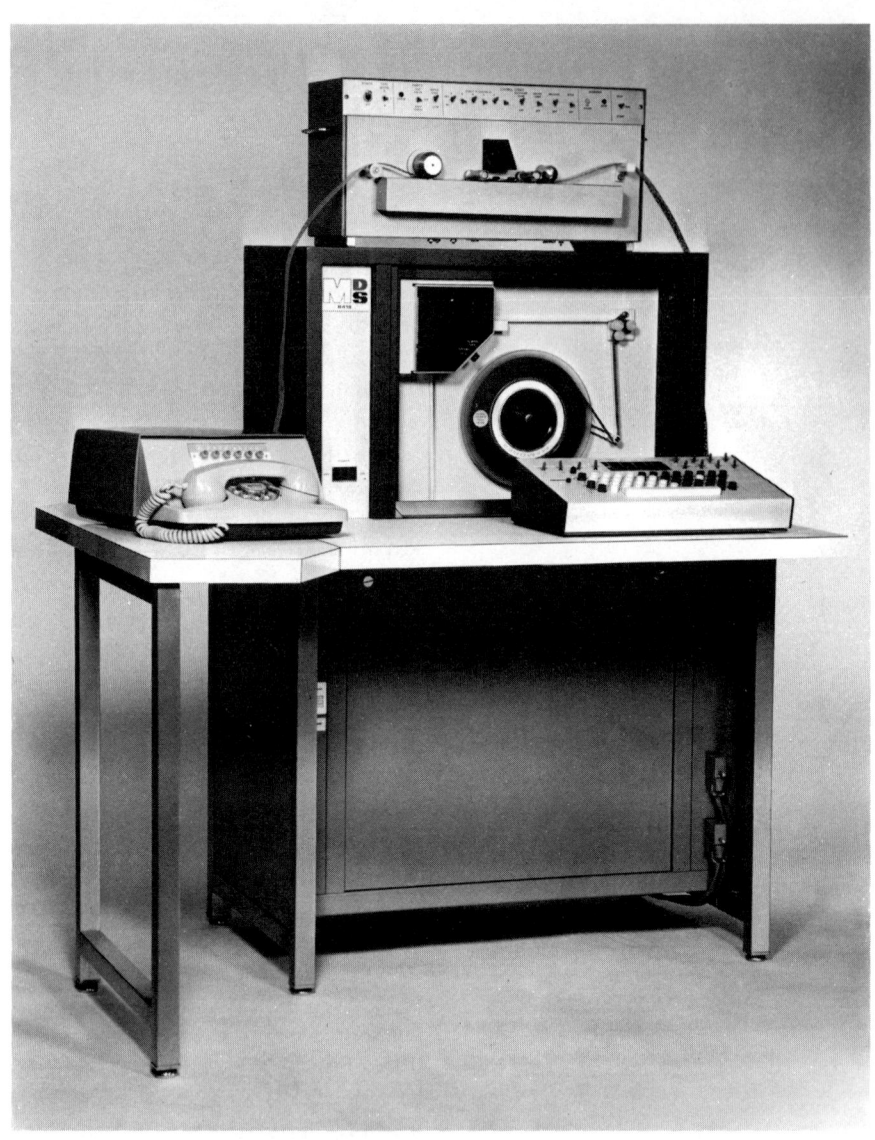

FIGURE 3.7
The Mohawk 6415 data recorder (Courtesy of Mohawk Data Sciences).

zone to 4 bits (for A, 0011) and reverse the zone bits (1100). The digit portion is the same. This method will work for letters and numbers but not for special characters. Since we are seldom concerned in data entry with interpreting such data, it is not of great importance.

However, you should know that there are three coding schemes used:[1]

1. The Hollerith code on cards.
2. The BCD code used on System/3 96-column cards and on some magnetic tapes.
3. The EBCDIC code used on magnetic tapes, disks, and on floppy disks (diskettes).

The keyboards of all data entry devices have certain operational characteristics in common. They look somewhat like typewriters. Figure 4.5 in Unit 4 shows an example of the IBM 129 keyboard. There are no lowercase letters

---

[1] There is a fourth code, the ASCII code (American National Standard Code for Information Interchange), that is used in data communications systems. This is a seven-bit code. It is used mainly with terminals.

24 PART 1 INTRODUCTION TO DATA ENTRY

as on the typewriter. Only capital letters are used. Special characters and numbers appear above many of the letters. On most machines, depressing the numeric shift key (in unprogrammed mode) will cause the upper character to be keyed.

Another difference from the typewriter is that the numbers are usually on the right rather than on the top row. This is because most data entry work is numeric work and it frees the left hand to hold paper and to move a ruler or guide down on a source document.

There are also special keys and switches on each machine that you will learn about when you use them.

SECTION D
RECORD DESIGN

No matter what recording media you use—card, tape, disk, or floppy disk—you will need to know how plans are made to record data and what the definitions involved are.

For example, in a college the state requires the following information for all the students in each class:

1. Social security number.
2. Name (first, middle initial, and last).
3. Address (house number, street, route, and/or box number).
4. City, state, and zip code.
5. Class number.

This information is to be recorded in a maximum of 80 positions.

Each of the above items is called a field of data. A *field* is a collection of characters that have some meaning. Fields may be subdivided into subfields (that is, the first name is a subfield). The position or arrangement of these fields is planned on record layout forms. If cards are involved, these forms are called *multi-card layouts*. An example is shown in Figure 3.8.

A collection of fields of data is called a *record*. A card can be considered a record. This is why machines that deal with cards are often called unit record (one record) machines. A *file* is a collection of records.

Before planning a record, you should consider several rules:

1. Fields that are to be duplicated or copied should be grouped together and placed in the left-most positions in the record. This increases the keying speed.
2. Fields that must be manually keyed should be grouped to the right of those that are being duplicated.
3. When possible all numeric fields should be grouped together and all alpha fields grouped together.

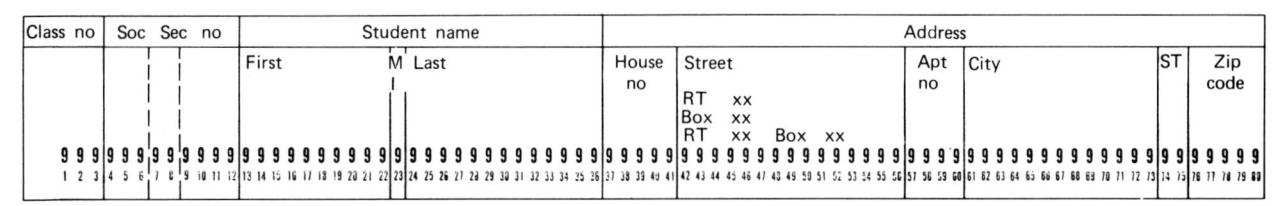

Class no	Soc Sec no	Student name			Address				
		First	M	Last	House no	Street RT xx Box xx RT xx Box xx	Apt no	City	ST	Zip code

FIGURE 3.8
Multi-card layout example.

4. Fields that are to be skipped or blank areas should be placed in the right-most positions of the record.
5. When several different records are used on the same job, any fields that are the same should have the same column numbers (relative position).

Therefore, record design steps should be:

1. Plan the order of the fields.
2. Plan the maximum size of the fields.
3. Draw the plan, labeling each field and subfields.

STEP 1   Considering the above rules, the fields needed should be in the following order:

1. Class number (since it will be duplicated). It is all numeric.
2. Social security number, all numeric.
3. Name.
4. Address.
5. City, state, and zip code (zip code is kept next to the state since it is in that position on the source document).

STEP 2   In determining the size of the field:

1. Consider the maximum size that could *ever* be encountered.
2. Place fields next to each other without any space between them. The computer, when asked to print them out, will be instructed to leave spaces between the fields.
3. Do not punch special characters, such as slashes in dates, dashes in social security numbers, or decimal points or commas in numbers. The computer will be instructed to insert these special characters when printing the data. People entering data for scientific applications sometimes do punch decimal points and commas in data but they are not normally punched in business data processing.

   Therefore, the choice of size of each field would be:
   a. Class number—three positions, the largest class number is 399.
   b. Social security number—nine digits, no dashes.
   c. Name—a problem exists here. If the names are from an area with German or Czech people, for example, you may encounter very long names. You could use the telephone directory to get an idea of the length of names in the community and then add one or two positions. For example, WESTMORELAND may be the longest last name and ELIZABETH the longest first name. Adding one position as a safeguard:
   > First name, 10 positions.
   > Middle initial, 1 position.
   > Last name, 13 positions.

   d. Address. Five-digit house numbers are not unusual in a large city. Consider these questions: (1) How should the treatment of apartment numbers, which can be letters or numbers, be planned? (2) What is the longest street name (consult the phone book or a city map)? (3) How should route and box numbers be handled? Our plan will be:

House number, 5 digits.
Street name, 15 positions.
Apartment number, 4 positions.

Your center should have standard abbreviations to be used in street names such as shown in Appendix B. Route and box numbers should be punched in the street name field leaving the house number blank.

e. City, state, and zip code. The post office zip code directory offers a method at the beginning of the directory for entering city, state, and zip code in 22 positions. The city is 13 positions. However, there is a two-page list of special abbreviations necessary for cities exceeding 13 positions. Therefore, we will use:

City, 13 positions.
State, 2 positions (use standard two-letter abbreviations).
Zip code, 5 positions.[2]

You will probably be asked to follow post office abbreviation rules where you work, and we will follow these in this textbook. They are listed in Appendix B.

STEP 3   Figure 3.8 shows the record layout plan. It can be seen that if a nine-position zip code or additional data are needed, there is no more space left on the card record. (One advantage of using tape, diskette, or disk media is that records may be less than or greater than 80 positions).

Field width is defined as: The highest column number minus the lowest column number plus 1. Therefore the field width of the street in Figure 3.8 is: 56 − 42 + 1 = 15 positions.

Figure 3.9 shows a form by which keying or job instructions for a job might be given.

In business applications numeric fields are normally keyed *right justified* and *zero filled*. That is, the house number 101 would be keyed:

```
 Ø   Ø   1   Ø   1      DATA
37  38  39  40  41      COLUMN NUMBERS
```

Notice that the zeros in the figure have a slash. In business data processing work, a written zero is slashed to distinguish it from the alphabetic letter O. Scientific personnel sometimes reverse this practice, which seems more sensible, since both groups slash the letter Z to distinguish it from the number 2. However, the notation used in this book will be that of slashing the zeros. Note that when the written zero is keyed, only a zero is keyed. You do *not* key both a zero and a slash.

In the field just shown, column 37 is said to be the high order field position and column 41 the low order field position. This seems backwards since the column number 37 is smaller than the number 41. But the terms arise from the number itself since the right-most 1 in 00101 is the units position of the number of the lowest digit position.

Therefore:

1. The *high order position* of a field is the left-most position.

2. The *low order position* of a field is the right-most position.

---

[2] The post office is discussing the use of nine-position zip codes. So in the future this may need to be changed.

JOB NAME Student List	JOB NO.	DATE IN	DATE DUE	PROGRAM NO.
RECEIVED FROM	SPECIAL INSTRUCTIONS			
DISPOSITION OF MATERIAL				
SOURCE DATA				
OUTPUT DATA				

DATA FIELD	POSITIONS		FUNC-	REMARKS
	FROM	TO	TION	
1. Class No.	1	3	DUP	**300** for all records
2: Social Security No.	4	12	PN	
3. First Name	13	22	PA	
4. Middle Initial	23	23	PA	
5. Last Name	24	36	PA	
6. House No.	37	41	P/N	LZ
7. Street Name	42	56	PA	Punch **RT** or **BOX** in this field or **RT XX BOX XX**
8. Apt. No.	57	60	PA/N	LJ
9. City	61	73	PA	
10. State	74	75	PA	**USE STANDARD ABBREV.**
11. Zip Code	76	80	PN	
12.				
13.				

FUNCTIONS -
P = PUNCH   SK = SKIP   LJ = LEFT JUSTIFY
V = VERIFY   LZ = LEFT ZERO
DUP = DUPLICATE LZ - = NEGATIVE LZ
N = NUMERIC   A = ALPHA

FIGURE 3.9
Job instructions.

An alphanumeric field (alphameric for short) is a field that may have numbers, letters, or special characters. In keying alphameric fields, they are *left justified* and *blank filled*. This means that the data is keyed beginning in the left-most column or high-order position and the unused portion of the field is left blank.

Therefore the first name REBECCA would be keyed as shown below:

R	E	B	E	C	C	A			
13	14	15	16	17	18	19	20	21	22

RULE   In business data processing normally,

1. Numeric fields are keyed right justified and zero filled.
2. Alphameric fields are keyed left justified and blank filled.

In keying numeric fields, if a number is to be subtracted by the computer, an 11 punch is often used. For example, the number −1238 to be keyed in columns 37 to 41 would be keyed:

Ø	1	2	3	8̄	DATA
37	38	39	40	41	COLUMN

An ampersand or 12 punch (on some computers it might be the character +) means the number is positive. For example:

				&	
Ø	1	2	3	8	DATA
37	38	39	40	41	COLUMN

Eleven punches are used more often than 12 punches. They are normally in the right-most position of the field. To key in an 11-8, a Q could be punched, but in most modern data entry machines a special key allows this to be done easily.

Some computers, such as Burroughs or NCR computers, expect the sign (+ or −) of a number to be shown in the left-most position of the field. But the most commonly used method is that described above.

Sometimes 12 or 11 punches are used in special situations. They do *not* mean a positive or negative number and are not always in the right-most position in the field. In these cases the punch has a special meaning and is called a *control punch*. Your supervisor or teacher will explain these situations to you when they arise. Often the use of signed numbers is not necessary since the computer could be programmed or instructed to subtract and thus give a negative number.

STUDY GUIDE

Answer these questions in your book. If asked to do so, tear out the pages and hand them in to your instructor.

1. List four factors that should be considered in record design.

    (1) _____

    _____

    (2) _____

    _____

    (3) _____

    _____

    (4) _____

    _____

2. On a record layout form, design a record layout for each of the following records. Label all fields and subfields.
    a. Record 1:
    Date, MM/DD/YY
    Company number, 2 digits
    Store number, 4 digits
    Department number, 3 digits
    Salesperson number, 2 digits

UNIT 3   HISTORY OF DATA ENTRY

Quantity (or number) sold, 3 digits
Description—longest name is 20 letters and spaces
Price—nn,nnn.nn

b. Record 2:
Card code, 1 character
Student social security number
Basis of admission code, 1 digit
County of residence code, 3 digits
High school information
(1) Year of graduation, last 2 digits
(2) Name of high school, maximum of 20 letters and spaces
(3) High school code, 9 digits
Code of institution transferred from, 6 digits
Major code, 4 digits
Date of birth, MM/DD/YY

3. Considering Records 1 and 2 that you just designed:
   a. Look at the price field in record 1:

   (1) The field width is _____ (how many) columns.

   (2) The field should be keyed _____ (right/left) justified

   and _____ (zero/blank) filled.

   (3) The high order position is column number _____ and

   the low order position is column number _____ .

   (4) State how the keying would differ if the price were negative.

   _____

   _____

   b. List any fields in Record 1 that have subfields.

   _____

   c. Look at the high school name field in Record 2.

   (1) The field width is _____ (how many) columns.

   (2) The field should be keyed _____ (right/left) justified

   and _____ (zero/blank) filled.

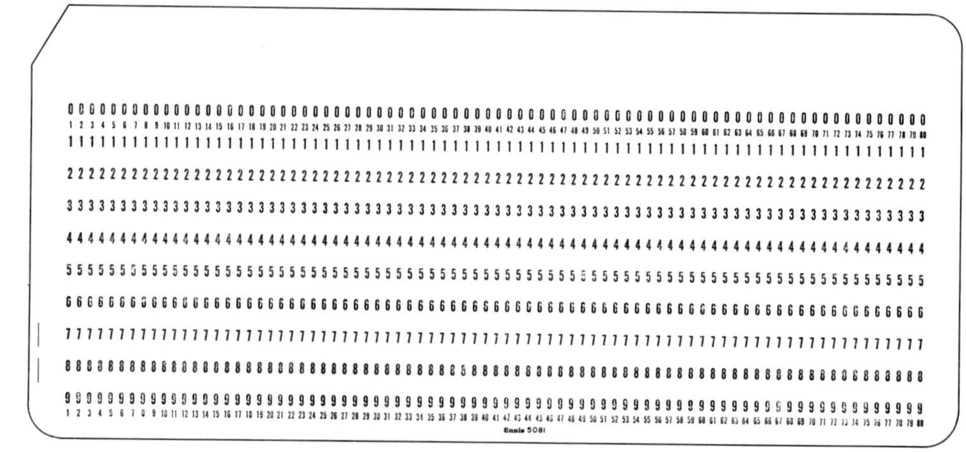

FIGURE 3.10

(3) The high order position is column number _____ and the low order position is column number _____.

    d. List any fields in record two that have subfields.

    _____

4. Given the Hollerith card in Figure 3.10, identify with arrows and names:
    a. 12 edge   e. Zone rows
    b. 9 edge   f. Digit rows
    c. 12 row   g. Corner cut
    d. 11 row

5. Complete the following chart:

Character	Hollerith Code	
	ZONE	DIGIT
B	_____	_____
M	_____	_____
W	_____	_____
5	_____	_____
/	_____	_____
-	_____	_____
&	_____	_____

6. Compare the Hollerith card and the System/3 card as to:

	Hollerith Card	System/3 Card
a. Number of punching columns.	_____	_____
b. Number of punching rows per character.	_____	_____
c. Shape of punched holes.	_____	_____

7. State two advantages of the System/3 card over the Hollerith card.

    (1) _____

    _____

    (2) _____

    _____

8. a. State four important coding systems that are used in data entry.

    (1) _____

    (2) _____

    (3) _____

    (4) _____

    b. What do all four of these codes have in common? _____

    _____

9. State three reasons why some persons prefer cards as a recording medium.

(1) _____

(2) _____

(3) _____

10. a. State the oldest data entry device. _____

b. State an advantage of data recorders over the older unbuffered keypunches. _____

11. State five disadvantages of cards as a recording medium.

(1) _____

(2) _____

(3) _____

(4) _____

(5) _____

12. State what type of code is used on the new data entry equipment.

_____

13. State at least four rules for the proper care and handling of cards.

(1) _____

(2) _____

(3) _____

(4) _____

14. State the purpose of:

a. Corner cuts _____

b. Colored or striped cards _____

15. Decode the message on the Hollerith card below:

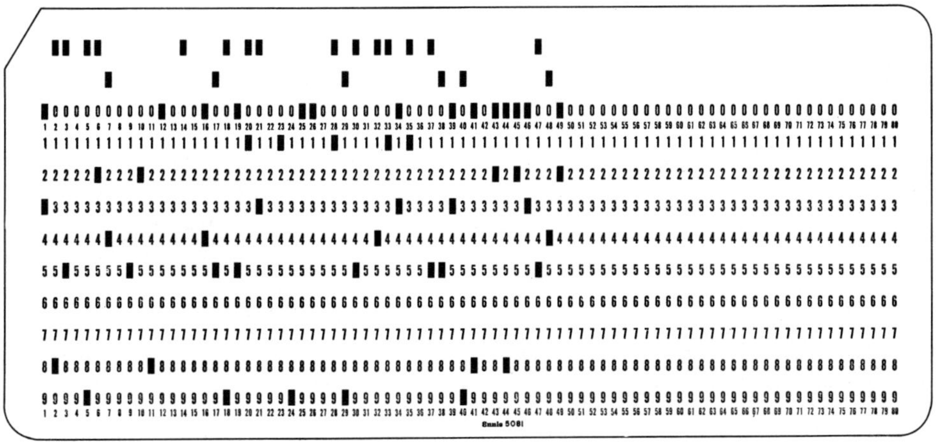

FIGURE 3.11

PART 2

Data Entry Equipment

UNIT 4
BUFFERED KEYPUNCHES

AFTER READING THIS UNIT YOU WILL KNOW:

The internal storage features of your buffered data entry device.
The external features of this device.
The special function keys on this device.
How cards are punched manually.
How error cards are corrected.
How cards are verified.
The program codes for your device.
How a program is loaded.
How a program can be punched out from memory.
How data is punched under program control.
The special features of your machine.
The conditions that cause keyboard lockups.
Proper maintenance and cleaning procedures for your device.
Other brands of buffered keypunches that are available.

What the following terms mean:

Buffer
Chaining
Duplicate
Left-zero (or right-adjust)
Program
Program code

SECTION A
INTRODUCTION

The death of keypunches and card recording media has been predicted for the last 10 years. Today there are still many card-oriented data entry devices being used in industry, especially in the data processing centers in smaller cities.

Modern keypunches are buffered which means that they have a memory. They are multi-functional. That is, they can be used to encode data on cards or to verify data that has already been punched. These buffered keypunches are also called data recorders. The memory has three storage areas as shown in Figure 4.1.

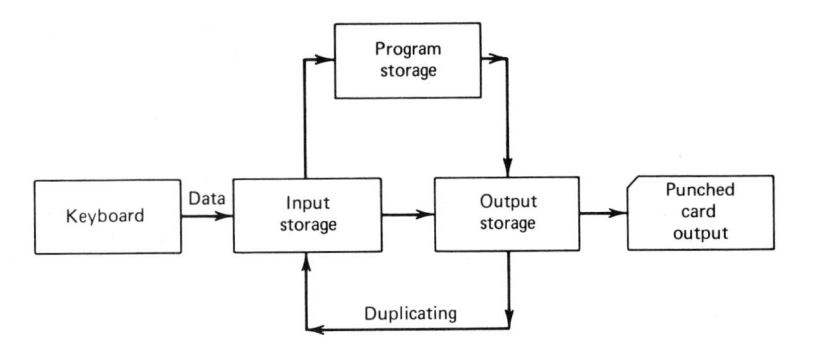

FIGURE 4.1
Buffered keypunch storage areas.

There are 80-column and 96-column buffered keypunches. The 96-column keypunch was made for the IBM System/3 computer, and its use is decreasing. Many companies that do not have huge amounts of data and do not have complicated and difficult data validation problems still use buffered keypunches. As mentioned in Unit 3, data that you can see on cards is reassuring to many individuals.

The buffered keypunches have many advantages over the old unbuffered keypunches. As you will see, they have:

1. The ability to correct an error that is sensed by the operator before the card is punched.
2. Greater speed.
3. The ability to verify and punch on the same machine.
4. More program levels than unbuffered keypunches.
5. Special features, such as production statistics, accumulating provisions, self-checking devices.

Card data entry devices have:

1. A keyboard console that contains special operating switches and controls.
2. A keyboard that has two types of keys:
   a. *Data keys* for entering data (numbers, letters, or special characters).
   b. *Function keys* that cause certain functions or controlling actions to take place.
3. Special indicator lights (on some keyboards).
4. A *card hopper* into which the blank cards to be punched are placed. Before you place cards in this hopper fan them to eliminate static electricity and joggle them to obtain a smooth block. Some devices also have an auxiliary input device into which only one card may be placed as input.
5. A *card stacker* where the punched cards are stacked. Some devices have an auxiliary stacker where unpunched or error cards are deposited.

Keying may be done two ways: *manually* with no program or *automatically* under program control. Because punched card data entry devices have a memory, instructions can be stored in their program storage unit. This is similar to the computer storage concept that was discussed in Unit 1. These instructions are called a *program.* When the program is activated, operations are said to be under *program control.*

Buffered data entry devices can store from two to eight different programs per device, depending on the brand of the device.

These devices are instructed or programmed by the use of a program card with programming codes punched on it. Other methods for programming

UNIT 4 BUFFERED KEYPUNCHES

some of the newer data entry equipment, such as key-to-disk equipment will be discussed in later units.

CAUTION

All of these devices have a variety of keyboards. The main differences in the keyboards are in the placement of the special characters. Some keyboards exist with the numbers on the top row, as on the typewriter. The special characters used in data entry must be what is expected by the brand of computer to be used. (There are ways to get around this by writing a special computer program to do a translation.) You should carefully note where the − (minus or hyphen), the _ (underline), the ' (apostrophe), and the | (a symbol for absolute value or the logical OR) sign are, if they exist on your keyboard.

SECTION B
THE IBM 129 DATA RECORDER (MODEL 3— PRINTS, PUNCHES, AND VERIFIES)

The IBM 129 Data Recorder is shown in Figure 4.2. In this figure the main features are numbered.

The IBM 129 is turned on by the *mainline switch* (13). When it is turned off, anything in memory or the storage areas is lost.

The *keyboard* (11) contains keys for 64 characters and functional keys that control the operation of the machine.

The *keyboard console* (10) contains operating switches and controls. A very important control is the *column indicator* (1) which shows the *next* card column to be keyed. It is very important to understand that nothing has been punched in that column.

Cards are placed face forward, 9 edge down, in the *card hopper* (7),

FIGURE 4.2
The IBM 129 data recorder (Courtesy of IBM Corporation).

PART 2   DATA ENTRY EQUIPMENT

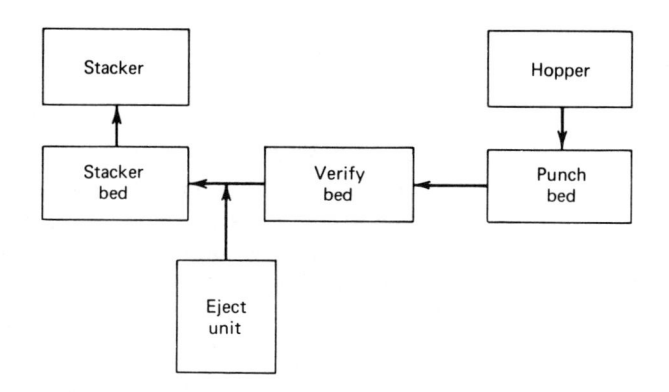

FIGURE 4.3
Card path for the IBM 129.

which holds about 500 cards. Cards feed down into the punch bed and are *registered* (positioned) against the *combination punch/read unit* (9). If cards are being punched, punching occurs here. As will be discussed later, if cards are being verified, a reading process takes place here. When the cards are punched, the paper chips fall into the *chip box* (12). This box needs to be emptied occasionally. Fuses are also in this area. The printing of the characters punched takes place in the *print unit* (8).

After punching or reading takes place, the card moves to the verify bed and the *eject unit* (3). At this point the card moves to the stacker bed and up into the *card stacker* (4). If a card becomes caught or jammed in the bed, under most conditions it can be removed by pressing the *card release button* (2). The card scale (5) gives an approximate card count.

The path of the card is shown in Figure 4.3.

Cards are placed in the hopper and come out in the stacker. If the stacker becomes full, the *stacker stop switch* (6) is activated. No more punching can take place until the cards are removed from the stacker.

OPERATING FEATURES

The IBM 129 can store up to six programs, or sets of instructions, in its program storage (see Figure 4.1). Using programs allows certain actions such as skipping or duplicating (copying) to be done faster. Parts of the *keyboard console,* as shown in Figure 4.4, are used under program control.

KEYBOARD CONSOLE

The keyboard console is made up of function controls and indicators. They are (from left to right in Figure 4.4):

1. PUNCH/VERIFY switch. When keying, the switch should be on PUNCH;

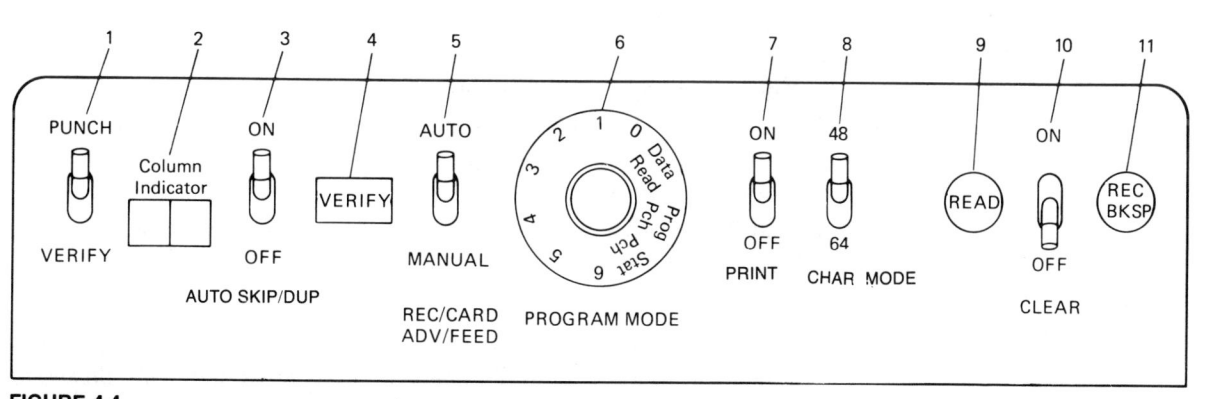

FIGURE 4.4
The IBM 129 data recorder keyboard console (Courtesy of IBM Corporation).

UNIT 4 BUFFERED KEYPUNCHES   41

when verifying, the switch should be on VERIFY. When this switch is changed, the CLEAR switch (10) should be used.

2. Column indicator. The indicator shows the *next* column in which data will be recorded.

3. AUTO SKIP/DUP switch. The Automatic Skip/Duplicate switch is set to ON when operating under programmed control. Automatic skipping and duplicating will take place when the appropriate key is pressed. When the AUTO SKIP/DUP switch is off, keying is done manually. Therefore to skip 10 spaces, the space bar must be pressed manually 10 times.

4. VERIFY light. When verifying, this light indicates that what was keyed does not agree with what has already been keyed on the card. If the machine has the special self-check feature (to be discussed later), it indicates a self-check error.

5. REC ADV/CARD FEED switch. The Record Advance/Card Feed switch when in:
   a. AUTO or *automatic* mode causes the column indicator to advance from 80 to 1 when the 80th column is keyed or the release key is pressed. A card will then be punched.
   b. MANUAL or *manual* mode stops at column 00 (column indicator reads 00). This is used for program selection or keying corrections. To continue, the FEED key can be pressed.

   Usually the REC ADV/CARD FEED switch should be on AUTO.

6. PROGRAM MODE dial.
   PROGRAM 0 indicates keying is taking place manually. The machine is *not* under program control.
   PROGRAMS 1 TO 6 indicate keying will take place under program control for the next record if the REC ADV/CARD FEED switch is set to AUTO. The program number will be indicated by the dial setting.
   DATA READ. This is used to load *data* into the output storage area for duplication purposes.
   PROG PCH. Program punch is used to punch out a program stored in the program storage area.
   STAT PCH. Statistics punch is used to punch out special statistics (not available on all machines).

7. PRINT switch. When ON, printing of the characters keyed takes place. When OFF, no printing takes place.

8. CHARACTER MODE switch. If this switch is set on 48, the +, _,), ¢, 0-8-2, >, :, ;, <, ', ?, ", =, !, (, ¬, |, characters are inoperative. The keyboard will lock up if these keys are pressed.

9. READ BUTTON. This button is used to:
   a. Read programs into program storage.
   b. Read data into output storage.

10. CLEAR switch. This switch is used to clear all of the cards out of the card bed.

11. REC BKSP BUTTON. When the record backspace button is pressed the column indicator returns to column 1 and erases what is in the input storage area.

KEYBOARD CONTROLS

The keyboard contains two types of keys: *data keys* and *function keys*. Data keys cause the entering of data. The blue, *function keys* cause the device to perform certain functions or controlling actions.

If *not* under program control, pressing a *data key* (key with a number, letter, or special character) will cause the character on the bottom of the key

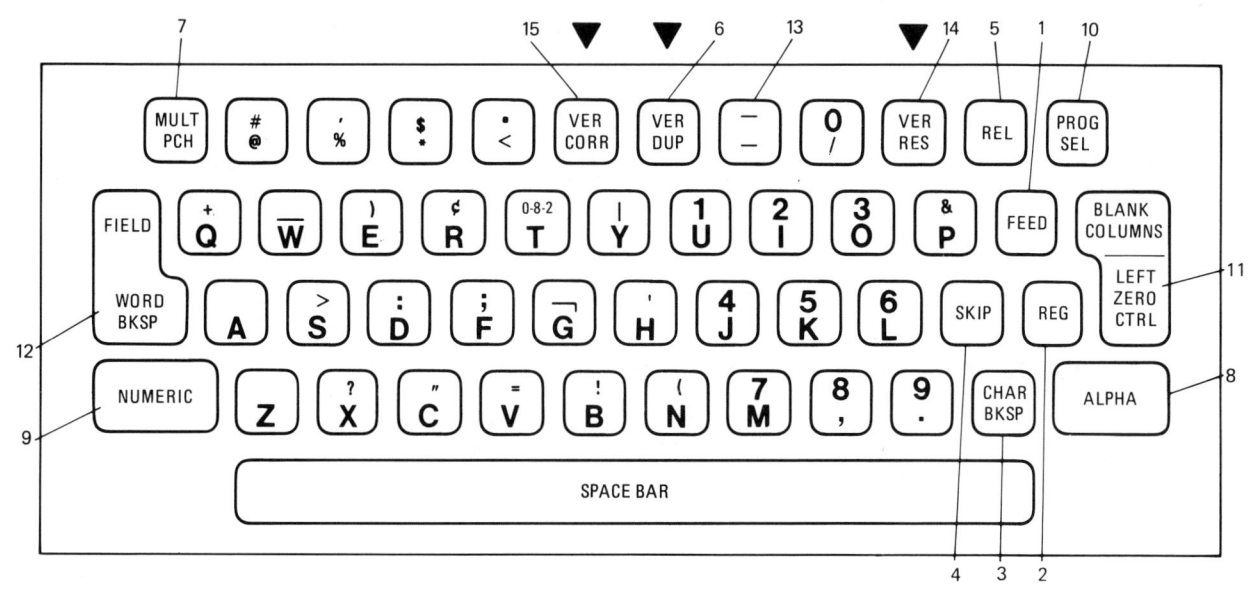

FIGURE 4.5
The IBM 129 data recorder keyboard
(Courtesy of IBM Corporation).

to be stored and later punched. If you wish the top character to be stored, hold down the numeric key at the same time that the data key is pressed.

Function Keys

The IBM 129 function keys shown in Figure 4.5 are:

1. *FEED key.* This key has two modes.
   a. In the *punch mode*, it feeds in two cards to the punch/read area, registering one card and preregistering the second card.
   b. In the verify mode, it feeds in one card.
2. *REG key.* This register key causes any card inserted manually or preregistered to be positioned against the punch/read station. A second card is not fed from the hopper.
3. *CHAR BKSP key.* The character backspace key causes:
   a. A backspace one column.
   b. The keyboard to be unlocked in an error condition.
4. *SKIP key.* This key has two modes.
   a. In *program mode*, it skips to the next field.
   b. In *manual mode*, it causes a single space.
5. *REL key.* Depression of the release key when keying:
   a. Moves the column indicator through column 80 and spaces are written for skipped columns.
   b. If the REC ADV/CARD FEED is set to AUTO, a card is read, and if the AUTO SKIP DUP switch is ON, any duplications at the beginning of the record are duplicated. If the REC ADV/CARD FEED is in MANUAL, the column indicator will read 00 and the card will not be punched until a FEED or a REG key is pressed.
6. *VER/DUP key.* The verify/duplicate key is used to duplicate or verify columns in a field of data. Depression of it causes more than one column to be duplicated.
7. *MULT PCH key.* Using the multiple punch key places the board in numeric shift and allows the operator to key several characters into one

UNIT 4 BUFFERED KEYPUNCHES

column. It provides a combination of characters that is not one of the standard 64 characters.

8. *ALPHA SHIFT key.* When depressed, this key places a numeric shift keyboard into an alpha shift (lower case).
9. *NUMERIC SHIFT key.* When depressed, this key places an alpha shift keyboard into NUMERIC shift (upper case).

The remaining function keys will be discussed in the PROGRAM and VERIFY sections.

OPERATOR PROCEDURES

Manual Punching (Program Level 0)

1. Set switches: PUNCH to ON, AUTO SKIP/DUP to ON, REC ADV/CARD FEED to ON, FEED to ON, PRINT to ON, CHARACTER MODE to 64 or 48 as instructed, PROGRAM MODE dial to 0.
2. Press the FEED key.
3. Key your card. If you make an error, use the CHAR BKSP key to backspace to the column in error. Rekey entering the correct data. If you press an invalid key, the CHAR BKSP key can be used to unlock the keyboard. For example, if you are in NUMERIC shift and press the "A" key, the keyboard will lock since no such character exists. In this case, press the CHAR BKSP key and the keyboard will unlock.
4. If there are not 80 characters to be keyed, press the REL key after keying the last character. This will move the column indicator to 01 and cause the card to be punched.

Error Corrections

If you detect an error immediately after keying the card, the card just punched will still be in the output storage area. Therefore you can feed a card in (FEED key) or manually insert and register it (REG key). Then press the duplication key (VER/DUP key) up to the column in error. Rekey the correction and press the duplication key through the last column. If the last column is not column 80, press the REL key.

However, if you discover an error after other cards have been keyed, the procedure is more complicated. First the data to be duplicated must be read back into the output storage area. To do this you follow the DATA READ procedure.

DATA READ Procedure

1. Set the PROGRAM MODE dial to DATA READ.
2. Manually insert the card in error in the punch bed. Do *not* register the card. Press the READ button. This reads the error card back into the output storage area.
3. Manually insert a blank card in the punch bed and press the REG key. Then duplicate up to the position where the error occurred, and duplicate the rest of the card.

When pressing the VER/DUP key if the card is punched and the column indicator has passed column 1, press the REC BKSP button on the console to get back to column 1. This must be done before keying the next record

Laboratory Work

Your instructor will now assign exercises from the text to key manually.

PART 2 DATA ENTRY EQUIPMENT

PROGRAMS The IBM 129 is instructed by the use of a program card which consists of programming codes. Each field in the program card has:

1. A punched code which describes the function needed.
2. A field definition code showing for how many columns this action is to take place.

A chart is shown below for the functions necessary in the laboratory exercises in this text.

Function	Character Code	Field Definition
Skip	- (11 punch)	& (12 punch)
Punch numeric	b (blank)	&
Duplicate numeric	0 (zero)	&
Punch alphanumeric	1	A (12 and 1 punches)
Duplicate alphameric	/	A (0 and 1 punches)
Left zero (verify only)	3 (1st and last column)	&

Your manual will have further codes.

EXAMPLE TO ILLUSTRATE OPERATIONS PROCEDURES A program card is to be planned for the following data:

Columns 1-6	Duplicate numeric date
Columns 7-11	Duplicate alphanumeric course abbreviation
Columns 12-20	Punch social security number
Columns 21-33	Punch last name
Columns 34-45	Punch first name
Column 46	Punch middle initial
Columns 47-52	Amount of tuition and fees (left zero) nnnn∧nn
Columns 53-80	Blank

A record layout with the planned codes is shown in Figure 4.6. Punch the program card and have your instructor inspect it.

Loading a Program

1. Set the AUTO SKIP/DUP key to OFF.
2. Set the PROGRAM MODE dial to the desired program number 1 through 6 (for this exercise use 1).
3. Insert the program card that has been punched at the punch/read station. Do *not* register the card.

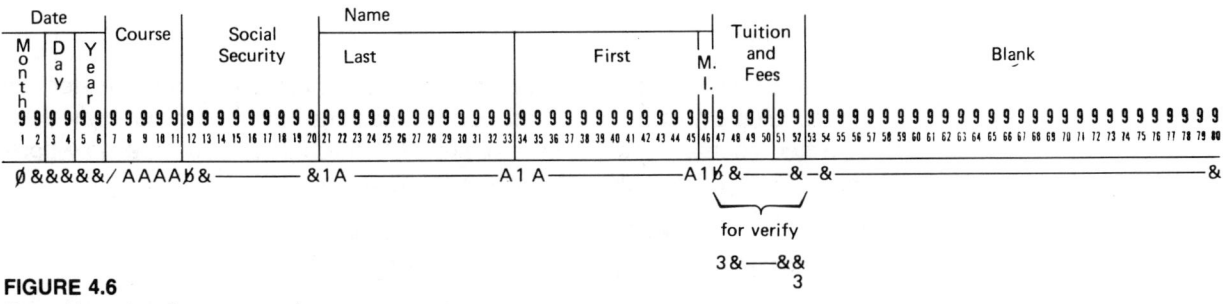

FIGURE 4.6
Record layout and program codes.

UNIT 4 BUFFERED KEYPUNCHES

4. Press the READ BUTTON.

This reads the program into program storage one.

Keying Under Program Control

At the beginning of a job there are no fields in the output storage area to be duplicated. Therefore for the first card the fields to be duplicated must be keyed manually.

1. Set the PUNCH/VERIFY switch to PUNCH.
2. Set the AUTO SKIP/DUP switch to OFF.
3. Set the REC ADV/CARD FEED switch to AUTO.
4. Set the PROGRAM MODE dial to the program number under which you loaded the program. (In the case of the example, 1)
5. Set the PRINT switch to ON.
6. Set your CHARACTER MODE switch to either 64 or 48 as directed by the instructor or job documentation.
7. Press the FEED key until two cards are fed.
8. Press the PROG SEL (number 10, Figure 4.5) key and the key with the program number used in Step 4 above. It is *not* necessary to hold down the NUMERIC shift key when the program number is keyed in. To get out of program control (for example, to correct or duplicate a card), the PROG SEL and zero keys can be pressed. Manual operations will then be possible. To get back under program control, press the PROG SEL and program number keys.
9. Since for the first card there is nothing in output storage to duplicate, the AUTO SKIP/DUP switch should be left off. The data to be duplicated will be manually keyed in. For our example, looking at Figure 4.6,
   a. Key in the current date. It will not be necessary to hold down the NUMERIC shift key since this field has been programmed numeric.
   b. Key in the course abbreviation and number. Use DP310 holding down NUMERIC for the 310.
   c. Key in your social security number (you need not hold down the NUMERIC shift key).
   d. Key in your last name. If you do not use the entire field, depress the SKIP key.
   e. Key in your first name. If you do not use the entire field, depress the SKIP key.
   f. Key in your middle initial. If you have none, press the SKIP key.
   g. Assume your tuition is $110.16. Key in 11016 and press the LEFT ZERO CTRL key (number 11, Figure 4.5). This inserts leading zeros without your having to determine how many should be keyed in.
   h. Press the REL key. This places what you keyed into the output storage area. There is now something to duplicate into the first two fields of the data card.
   i. Turn the AUTO SKIP/DUP switch to ON.

Now try keying the next two records. Note that the column indicator has moved to column 12. This is because the machine has already duplicated the date and course abbreviation in columns 1 through 11. You are now positioned for the third field, the social security number.

SS #	Name	Tuition
123-45-6754	Lee, Iva H	150.00
675-88-9766	Harbaugh, Maggie	34.67

PART 2 DATA ENTRY EQUIPMENT

Note that duplication and skipping operations are now fully automatic.

A long job must sometimes be interrupted. In this case do not key the first card again manually. Read the data for the last card punched into output storage with DATA READ procedure (page 44). Then load the program as before (page 45). Press the PROG SEL and program number keys. This procedure permits the AUTO SKIP/DUP switch to be set on at the beginning.

MORE SPECIAL FUNCTION KEYS

1. FIELD/WORD BKSP key (number 12, Figure 4.5). The field word backspace key can be used under program control to backspace an entire *field*. If *not* under program control, the key acts as the CHAR BKSP key and backspaces only one column.
2. -LZ key (number 13, Figure 4.5). The minus left zero key under program control is used to left zero and punch negative amounts. If this had been used in Step g above, leading zeros would have been inserted on the left *and* a minus or 11 punch and the digit 6 would have been punched in the right-most position.

NOTE There are two keys for the comma and period; their use depends on whether you are in NUMERIC or ALPHA shifts.

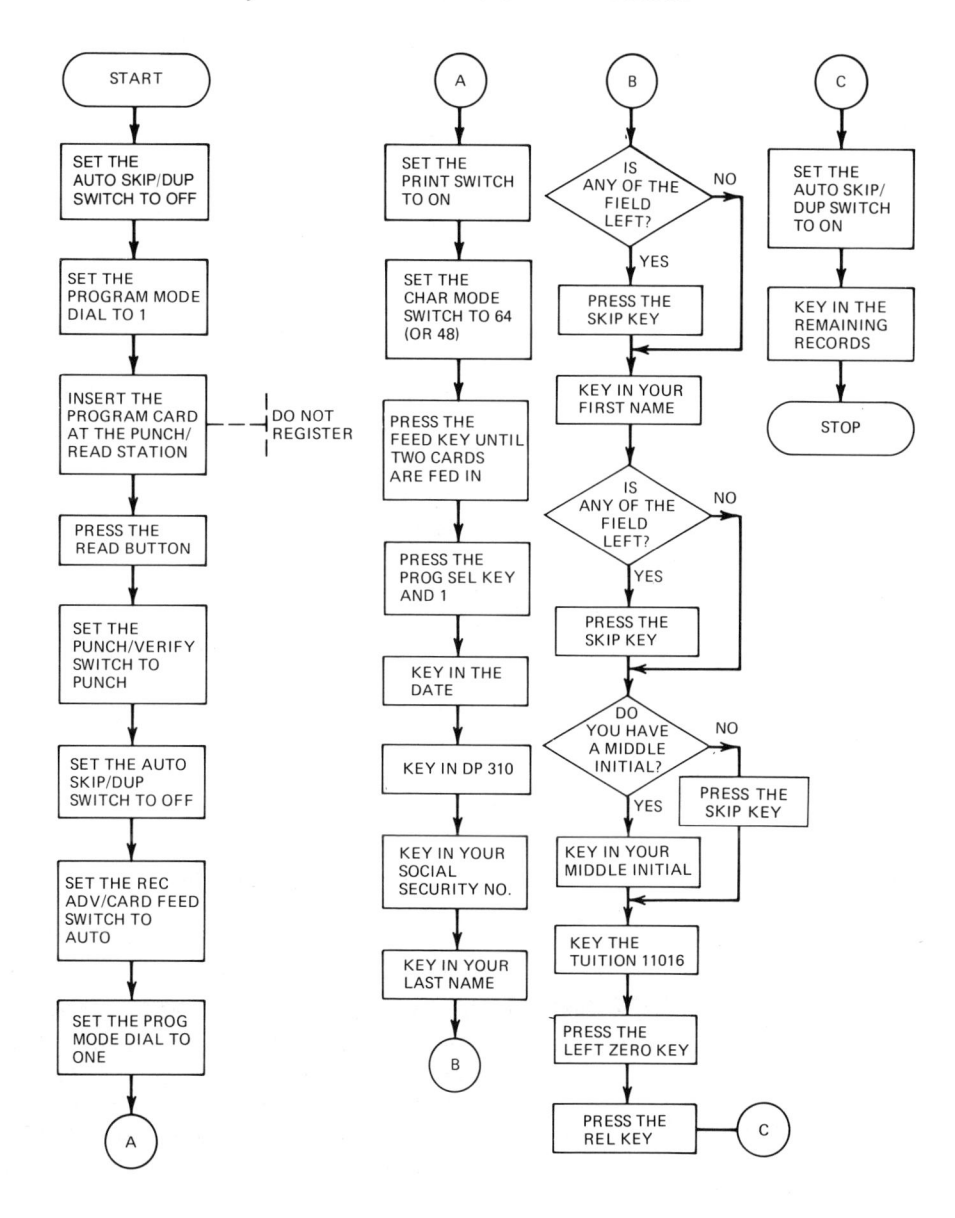

FIGURE 4.7
Keying data under program control on the IBM 129.

PUNCHING OUT A PROGRAM

If you are not sure what program is in storage, you can punch out the program on a blank card to check. The steps are:

1. Set the PUNCH/VERIFY switch to PUNCH.
2. Set the AUTO SKIP/DUP switch to OFF.
3. Set the REC ADV/CARD FEED switch to MANUAL.
4. Set the PROGRAM MODE dial to PROG PCH.
5. Insert a blank card at the punch station and press the REG key.
6. Press the REL key. Note that the column indicator reads 00.
7. Press the PROG SEL and program level number keys.

The program will be punched out.

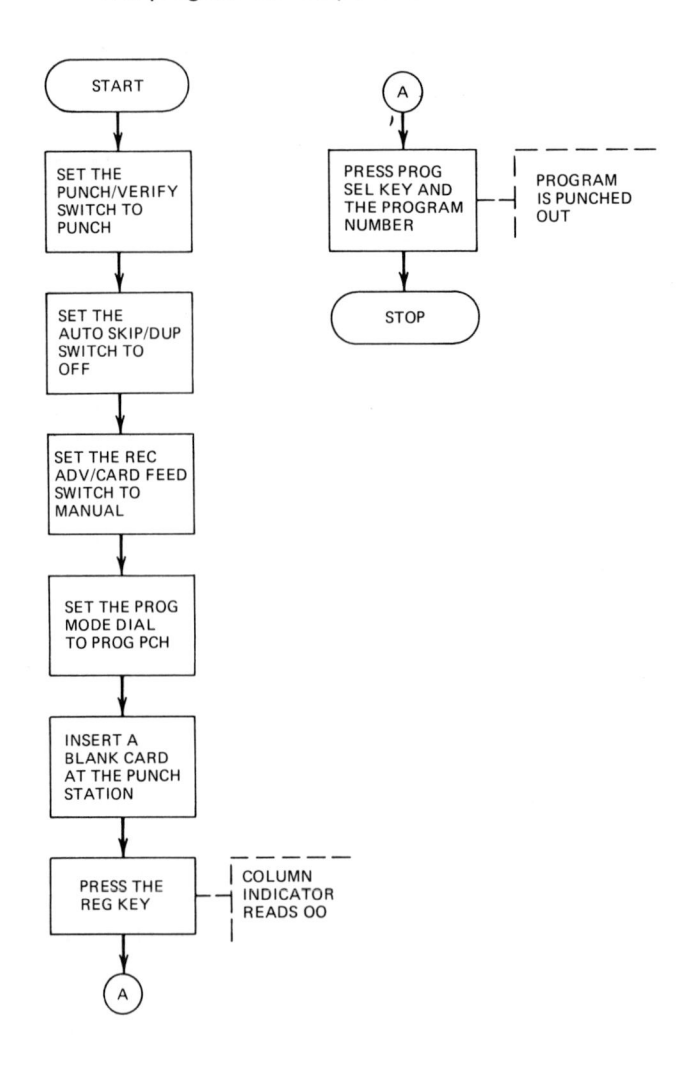

FIGURE 4.8
Punching out a program on the IBM 129.

Laboratory Exercises

Your instructor will assign programmed exercises to you from this textbook.

VERIFYING

Verifying is done as a check, normally by a person other than the one who keyed the original data. Some industries spot verify; that is, they verify only certain batches of data. Such a practice has obvious dangers. Verifying should be done by experienced operators.

In the previous example in Figure 4.6, the only change necessary for a verifying program card would be the change shown in the tuition and fees

PART 2 DATA ENTRY EQUIPMENT

field (columns 47 to 52). The code of a 3 occurs in column 47, ampersands until column 52, and codes of 3 and & in column 52.

Loading the program is done as previously described. Duplicated data can be loaded with a DATA READ. Then the program should be selected and switches set as before. The PUNCH/VERIFY switch must be set to VERIFY.

Verifying steps are:

1. Place punched cards in the hopper. Load the program. Load the data to be duplicated. Set switches to VERIFY and to ON for AUTO SKIP/DUP and REC ADV/CARD FEED.
2. Press the FEED key. The card will *pass through* the PUNCH/READ unit, which is now acting as a reader. An image of the data just read has been placed in input storage.
3. Key as you would if punching. If there are no errors (that is, what you key agrees with what was read into input storage), two punches occur in the right edge (called column 81) of the card opposite the 2 and 3 rows.
4. If there is a disagreement between what you key and what is in the input storage, the read verify light will come on. Then:

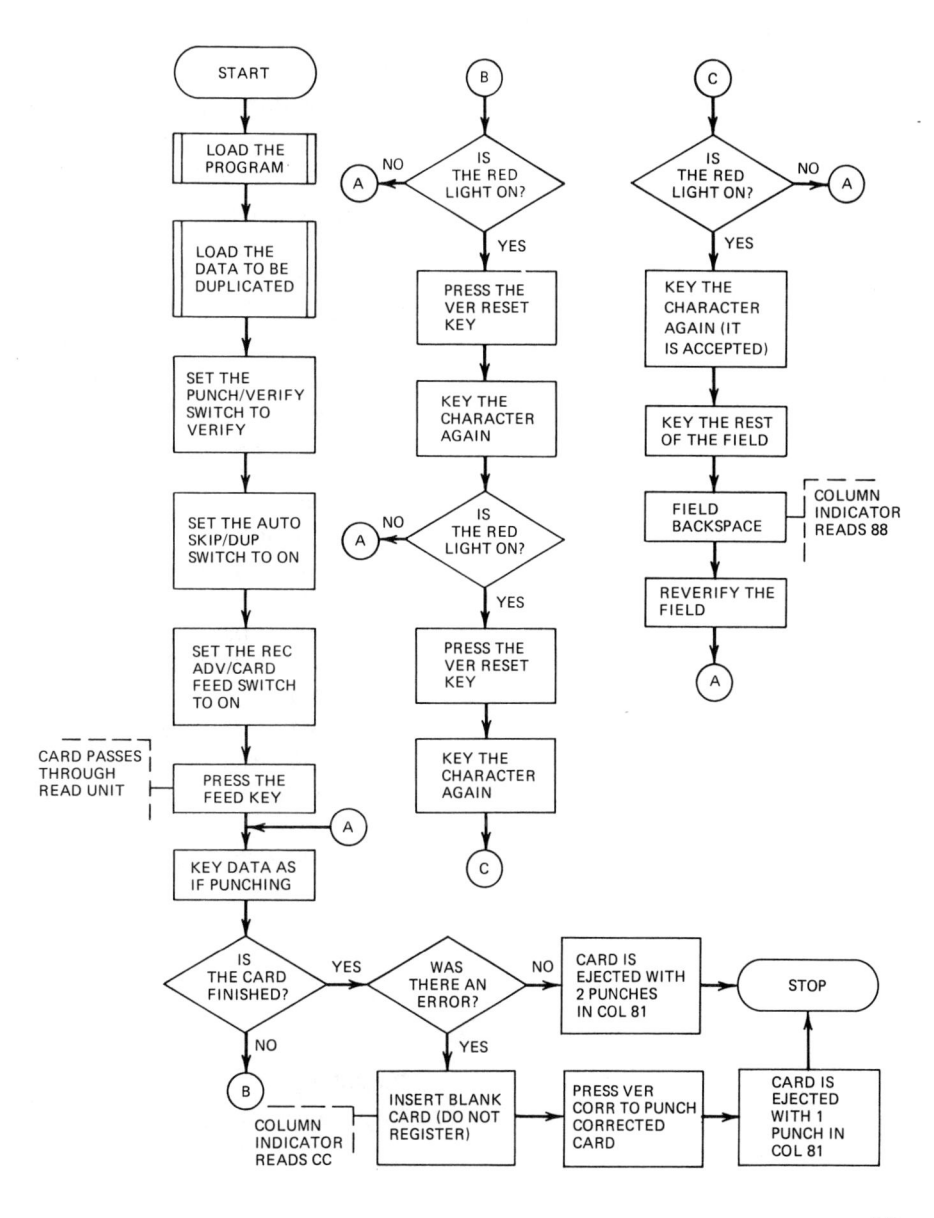

FIGURE 4.9
Verifying on the IBM 129.

UNIT 4 BUFFERED KEYPUNCHES

a. Press the VER RES (verify reset) key, (number 14, Figure 4.5) and key in the character again.
b. If the red light comes on again, repeat Step a.
c. If the red light comes on again, repeat Step a again. What you key is accepted, and it replaces the originally keyed information. (You are allowed three tries in case you have made a mistake.)
d. Finish keying the field. The 88 will appear in the column indicator.
e. Press FIELD BKSP and reverify the entire field.
f. Continue.
g. When keying is completed for the record, **CC** will appear in the column indicator. This means a *c*orrection *c*ard should be inserted manually at the punch/read unit. Do *not* register this blank card.
h. Press the VER CORR (verify correct) key (number 15, Figure 4.5). A new corrected card will be punched. This card will have only a 2 punch in column 81. The error card should be discarded.

Laboratory Exercises

Your instructor will assign some verifying exercises.

MAINTENANCE AND UNUSUAL CONDITIONS

1. You may be required to change the printer ribbon. Your reference manual will give directions for this operation.
2. You may wish to dust or wipe off the keyboard. You may use a soft damp cloth, but never spray cleaning solutions or water on the machine. Do not consume food or drinks at the keyboard.
3. Empty the chip box periodically.
4. Cards sometimes jam.
   If the jam is in the hopper, remove the cover of the hopper. Pull the handle underneath it forward to allow removal of the card.
   If the jam is in the card bed:
   a. Try pressing the card release button and gently pull out the card. If the card tears, try pushing out the pieces with another card.
   b. Piece these parts of the card together to see that all the pieces have been removed from the machine.
   c. If pieces still remain in the machine:
      (1) Set the PRINT and AUTO SKIP/DUP switches to OFF and set the REC ADV/CARD FEED switch to MANUAL.
      (2) Press PROG SEL and the zero key.
      (3) Hold down the MULT PCH key and key in all 12 punches using &, -, and digits 0 to 9 keys sequentially. (This uses all of the punch dies.)
      (4) Manually insert a card at the PUNCH/READ station and press the REG key.
      (5) While holding down the CARD RELEASE button press PROG SEL and the zero key. Punch out follows but the card will not move while you are holding down the CARD RELEASE button.
      (6) Tear a strip of card (about 1 inch wide) and use it to push the pieces of card out from under the PUNCH/READ unit.
      (7) Repeat using the DUP key if necessary for step (3).
   If repeating the above procedure several times does not work, call your instructor or supervisor. The use of a card saw (Figure 4.10) may be necessary. Caution should be used with this instrument. Punch dies can be damaged if too much force is used.
5. Keyboard lockups sometimes occur. The keys do not respond to pressure. Some possible causes of keyboard lockups are:

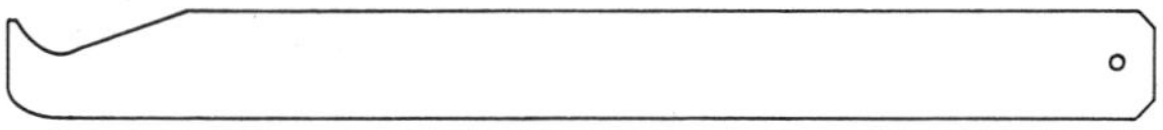

FIGURE 4.10
Card saw.

    a. Invalid character key was pressed. For example, the "A" key was pressed while in numeric control. (No such character exists.) Press the CHAR BKSP key and rekey.
    b. Attempted duplication after a CLEAR. Character backspace and manually key in data.
    c. Invalid program selection. Character backspace and select program.
    d. Hopper out of cards. Add cards and press the FEED key.
    e. Stacker full. Remove cards.
    f. Column indicator reads **00** and REC ADV/CARD FEED switch is on MANUAL. Set on AUTO or manually select program and feed a card.
    g. Compare error. Press VER RES and rekey.
    h. Failure to reverify a field when the column indicator reads 88. FLD BKSP and reverify.

Other lockup conditions are explained in your reference manual.

SPECIAL FEATURES

The IBM 129 has 12 special features available which cost extra money. They are described in the IBM 129 reference manual. Some of them are:

1. *Production Statistics.* The word *statistics* means the collection, organization, and interpretation of numerical data. Many people mispronounce this word. It is pronounced sta-tis'-ticks. Production statistic features give counts on keystrokes or cards punched. They are sometimes used to measure the productivity or output of data entry operators.

2. *Accumulate Feature.* This allows the user to balance to a predetermined total, to create a hash total for a group of cards, and other features. A *hash total* is the arithmetic total of the numbers in a specific field.

3. *Self-Checking Number Device (Modulus 10 or 11).* This is a method of catching substitution and transposition errors in keying. For an explanation of these terms and the methods used, see Appendix D.

4. *A Card I/O Attachment.* This attachment allows the IBM 129 to be on-line to the IBM System/3 Model 6 and gives 80-column-card punching capabilities. In this way computer output can be punched onto cards.

5. *Variable Length Cards.* This feature allows handling of cards with 51, 60, 66, or 80 columns.

SECTION C
THE UNIVAC 1710

Other companies such as Sperry UNIVAC make card data recorders. UNIVAC makes the UNIVAC 1710 and 1810 VIPs.

A picture of the UNIVAC 1710 and its keyboard are shown in Figures 4.11 and 4.12. The UNIVAC 1710 and 1810 are called VIPs because the verify, interpret, and punch functions are all done on the same machine.

Interpreting is printing on the top of a card information that has already been punched. Sometimes, when cards are punched on a computer no printing occurs. Punches can then be decoded and printed at the top of the card on the UNIVAC 1710 and 1810.

The UNIVAC machines operate on the same principle as the IBM 129. Examine the schematic picture of the parts of the VIP shown in Figure 4.13.

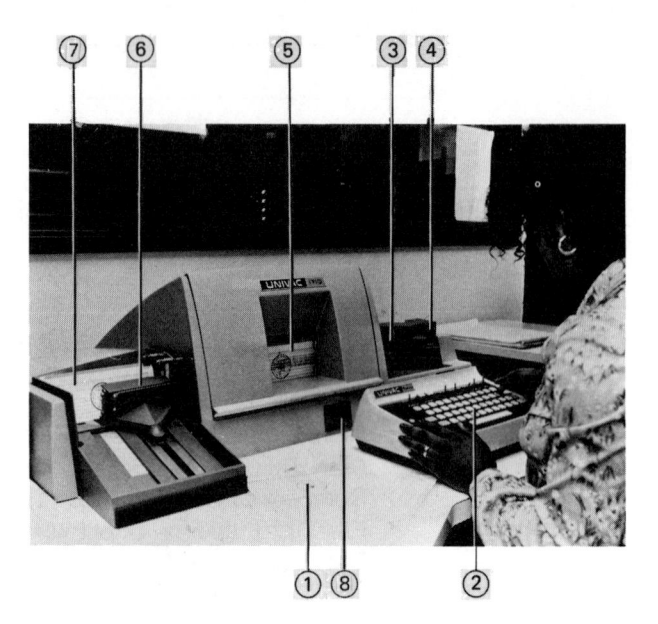

FIGURE 4.11
The UNIVAC 1710 VIP.

1. Reading board
2. Keyboard
3. Input magazine
4. Auxiliary input
5. Visible station
6. Output stacker
7. Select stacker
8. Column indicator

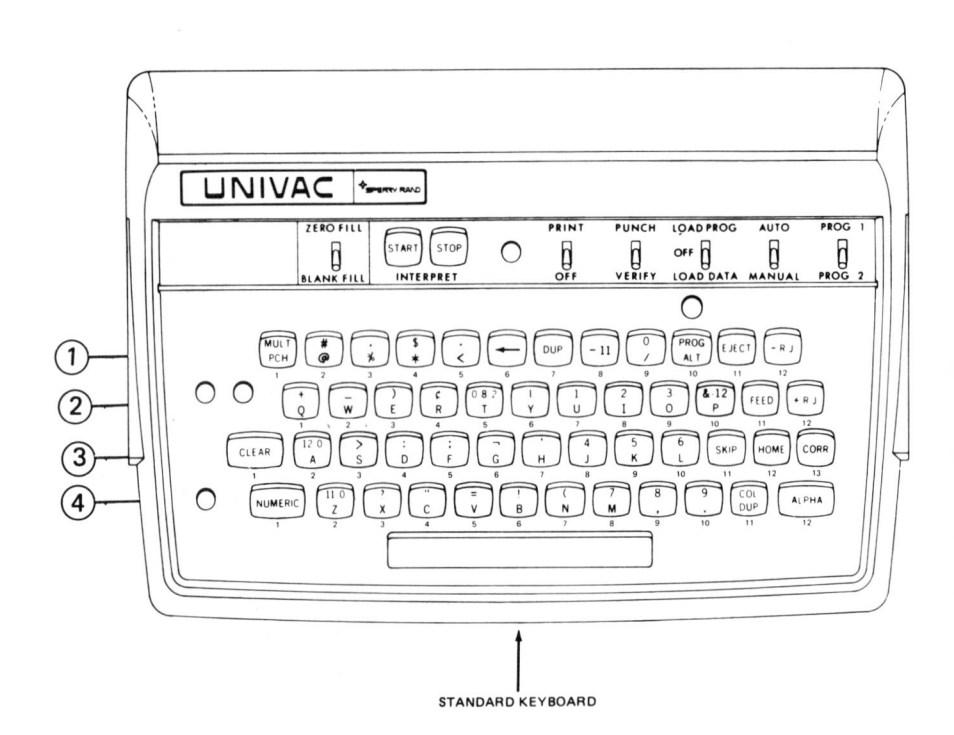

FIGURE 4.12
The UNIVAC 1710 keyboard (Courtesy of Sperry UNIVAC).

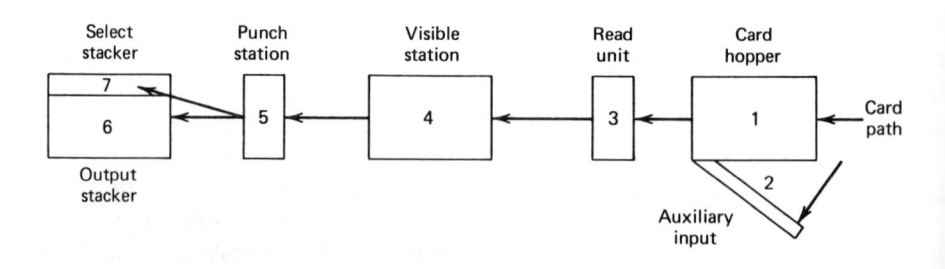

FIGURE 4.13
Univac 1710 and 1810 card path.

PART 2 DATA ENTRY EQUIPMENT

Cards are normally placed in the card hopper (1), which holds about 600 cards. However, if only one card is to be read or punched, the card can be inserted in the auxiliary input slot (2). The card passes to the read unit (3) where it is read if it is being duplicated or verified. The card then passes to the visible station (4) and remains there until the record has been keyed (or duplicated). The card then passes through the punch station (5) where it is punched and passed to the output stacker (6). When a program or data are being loaded, the card may go instead to the select stacker (7).

Two advantages of the VIP over the IBM 129 are immediately obvious:

1. The entire card is visible at all times. This feature eliminates card design problems.
2. The column indicator is larger and much easier to read.

These machines can also store instructions or programs in program storage just as the IBM 129 does (see Figure 4.1). The 1710 can store only two programs which makes it similar to the old IBM 029, except that the 1710 is buffered. But the UNIVAC 1810 can store up to *eight* programs.

Referring to Figure 4.12, the two right-most console switches on the UNIVAC 1710 VIP control the modes of operation. The modes are:

1. AUTOmatic. Operation is under program control.
2. MANUAL. Punching is done manually with no program control.
3. LOAD DATA. Data is being read into the output storage area for duplication purposes.
4. LOAD PROGRAM. A program card is being read into program storage. The program 1 and 2 switch determines the program number.

Other switches are:

1. PRINT switch. This switch should be ON for printing of what is punched.
2. PUNCH/VERIFY switch. This switch should be on PUNCH for punching or on VERIFY for verifying.
3. BLANK/ZERO FILL switch. This switch is used with the RJ or right justify key. It fills with blanks or zeros depending on the switch setting.
4. The START and STOP switches. These switches are used when interpreting punched cards with no printing.

MANUAL KEYING The 1710 and 1810 VIPs differ from the IBM 129 in that they are normally in NUMERIC shift. The IBM 129 is normally in ALPHA shift. To key the lower set of characters the ALPHA key must be pressed. The ALPHA shift continues until the NUMERIC shift is pressed. When the ALPHA shift is established, the green ALPHA indicator light on the keyboard comes on.

SPECIAL LIGHTS Locate these lights on your 1710 keyboard as you read the following material:

1. ALPHA LIGHT
   The ALPHA LIGHT is next to the PRINT switch at the top center of the keyboard. When this light is green (ON), keying is in alpha shift (lower case or the symbols on the bottom of the key).
2. INTERLOCK LIGHT
   The INTERLOCK LIGHT is the red light opposite the NUMERIC shift key. It indicates a keyboard lockup. Some causes for the interlock light being ON are:
   a. Output stacker is full. Correct and press CLEAR key.
   b. Card jam. Correct and press CLEAR key.
   c. FEED key was depressed when nothing was in the visible station. Press CLEAR key.

UNIT 4 BUFFERED KEYPUNCHES

3. **PROGRAM 2 LIGHT**
The PROGRAM 2 LIGHT is the green light above the PROG ALT key. When this light is on, it indicates program 2 is under control.

4. **ERROR LIGHT**
The ERROR LIGHT is the red light just to the left of the "Q" key. When verifying, it indicates:
a. What was keyed does not agree with what was punched.
b. A non-match situation (see below).

5. **NON-MATCH LIGHT**
The NON-MATCH LIGHT is the yellow light opposite the "Q" key, to the left of the ERROR LIGHT. Under program control a field may be programmed for the STOP RIGHT JUSTIFY code. The yellow light then comes on if too many characters are keyed for the size of the field. The STOP RIGHT JUSTIFY code prevents keying too many characters in a field.

SPECIAL FUNCTION KEYS

1. **DUP KEY**
The DUPLICATE key duplicates one column or initiates programmed duplication of a field.

2. **COL DUP KEY**
The COLUMN DUPLICATE key causes a continuous duplication until released. It will *not* initiate programmed duplication.

3. **FEED KEY**
The FEED key causes a card to be moved to the next position in the card path in either manual or automatic mode. In Figure 4.13 it causes a card to move from the card hopper to the visible station. If a card had been in the visible station, it would have caused that card to be punched and moved to the output stacker.

4. **EJECT KEY**
Depressing the EJECT key causes the card in the visible station to move to the select stacker (number 7, Figure 4.13). The column indicator returns to 1, but no punching takes place. What was in output storage does not change. A new card is *not* fed into the visible station. There is an optional REL/EJT key. If your device has this key, your instructor will discuss this feature or refer you to the manual.

5. **BACKSPACE KEY (←)**
This key with an arrow causes the column indicator to go back one column. It does not change anything in input storage. You may correct errors by using this key to backspace and then rekey.

6. **SKIP KEY**
The SKIP key is similar to the TAB key on a typewriter. Under programmed control, it causes a skip to the next field and input storage is set to blanks for those columns skipped. Under manual control, the first depression causes a skip from the current column position through column 80, clearing these positions in storage to blanks.

7. **HOME KEY**
The HOME key causes the column indicator to return to column 1 without clearing anything in the input storage area.

8. **+RJ and −RJ KEYS**
Under programmed control these RIGHT ADJUST keys cause leading zeros to be inserted when only the significant digits have been keyed. For example if 101 were keyed in a five position field and the +RJ key were pressed,

Ø	Ø	1	Ø	1
32	33	34	35	36

would be entered in storage. If the −RJ key had been pressed, the only change would be that an 11 punch and a 1 punch would be placed in position 36 making it a negative number. These keys on other devices are sometimes called the LZ and −LZ keys.

9. PROG ALT KEY

   The PROG ALT key allows you to change programs without changing the console program switch.

10. CORR KEY

    The CORR key is used to make corrections when verifying.

Manual Keying Procedure

1. Load cards in the hopper.
2. Set switches to PRINT, PUNCH, OFF, and MANUAL.
3. Press the FEED key to feed a card into the visible station.
4. Press the CLEAR key to turn off the red interlock light.
5. Key in the data, remembering to press the ALPHA SHIFT key to get the lower shift.
6. When you finish keying, press the FEED key to punch the card.

Error Corrections

1. If you detect an error immediately after keying the card, then a copy still remains in the output storage area.
   a. If a card is not in the visible station, press the FEED and CLEAR keys or insert a card manually in the auxiliary input. Press the FEED and CLEAR keys.
   b. Press the COL DUP key up to the column in error.
   c. Key the correction.
   d. Press the COL DUP key to the end of the card or to the last position on the record.
   e. Press the FEED key and the card will be punched.
2. If the error is discovered at a later date, the data is no longer in the output storage area. Therefore data needs to be loaded into the output area.

Load Data Procedure

1. Insert the data card (or in this case the error card) in the auxiliary input.
2. Set the console switch to LOAD DATA.
3. Press the FEED key. This reads the card into output storage.
4. Set the LOAD DATA switch to OFF.
5. Now the card is ready to be duplicated. Do Steps a through e in Part 1 of the error correction procedure above.

Laboratory Work

Your instructor will now assign exercises to key manually.

PROGRAMS The UNIVAC 1710 is instructed by a program card. The program card consists of programming codes. Each field in the program card has:

1. A punched code which describes the function needed.

UNIT 4 BUFFERED KEYPUNCHES

2. A field definition code showing for how many columns this action is to take place.

This table shows the functions needed to do the laboratory exercises in this text.

	Character Code		Field Definition	
Function	Program 1	Program 2	Program 1	Program 2
Skip	-	5	&	4
Punch numeric	ᵇ	ᵇ	&	4
Duplicate numeric	0	6	&	4
Punch alpha	1	7	A	4-7
Duplicate alpha	/	6-7	A	4-7
Start right justify	J	5-7	&	4
Stop right justify	12-11-1	4-5-7		

Your manual will have further codes.

Programs 1 and 2 are both punched on the same card if two programs are to be used in the same job. This method is similar to the method used on the IBM 029 described in Appendix H. Program 1 uses rows 12, 11, 0, 1, 2, and 3. Program 2 uses rows 4, 5, 6, 7, 8, and 9. To obtain some of the multiple punches in the above chart, you must use the MULT PCH key.

EXAMPLE TO ILLUSTRATE OPERATIONS PROCEDURES

A program card is to be planned for the following data:

Columns 1-6	Duplicate numeric data.
Columns 7-11	Duplicate alphameric course abbreviation.
Columns 12-20	Punch social security number.
Columns 21-33	Punch last name.
Columns 34-45	Punch first name.
Column 46	Punch middle initial.
Columns 47-52	Punch amount of tuition and fees (right justify) nnnn‸nn.
Columns 53-80	Blank.

A record layout with the planned codes is shown in Figure 4.14. Punch the program card and have your instructor inspect it.

Program Load Procedure

1. Insert the program card in the auxiliary input slot.
2. Set the LOAD switch to LOAD PROG.

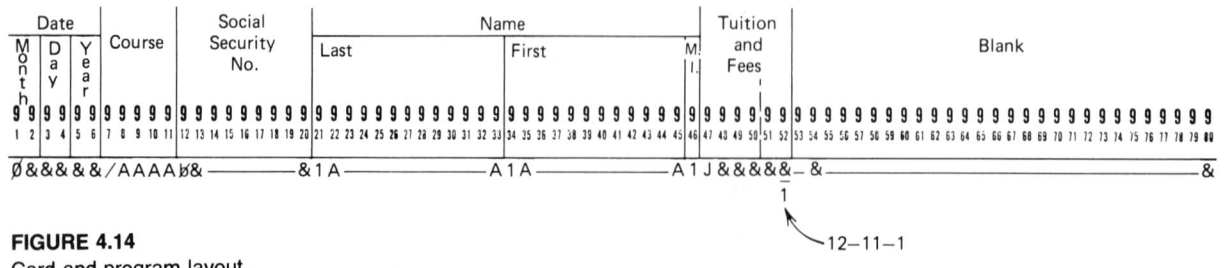

FIGURE 4.14
Card and program layout.

3. Press the FEED key. The program card is read into program storage and then passes into the select stacker.
4. Set the LOAD switch back to OFF.

Keying Under Program Control

1. Prepare a master card for the data to be duplicated. Load this data.
   a. In our example, punch the correct data in columns 1 to 6 and punch DP310 in columns 7 to 11.
   b. Using the LOAD DATA PROCEDURE on page 55, load the duplication data into output storage.
2. Load your program (in the example, load into PROG 1) using the PROGRAM LOAD PROCEDURE above.
3. Set the console switches (from left to right) on ZERO FILL, PRINT, PUNCH, OFF, AUTO, and PROG 1.
4. Press the FEED key and the CLEAR key.

In our example, the keying would be:

1. Since you are under programmed control, columns 1 to 11 will be duplicated immediately and the column indicator should read 12.
2. Key in your social security number.
3. When column 21 is reached, the green ALPHA SHIFT light will come on because the last name field has been programmed in ALPHA SHIFT. Therefore it is *not* necessary to press the ALPHA SHIFT key as in manual keying. Key in your last name and press SKIP unless you used the entire field.
4. Key in your first name and press SKIP unless you used the entire field.
5. Key in your middle initial. If you have none, press the SKIP key.
6. Assume your tuition is $110.16. Key in 11016 and press the +RJ key. This inserts leading zeros to the left without your having to determine how many zeros should be keyed and keying them. The device should then automatically skip to column 80 and punch a card since you programmed the last field to skip.

Now try keying the records below:

SS#	Name	Tuition
124-45-6754	Lee, Iva H	150.00
675-88-9766	Harbaugh, Maggie	34.67

Laboratory Exercises

Your instructor will assign programmed exercises to you from this textbook.

VERIFYING Verifying is normally done by a person who did not key the original data. Verifying is done as a check. Some industries spot verify; that is, they verify only certain batches of data. Such a practice has obvious dangers. Verifying is usually done by experienced operators.

Verifying steps are:

1. Load the program card with the PROGRAM LOAD PROCEDURE.
2. Load a master data card with fields to be duplicated with the LOAD DATA PROCEDURE.
3. Set the console switches to ZERO FILL, VERIFY, OFF, AUTO, and PROG 1 (in the case of our example).

4. Press the FEED and CLEAR keys.
5. Key as you would if punching. If there are no errors, punches will appear in the left margin of the card, sometimes called column −1. If punches appear opposite rows 0 and 1 in the left margin, the card was verified as correct.
6. If there is a disagreement between what you key and what was in input storage, the yellow NON-MATCH indicator light will come on. The keyboard then locks up. Action should be taken as follows:
   a. Press the CLEAR key, and key the character again. If the yellow light does not come on again (*you* made the mistake while verifying), you may proceed.
   b. If the yellow light comes on again, repeat step (a) again.
   c. If the yellow light comes on again, you may try once more to rekey. After the third non match, the red ERROR indicator light comes on. This means that the keyboard is set for you to enter the correct data. Rekey the correct data.
   d. Keying should continue. When keying of the card is finished, the card will *not* feed automatically. Insert a blank card in the auxiliary input to be used for correction purposes.
   e. Press the FEED key. The error card will be ejected into the select stacker. The corrected card will be punched with a punch opposite row 1 in the left margin; the corrected card will be deposited in the output stacker with the cards previously verified.

Laboratory Exercises

Your instructor will assign verifying exercises.

MAINTENANCE AND UNUSUAL CONDITIONS

1. The ink roller may need to be changed because the printing is becoming dim. Your instructor will either demonstrate how this may be done or will refer you to the manual.
2. You may use a soft damp cloth to wipe off the keyboard but do not use cleaning solutions or water. Do not consume food or drinks at the keyboard.
3. Empty the chip box periodically.
4. Every two weeks:
   a. You should remove the read unit and post punch for dusting purposes. Use a small brush to brush the lint into an envelope, not into the lower mechanism.
   b. Remove lint and card dust from the input and output stacker.
   c. Wipe the glass plate, reader surface and rolls, and post punch plate with a lint free cloth. Ink smears on the glass plate and other interior areas can be removed with furniture cleaner. Do not get ink on the table top or covers. Your instructor will demonstrate these cleaning procedures.
5. Card Jams
   a. Open the cover and release the two clips holding the glass plate in the visible station. Lower the glass plate.
   b. If a card is caught in the read unit, it can be removed by removing the optical fiber block of the read unit. Turn the wing fastener and pull out. The unit, if lowered, will be free of the spring unit at the top. Remove the card by turning the disk at the top in a clockwise direction.
   c. If the card is caught in the punch unit, unscrew the two screws on the punch unit. Then pull it out to the right.

d. If a card jams in the stacker, remove it by pulling it on through.
e. It is always wise to piece together the pieces of a torn card to be sure you have all the card out.

Your instructor will demonstrate the above procedures when jams occur.

6. *Blown Fuses.* If too much electricity surges through the device, the circuit breaker may be thrown. Press the reset button next to the Power ON-OFF switch. If the trouble continues, your customer engineer (repair person) may have to be called.

7. *Leaving the Machine On for a Period of Time.* If the cover of the visible station is raised, the current to the motor is cut off. None of the contents of internal storage are disturbed as they would be if the machine were turned off. Work can be resumed by closing the cover. If you leave your machine for a few minutes, raise the cover.

8. *Keyboard Interlocks.* Keyboard interlocks can be caused by:
    a. A full output stacker (red light). Clear stacker.
    b. Feeding when the visible station is empty (red light). Press the CLEAR key.
    c. A card jam in the read station, visible station, punch station (red light), or output stacker (no light). Remove the jam and press CLEAR.
    d. Exceeding the length of a right adjusted field or not depressing the right adjust key at the end of the field (yellow light). Rekey or press the RJ key.
    e. Depressing the FEED key when there are no cards in the hopper (red light) or when the visible station cover is open Correct the situation.
    f. Keying an incorrect character while verifying (yellow or red light). See directions for verifying.
    g. Keying when the LOAD PROGRAM or LOAD DATA switch is on.

SPECIAL FEATURES

As with other buffered keypunches, special features are available on the 1710 for extra cost. They are:

1. *Production Counters.* These counters give keystroke and card counts. Error counts exist for verifying. This feature is used to monitor operator production.

2. *Acoustical Covers.* This cover is said to reduce the noise level by 50%.

3. *Column 81 Verification Punching.* This feature makes verification punches compatible with the IBM 129 and other devices.

4. *Release Key.* The EJECT key is modified so that in AUTO mode it will feed a card after duplicating programmed duplication fields and clearing by skipping all other fields.

5. *Modulus 10 or 11.* Check digits are generated on special fields to catch errors in keying (see Appendix D).

6. *Variable Length Cards.* This feature allows the feeding of cards that are 51 or 66 columns in length.

7. *Interspersed Master Card.* This feature allows the punching of duplicated data from a master card with, for example, a left corner cut into following cards with a right corner cut (or vice versa).

8. The UNIVAC 1710 has an expanded feature which allows six program levels rather than two. This is implemented through a program level control auxiliary board (see Figure 4.15). Programs are selected by the program select keys rather than the program switch. Chaining is also possible as on the UNIVAC 1810 (see Section D below). The *chaining feature* causes the machine to switch automatically from one program

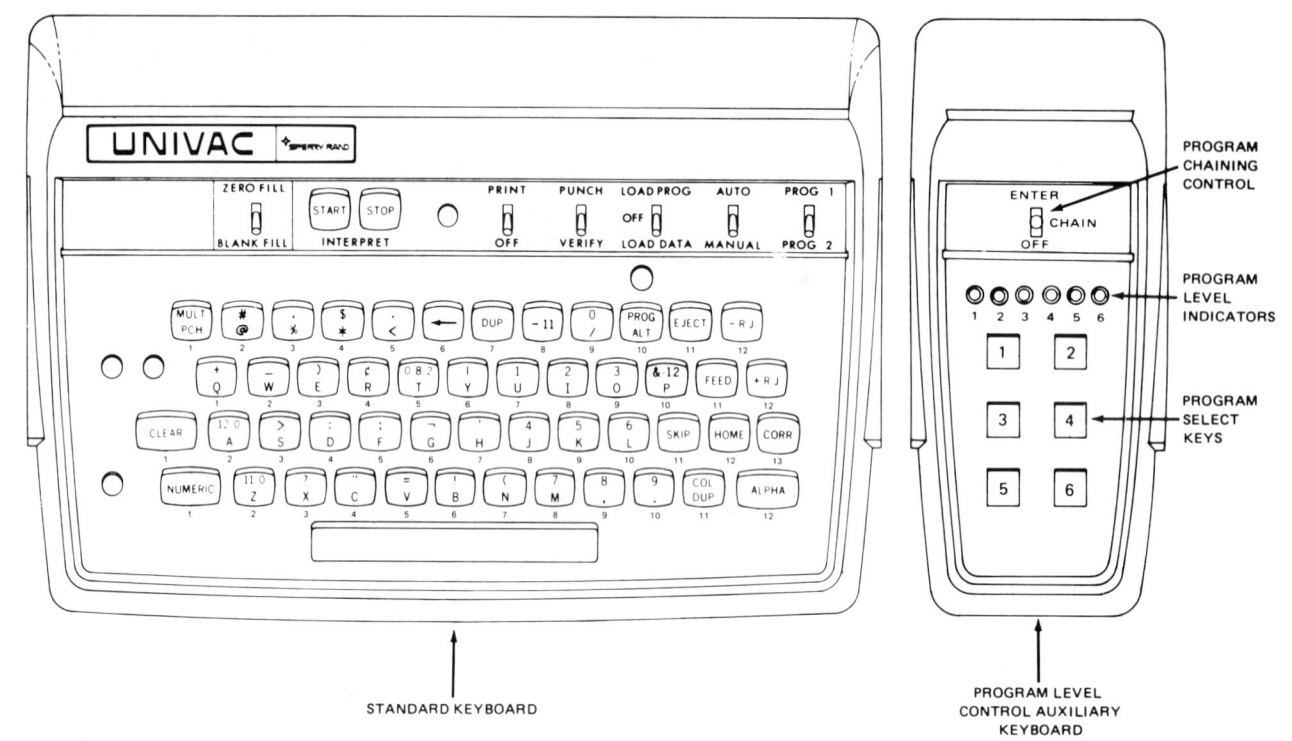

FIGURE 4.15
Sperry UNIVAC 1710 VIP with six-program level expansion (Courtesy of Sperry UNIVAC).

level to another without the necessity of the operator keying in the program selection change.

INTERPRETING The steps to interpret a deck of punched cards are:

1. Place the punched cards in the hopper.
2. Set switches on PRINT, PUNCH, OFF, MANUAL, PROG 1 or 2.
3. Press the START (INTERPRET) key.
4. Press the CLEAR key.
5. Press the START key. Interpreting should begin.

If you wish to stop the interpreting to inspect cards or for some other reason, press the STOP (INTERPRET) key.

Interpreting can be done under program control. In this case the program must be loaded and the mode switch set on AUTO rather than MANUAL. This procedure is normally used if it is desired *not* to print certain fields (code 11 and field definition & for program 1).

SECTION D
OTHER EQUIPMENT

THE UNIVAC 1810 The UNIVAC 1810, shown in Figure 4.16, differs from the IBM 129 and UNIVAC 1710 in that:

1. It has more program levels (eight plus manual mode).

PART 2 DATA ENTRY EQUIPMENT

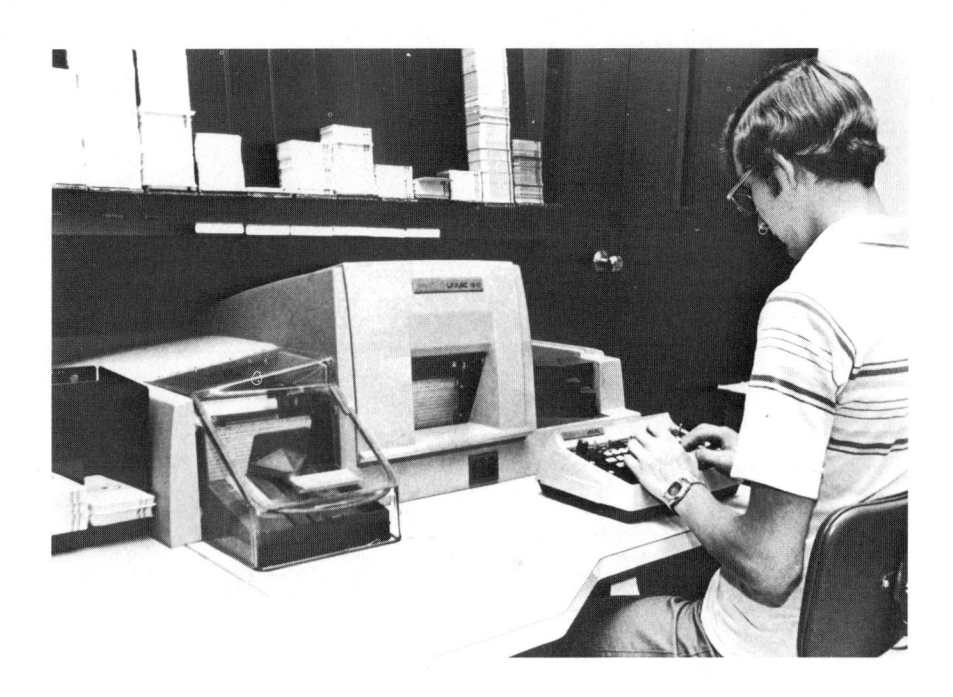

FIGURE 4.16
The UNIVAC 1810 VIP.

2. In addition to program storage and data storage, it has four auxiliary data storage levels.
3. It has an extra column on the extreme left of the card called column 00. This column contains an address for each program and auxiliary card. Program addresses contain an 11 punch and one or more digit punches in column 00. An auxiliary storage card has only digit punches in column 00.
4. It has a program chaining feature.

The 1810 differs considerably from the IBM 129 and UNIVAC 1710 in program codes, console keyboard switches and controls, and methods of loading programs and auxiliary data. Its chaining feature and its greater number of program levels make it superior to the 129 and 1710.

If you have the 1810, you will need to refer to your manual for further instructions on its use.

THE IBM 5496 DATA RECORDER

The IBM 5496 Data Recorder punches the 96-column cards used on the System/3. The codes used are shown in Appendix E. Figure 4.17 illustrates the 5496. The console switches and keyboard are shown in Figures 4.18 and 4.19.

Viewing Figures 4.13 and 4.14, we see that:

1. The ALPHA SHIFT key is called the LOWER SHIFT key and the NUMERIC SHIFT key is called the UPPER SHIFT key. This machine is normally in lower shift.
2. The LEFT ZERO key is called a RIGHT ADJUST key. This device has no negative right adjust or −RJ key. Therefore to key a negative number, one must use the MULT PCH key and key the minus sign and digit.
3. The FLD ERASE function key corresponds to the FLD BKSP key on the IBM 129.
4. The RECORD ERASE console switch corresponds to the RECORD BKSP button on the IBM 129.
5. Only four program levels are available.

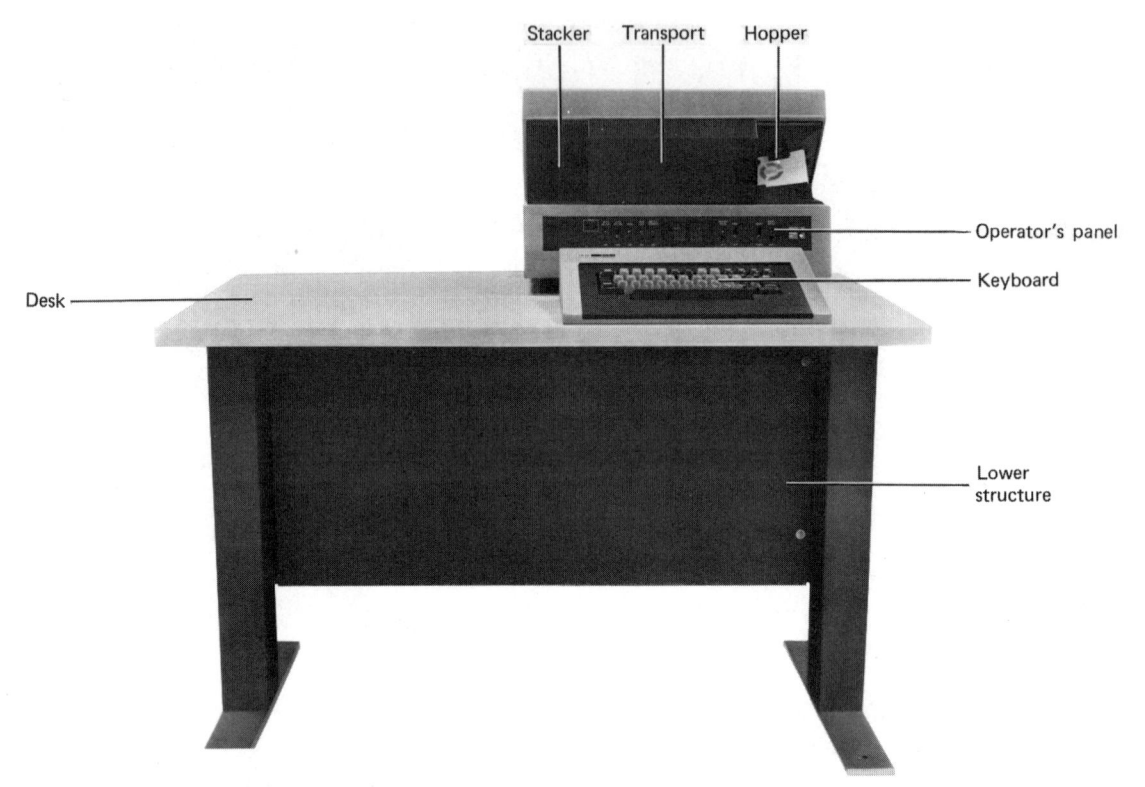

FIGURE 4.17
The IBM 5496 data recorder (Courtesy of IBM Corporation).

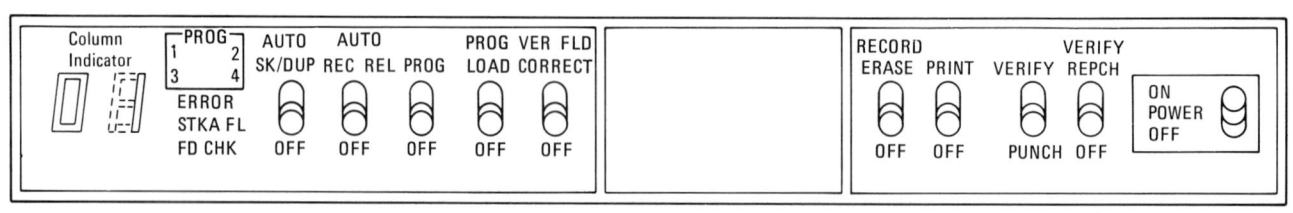

FIGURE 4.18
IBM 5496 keyboard (Courtesy of IBM Corporation).

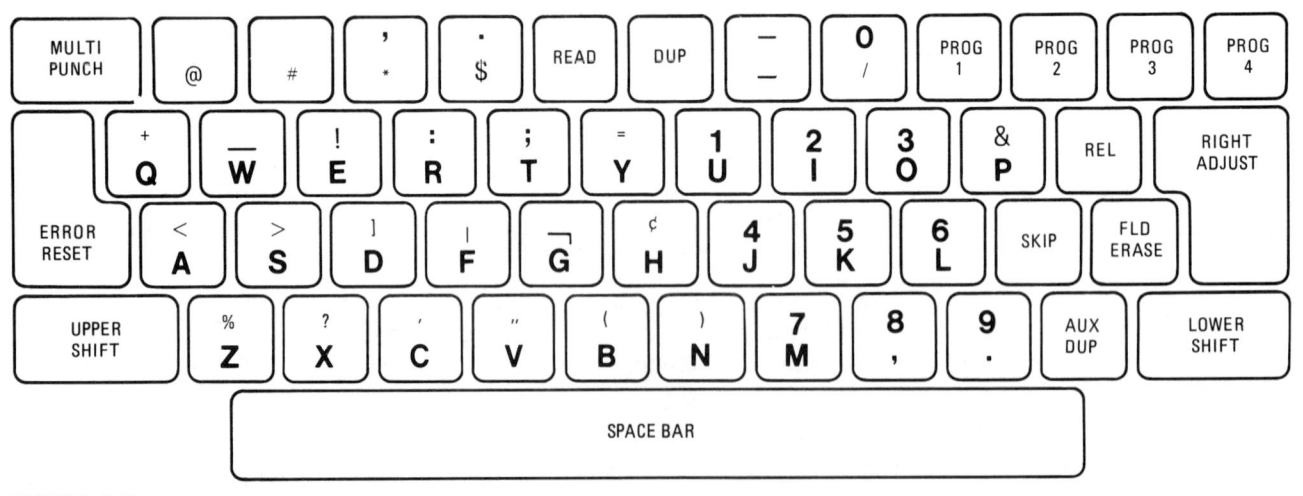

FIGURE 4.19
The IBM 5496 CONSOLE AND KEYBOARD (Courtesy of IBM Corporation).

PART 2 DATA ENTRY EQUIPMENT

6. Data can be loaded into program level four. When the AUX DUP key is pressed, the data will be duplicated into the same columns in the key entry area.
7. The AUTO REC REL switch is the same as the IBM 129's REC ADV/CARD FEED switch.
8. The VER FLD CORRECT and VERIFY REPCH switches are used in verifying. (On the IBM 129, VER CORR and VER RES.)
9. The ERROR RESET function unlocks the keyboard.

Disadvantages of the IBM 5496 are that:

1. There is no negative LZ or RJ key.
2. Only four program levels are available in contrast to six on the IBM 129 and eight on the UNIVAC 1810 and TAB 501.
3. Verifying is somewhat less convenient because one must use switches rather than keys.
4. Only two special features are available. They are a selfcheck number and an on-line reader/punch feature allowing the machine to act as a card reader or punch for a computer.

If you have this machine, it will be necessary for you to use your manual with this book.

THE TAB 501 PUNCH/VERIFIER

The TAB 501 Punch/Verifier, shown in Figure 4.20, is another type of buffered keypunch produced by TAB PRODUCTS COMPANY. Some of its features are:

1. It has 8 program levels rivaling the UNIVAC 1810. Options are available allowing as many as 28 program levels.
2. It can store up to 58 constants in memory and make them available for different program levels. When called forth, the constants are automatically duplicated, thus saving keying time. Options are available allowing up to 220 constants in memory.

FIGURE 4.20
The TAB 501 punch/verifier (Copyright © 1980, TAB Products, Co., Palo Alto, CA).

FIGURE 4.21
The TAB 501 punch/verifier keyboard (Copyright © 1980, TAB Products, Co., Palo Alto, CA).

3. Its card is completely visible as on the UNIVAC 1710 and 1810.
4. It has −RJ and +RJ function keys.
5. It has a chaining feature called *automatic program sequencing* which saves time in selection programs.
6. This machine can also communicate with computers, plotters, and printers.
7. It has selfcheck and statistical special features.

A picture of the TAB 501 keyboard is shown in Figure 4.21.

If you have this machine, you will need to use your manual with this textbook.

STUDY GUIDE

Answer these questions in your book. If asked to do so, tear out the pages and hand them to your instructor.

1. List the internal storage features of your buffered keypunch.

    (1) _____

    (2) _____

    (3) _____

    (4) _____

2. List the external features of your buffered keypunch, giving the purpose of each main part.

    (1) _____

(2) _____
(3) _____
(4) _____
(5) _____
(6) _____
(7) _____
(8) _____
(9) _____
(10) _____
(11) _____
(12) _____

3. List each special switch or control on your keyboard console and give the purpose of each.

(1) _____
(2) _____
(3) _____
(4) _____
(5) _____
(6) _____
(7) _____
(8) _____
(9) _____
(10) _____
(11) _____
(12) _____

4. List each special function key on your keyboard and give the purpose of each.

(1) _____
(2) _____
(3) _____
(4) _____
(5) _____
(6) _____
(7) _____
(8) _____
(9) _____
(10) _____
(11) _____

(12) _____

(13) _____

5. If your buffered keypunch has any special keyboard lights, list them and tell the meaning of each.

   (1) _____

   (2) _____

   (3) _____

   (4) _____

6. Define:

   a. Duplicate _____
   _____

   b. Program _____
   _____

   c. Program code _____
   _____

   d. Buffer _____
   _____

   e. Chaining _____
   _____

   f. Left zero; right adjust _____
   _____

7. State your program and field definition codes for:

Operation	Character Code	Field Definition Code
a. Punching alphameric	_____	_____
b. Duplicating alphameric	_____	_____
c. Punching numeric	_____	_____
d. Duplicating numeric	_____	_____
e. Skipping	_____	_____
f. Left zero (right adjust and zero fill)	_____	_____

8. List the conditions under which keyboard lockups may occur on your device and state the corrective actions necessary.

   (1) _____

   (2) _____

   (3) _____

   (4) _____

   (5) _____

   (6) _____

(7) _____

(8) _____

9. Describe on a separate sheet of paper or demonstrate to your instructor how to:
   a. Prepare the machine for operation.
   b. Manually key in a record.
   c. Correct an error in a record as it is being keyed.
   d. Duplicate and correct an error on the last record keyed.
   e. Duplicate and correct an error in a record that is not the last record keyed.
   f. Design and prepare a program card.
   g. Load a program.
   h. Key under program control.
   i. Verify two records, one with an error.
   j. Remove card jams.
   k. Change the printing ribbon or print ink roll when needed.
   l. Clean your machine.
   m. Punch out a program in storage (if possible).
   n. Use any special features that your instructor designates.

10. List four advantages of buffered keypunches over the older unbuffered keypunches.

    (1) _____

    (2) _____

    (3) _____

    (4) _____

11. Study your manual and text and list all special features that your data recorder has, explaining the function of each special feature.

    (1) _____
    (2) _____
    (3) _____
    (4) _____
    (5) _____
    (6) _____

12. If your device has any special halt displays using the column indicator, list these and give the meaning of each.

    _____
    _____
    _____
    _____
    _____

UNIT 4 BUFFERED KEYPUNCHES

13. Describe the maintenance and cleaning instructions recommended for your device.

AFTER READING THIS UNIT YOU WILL KNOW:

The features of your floppy disk.
How diskettes should be handled.
What the external features of your device are
What the internal features of your device are.
What the main display features are.
What information is given in a status line.
What the special keys and switches are.
What the machine modes are.
What the program codes are.
How data is keyed manually.
How a program is loaded.
How data is keyed under program control.
How records are found and deleted.
How records are added.
How records are verified.
What types of error conditions can occur.
What special features are available.
What advantages the key-to-diskette has over the buffered keypunch.
What other brands of key-to-diskette devices exist.
How data set labels are changed.

What the following terms mean:

BOE
Buffer
Chaining
CRT
Cursor
Data set
Data set Label
EOD
EOE
Extent
Mode of operation
Program
Program code
Prompt
Random access
Sector
Status line
Track

UNIT 5
KEY-TO-DISKETTE DEVICES

SECTION A
THE DISKETTE

Key-to-diskette devices, introduced by IBM in 1973, use a "floppy disk" or diskette as the recording media. Figure 5.1 shows its external features. A diskette is flexible (can be bent), thus the name "floppy disk." It resembles a 45-RPM phonograph record, but it always remains in its semi-rigid protective plastic jacket. As the diskette turns in the stationary jacket, a liner material cleans it. The diskette surface is coated with a magnetic material, and data is written on it in a series of magnetized spots. The EBCDIC code that was discussed in Unit 3 is used in recording data on the diskette.

Data written on a diskette remains there until it is overwritten by other data or blanks. When a diskette with data on it is read, the data is not changed. When not in use, the diskette should be kept in the paper envelope provided with it. Figure 5.1 shows its:

1. *Head slot.* The read/write mechanism reads and writes data on the diskette through this area.
2. *Drive spindle hole.* This is similar to the hole in a 45 RPM record.
3. *Index hole.* When the hole in the protective cover and the hole in the diskette coincide, a beam of light shines through this hole. This action controls the timing.
4. *Temporary* adhesive *label.* This label is used to identify the user, the job, or the type of data. You should record your name and lab number on this label.
5. *Permanent* diskette *label.* Every center should have a permanent ID number on this label along with such information as the date first used and the location of defective tracks (to be discussed later).

The diskettes that you use will probably have only one side that can be written on. However information can be written on both sides of some diskettes. These two-sided diskettes are sometimes called *flippy disks.*

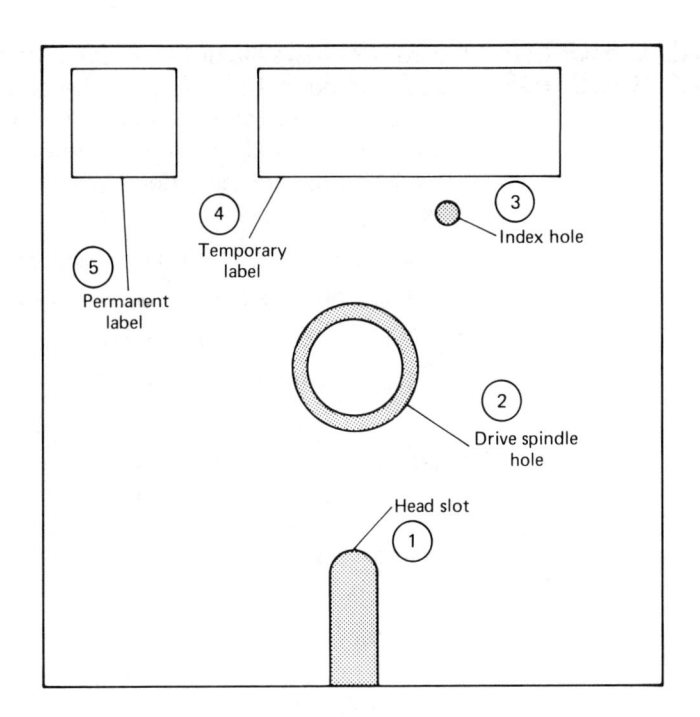

FIGURE 5.1
A diskette in its protective cover.

ADVANTAGES OF DISKETTES

The advantages of diskettes over cards as a recording media are:
1. They can be reused and cards cannot.
2. Incorrect data can be corrected on the diskette, but cards in error must be replaced.
3. Data stored on a diskette is much easier to use and store.
4. In a search mode, a specific record can be found easily.

CARE AND HANDLING OF DISKETTES

1. Keep diskettes in a cool dry place. Do *not* leave them in your car. Heat and humidity cause diskettes to warp. Warped diskettes will not function properly.
2. Do not use diskettes that have been contaminated (by coffee, soft drinks, etc.). You can damage the read/write mechanism of the machine by using dirty diskettes.
3. Do not bend them.
4. Handle the diskette on its upper edge by the label. Do not touch exposed surfaces such as in the head slot.
5. Do not use rubber bands or paper clips on a diskette.
6. Do not smoke, drink, or eat while working with diskettes.
7. Do not place heavy objects, such as books, on a diskette.
8. Do not expose a diskette to a strong magnetic field. It can destroy the data.
9. Use a fiber-tip or ball-point pen to write on diskette labels. Eraser dust can damage diskettes. It is better to peel off the old label and put on a new label.
10. The diskette should be kept in the paper envelope provided, when not in use.

INTERNAL DISKETTE CHARACTERISTICS

Figure 5.2 shows the diskette itself. The diskette has 77 circular *tracks* numbered 0 through 76. A *track* is the path on which data is recorded. Track number 00 or the *index track* is used to identify data in tracks 1 through 73. Tracks 74, 75, and 76 are reserved by the system for recording data that cannot be recorded on a defective track. These are sometimes called alternate or spare tracks. In summary:

1. A diskette has 77 tracks numbered 0 through 76.
2. Track 00 is an index track and is reserved for indices called data labels.
3. Tracks 74, 75, 76 are alternate or reserved tracks.
4. Tracks 1 through 73 can be used for data.

Each track is subdivided into *sectors*. There are several different formats used on diskettes. Key-to-diskette devices differ in the number of characters per sector and the number of sectors per track. Devices also differ in the number of tracks reserved for the system. In this textbook the *basic data exchange* format will be used.

In the basic data exchange format:

1. A track has 26 sectors or subdivisions.
2. One 80-character record can be written per sector. (If the key-to-diskette device has the 128-character feature, 128 characters can be keyed per record.)
3. With 80-character records, 1 track = 26 card records and 1 diskette = 26 × 73 tracks = 1898 card records. This is about a box of Hollerith cards.
4. In the IBM 3742 format only one track is reserved at the end, track number 74. Tracks 75 and 76 are not used. However, the TAB 700 series uses all three alternate tracks.

DEFINITIONS

1. A *data set* is a group of records for a particular job. It might be thought of as a file. More than one data set (or job) can be recorded on a diskette. The index track contains labels for each data set.

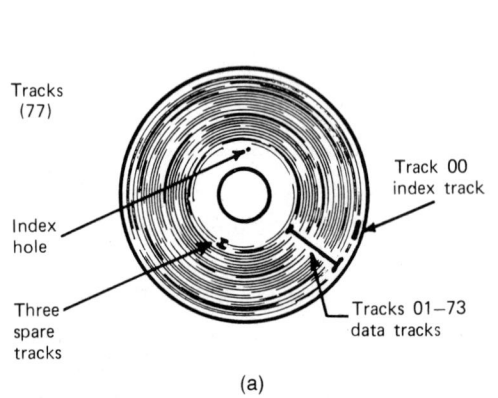

FIGURE 5.2
Diskette features (Copyright © 1980, TAB Products Co., Palo Alto, CA).

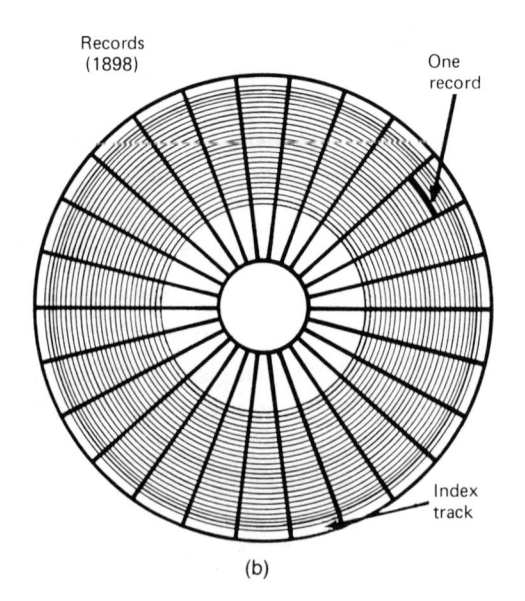

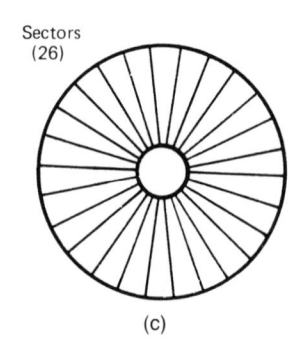

PART 2 DATA ENTRY EQUIPMENT

2. A *data set label* is an internal label which identifies the data in a data set. This label contains a name or ID, and it gives the length of the record and the record's location.
3. An *extent* is an area or the sectors on the diskette within which a data set or job is recorded.
4. *BOE* means *beginning of extent* or the address at which the data for a job begins.
5. *EOE* means *end of extent* or the last address at which data for a job *may* be keyed.
6. *EOD* means *end of data* or the last address at which data has *actually* been keyed plus one record.
7. A *volume* is defined as a recording medium that is available to one read/write mechanism. You may think of a volume as a diskette (or a magnetic tape or disk).
8. A *volume label* is an internal label that identifies the diskette. This 80-position label has the characters VOL1 in positions 1 to 4 and a volume ID or blanks in positions 5 to 10.
9. *Disk initialization* is achieved when an internal volume label is written on the diskette. Diskettes come initialized (labeled internally) from the factory and are seldom reinitialized except under special conditions (explained in the reference manual under "disk initialization"). Diskettes may be obtained from many data processing supply firms.

SECTION B
KEY-TO-DISKETTE DEVICE CHARACTERISTICS

Figure 5.4 is an example of a key-to-diskette device. All the key-to-diskette devices have:

1. *A Disk Unit.* This is a hopper that holds the diskette and contains the read/write mechanism.
2. *A Display Unit or CRT.* CRT means cathode-ray tube. This display unit or screen shows program status information and data that has been keyed.
3. *A Keyboard.* The keyboard consists of:
   a. *Data keys* used for entering data (numbers, letters, or special characters).
   b. *Function keys* that cause certain functions or controlling actions to take place.
   c. *Function select keys* that redefine the top row of keys as indicated by the row of labels above.
   d. *Operating switches* to control certain operations.

   Figure 5.5 shows an example of such a keyboard.

INTERNAL CHARACTERISTICS

Because these devices are buffered, or have a memory, data and instructions can be stored. They have four buffers:

1. *Current Record Buffer or Storage.* This buffer holds data currently being keyed. This is what is displayed on the CRT or display screen.

2. *Previous Record Buffer or Storage.* This holds the data from the previous record keyed and entered on the diskette.

3. *Hold Buffer or Storage.* This area contains the next record to be verified in verify mode.

4. *Program Buffers or Storage.* These areas contain programs or instructions.

Keying may be done two ways: *manually* with no program or *automatically* under program control.

Instructions that are stored are called *programs*. When a program is activated, operations are said to be under *program control*. Different kinds of buffered devices can store different numbers of programs. These devices are instructed or programmed by keying in program codes for each field and loading the program. Other methods exist for programming some of the newer key-to-diskette data entry equipment, that involve minicomputers. This type of programming will be discussed in the key-to-disk unit.

Some devices also allow prompting formats to be loaded for each program level or number. *Prompts* are programmed messages which are displayed to indicate what data is to be keyed in a field. In other words, prompts give special instructions.

CAUTION

A variety of keyboards are available for these devices. The main differences are in the placement of the special characters. They must match what is expected by a computer brand. (There are ways to get around this by writing special computer programs to do a translation.) You should note very carefully on your keyboard the difference between the - (minus or hyphen) and the _ (underline), and the ' (apostrophe) and the | sign if they exist on your keyboard.

These devices have *random access* capabilities. This means that a record can be located by keying in an ID or a disk address. The operator does *not* need to search sequentially from the beginning to find the record. A *disk address* on the diskettes that we will use is a five-digit number indicating the track and sector in the form TTOSS where TT is the track and SS is the sector number. The middle digit is always 0. See Figure 5.3. Some diskettes have a six-digit address where the middle two digits represent a read/write head number.

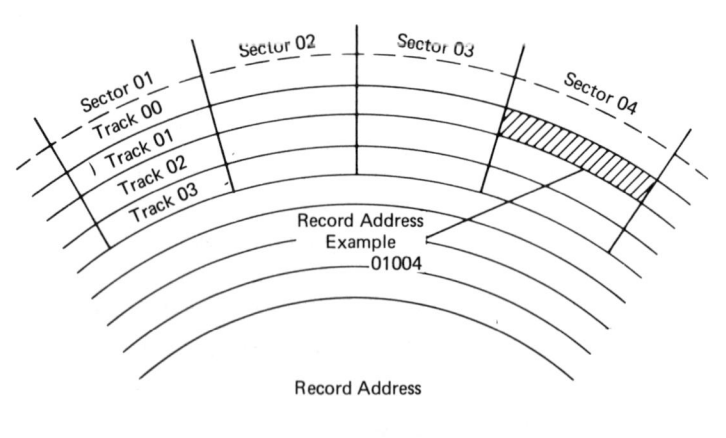

FIGURE 5.3
Diskette addresses (Copyright © 1980, TAB Products Co., Palo Alto, CA).

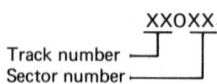

SECTION C
THE IBM 3740 SERIES AND THE IBM 3742

IBM has two key-to-diskette devices currently in use, the IBM 3741 and 3742. (A new key-to-diskette entry device appeared on the market in 1980. This is the IBM 5280 and will be discussed later.) Both the 3741 and 3742 record data on a diskette. The 3742 can accommodate two operators and is mainly used in centralized large-volume data processing. *No prompting* is possible. Six program levels are available on the 3742, although 10 are available with a special feature.

The 3741 is often used as a stand-alone station (not connected to any other device) in decentralized data processing. It has a prompting feature and 10 program levels are available. It is possible to connect it to a printer to obtain *hard copies* (printed data that can be kept as a reference) of the keyed information. The 3741 can be used as a remote on-line terminal.

Because the IBM 3742 is used more in training institutions, it will be discussed in detail.

IBM 3742 DUAL DATA STATION

The IBM 3742 Dual Data Station is shown in Figure 5.4. It is a stand-alone device with two operator stations. Since it has only one main-line switch, care must be taken at the end of a job *not* to turn the machine off while another person is working at the second station.

The *mode* of the machine determines the operation the machine will perform. The 3742 modes are:

Mode	Code	How Used
ENTER	E	To record new data.
VERIFY	V	To check the accuracy of data already entered on a diskette.
UPDATE	U	To retrieve or alter data already entered on a diskette.
SEARCH	S	To search or look for a particular record.

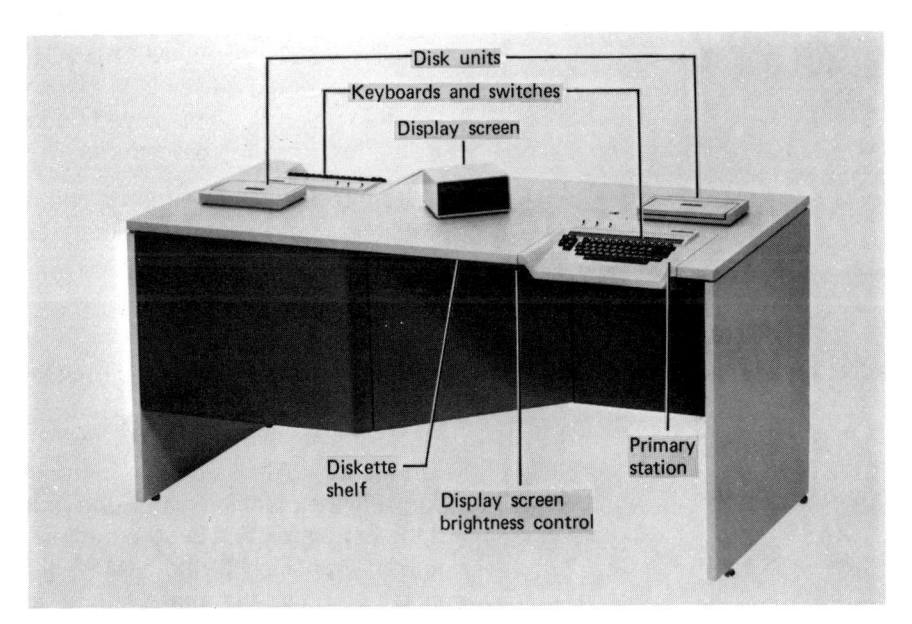

FIGURE 5.4
IBM 3742 dual data station (Courtesy of IBM Corporation).

FIELD CORRECT	C	To correct an error in verifying.
MODIFY INDEX	M	To change index information.
FIELD TOTALS	F	To display totals in accumulators.
READ INDEX	X	To display index information.
RECORD INSERT	N	To insert a record between records already keyed.

OPERATING FEATURES

The Display Screen

The DISPLAY SCREEN (Figure 5.7) shows:

1. *STATUS INFORMATION* on the first line of the screen. This status line gives information such as the current position in the record, the machine mode, error codes, and other items.

2. *DATA LINES* on the second and third lines of the screen. Each of these data lines can have a maximum of 40 characters giving an 80-character record display.

   If the device has the 128-character feature, after position 80 is keyed, the first data line disappears and the two data lines displayed are:

   ----------------------------**POSITIONS 41 THRU 80**----------------------------
   ----------------------------**POSITIONS 81 THRU 120**----------------------------

   When position 121 is keyed, the two data lines displayed are:

   ----------------------------**POSITIONS 81 THRU 120**----------------------------
   ----------------------------**POSITIONS 121 THRU 128**----------------------------

   The next character to be keyed or the keying position is shown on the screen by:
   a. The first piece of information in the status line.
   b. The underscore character, called a *cursor*.
   For example,

                  BRISCOE_

   shows the eighth character is about to be keyed.

3. DATA SET LABEL INFORMATION on the second and third lines of the screen. If the device is in index mode, data set label information rather than data will be displayed under the status line. This will be discussed under operating procedures. See Figure 5.6.

   Brightness of the screen is controlled by a knob below the tabletop under the display screen on the primary side (the side for which the on-off switch labels face you). See Figure 5.4.

Keyboard

A picture of the 3742 keyboard is shown in Figure 5.5. The keyboard contains:

Data Keys. The data keys cause the entering of 64 possible characters. Normally the machine is in alpha or lower shift, which causes the characters at the bottom of the key to be entered. If a character at the top of the key is desired (upper shift), the NUM SHIFT (numeric shift) key must be used. It should be noted that the A and Z keys have nothing on the top of the key.

FIGURE 5.5
The IBM 3742 keyboard and console switches (Courtesy of IBM Corporation).

Switches

1. *The AUTO DUP/SKIP Switch.* The *automatic duplicate/skip* switch when on and under program control causes:
   a. Automatic duplication of corresponding fields from the last record into the record being currently keyed.
   b. Automatic fill with blanks for any fields skipped.
   When this switch is off, keying is manual.

2. *The AUTO REC ADV Switch.* When the *automatic record advance* switch is on, records are entered automatically on the diskette. This means that when the last position in the record is keyed or the end character of the program is reached, the 3742 automatically advances to the next record and stores what has been keyed into the current record buffer on the diskette.
   If this switch is off, the REC ADV function key must be pressed to write a record on the diskette.

3. *The PROG NUM SHIFT Switch.* The *programmed numeric* switch is used when keying fields programmed for numeric shift.
   a. In NUMBERS ONLY position, only the characters 0 to 9, -, blank, and + are valid in programmed numeric shift. (However, the ALPHA SHIFT key will override this.)
   b. In ALL CHAR position, all keys can be used. Regardless of its setting, all keys can be used.
   In manual mode (no program), this switch has no effect.

UNIT 5 KEY-TO-DISKETTE DEVICES   77

Special Functions Keys. The darker keys (except those at the extreme left) in Figure 5.5 are the *special function* keys:

1. *NUM SHIFT Key.* This key is used to obtain the *numeric* or upper shift.

2. *ALPHA SHIFT Key.* This *alphabetic shift* key is used only under programmed numeric shift when a character in the lower shift is desired.

3. *CHAR ADV Key.* The *character advance* key advances the cursor without destroying data that has already been keyed. (Pressing the space bar would destroy data already keyed.)

4. *CHAR BKSP Key.* The *Character backspace* key backspaces one character without destroying what has already been keyed.

5. *FIELD BKSP Key.* The *field backspace* key, under program control, moves the cursor back to the first position of the field currently being keyed. If already in the first position, it backspaces to the first position of the previous field. No data is destroyed or changed.

6. *FIELD ADV Key.* The *field advance* key (unless verifying) under program control moves the cursor to the first position of the next field to be keyed. Pressing this key when verifying causes an error.

7. *REC ADV Key.* The *record advance* key action varies according to the mode the device is in.
    a. In ENTER mode this key causes the record to be written on the diskette. The cursor advances to the first position of the next record.
    b. In INDEX mode this key causes the next data-set label record to be displayed on the screen.
    c. In UPDATE mode this key enters the changed record on the diskette and advances to the first position of the next record.

8. *The Hex Key.* The *hexadecimal* key takes the place of the MULT PCH key in the buffered and unbuffered keypunches. Zone punches are keyed as follows:

12 zone	letter C
11 zone	letter D
0 zone	letter E

    Therefore, the procedure for keying the number 101 or −101 would be:
    a. Press the hex key.
    b. Key the letter D.
    c. Key the number 1.
    If you were to study the EBCDIC code and base-16 or hexadecimal number system in detail, the reason for this procedure would be clear. This is why it is important that you go on and take introduction to computers and computer operations courses.

9. *The DUP Key.* The *duplicate* key causes data from the previous record to be transferred into the corresponding positions of the current record.

10. *The REP Key.* The *repeat* key when used with another key causes this character or function to be repeated until either key is released. If manual duplication is desired for several characters, the DUP and REP keys can be used for faster duplication. Or if several minus signs are desired, the REP and minus key could be used.

11. *The RESET Key.* The *reset* key is used to reactivate or reset the keyboard after an error. It will unlock the keyboard. This key will be discussed later in detail.

12. *The RIGHT ADJUST Key.* Under program control, the *right adjust* key causes leading zeros to be inserted when only significant digits have been keyed. For example, if 101 were keyed in a five-position field and then the RIGHT ADJUST key were pressed, the following would be entered in storage:

```
 Ø   Ø   1   Ø   1
32  33  34  35  36   (column positions)
```

To key a −101 or 101 in a five-position, right-adjust field programmed for numeric shift:
a. Key the digits 1, 0, and 1.
b. Key the hyphen (minus sign).
c. The field will be right-adjusted when the minus key is pressed.

13. *The SEL PROG Key.* The *select program* key is used to select a program number. This key will be discussed later when keying under program control.

14. *The FIELD CORR Key.* The *field correct* key is used when verifying and will be discussed under verifying.

15. *The SKIP Key.* The *skip* key, under program control, causes a skip to the next field and enters blanks in storage for the positions skipped.

The function select keys. The darker keys in Figure 5.5 set off to the left of the keyboard are the function select keys. These keys are used to redefine (or give another meaning to) the top row of keys as indicated by the two rows of labels above the top row of keys.

1. FUNC SEL (upper) key. The green FUNC SEL key at the extreme left is called the *function select upper* key and is associated with the upper row of green labels. That is, FUNC SEL UPPER redefines the top row of keys according to the top row of labels.

2. FUNC SEL (lower) key. The white FUNC SEL key at the extreme right is called *function select lower* and is associated with the bottom row of white labels. The FUNC SEL LOWER key redefines the top row of keys according to the lower row of labels.
    Using function select keys and a key in top row, you can:
   a. Delete a record.
   b. Display data.
   c. Display a program.
   d. Enter.
   e. Load a program.
   f. Return to index.
   g. Search an address.
   h. Search content.
   i. Search end of data.
   j. Search sequential content.

   These actions will be discussed under operating procedures.

3. *REC BKSP Key.* The *record backspace* key (except in verifying) moves the cursor back to the first position of the current record. If in the first position, it moves the cursor to the first position of the previous record.

4. *SCRL BKWD Key.* The *scroll backward* key is used to backspace if the device has the 128-character feature.
    Possible data lines on the display screen are:

CASE A

---------------------------- POSITIONS 1   THRU 40 ---------------------------
---------------------------- POSITIONS 41 THRU 80 ---------------------------

CASE B

---------------------------- POSITIONS 41 THRU 80 --------------------------
---------------------------- POSITIONS 81 THRU 120 --------------------------

CASE C

---------------------------- POSITIONS 81 THRU 120 --------------------------
---------------------------- POSITIONS 121 THRU 128 --------------------------

    a. In Case A if SCRL BKWD is pressed, the cursor moves to position 1 of Case A.
    b. In Case B if SCRL BKWD is pressed, the cursor moves to position 1 of Case A.
    c. In Case C if SCRL BKWD is pressed, the cursor moves to position 1 of Case B.

5. *The SCRL FWD Key.* The *scroll forward* key is used to move forward on the display screen if your device has the 128-character feature.
    In the cases shown above:
    a. In Case A if SCRL FWD is pressed, the cursor moves to position 81 of Case B.
    b. In Case B if SCRL FWD is pressed, the cursor moves to position 121 of Case C.
    c. In Case C if the AUTO REC ADV switch is on, the cursor moves to the first position of the next record; if the switch is off, the cursor moves to position 000 of Case C.

OPERATING PROCEDURES

To Begin (see Figure 5.4):

1. Set the POWER ON switch to ON.
2. Remove the diskette from its envelope.
3. Press the rectangular lever on the diskette unit cover. The cover will move toward you leaving an opening, or hopper, into which the diskette may be inserted.
4. Insert the diskette with the permanent label in the left corner facing you.
5. Push the diskette unit cover forward until you hear a click. The lever on the cover does not need to be held down. You will hear a short buzz. (If the buzz continues, open and close the cover. If the buzz still continues, turn the power off and call the supervisor.)
6. A data set label and status line should be displayed on the screen. (See Figure 5.6)

Status Line

The status line, is the first line on the screen. Looking at Figure 5.7 and the first line on your display screen, the fields displayed are:

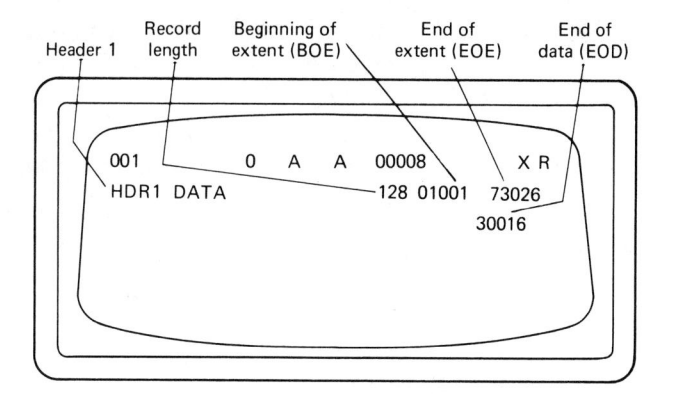

FIGURE 5.6
The IBM 3742 STATUS LINE and data set label (Courtesy of IBM Corporation).

```
                    Record    Beginning of    End of      End of
         Header 1   length    extent (BOE)    extent (EOE) data (EOD)

         001              0    A    A    00008          X R
         HDR1 DATA                 128 01001    73026
                                                30016
```

1. *The Cursor Position.* This field shows the cursor position, which is 001 in this case.
2. *An Error Code.* This field shows a code for the type of error that has occurred. If it is blank, no error has occurred.
3. *Program Number.* This field is zero at this time because no program is being used.
4. *Begin Field Code.* This field will be an A for ALPHA because we are not in automatic mode, and the 3742 is normally in the alphameric shift. Under program control this code (N or A) shows if the current field being keyed is programmed for numeric or alpha shift.
5. *Program Shift Code.* This field shows the program shift for the *current* position (numeric or alpha). Since we are *not* under program control, this shows A for alpha.
6. *Disk 1 Address.* This field shows the disk address of the track currently in use. As explained later under the INDEX TRACK section, the diskette is positioned on track 0, sector 8. Therefore you see 00008.
7. *Disk 2 Address.* This field is used only in disk copying procedures. It may be blank if no copying is taking place.

STATUS LINE

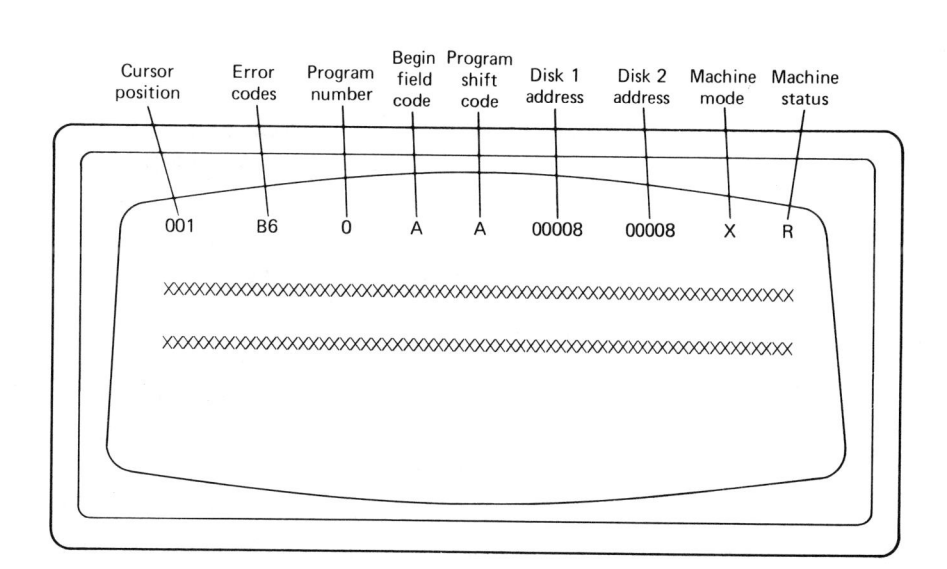

```
                              Begin  Program
  Cursor   Error    Program   field  shift    Disk 1    Disk 2    Machine  Machine
  position codes    number    code   code     address   address   mode     status

   001      B6        0        A      A       00008     00008      X        R
```

FIGURE 5.7
The IBM 3742 STATUS LINE fields (Courtesy of IBM Corporation).

UNIT 5 KEY-TO-DISKETTE DEVICES

8. *Machine Mode.* This field shows an X. Looking back at the machine mode discussion on page 76, you will see that the machine is in *index* mode.

9. *Machine Status.* This last field in the status line shows the ready status code (R). The three status codes are:

        R   Ready
        N   Not ready
        W   Wait

Errors

An error is shown by a flashing screen and an error code on the status line. To demonstrate this (assuming that you have inserted the diskette given you as directed above):

1. Press the field correct key.
2. Observe the flashing screen and the error code M on the status line.

RULE 1   If the error code is a *letter,* press the *reset* key and continue.

3. Press the RESET key.
4. Open the diskette holder cover and close it.
5. Press the REC ADV key.
6. Observe the flashing screen and the error code 6.

RULE 2   If the error code is a *number,* press the NUM SHIFT key and the RESET key.

7. Press the NUM SHIFT and while holding it down press the RESET key.

THE INDEX TRACK OR TRACK ZERO

So that you will understand the index track, its construction will be discussed. If you still do not have a diskette in the machine, put one in. The second and third lines on the screen are displaying information in sector 8 of track 0.

The construction of *track zero* is as follows:

Sector 1	Blank.
Sector 2	Blank.
Sector 3	Contains a machine-test character in position 1 for a write test.
Sector 4	Blank.
Sector 5	Contains bad-track information.
Sector 6	Blank.
Sector 7	A volume label.

        Positions 1-4   Characters VOL1.

        Positions 5-10   A volume ID or blank. IBM puts a volume ID of IBMIRD here.

        Position 11   Accessibility code. If non-blank this means the diskette cannot be used.

        Positions 12-76   Blank.

	Positions 77-78 Sector sequence information, usually blank or 01 (for details see the reference manual).
	Position 79 Blank.
	Position 80 The character W.
Sector 8	First data set label: data set name DATA.
Sector 9	Second data set label: data set name DATA09.
Sector 10	Third data set label: data set name DATA10.
↓	etc.
Sector 26	Nineteenth data set label: data set name DATA19.

The above discussion shows that it is possible to have 19 sets of data or programs on a diskette since sectors 8 through 26, or 19 sectors, are labels for 19 possible sets of data or programs.

Examining the volume label in sector 7:

1. Press the REC BKSP key. You should see the volume label discussed above with VOL1 in positions 1 through 4. (If you backspaced further, you would see the other sectors described above.)

2. Press REC ADV to get back to sector 8.

Data Set Label

Examine the data set label on the second line of your display screen. The parts of the data set label are:

Positions 1-4	The characters HDR1.
Position 5	Reserved.
Positions 6-13	The data set name DATA. This name may be changed as discussed below.
Positions 14-22	Reserved.
Positions 23-27	Logical record length (080 or 128).
Position 28	Reserved.
Positions 29-33	Disk address of the first sector of the data set. (For your case, it should be 01001—track 1, sector 1.)
Position 34	Reserved.
Positions 35-39	Disk address of the last sector reserved for this data set. (For your case, it is probably 73026—track 73, sector 26. Remember track 74 is reserved and 75 and 76 are not used on the 3742 unless substituted for bad tracks in a disk initialization.)
Position 40	Reserved.
Position 41	A by-pass data set indicator that is a character B or blank. For our purposes this will be blank. It is used in data communications and with other equipment.
Position 42	Accessability code. This should be blank.

Position 43	Write protect code:
	Blank = Diskette can be used for both reading and writing.
	P = Diskette can be read only (ours is blank).
Position 44	Interchange type indicator. This should be blank.
Position 45	Multivolume indicator:
	Blank = Data set is all on one diskette.
	C = Data set is continued on another diskette.
	L = This is the last diskette for a data set occupying more than one diskette.
Positions 46-47	Volume sequence number.
	Blank if position 45 is blank.
	1-99 if the data set takes up more than one diskette.
Positions 48-53	Creation date. This may contain the date when the data on the diskette was first created, keyed in the form YYMMDD (year, month, day). (For our purposes it is blank.)
Positions 54-66	Reserved.
Positions 67-72	Expiration date. This is the date when the data on this data set expires, in the form YYMMDD. (For our purposes, it will be blank.) If this diskette were later to be written on by the computer using the IBM 3540 Diskette I/O Unit, an expiration date would have to be present.)
Position 73	Verify indicator:
	Blank = Data set is not verified.
	V = Data set is verified.
Position 74	Reserved.
Positions 75-79	Identifies the disk address of the next available sector to be written on. (Yours should read 01001, which indicates no data records have yet been keyed.) As data records are keyed, this disk address increases by one.
Position 80	Reserved.

Any of the information in this data set label can be changed by the following procedure.

Modifying or Changing Data Set Label Information

As an example, assume that your supervisor has instructed you to change the name of the first data set label from DATA to PAYROLL. Using the keys shown in Figure 5.5:

1. Character advance to position 6. Use the [CHAR ADV] key.
2. Key in PAYROLL.
3. Press the white FUNCT SEL (LOWER) key and the [FUNCT SEL] M key (for MODIFY) [7 M]
4. Press the REC ADV key.
5. The data set label should reappear with your change.

Now repeat Steps 1 through 5 above, changing the label PAYROLL back to DATA. You will need to use the space bar to blank out all characters through position 13.

Any field in the data set label may be changed by the above method. Now investigate some of the remaining data set labels.

1. Press the REC ADV key. Notice that the display screen flashes and that the second field on the status line (first line) shows error code 6. The rule on page 82 for a numeric error code was to press NUM SHIFT and RESET.
2. Press the NUM SHIFT and while holding it [RESET] [NUM SHIFT]

press the RESET key. The screen should stop flashing. You are now positioned on section 9 of track 0, the second data set label—DATA09. Notice the D in position 1. This means that the record is a delete record. A *delete record* is a record that is still physically on the diskette, but is not being used.

Second Data Set Label Creation Procedure

If a second set of data or information were to be entered on the diskette and the first set in the sector 8 data set were finished at disk address 20020 (track 20, sector 20), the procedure would be:

1. Decide if any space is to be left in the first data set for later additions. As an example, suppose it is decided that space will be left through 24026. Then the data set label disk address (BOE) for the second set would be 25000.
2. Change the D in position 1 to an H.
3. Use the CHAR ADV and REP keys to move the cursor to position 29. Key in 25000.
4. Press FUNCT SEL LOWER (the white key) and the M key.
5. Press the REC ADV key.
6. The modified data set label should appear.
7. Press the REC BKSP key. This positions you in sector 8 or the first data set label. The disk address for the end of extent (EOE) needs to be changed to 24026 because of the decision in step 1.
8. Press the CHAR ADV and the REP keys until position 35 is reached.
9. Key in 24026, press FUNCT SEL LOWER and the M key.
10. Press the REC ADV key and the changed data set label in sector 8 will be displayed.

Now the diskette is prepared for a second set of data. Do the above procedure only if your instructor tells you to do so.

MANUAL KEYING The following data is to be keyed in the first data set.

Position	1	15	20	25
	↓	↓	↓	↓
Record 1	JOHN A BROWN	DP310	B	461-82-9981
Record 2	MARY V SMITH	DP300	C	421-88-6540
Record 3	JENNY L REJCEK	DP456	A	231-81-4444
Record 4	JAMES WILLIAMS	DP452	A	886-00-1042

The keys and labels shown in Figure 5.8 will be used. Do not key in the dashes in the social security number.

Entering records 1 to 3

1. Press FUNCT SEL LOWER AND ENTER (press the white FUNCT SEL and HEX keys as shown in Figure 5.9).
2. Notice that the data set label has disappeared. Blanks are under the status line.
3. Key in the first record remembering to press NUM SHIFT for the numbers. If you make a mistake, simply press the CHAR BKSP key and rekey. Your fingers should be positioned as shown in Figure 5.11.
4. Key in the second record and press REC ADV.
5. Key in the third record and press REC ADV.
6. Assume time is at an end and you must stop. Press FUNCT SEL LOWER and RETURN TO INDEX. (This means that you press the white FUNCT SEL key and the − key as shown in Figure 5.10.)
7. Wait until an **X** shows up on the status line in the machine status field. Open the disk-unit cover and remove the diskette.

Continuing your work

1. Insert your diskette and close the disk-unit cover.
2. Look at the data set label on the screen. The last field (or the disk

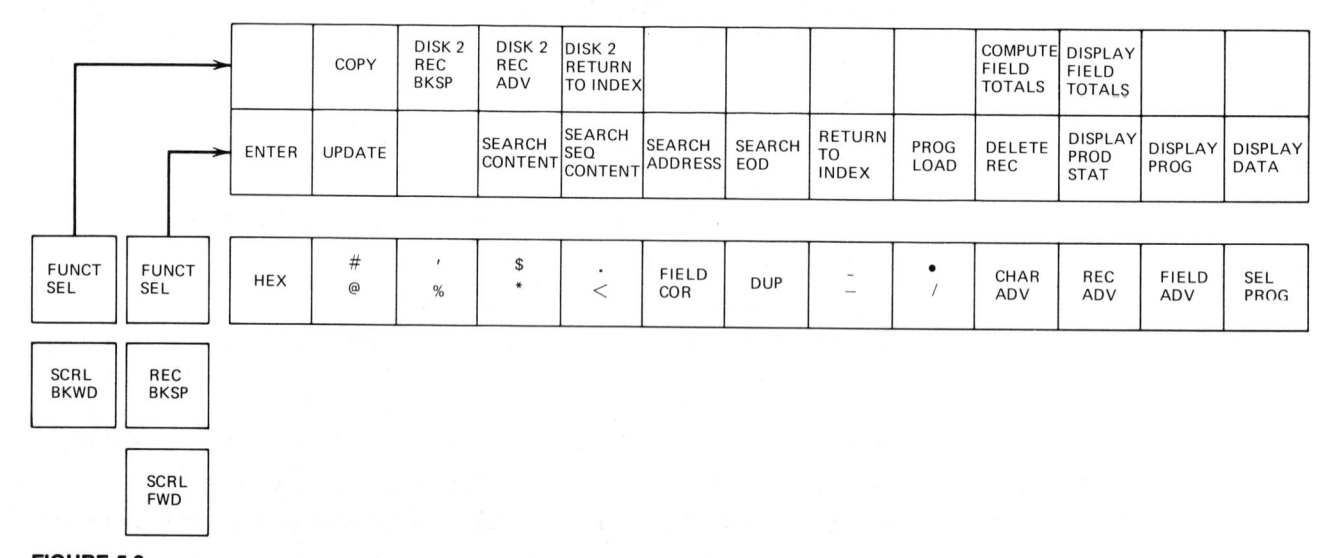

FIGURE 5.8
The IBM 3742 FUNCTION SELECT keys.

PART 2 DATA ENTRY EQUIPMENT

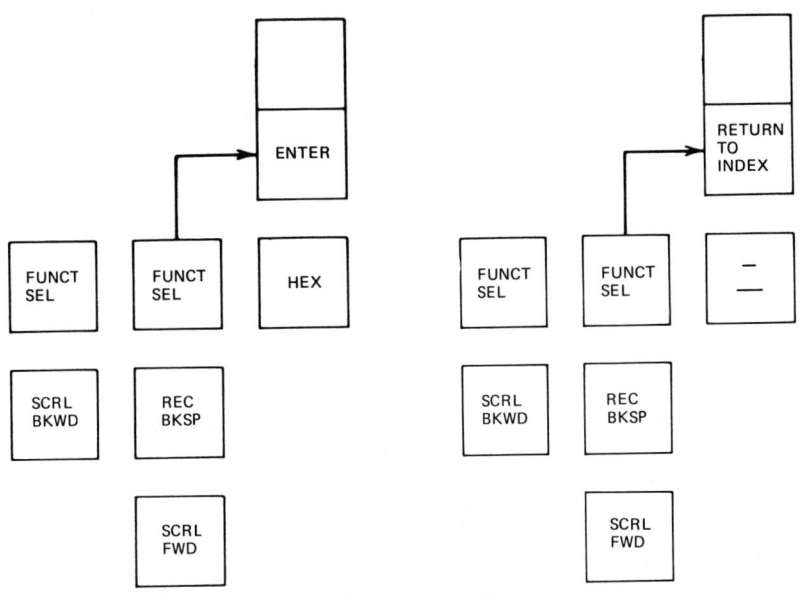

FIGURE 5.9
The IBM enter mode key.

FIGURE 5.10
The IBM 3742 RETURN TO INDEX MODE keys.

addresses of the next available sector) reads 01004 because you have already keyed three records in the first three sectors of track 1.

3. You do *not* use FUNCT SEL and ENTER keys because this would position you in sector 1 and cause you to *overwrite* or *destroy* the JOHN BROWN record.

4. Press FUNCT SEL LOWER and SEARCH EOD. (This means that you press the white FUNCT SEL key and the DUP key as shown in Figure 5.12.) Using the SEARCH EOD key is called *searching for the end of data* (EOD) or the *last record*.

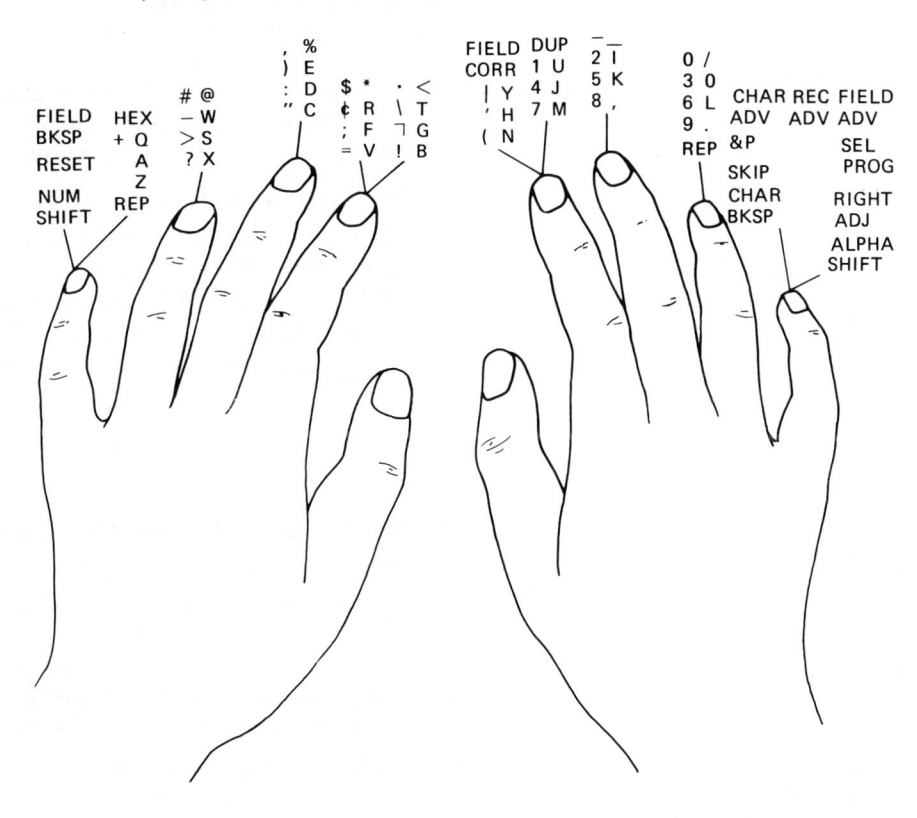

FIGURE 5.11
Home Finger Positions.

UNIT 5 KEY-TO-DISKETTE DEVICES

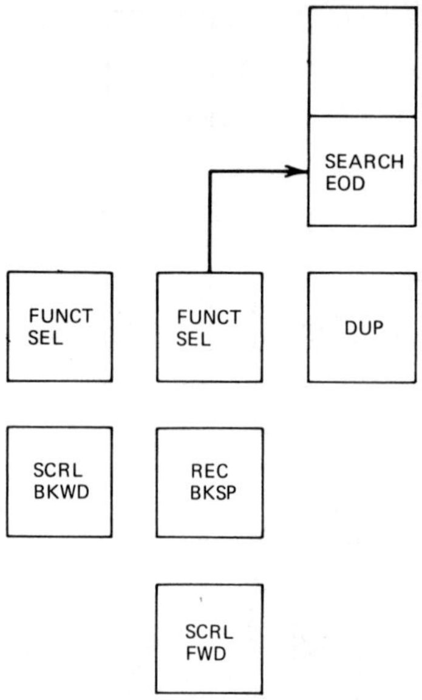

FIGURE 5.12
The IBM 3742 SEARCH EOD keys.

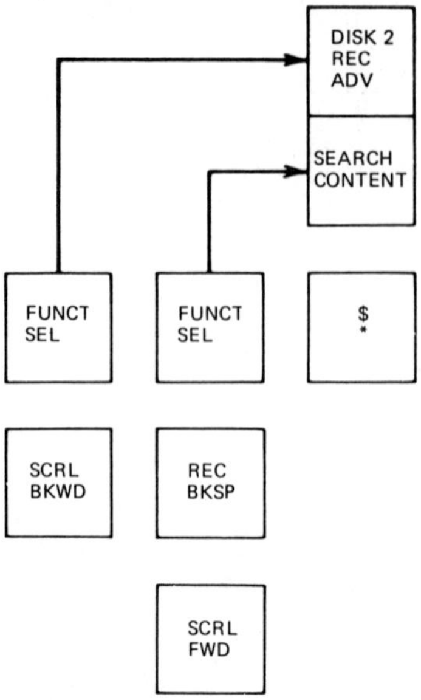

FIGURE 5.13
The IBM 3742 SEARCH CONTENT and RECORD ADVANCE FOR DISK 2 keys.

5. The last record that you keyed (JENNY L REJCEK) will appear. Press the REC ADV key.

6. The screen will blank out. Key in the fourth record (JAMES WILLIAMS) and press the REC ADV key.

7. Work would be continued as before if there were more records. Press FUNCT SEL LOWER and RETURN TO INDEX.

Correction procedure. Suppose that you have found that JENNY L REJCEK should be JENNY M REJCEK.

1. Press FUNCT SEL LOWER and SEARCH CONTENT. (This means press the white FUNCT SEL key and the * $ key as shown in Figure 5.13.) The screen should go blank.

2. Key in a search field after character-advancing to the beginning position of the field. (In our case the social security number would be unique, so press the CHAR ADV and REP keys until the cursor is on position 25. Key in the social security number 231814444.) This process is called searching for a record by the *content of the field.*

3. Press REC ADV. The JENNY L REJCEK record should eventually appear.

4. CHAR ADV and make the necessary correction. (Change the middle initial to an M.)

5. Press REC ADV. This enters the change on the diskette.

6. If further corrections are necessary on other records, repeat Steps 1 to 5. *But* the screen may *not* go completely blank on Step 2. It may have the last record that you keyed in, which is rather confusing. Blank this out by pressing FUNCT SEL LOWER and DEL REC (see Figure 5.14). Key in the new search record field and press REC ADV in Step 3. (If you wish to try another example, find the JAMES WILLIAMS record by using the social security number and give him a middle initial.)

Deleting a record

1. Insert the diskette and turn off the AUTO SKIP/DUP and REC ADV switches.
2. Press the FUNCT SEL and SEARCH CONTENT keys. The screen will go blank.
3. Type in a *unique* field after character-advancing to its beginning position. Press REC ADV and the record should appear.
4. Press FUNCT SEL and DELETE REC. (This means press the white FUNCT SEL key and the CHAR ADV key as shown in Figure 5.14.) The letter D will appear in position 1. The record is deleted.

   Try this procedure deleting the REJCEK record.

Adding or inserting a new record. You have just deleted record 3 or the REJECK record. The records that remain are BROWN, SMITH, and WILLIAMS. Suppose you wish to insert

```
1                  15          20      25
↓                  ↓           ↓       ↓
JANE A LITTLE      DP 453      A       661-82-9456
```

between the SMITH AND WILLIAMS records. Use the following procedure to insert the record.

1. Insert the diskette and turn off the AUTO SKIP/DUP and REC ADV switches.
2. Press the FUNCT SEL and SEARCH CONTENT keys. The screen will go blank.
3. Type in the unique field for the first record that must be moved down after character-advancing to the field's beginning position. (In this case the social security number for the WILLIAMS record.) Press REC ADV and the record should appear.
4. Press FUNCT SEL and SEARCH ADDRESS. (This means press the white FUNCT SEL key and the FIELD COR key as shown in Figure 5.15.)

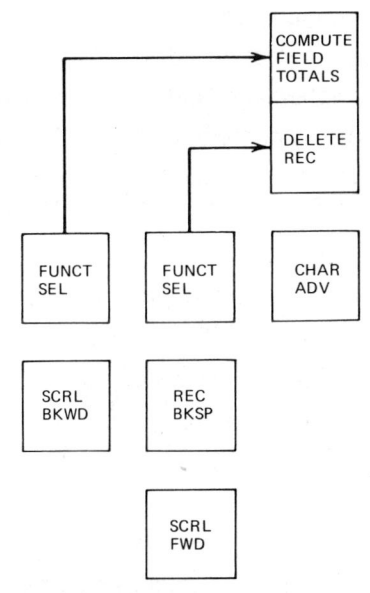

FIGURE 5.14
The IBM 3742 DELETE RECORD and COMPUTE FIELD TOTAL keys.

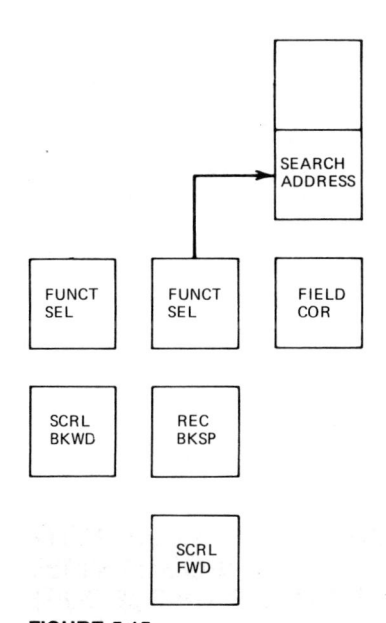

FIGURE 5.15
The IBM 3742 SEARCH ADDRESS keys.

UNIT 5　KEY-TO-DISKETTE DEVICES

5. Key in a *two*-digit number indicating the number of records that you intend to insert *here*. (In this case 01.)
6. Press the white FUNCT SEL LOWER key and the RIGHT ADJUST key. There will be a pause while all the records are being shifted down. The machine mode changes to N (not ready) on the status line and the machine status changes to W (wait) and the data is blanked out. When all the records are moved down, a flashing screen and error code 6 will appear.
7. Press the NUM SHIFT key and RESET key.
8. Key in the record or records that you wish to insert, pressing REC ADV each time.
9. Press FUNCT SEL LOWER and RETURN TO INDEX.

Laboratory Exercises

Your instructor will give you some exercises to key manually.

PROGRAMS

The IBM 3742 is instructed by the use of a program record with programming codes. This program controls the record format and assists in making keying faster and easier. The 3742 can store a maximum of six programs, numbered 1 through 6. The program number is displayed in the field of the status line. Each field in the program record has:

1. A code that describes the function needed.
2. A field-definition code showing for how many positions this action is to take place.

A program chart is shown in Figure 5.16. However, the following chart shows only the functions you will need to do the next programmed laboratory exercises.

Function	Character Code	Field Definition
Skip numeric field	S	—
Skip alphameric field	K	.
Punch numeric field	N	—
Duplicate numeric field	D	—
Punch alphameric field	A	.
Duplicate alphameric field	U	.
Right adjust a numeric field and zero fill	R	—
End of program	E	

NOTE If the record length is 80 and the program is for 80 positions, the E for end of program is not necessary.

There are two ways of loading programs on the 3742.

1. From the keyboard.
2. From a diskette.

EXAMPLE TO ILLUSTRATE PROGRAMMED OPERATIONS PROCEDURE

A program is to be planned on the 3742 for the following data:

Positions 1-6   Duplicate numeric date.
Positions 7-11   Duplicate alphameric course abbreviation.

PROGRAM CODE CHART

	Code	Verify Bypass Equivalent	Shift	Function
Begin Field Codes	N	V	Numeric	Manual Fields
	A	W	Alpha	Manual Fields
	J	Y	Numeric	Right-Adjust, blank fill
	R	X	Numeric	Right-Adjust, zero fill
	I	Z	Alpha	Right-Adjust, blank fill
	B	– – – –		Bypass
	D		Numeric	Automatically Duplicates
	U		Alpha	Automatically Duplicates
	S		Numeric	Automatically Skips
	K		Alpha	Automatically Skips
Continue Field Codes	–		Numeric	Continues Field in Numeric Shift
	.		Alpha	Continues Field in Alpha Shift
End Program Codes	E			Marks End of Program
Feature Begin Field Codes	H		Numeric	Self-Check, Modulus 10
	C		Numeric	Self-Check, Modulus 11
	F		Numeric	Auto Skip Self-Check, Modulus 10
	G		Numeric	Auto Skip Self-Check, Modulus 11
	L		Numeric	Auto Dup Self-Check, Modulus 10
	M		Numeric	Auto Dup Self-Check, Modulus 11 (See "Self-Check" in either reference manual*)
	Any Begin Field character followed by 1, 2, or 3.			Field Totals Entry (See "Field Totals" in either reference manual*)
	B Bypass character followed by 4, 5, or 6.			Field Totals Read Out (See "Field Totals" in either reference manual*)
	B Bypass character followed by 7, 8, or 9.			Field Totals and Readout and Reset Field (See "Field Totals" in either reference manual*)

* *IBM 3741 Data Station Reference Manual*, GA21-9183, or *IBM 3742 Dual Data Station Reference Manual*, GA21-9184.

FIGURE 5.16
IBM 3742 program code chart (Courtesy of IBM Corporation).

Positions 12–20	Key social security number.
Positions 21–33	Key last name.
Positions 34–45	Key first name.
Position 46	Key middle initial.
Positions 47–52	Amount of tuition and fees (right justify) nnnn̬nn.
Positions 53–80	Blank.

A record layout with the planned codes is shown in Figure 5.17.

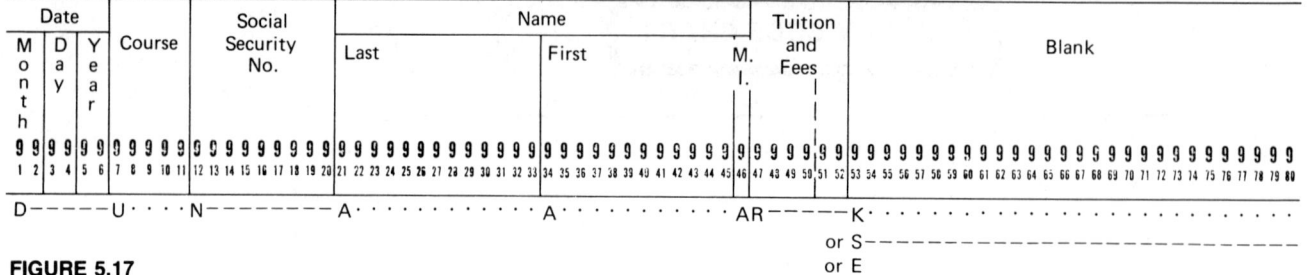

FIGURE 5.17
IBM 3742 record layout and program codes.

Loading a Program from the Keyboard

1. Insert the diskette.
2. Set the AUTO REC ADV and AUTO DUP/SKIP switches to OFF.
3. Press FUNCT SEL LOWER and DELETE REC (Press the white FUNCT SEL key and the CHAR ADV key as shown in Figure 5.14.)
4. Key in the program. (In this example key in the program shown in Figure 5.17.)
5. Press FUNCT SEL LOWER and PROG LOAD (Press the white FUNCT SEL key and the 0/ key as shown in Figure 5.18). Press the program number key (use 1 in this case). The NUM SHIFT key does not need to be held down when keying the program number.
6. Load the program into memory by pressing the SEL PROG key and the key with the program number you wish to activate (for our example, 1). It is not necessary to hold down the NUM SHIFT key. The screen will blank out.
7. If more than one program is to be loaded, Steps 4 through 6 can be repeated.

The important thing to understand is that in the beginning there are no fields in the output storage area to be duplicated. Therefore, on the *first* record, these fields to be duplicated must be keyed manually.

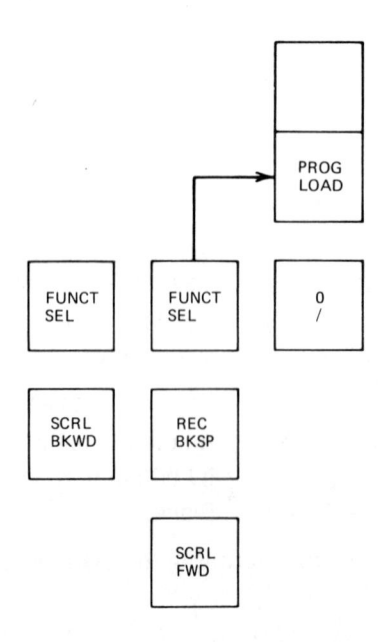

FIGURE 5.18
The IBM 3742 program load keys.

PART 2 DATA ENTRY EQUIPMENT

Keying Under Program Control (Program Has Been Loaded)

1. Set the AUTO REC ADV switch to ON; set the AUTO DUP/SKIP to OFF.
2. Press FUNCT SEL LOWER and ENTER.
3. Press SEL PROG and the program number (in our case 1). If you ever need to get *out* of program control or into manual mode, you can key SEL PROG and a 0.
4. Since there is nothing in the output storage area to duplicate, you must key in the duplicated fields on the first record (only). Looking at the record format in Figure 5.17, key in the current date. You do not need to hold down the NUMERIC SHIFT key since this field has been programmed in the numeric shift.
5. Key in a course abbreviation and number. (Use DP 300.) Since this field has been programmed alphameric, you will need to hold down the NUM SHIFT key for the 300.
6. Key in your social security number. (You need not hold down the NUM SHIFT key.)
7. Key in your last name and press SKIP unless you used the entire field.
8. Key in your first name and press SKIP unless you used the entire field.
9. Key in your middle initial. If you have no middle initial, press the SKIP key.
10. Assume your tuition is $110.16. Key in 11016 and press the RIGHT ADJ key. This inserts leading zeros to the left and forces the number you keyed to the right part of the field. This makes keying easier since you do not have to determine how many leading zeros should be keyed and then key them.
11. Press the REC ADV key. This places what you keyed in the previous-record buffer area and writes what you keyed on the diskette. There is now something in the storage area to be duplicated.
12. Turn on the AUTO DUP/SKIP switch. Now try keying the next two records below; but note that the cursor position has moved to position 12. This is because the machine has already duplicated the date and course abbreviation in positions 1 to 12, and the cursor is now positioned for the third field, the social security number.

SS	Name	Tuition
123-45-6754	Lee, Iva H	150.00
675-88-9766	Harbaugh, Maggie	34.67

Note that all operations are now fully automatic.

CAUTION

1. Assume that you use the REC BKSP key to backspace in order to look at data. You then plan to go forward with a REC ADV. Turn off your AUTO DUP/SKIP switch if more than one record format or type is involved. You may duplicate data that you do not wish to duplicate as you record-advance.
2. If you decide to delete or insert new records in the middle of a job under program control:
    a. Key in SEL PROG and 0. This gets you out of program control into manual mode.
    b. Make your corrections and then key in SEL PROG and the program number, then continue.

3. In loading your program from the keyboard: If you must stop and continue later, the program must be rekeyed and loaded as described above.

Laboratory Exercises

Your instructor will assign exercises from the textbook to do under program control.

STORING AND LOADING PROGRAMS ON A DISKETTE

There are two ways of storing programs on a diskette:

1. Using a separate diskette for the programs.
2. Recording the programs on the same diskette that the data is recorded on.

In installations where the first method is used, the supervisor creates all of the programs on a diskette and makes copies for each operator. Thus the supervisor is responsible for the accuracy of the programs. Dates are maintained in the label-creation-date area, thus ensuring that an operator is using the correct version.

The individual operator can also maintain a separate diskette for programs. No matter who creates the diskette, a record must be kept of where the programs are. One might have the programs arranged as follows:

Track	Sector		Program
01	0	01	Job 1, program 1
01	0	02	Job 1, program 2
01	0	03	Job 1, program 3
02	0	01	Job 2, program 1
02	0	02	Job 2, program 2

If the second method is used, the operator is probably maintaining the programs. An area must be created on the diskette for the programs. For example, one can put the programs in the last track, track 73. This would allow for 26 programs since there are 26 sectors per track.

Storing Your Program on a Diskette with Data

There are 19 labels on your diskette. You have been entering data in the first label with an ID of DATA. Earlier we discovered that the remaining labels had a delete code in position 1. This code was placed there by the manufacturer.

To store a program on your diskette, follow these steps:

1. If the machine is not in INDEX (X) mode, press FUNCT SEL LOWER and RETURN TO INDEX.
2. Press the REC ADV key until you find the first deleted label record. The screen will flash and there will be an error code 6 on the status line.
3. Press NUM SHIFT and RESET.
4. Key in an H in position 1. This restores positions 1 through 4 to HDR1.
5. Create a name for the label in positions 6 through 13. For example, you might use PROGRAMS or PAYROLL, and so forth.
6. Positions 25 through 27 should be 80 or 128. (Use 80.)
7. Positions 29 through 33 show the beginning track and sector (disk address) for the extent. (Use 73001.)
8. Positions 35 through 39 show the disk address for the end of the extent.

PART 2 DATA ENTRY EQUIPMENT

For our purposes one track should be enough. This would allow twenty-six programs, one per sector. Therefore, use 73026.

9. Positions 75 through 79 show the disk address for the end of the data. It should be the same as in positions 29 through 33 since no program data has been entered under this label. Therefore use 73001.
10. Press FUNCT SEL LOWER, the letter M, and REC ADV. This enters the new changes in the data set label.
11. Press FUNCT SEL LOWER and ENTER.
12. Key in your program and REC ADV.
13. Repeat Step 12 for any other programs up to 26 times.
14. REC BKSP to the program you wish to load.
15. Press FUNCT SEL LOWER and PROG LOAD and the program number that the program is to be used under. The screen is cleared.

If you need over 26 programs, steps 1 through 13 can be repeated creating another label and using, for example, track 72. Programs can be placed in track 1 at the beginning of the diskette. To prevent these programs from being later read as data, a B can be placed in position 41 of the label, the bypass data set indicator.

Loading a Program from Diskette at a Later Time

1. Insert the diskette and turn off the AUTO SKIP/DUP and REC ADV switches. (For method 2, REC ADV to the program index label.)
2. Press FUNCT SEL LOWER and UPDATE.
3. Press REC ADV until you find the program that you want to load. (You can also do a SEARCH.)
4. When the program you want is displayed, press FUNCT SEL LOWER, PROG LOAD, and the program number. The screen goes blank after the program is loaded.
5. To load more programs, repeat Steps 1 thorugh 4.
6. Press FUNCT SEL LOWER and RETURN TO INDEX.
7. Then set your switches and proceed.

SEARCHING FOR RECORDS

There are four methods of searching for records. These methods are not always available on all 3742s. Availability depends on what was requested when the machine was purchased. Your instructor will tell you what methods are available on your device. Even if you can't use them all now, you should know the four methods of searching for a record. Two methods have already been discussed:

1. Searching for EOD or last record.
2. Searching for a field with a specific content.

There are a third and fourth method.

3. Searching for a specific disk address. In this case the SEARCH ADDRESS feature is used and a specific disk address is keyed in the form TTOSS where TT equals the track number and SS equals the sector number.
4. Searching for a record in sequence. In this case, the SEARCH SEQ CONTENT is used. There is a field that is in ascending sequence and acts as a search field. The field must be in the same positions in all records.

UNIT 5 KEY-TO-DISKETTE DEVICES

DISK COPY OPERATIONS

When performing disk copy operations, data can be copied from a diskette inserted in the secondary station to one in the primary station.

The following may be copied;

1. All of disk(ette) 2.
2. A data set of disk(ette) 2.
3. Data up to a specified record on disk(ette) 2.
4. A single record.

For example, a diskette is to be cleared. The supervisor has given you a diskette with blanks in all tracks and the index tracks are properly set up.

1. Insert the cleared diskette in the secondary station disk unit.
2. Press FUNCT SEL LOWER and the letter A on the secondary keyboard. An A should appear in position 36 of the status line.
3. Insert the diskette to be cleared in the primary station disk unit.
4. The primary diskette should be positioned on the index track to the sector where copying is to begin. In our case it would be sector 08.
5. Position the secondary diskette (disk 2) at the data set label at which copying is to stop (EOE), by pressing FUNCT SEL UPPER and DISK 2 REC ADV on the primary station. (See Figure 5.13.)
6. Press FUNCT SEL UPPER (green key), NUM SHIFT, and COPY on the primary station to start the copying.
7. When the copying is complete, press FUNCT SEL LOWER and RETURN TO INDEX to return the primary station to the index track.
8. Press FUNCT SEL LOWER and the letter A on the primary station to return to the normal two-station control.

You may be asked by your instructor to use this procedure to clear a diskette after an exercise has been graded. Your manufacturer's manual describes further copying procedures.

VERIFYING

Verifying is normally done by an experienced operator who has not keyed the original data. It is done to check the accuracy of the data recorded on the diskette. Some industries spot verify; that is, they verify only certain batches of data. Such a practice has obvious dangers.

The program for verifying our sample data on page 93 would be the same as it was for keying. However, the program code chart in Figure 5.16 shows that additional codes do exist. The B code can be used to bypass verifying a field. Also, if a field is to be right-adjusted when entered but bypassed when verifying, the codes V, W, X, and Z may be used.

Insert the diskette with the data you keyed on page 93. If the data is lost, rekey the three records. Locate the second record and make two deliberate errors. Key the social security number as 123-46-6754 and the last name as ROBERTSON rather than LEE.

Verifying steps are as follows:

1. Insert the diskette with the data to be verified (and the program to be loaded if this is the case).
2. Load the program by rekeying as described on page 92 (our case) or by loading from the diskette as described on page 95.
3. Press SEL PROG and the program number (1 in our case).
4. Press FUNCT SEL LOWER and VERIFY (the white FUNCT SEL key

and the ⸱/% key as shown in Figure 5.19. Notice that the machine mode displayed at the right of the status line is V.

The VERIFY (V) mode may be selected from the INDEX (X) mode or from the UPDATE (U) mode.

5. Key the first record, your individual record, as you did originally. Notice that after the first character is keyed, the remaining ones on the screen are blanked out. Therefore you are forced to key what is on the source document.

Verifying Errors or Mismatches

When the verifier keys a character which differs with the data already on the diskette, a *mismatch* is said to occur. The error-code field on the status line (second field from the left) will show a V error and the screen will display a flashing light.

Mismatch errors can be made in a number of ways.

1. The verifying operator pressed the wrong key.
2. The original operator placed an incorrect character on the diskette.
3. More than one character or the entire field is incorrect. (In our case ROBERTSON should be LEE.)
4. Too many or too few characters were keyed in a field that was right adjusted.
5. An extra record has been keyed. (This often happens when an operator's attention is distracted and he or she keys in the same record a second time.)
6. A record has been entirely left out during the original keying.

The above cases are handled in the following way:

CASE 1   Verifying operator pressed the wrong key.

1. Press the RESET key.
2. Rekey the correct character and continue.

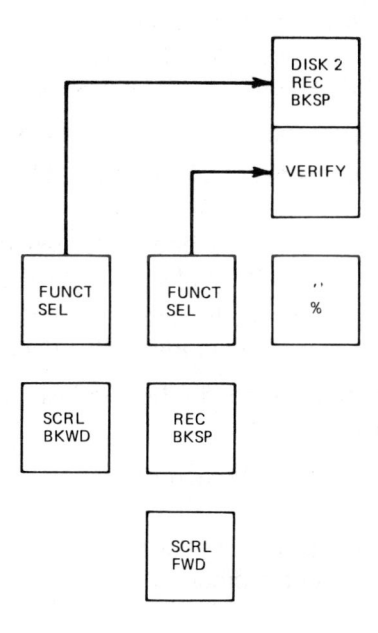

FIGURE 5.19
The IBM 3742 verify mode keys.

UNIT 5   KEY-TO-DISKETTE DEVICES   **97**

CASE 2 Character on the diskette is incorrect. Same procedure as in Case 1.

CASE 3 Entire field (or most of it) is incorrect.

1. Press the FIELD COR (field correct) key. The cursor will return to the first position of the field. Note also that the machine mode on the status line has changed to C.

2. Key the corrected field. (In our case key LEE and press the SKIP key.) When the field is completely keyed, the cursor goes back to the first position of the field for you to reverify what you have just keyed.

CASE 4 An error in a RIGHT ADJUST field.
Use the same procedure as in Case 3 but use the RIGHT ADJ key after the field has been keyed. When the verify error occurs in this case, an R error will be displayed on the status line rather than a V error.

CASE 5 An extra record has been keyed.
It is the verifying operator's responsibility to delete this extra record. Use the FUNCT SEL (lower) and DELETE REC keys to delete the record. (The character D will be placed in position 1 of the record.)

CASE 6 A record has been left out.

1. If a record has been left out and the record insert feature is available, get the system into the UPDATE mode and use the INSERT RECORD PROCEDURE, discussed earlier, for your device. If you do not have this feature, the instructor will tell you what to do.

2. When all missing records have been keyed, do a RCD BKSP or SEARCH ADDRESS for the first record inserted.

3. Press the FUNCT SEL (lower) and VERIFY to get back in VERIFY mode.

Now verify record 2 in the example using Case 2 to correct the social security number and Case 3 to correct the last name. Verify record 3.

When a verifying job is finished:

1. The machine automatically returns to INDEX mode.

2. An examination of the data set label will show that a V has been placed in position 73 of the label.

3. The device has been returned to manual control (the program-level number on the status line shows 0).

4. The error code E shown on the status line does *not* mean an error. It just shows the end of the verifying job.

If you have not finished verifying a job and you must stop work, do the following:

1. Write down the address of the next record to be verified and RETURN TO INDEX.

2. When continuing later:
   a. Load the program.

b. Press FUNCT SEL LOWER and SEARCH ADDRESS. (Press the white FUNCT SEL key and the FIELD CORR key as shown in Figure 5.15.)
c. Key in the disk address that you recorded.
d. Press the REC ADV key.
e. Key in SEL PROG and the program number.
f. Press FUNCT SEL LOWER and VERIFY.
g. Continue verifying.

CAUTION

1. Be careful about pressing REC ADV when verifying. In the first manual keying position of the record, this will bypass the record without verifying it. *But* if the cursor is past the first manual position, the machine will verify manual fields as blanks. Therefore, if there is something in the field, a verify error will occur. Also, in this case the DUP fields must match the previous record or a verify error will occur.

2. When using REC ADV, deleted records are *not* displayed. When using REC BKSP, deleted records *are* displayed.

Laboratory Exercises

Your instructor will assign verifying exercises from the textbook.

CHAINING

Program *chaining* is a method of programming a data entry device so that it switches automatically from one program to another without the operator having to select the program manually (using the SEL PROG key). This feature would be used if a job involved two or more different record formats.

With the 80-character feature, positions 79 and 80 of the program (positions 127 and 128 with the 128 feature) are used for chaining. Acceptable characters for these positions for the 80-character feature are the program numbers 1 through 6.

1. Position 79 controls what program number will be used for a REC BKSP. If this position is blank, the current program number will be in control.
2. Position 80 controls the program that will be in control after the next REC ADV.

If positions 79 and 80 also contain data that is keyed (in other words, all 80 positions of the record have data), a *numeric-continuation field* is assumed. This fact might influence one's record-format design plans.

Laboratory Exercises

Your instructor will assign chaining exercises from the textbook.

SPECIAL FEATURES AVAILABLE FOR THE 3742

Certain special features may be obtained for the 3742 at extra cost. They are:

1. *Search on Content.* This allows a search on the *contents* of a particular field. This feature is very helpful.
2. *Disk Copy.* This feature allows copying all or part of the contents of a diskette in the secondary station to a diskette in the primary station. This feature is also very helpful.
3. *Self-Checking Number.* The self-checking feature is a method for the detection of substitution and transposition keying errors. For an explanation see the modulus 10 and 11 discussion in Appendix D.

4. *Off-Line Field Totals.* Program codes may be used to indicate that accumulators with this special feature are to accumulate field totals. These totals can then be "read out" and placed in a data record on the diskette.
5. *Disk Initialization.* This feature allows reinitialization of a diskette when necessitated by unusual conditions. An example of an unusual condition would be the exposure of a diskette to a strong magnetic field.
6. *Variable Record Length from 1 to 128.* This feature allows records to be of different lengths to be entered.
7. *Four Additional Program Buffers.* Ten programs per operator are possible (1 through 9 and A)
8. *Record Insert.* This feature allows a record to be inserted, and eliminates the need of using the disk-copy routine. This is a very helpful feature.
9. *Proof Keyboard.* The proof keyboard has an adding-machine arrangement for the numeric keys.

MAINTENANCE AND UNUSUAL CONDITIONS

1. To dust or wipe off the keyboard use a soft damp cloth, but don't spray cleaning solutions or water on it. Do not consume food or drinks at the keyboard.
   Wipe the screen with a very soft cloth that will not scratch the surface.
2. Error condition causes and proper actions are listed in the ERROR RECOVERY chart. (See Figure 5.20.)
3. Data is sometimes lost but can be recovered. The EOD address can sometimes be lost by:
   a. Pressing FUNCT SEL LOWER and ENTER, keying a record, and pressing REC ADV. (A SEARCH EOD or FUNCT SEL LOWER and UPDATE should have been used.)
   b. Removing the diskette from the drive before the RETURN TO INDEX was completed.
   c. Cutting off the power.
   d. Getting into the CE (customer engineer mode) accidentally. Only the repair-person should use this mode. (CER is displayed in positions 38 to 40 of the status line.) To get out of this mode, press RESET several times.

   Recovery procedure for all of the above except (d) is:
   a. Estimate an EOD disk address and enter it in the EOD field in the data set label.
   b. Execute a search EOD.
   c. Repeat steps (a) and (b) adjusting the estimated EOD's address until the last record is found.
   d. Return to INDEX.
   e. Use the MODIFY routine (see page 85) to change the EOD disk-address field in the label to what you wrote down.
   f. Execute a search EOD to be sure the EOD address is now correct.
   g. If any records were keyed over, go back and correct these records.
4. Disk-write errors may occur due to defective (or bad) tracks. You may need to copy the disk and rekey the corrections.

IBM 3741/3742 REFERENCE CARD
GX21-9172-1

ERROR RECOVERY

Applicable to all errors except those that occur during initialization or communications procedures. For communications or initialization error recovery, see *IBM 3741 Data Station Reference Manual*, GA21-9183, and *IBM 3742 Dual Data Station Reference Manual*, GA21-9184.

Error Code	Description and Resolution
A	This diskette is not to be used. Remove diskette.
B	The data set label is wrong. Reset and correct the label.
C	The self-check digit shows an error. Reset, field backspace, and rekey the field.
D	Disk 2 is not installed or not ready. Reset and make disk 2 ready.
E	An attempt was made to go past the End of Extent. Reset and continue with a new data set or disk. This occurs after the last record of a data set is verified. Not an error—reset and go on.
F	Function selected is not available. Move job to a different machine.
G	An attempt to write was made on protected data set. Reset and inspect label.
H	A disk copy was attempted with an improper setup. Reset and check the following: (1) Disk 2 address. (2) Disk 2 readiness. (3) Was shift key pressed with copy key? (4) Disk 1 address.
I	The search address is invalid. Reset and check the following: (1) Address incorrectly keyed? (2) Address outside data set?

Error Code	Description and Resolution
J	Printing is completed for this diskette. Change diskettes and continue.
K	An invalid key was pressed. Reset and rekey.
L	In wrong mode for key pressed. Reset and rekey or change mode.
M	In wrong mode for mode selection attempted. Reset and select another mode.
N	Keying too fast for machine. Reset and continue.
O	An incorrect operation was attempted. Reset and continue, using the correct procedure.
P	Program or program selection wrong. Reset and correct the problem.
Q	The field totals control statement is incorrect. Reset and rewrite the control statement.
R	Right adjust key not pressed or pressed early in verify mode. Reset and perform necessary action.
S	No such record found during search. Reset; check search information and data set label.

Error Code	Description and Resolution
T	Attempt was made to key beyond end of record. Reset and advance to next record. (Check the auto record advance switch.)
U	Printer out of paper (or cover open). Reset and load paper.
V	Character keyed in Verify does not match the character from the record. Reset and rekey.
W	Invalid printer format character. Reset and correct. (Check program level A.)
X	In verifying a right adjust field, the right adjust key was used for a negative number or the dash key was used for a positive number. Reset and key correctly.

Error Code	Description and Resolution
Y	Search, Update, or Verify was selected for an empty data set. Reset and inspect label.
0	The disk cover was opened before RETURN TO INDEX was completed. Check the *Error Recovery* section of the Operator's Guide.
Z, 1 2, 3 4, 5	Machine or disk problem. Check the *Error Recovery* sections of either the 3741 Operator's Guide, GA21-9131, or the 3742 Operator's Guide, GA21-9136.
6	The record just read is a deleted record. Numeric reset and continue.
7	No such record found during search. Reset; check search information and data set label.

FIGURE 5.20
The IBM 3741/3742 error recovery reference card (Courtesy of IBM Corporation).

SECTION D
THE TAB 700 SERIES

TAB PRODUCTS has two key-to-diskette devices, the 701 and 702.

The 702 accommodates two operators and is used for centralized large volume data processing; whereas, the 701 accommodates one operator and can be used for remote job entry. The 701 can have a printer attached for hard copy (printed reports that can be used for reference).

Both models have prompting capabilities. Prompting is the display of programming messages at the bottom of the screen to assist the operator in keying.

The 701 can store up to 168 characters in a constant buffer; the 702 can store up to 84 characters. The 701 has 20 programs; each operator on the 702 has 10 program levels.

It is interesting to compare the differences in optional and standard features between the IBM 3742 and the TAB 702.

TAB Standard Features	IBM 3742	TAB 702
Program levels	6	10
Lines of display per operator	3	6
Displayable characters per operator	120	240
Characters/record	80 (128 at extra cost)	128
Variable-length record	Extra cost	Standard
Record insert	Extra cost	Standard
Search content	Extra cost	Standard
Search sequential content	Extra cost	Standard
Disk copy	Extra cost	Standard
Character insert/delete	Not available	Standard
Operator prompting	Not available	Standard
Consecutive numbering	Not available	Standard
Constants from memory	Not available	Standard
TAB Optional Features at Extra Cost		
Check digit validate	Included	Included
Check digit generate	Not available	Included
Offline field totals	3 accumulators	5 accumulators
Record pool	Not available	Included
Disk initialization	Available	Available
Printer Interface	Not available	Available
Additional Program levels	Not available	Available

TAB 702 DATA ENTRY DEVICE The TAB 702 Data entry device is shown in Figure 5.21. It is a stand-alone device (not connected to another device) with two operator stations. It has only one main line switch so care must be taken at the end of a job *not* to cut the machine off while another person is working at the second station.

The *mode* of the machine determines the operation the machine will perform. The 700 modes are:

Mode	Character	How Used
ENTER	E	To record new data.
VERIFY	V	To check the accuracy of data already entered on a diskette.

FIGURE 5.21
The TAB System 700 KEY-TO-DISKETTE
(Copyright © 1980, TAB Products Co., Palo
Alto, CA).

UPDATE	U	To retrieve or alter data already entered on a diskette.
SEARCH	S	To search or look for a particular record.
CORRECT	C	To correct an error in verifying.
MODIFY	M	To change index information.
FIELD TOTALS	F	To display totals in accumulators.
INDEX	X	To display index information.
RECORD INSERT	N	To insert a record between records already keyed.
COPY	K	To copy information from one diskette to the other.

The Display Screen

Six lines of 40 characters each are displayed on the TAB 702 display screen shown in Figure 5.23.

1. STATUS LINE

    Turn to page 80 and read about the IBM 3742 status line if you have not done so. The TAB 700 Series status line is shown in Figure 5.22. There are very few differences.

    a. The BEGIN FIELD CODE is called a COMMAND CODE by TAB.
    b. There is a RETRY COUNTER. This is a *hex* character which indicates the number of times the system has tried to read or write at the current address. Ten tries are allowed before a disk read or write error is displayed. (For a discussion of the hexadecimal numbering system, see Appendix C. The digits 0 to 9 in our number system and the hex system are the same. Our 10 is the letter A in hex.)
    c. The Alternate Record Advance Field is blank unless the alternate record advance is in use. A minus sign is then displayed.

2. DATA LINES

    Data or program information lines are shown in lines 2 to 5.

    Line 2 ------------------**POSITIONS 1 THRU 40**---------------------------
    Line 3 ------------------**POSITIONS 41 THRU 80**---------------------------
    Line 4 ------------------**POSITIONS 81 THRU 120**---------------------------
    Line 5 ------------------**POSITIONS 121 THRU 128**---------------------------

3. PROMPTING LINE

    The last 30 characters of line 5 can contain prompting messages to assist the operator in keying. A message no longer than 30 characters can be displayed telling the operator what field to key in.

4. FIELD DEFINITION

    The slashes in the last 30 positions of line 6 on the display screen show the field length. For example:

	Prompting Message
LINE 5	**CO NAME**
LINE 6	**TAB PRODUCTS** ////////

    CO NAME is the prompting message. TAB PRODUCTS has been keyed in and the slashes show that there are eight positions left in the company-name field.

5. DATA SET LABEL INFORMATION

    When the device is in INDEX (X) mode, a data set label rather than data is displayed on lines 2 and 3 of the screen.

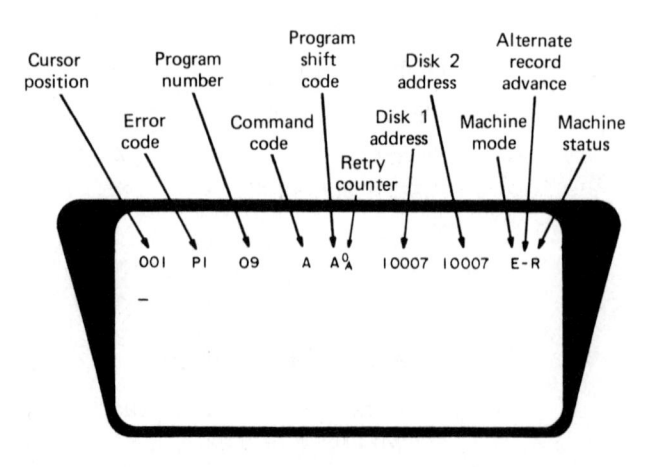

FIGURE 5.22
The TAB 702 status line (Copyright © 1980, TAB Products Co., Palo Alto, CA).

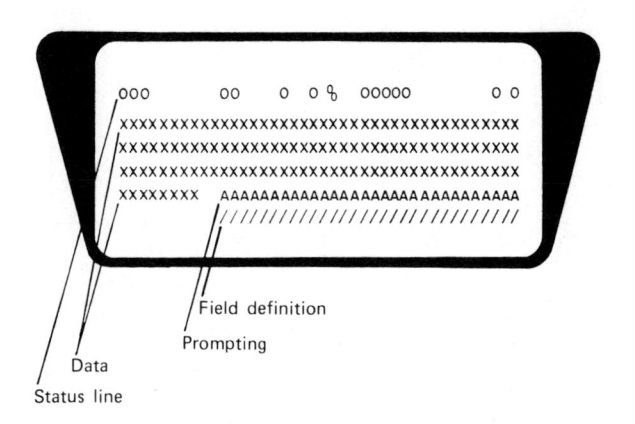

FIGURE 5.23
The TAB 702 display screen (Copyright © 1980, TAB Products Co., Palo Alto, CA).

Power-On Information

The power ON/OFF switch is found on the right side of the keyboard at the back near the bottom of the board. The switch should be pulled toward the operator. Only one keyboard has the power ON/OFF switch.

The diskette unit is to the right of the keyboard. It has a rectangular handle with a red dot on it. When the red dot is lit, the cover cannot be opened. The machine must be in RETURN TO INDEX mode before the cover will open.

To load the diskette:

1. Open the diskette unit by pressing down on the rectangular handle with the red dot on it.
2. Insert the diskette with the label away from the CRT as directed on the disk unit.
3. Push the diskette down until it locks or clicks.
4. Close the cover.

When the red light goes out and the data set label appears on the screen, the machine is ready.

You can adjust the tilt of the CRT screen for better viewing by using the tab on the upper left corner of the mirror. The brightness control knob is on the left side (if you are sitting at disk 1 position) of the table. It can be used to adjust the brightness of the screen.

Unloading a Diskette

1. Depress the FUNC SEL (lower) and RET TO INDEX keys to get the machine into the RETURN TO INDEX MODE. (These keys are discussed in the keyboard section.)
2. When the red light on the rectangular handle goes out, press the diskette unit handle. The diskette will pop up.
3. Close the unit by moving the cover toward the red dot. Do *not* leave this cover open.
4. Place the diskette in its protective envelope.

The 702 Keyboard

Data Keys. Figure 5.24 shows a picture of the TAB 702 keyboard. The data keys cause the entering of 64 possible characters. Normally the machine is in alpha or lower shift which causes the characters at the bottom of the key to

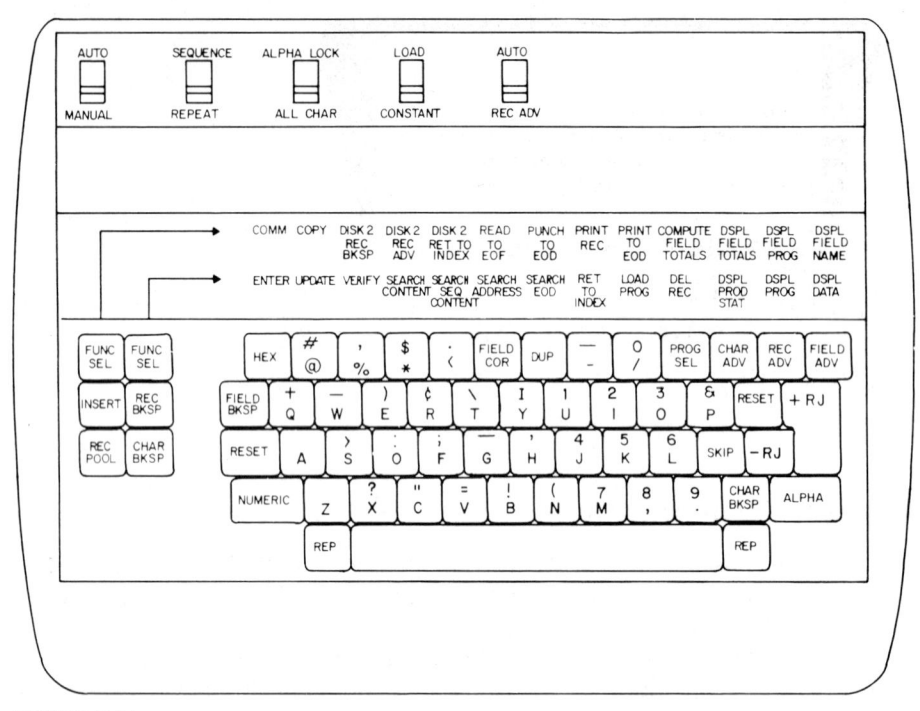

FIGURE 5.24
The TAB 700 keyboard (Copyright © 1980, TAB Products Co., Palo Alto, CA).

be entered. To get a character at the top of the key (upper shift), use the NUM SHIFT (numeric shift) key. Note the A and Z keys have nothing on the top of the key.

Switches

1. *AUTO/MANUAL Switch.* This switch has the same function as that of the 3742 AUTO DUP/SKIP switch described on page 77.
2. *SEQUENCE/REPEAT Switch.* This switch controls program sequencing (chaining). If set on SEQUENCE it will automatically select the program

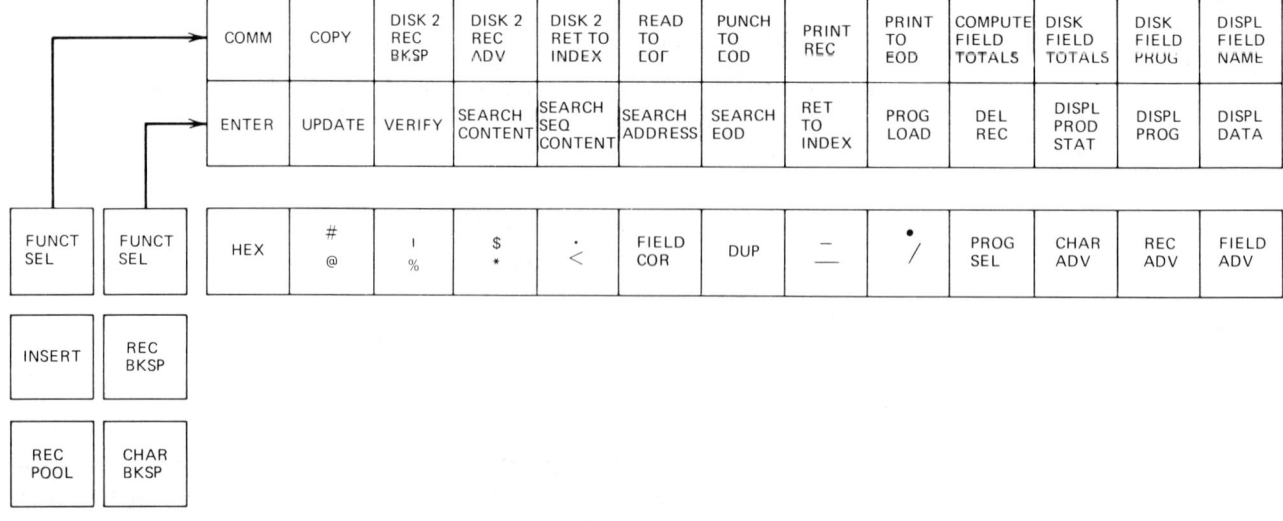

FIGURE 5.25
TAB 702 FUNCTION SELECT keys.

106 PART 2 DATA ENTRY EQUIPMENT

level for the next record. On REPEAT, control remains in the same program level. However, an operator may manually select a program from the keyboard at any time.

3. *ALPHA LOCK/ALL CHAR Switch.* This switch is similar to the 3742 PROG NUM SHIFT switch described on page 77. The ALPHA LOCK is the same as the NUMBERS ONLY setting on the 3742 switch.

4. *LOAD/CONSTANT Switch.* The 702 has an additional buffer area called a *constant buffer area.* (The buffer areas were discussed on page 74.) The 702 operator may store up to 84 characters of constants. Under program control this data is emitted or placed in a specified field of each record. Turning the machine off or loading a new program erases this information.

    On LOAD this switch allows the operator to load information into memory. He or she keys data into the first record manually while the switch is set on LOAD. With the switch set on CONSTANT, the data is automatically emitted into the record as programmed.

5. *AUTO REC ADV Switch.* This switch works the same as the AUTO REC ADV on the 3742 (see page 77).

Special function keys. Read pages 78 and 79 on the 3742 special function keys.

On the 702 the dark blue keys, except those at the extreme left, are called the special function keys. These keys work exactly the same as those on the 3742 except for the following differences:

1. The 702 select program key is called the PROG SEL key (rather than the SEL PROG key).
2. There are two RESET keys on the 702.
3. There are two right adjust keys, the +RJ and the −RJ, which makes keying of negative right-adjusted fields much easier than on the 3742. For a negative field, the −RJ key is pressed. For a positive field the +RJ key is used.
4. There are two repeat (REP) keys on each side of the space bar. They are white in color.

Function select keys. These keys, as on the 3742, are used to redefine (or give another meaning to) the top row of keys. The new meanings are indicated by the two rows of labels above the top row of keys. The colors are *blue* and white rather than the green and white used on the 3742. The possible actions with these function select keys and a key in the top row are:

1. *FUNC SEL (Upper) Key.* The blue FUNC SEL key at the extreme left is called the *upper function select* key and is associated with the upper row of labels in blue. FUNC SEL UPPER redefines the top row of keys according to the top row of labels.
2. *FUNC SEL (Lower) Key.* The white FUNC SEL key at the extreme right is called *function select lower* and is associated with the bottom row of white labels. FUNC SEL LOWER redefines the top row of keys according to the lower row of labels.

    Using these function select keys allows:
    a. Copying of data from a diskette in unit 2 to a diskette in unit 1.
    b. Starting of transmission of data on a communications line.
    c. Record backspacing and forward spacing and returning to index mode on diskette 2 from unit one (DISK 2 REC BKSP, REC ADV, RET TO INDEX).

UNIT 5 KEY-TO-DISKETTE DEVICES

d. Cards to be read from an interfaced card machine (READ TO EOF).
  e. Punching of cards on an interfaced card machine (PUNCH TO EOD).
  f. Printing of records on an interfaced printer (PRINT REC or PRINT EOD).
  g. Initialization of accumulators; and begins accumulation of totals (COMPUTE FIELD TOTALS) or displays totals on the screen (DSPLY FIELD TOTALS).
  h. The display of the program for the field being keyed on the prompting line (DSPL FIELD PROG) and is turned off by DSPL FIELD NAME.
  i. Selection of ENTER mode.
  j. Selection of UPDATE mode.
  k. Selection of VERIFY mode.
  l. Search for a field with the same content, for sequential content, or end of data.
  m. Selection of RETURN TO INDEX mode.
  n. Loading of a program.
  o. Deletion of a record.
  p. Display of production statistics, a program, or the prompting data following the program.
3. *REC BKSP Key.* This key causes the cursor to be returned to position 1 of the record. If the cursor is already in position 1, the key will move the cursor to position 1 of the previous record.

    Under program control, action is the same except the cursor returns to the first *manual* field in the record. Any programmed duplications or skips will be executed at the beginning of the record.

4. *INSERT Key.* This key allows the operator to insert characters, records, or blanks.
    a. Pressing FUNC SEL (upper) and the INSERT key allows the operator to insert a character. All characters to the right are moved one position to the right.
    b. Pressing the INSERT key and then holding the NUMERIC shift key and keying two digits (nn) will insert nn blanks from the cursor position to the end of the record. All data to the right is moved toward the end of the record.
    c. Depressing FUNC SEL (lower) and SEARCH ADDRESS, keying in two digits for the number of records, then depressing FUNC SEL (lower) and the INSERT key will insert the number of records keyed for the two digits. These records are blank and can later have data inserted. (See section on insertion of records.)

5. *REC POOL Key.* When pressed, the record pool key begins record pooling. *Record pooling* allows up to 26 records (each up to 128 characters in length) to be stored in track 73 of the diskette. These records can be retrieved later by using the REC POOL key and keying the two-digit sector number of the record. The data is copied and thus saves keying time.

6. *CHAR BKSP Key.* There are two character backspace keys, a white one on the left and a blue one on the right. Either key moves the cursor back one position to the previous manual position.

Errors

An error is shown by a flashing screen and an error code on the status line. To demonstrate this, assume you have inserted the diskette given you as directed above:

1. Press the FIELD COR key.
2. Observe the flashing screen and the error code of M on the status line.

These error codes may consist of one or two alpha characters or a combination of one alpha and one numeric character. The recovery procedure should be:

1. Look up the error code in the Error Codes and Recovery Section.
2. Press the RESET key. This stops the blinking and erases the error code from the status line.

The Index Track or Track Zero

Read pages 82 to 84 of the 3742 section on the index track or track zero.

Modifying or Changing a Data Set Label

Note that when a data set label is displayed, the program level displayed on the status line is program Q. On the 702 this program should be used when keying a new label or modifying an old one. This makes it easier to change or modify labels than on the 3742.

Turning on the AUTO/MANUAL switch and pressing the FIELD ADV key will cause the system to stop at the six fields of the label that are mandatory. The shift (A or N) for the field is displayed in the status line, and the slashes on the prompt line show the number of positions to be entered. To try this (the diskette should be inserted and the machine should be in RETURN TO INDEX mode):

1. Turn the AUTO/MANUAL switch to AUTO. Observe the record number, shift, and characters on the status line as you proceed.
2. Press the FIELD ADV key. The cursor should be in position 4 of the label.
3. Press the FIELD ADV key. The cursor should be in position 6 of the label, which is the name of the data-set field. Change DATA to PAYROLL.
4. Press FUNC SEL (lower) and the letter M.
5. Press REC ADV. The cursor will go back to position 1 of the label. The label will reappear with the change.

Now repeat Steps 1 through 5 above, changing the label PAYROLL back to DATA. You will need to use the space bar to blank out all characters through position 13.

Any field in the data set label may be changed by the above method. Now investigating some of the remaining data set labels:

1. Press the REC ADV key. Notice that the display screen flashes and that the second field on the status line (first line) shows a DR error code. As listed in the section on error messages, this code indicates a deleted record.
2. Press the RESET key. The screen should stop flashing. You are now positioned on sector 10 of track 0, the second data set label—DATA09. Notice the D in position 1. This means that the record is a delete record. A *delete record* is a record that is still physically on the diskette, but is not being used.

UNIT 5   KEY-TO-DISKETTE DEVICES

Second Data Set Label Creation Procedure

Read this section for the 3742 on pages 85-86. Follow the steps, but in Step 3 use the FIELD ADV key instead of the CHAR ADV and REP keys to move the cursor.

Manual Keying

Read pages 86 beginning with MANUAL KEYING through page 88 ending with DELETING A RECORD for the 3742. However, look at Figure 5.25 for the 702 function keys.

Adding or Inserting a Record on the 702

You have just deleted record 3 or the REJCEK record. The records that remain are BROWN, SMITH, and WILLIAMS. Suppose you wish to insert

        JANE A LITTLE   DP 453   A   661-82-9456

between the SMITH and WILLIAMS records. Try this with the following procedure:

1. Insert the diskette and turn the AUTO/MANUAL switch to MANUAL and the AUTO/REC ADV switch to REC ADV.
2. Press the FUNC SEL and SEARCH CONTENT keys. The screen will go blank.
3. Determine the first record that will be moved down after the insertion. Character advance to a unique field in this record. Key in the unique field (in this example the social security number for the WILLIAMS record). Press REC ADV and the record should appear.
4. Press FUNC SEL and SEARCH ADDRESS. (This means press the white FUNC SEL key and the FIELD COR key as shown in Figure 5.15.)
5. Key in a *two*-digit number indicating the number of records that you intend to insert *here* (in this case 01).
6. Depress the FUNC SEL (lower) and INSERT keys. This procedure does not lock out the other operator on a dual station. To do a fast record-insert and lock out the other operator, depress and hold down the ALPHA key while depressing the INSERT key. The system enters the RECORD INSERT mode moving the records to the right. The status line will show an **N** for RECORD INSERT mode and a **W** for WAIT in the two fields at the right.
7. When the insertion is complete, the cursor will appear in position 1 of the first deleted record and a flashing screen will show a **DR** error code. A **D/** will be placed in the first two positions of each inserted record.
8. Press the RESET key.
9. Key in the record to be inserted and press the REC ADV key.
10. Repeat step 9 until all records have been inserted. If you were using a program, you would have to select it before the keying.

Laboratory Exercises

Your instructor will now give you exercises to key manually on the TAB 702.

PROGRAMS   The TAB 702 is instructed by the use of a (program) record with programming codes. Loaded into the program buffer, this program controls the record format and assists in faster and easier keying.

There are two ways of loading a program on the 702:

1. From the keyboard.
2. From a diskette.

The program buffer on the TAB 702 is used to store programs that control:

1. The record format.
2. Statements for field totals.
3. Prompting.

Ten programs may be stored on the 702. If prompting is not used, ten format programs may be stored; otherwise five format and five prompting programs may be stored. In the latter case format programs are sorted in odd numered levels (01,03,05,07,09), and prompting programs are sorted in even number levels (02,04,06,08,10). When a new format program is loaded, the prompting program is erased.

Each field in a program format has:

1. A code that describes the function needed.
2. A field definition code showing for how many positions this action is to take place.

Figure 5.26 shows the TAB 702 program chart.

A short chart is shown below for the functions necessary in the programmed laboratory exercises for this text.

Function	Character Code	Field Definition
Skip numeric field	S	—
Skip alphanumeric field	K	.
Punch numeric field	N	—
Duplicate numeric field	D	—
Punch alphameric field	A	.
Duplicate alphanumeric field	U	.
Right adjust a numeric field and zero fill	R	—
End of program	E	

NOTE If the record length is 80 and the program is for 80 positions, the E for end of program is not necessary.

EXAMPLE TO ILLUSTRATE PROGRAMMED OPERATIONS PROCEDURE

A program is to be planned on the TAB 702 for the following data:

Positions 1–6	Duplicate numeric date.
Positions 7–11	Duplicate alphameric course abbreviation.
Positions 12–20	Key social security number.
Positions 21–33	Key last name.
Positions 34–45	Key first name.
Position 46	Key middle initial.

UNIT 5 KEY-TO-DISKETTE DEVICES

CHART OF PROGRAMMING CODES

PROGRAM CODES FOR STANDARD FEATURES

COMMAND CODES	FUNCTION DEFINITION	SHIFT
N	Manual Field	Numeric
A	Manual Field	Alpha
R	Right Justify Field/Zero Fill	Numeric
J	Right Justify Field/Blank Fill	Numeric
I	Right Justify Field/Blank Fill	Alpha
V	Manual Field/Bypass in Verify Mode Only	Numeric
W	Manual Field/Bypass in Verify Mode Only	Alpha
X	Right Justify Field/Zero Fill/ Bypass in Verify Mode	Numeric
Y	Right Justify Field/Blank Fill/ Bypass to Verify Mode	Numeric
Z	Right Justify Field/Blank Fill/ Bypass in Verify Mode	Alpha
DA**	Must Enter, W/RJ/Zero Fill	Numeric
DB**	Must Enter, W/RJ/Blank Fill	Numeric
DC**	Must Enter, W/RJ/Blank Fill	Alpha
DD**	Consecutive Numbering/Zero Fill	Numeric
DE**	Consecutive Numbering/Blank Fill	Numeric
CC**	Insert Constant	Numeric
CD**	Insert Constant	Alpha
CE**	Must Enter	Numeric
CF**	Must Enter	Alpha
D	Auto Duplicate	Numeric
U	Auto Duplicate	Alpha
S	Auto Skip	Numeric
K	Auto Skip	Alpha
E	End of Program	------
* (asterisk)	Prompting Delimiter (Breaker)	------
B	Bypass	------

CONTINUATION CODES	FUNCTION DEFINITION	SHIFT
- (dash)	Field Continuation	Numeric
. (period)	Field Continuation	Alpha

FIGURE 5.26
TAB 702 programming codes (Copyright © 1980, TAB Products, Co., Palo Alto, CA).

Positions 47-52   Amount of tuition and fees (right justify) nnnn‸nn.

Positions 53-80   Blank.

A record layout with the planned codes is shown in Figure 5.27.

Prompting Programs

Rules for writing a prompting program are:

1. Each prompting program begins and ends with *two* asterisks.
2. Prompts for each field are separated by *one* asterisk.
3. Prompts cannot be over 30 characters long.

For our sample format program, the prompting program might be:

DATE*COURSE*SS#*LAST NAME*FIRST NAME*MI* TUITION(RJ)

Figure 5.27 also shows this prompting program.

PROGRAM CODES FOR OPTIONAL FEATURES

OPTION COMMAND CODES	FUNCTION DEFINITION	SHIFT
H	Check Digit Validate - Modulus 10	Numeric
C	Check Digit Validate - Modulus 11	Numeric
F	Auto/Skip/Check Digit Validate/ Modulus 10	Numeric
G	Auto Skip/Check Digit Validate/ Modulus 11	Numeric
L	Auto Dup/Check Digit Validate/ Modulus 10	Numeric
M	Auto Dup/Check Digit Validate/ Modulus 11	Numeric
CA**	Generate Check Digit/Modulus 10	Numeric
CB**	Generate Check Digit/Modulus 11	Numeric
Any command code followed by a 1, 2, 3, 10 or 11 **	Add Field Totals - any amount keyed in this field will be added or subtracted in the accumulator designated.	------
Bypass code followed by a 4, 5, 6, 12 or 13 **	Field Totals Readout - this field will be automatically bypassed and the total will be displayed as a Field Totals Field. Use during Off Line Field Totals ONLY.	------
Bypass code followed by a 7, 8, 9, 14 or 15 **	Field Totals Readout & Reset - field will be automatically bypassed, totals will be displayed, and the accumulators reset to zeroes.	------

** any two digits code needed must be keyed in one position by depressing the HEX key and keying the two digits.

FIGURE 5.26 *(Continued)*

Loading a Program From the Keyboard

1. Insert the diskette.
2. Set the AUTO/MANUAL switch to MANUAL and the AUTO/REC ADV switch to REC ADV.
3. Press FUNC SEL (lower) and DELETE REC.
4. Key in the format program as shown in Figure 5.27.
5. Press FUNC SEL (lower) and PROG LOAD. Key the *two*-digit program number (01 in our case). You do not need to hold down the NUMERIC shift key when keying in this program number. The screen will blank out.

Prompting format: ****DATE*COURSE*SS#*LAST NAME*FIRST NAME*MI*TUITION[RJ]****

FIGURE 5.27
TAB 702 record layout, program, and prompt codes.

UNIT 5 KEY-TO-DISKETTE DEVICES

6. Key in the prompting program.
7. Press FUNC SEL (lower) and PROG LOAD. Key in the even numbered *two*-digit program number (02 in our case). The screen will blank out again.
8. To load more programs, repeat Steps 4 to 7.
9. Press FUNC SEL and RETURN TO INDEX.
10. Press FUNC SEL and ENTER. If the data set being used already has data in it, a DP error code will appear on the status line. Either:
    (a) RETURN TO INDEX and use another data set, or
    (b) Override by pressing the RESET key.
    This error stop is a protection against accidental destruction of good data.
11. Load the program into memory by pressing PROG SEL and keying in the two-digit program number (in our case 01). The prompting program is loaded with the format program.

The important thing to understand is that in the beginning there are no fields in the output storage area to be duplicated. Therefore on the *first* record, these fields to be duplicated must be keyed manually.

Keying Under Program Control (Program Has Been Loaded)

Read pages 93 to 94, 3742 keying under program control, remembering that the 3742 AUTO REC ADV and AUTO SKIP/DUP switches are called the AUTO/REC ADV and AUTO/MANUAL switches on the 702.

1. Step 1 would read for the 702:
   "Set the AUTO/MANUAL switch to MANUAL; set the AUTO/REC ADV switch to REC ADV."
2. Step 12 would read:
   "Turn the AUTO/MANUAL switch to AUTO and the AUTO/REC ADV switch to AUTO."

Laboratory Exercises

Your instructor will assign some exercises from the textbook to do under program control.

STORING AND LOADING PROGRAMS ON A DISKETTE

Read pages 94 to 95, storing and loading programs on a diskette, remembering that Step 3 would read: "Press the RESET key."
The steps for loading a program from diskette at a later time are also the same except for the AUTO/MANUAL and AUTO/REC ADV switch names.

SEARCHING FOR RECORDS

Read the 3742 searching for records section on page 95.

DISK COPY OPERATIONS

Read the 3742 disk copy operations section on page 96.

VERIFYING

The verifying process is the same on the 702 as on the 3742 except that when verifying is completed an error code of E1 rather than E will appear on the status line.
Read the section on verifying on pages 96 to 99. Then your instructor will assign some verifying exercises.

PART 2 DATA ENTRY EQUIPMENT

CHAINING Program *chaining* is a method of programming a data entry device so that it switches automatically from one program to another without the operator having to select the program manually (using the PROG SEL key). This feature would be used if a job involved two or more different record formats. TAB uses the term *automatic program sequencing* rather than chaining.

With the 80-character feature, positions 127 and 128 of the format program are used for program sequencing. If the SEQUENCE/REPEAT switch in on SEQUENCE, control changes to the program level number coded in positions 127 and 128. If the switch is on REPEAT, the program format remains the same.

If data is to be keyed into positions 127 and 128, the sequence code also acts as a numeric or alpha field continuation code depending on the last field definition code before column 127.

Laboratory Exercises

Your instructor will assign chaining or automatic program sequencing exercises from the textbook.

SUMMARY As stated previously, the TAB 702 has many features considered special features on the IBM 3742. Details for these features and the use of the constant buffer available on the 702 may be found in the *TAB 700 Concepts and Operating Techniques Manual*.

TAB 702 ERROR CODES AND RECOVERY PROCEDURES

Code	Type of Error	Mode	Cause	Recovery Procedure
C1	Constant Error	E, U, V	Constant memory has not been loaded.	Raise LOAD/CONSTANT switch and reset. Key all constants.
C2	Constant Error	E, U, V	All standard and additional constant memory has been utilized.	Reset and lower the LOAD/CONSTANT switch. No more constants may be loaded. Program should be changed to make the remainder of the field a manual field. NOTE: If you need more than 168/84 character of constant data already stored, call your TAB Sales Representative.
CD	Check Digit	E, U, V	The Check Digit keyed does not validate (compare). In Verify mode: it has been keyed incorrectly or it was left blank.	Reset and rekey the Check Digit. If the error persists, depress Field Backspace and rekey the entire field. If the Check Digit Field cannot be validated, depress the Skip key while in the first column of the field. The Skip key takes you to the next field, leaving the Check Digit Field blank.
			You tried to Skip, Dup, Field Adv, or Rec Adv while not in the first position of the Check Digit Validate Field.	Reset and key the remainder of the Check Digit field or return to the beginning of the field. Then depress the Skip, Dup, Field Adv, or Rec Adv key.
CN	Consecutive Record Numbering	E, U	Field length for consecutive numbering has been programmed for more than 6 positions.	Put AUTO/MANUAL down. Reset and change the program.

Code	Type of Error	Mode	Cause	Recovery Procedure
CP	Copy	X, E, U	Data set label in disk 1 or 2 is invalid.	Modify the data set label until it is valid; see "Data Set Labels."
			OR	OR
			Numeric Shift key is not being held while COPY is depressed.	Hold down NUMERIC key while COPY is depressed.
			OR	OR
			All of the above.	Call TAB Field Service.
D2	Disk 2 Error	All	The Disk 2 drive is not ready.	Reset. Depress the FUNC SEL (upper), and DISK 2 REC ADV.
DI	Disk Initialization Error	I	A track on the disk cannot be initialized	Reset. This disk cannot be initialized.
			OR	OR
			During Track Checking procedure, system has listed tracks with any of the following problems: 1. Bad track code. 2. Track with read/write error. 3. Track with deleted records.	Reset. Select Update mode and look at specified tracks to find problem; or, initialize the disk.
DP	Keying in a Data Set that has already been used.	E	You selected Enter mode in a data set that already has data in it.	Reset and use another data set or go ahead and key over the data after checking to make sure it is no longer needed.
DR	Deleted	All	This code does not indicate an error, but only shows that the record is deleted. This code may show up during Search Operations, Disk Copy, etc., as the deleted record is passed.	Reset and continue.
			OR	OR
			Data set label is deleted.	Reset and modify label if needed.
E1	End of Extent	V	Disk has returned to the Index track because the last record in the data set has been verified.	Reset and go to the next job.
E2	End of Extent	E, U	You tried to Record Advance on Disk 1 beyond the EOE.	Reset and modify the EOE in the data set label, if possible, or go to another data set—use another disk if necessary.
E3	End of Extent	E	You tried to copy from Disk 2 beyond the last record in the data set.	Reset and continue on another data set for diskette.
			OR	OR
			Encountered EOE on Disk 1 during a copy operation.	Reset and modify the EOE in the data set label or continue on another diskette.
F1	Function not Available	ALL	You have selected a function that is not installed in your model. If you need more optional functions, call your TAB Sales Representative.	Reset and key a function that is installed in your model.
HX	Keying Error	ALL	One of the two keys depressed, following the Hex key, is not a Hex character.	Reset, depress the Hex key and the two Hex characters. The acceptable HEX characters are Numeric K, 0 through 9, and letters A through F.

Code	Type of Error	Mode	Cause	Recovery Procedure
I	Insert Error	E, U C	Char/Line Insert: The number of spaces selected is greater than spaces left in the field.	Reset. Key a digit that fits or rekey the entire field.
IE	Illegal Entry	E, U	You tried to select Search "E" with AUTO/REC ADV switch up.	Reset and lower AUTO/REC ADV switch.
IF	Incorrect Function	ALL	Depressed the CHAR ADV or FIELD ADV in the Verify mode.	Reset and depress the correct key.
			OR	OR
			You depressed a function key after the Insert key.	Reset and depress the correct key.
			OR	OR
			Depressed the REC BKSP or REC ADV in the Correct mode.	Reset and depress the correct key.
			OR	OR
			Depressed a Disk 1 key when in Verify or Correct mode.	Reset and select the correct key.
			OR	OR
			Selected function not available on the system.	Reset and check function desired.
IV	Insert Error	V	Insert function selected while in Verify mode.	Reset. Depress Update mode, then select Insert.
K1	Keying Error	ALL	You depressed the A or Z key in Numeric mode.	Reset and depress the correct key.
			OR	OR
			A character key other than a 0 through 9, a dash, a space, or a plus has been keyed in a Numeric Field with the ALPHA LOCK/ALL CHAR switch in the Alpha position.	Reset and key the proper keys or set the ALPHA LOCK/ALL CHAR switch to ALL CHAR. (Alpha Shift can override ALPHA LOCK/ALL CHAR switch.)
			OR	OR
			DUP key is being depressed within a constant field.	Reset. Manually key or Skip the remainder of field.
K2	Keying Error	ALL	Depressed Skip or CHAR ADV in a Must Enter field.	Reset and key.
L1	Data Set Label Incorrect	X	Label has one or more extents missing or incorrect:	
			BOE is greater than the EOE or the EOD.	Depress the Reset key and then correct the BOE and/or the EOE and the EOD.
			BOE is less than track 01, sector 01.	Reset and Correct the BOE.
			EOE, is greater than track 73, sector 26. (Track 74 is reserved and should not be used.)	Reset and correct the EOE.
			Sector number is 00 or is greater than 26 in either the BOE, EOE, or EOD.	Reset and enter the correct number.
			The third position in the BOE, EOE, or EOD is not a zero.	Reset and key a zero in the third position.

Code	Type of Error	Mode	Cause	Recovery Procedure
			EOD is greater than the EOE plus 1.	Reset and correct the EOD and/or the EOE.
			EOD is greater than track 74, sector 01.	Reset and correct the EOD.
L2	Data Set Label Incorrect	X	Record length is either missing, is 00, or larger than 128.	Reset and enter the correct record length.
			OR	OR
			Data has been keyed into a position that should have been left blank.	Reset and correct by keying blanks into these positions.
			OR	OR
			Position four in the data set label is not a "1".	Reset and key a "1" into position four.
			OR	OR
			Non-numeric was keyed in one of the extents.	Reset and correct.
			OR	OR
			BOE higher than EOD.	Reset and correct.
M	Mode Error	X, E, U	Attempted to select a mode while current sector is either 01, 02, 03, 04, 05, 06, or 07 of the Index track. (Modify mode is allowed.)	Reset and REC ADV to the label desired.
			OR	OR
			Tried to select FIELD COR when not in the Verify mode.	Reset and rekey the data. It is not necessary to depress CORR in Enter or Update mode before rewriting data.
			OR	OR
		U, V, S	Tried to select Enter mode when not in the Index mode. (Enter could be selected while in Enter mode to begin data set over.)	Reset. Return to Index mode, then depress the Function Select (lower) and Enter.
			OR	OR
		X, E	Operator selected Update mode in a data set where EOD equals BOE. (No records to update.)	Reset and select Enter mode or advance to data set that is to be updated.
			OR	OR
		S	Update mode selected while in the Search mode.	Reset and return to the Index depress the FUNC SEL (lower) and Update.
			OR	OR
		E, U, V, X	Selected Disk Initialization while in the wrong mode.	Reset and follow proper procedure for disk initialization.
			OR	OR
			There is a disk in Disk Drive 2.	Reset. Remove disk from Disk Drive 2.
M1	Modify Error	X	Incorrect key after Modify.	Reset and perform Modify function again.
N	Buffers Full	ALL	You are keying ahead of the machine and the buffers are loaded.	Reset and continue to key data.

Code	Type of Error	Mode	Cause	Recovery Procedure
NR	Disk Error	ALL	You just loaded the diskette or selected to return to Index and no track 00 was found.	Reset. Change the diskette, and try again. If the problem persists, call your TAB Service Representative.
			OR	OR
			Disk not ready.	Reset and check the disk drive cover. Try again. If the problem persists, call your TAB Service Representative.
			OR	OR
	System Not Ready	ALL	You depressed REC BKSP key without a diskette in the drive.	Load diskette in the drive and RESET, if necessary.
P1	Program Error	E, U, V	While attempting to load a program, you keyed a program number above the number of programs available on your model. If you need more optional program levels installed, call your TAB Sales Representative.	Reset and use only the programs available.
			OR	OR
			The key depressed for Program Select is not 00 through 10, on a dual station or 00 through 20 on a single station.	Reset and depress an acceptable program number.
			OR	OR
		E, U, V, X, S	Incorrect Program:	When an incorrect program is loaded, the program will be displayed by the first key pressed after the error has been reset.
			You have programmed functions that are not available on your model.	Reset and check the program to see if the functions programmed are installed on your station.
			OR	OR
			"E" code missing at end of program when the program is less than designated record length.	Reset. Insert the "E" at the end of the program.
			OR	OR
			Illegal combination of program codes, or you have used codes for a function not available on your system.	Reset. Check program.
			OR	OR
			You tried to select a program level that has a prompting program in it.	Reset. Check program.
P2	Program Error	E, U, V	You selected a program while not at the beginning of a field (in the program selected or in the program being selected).	Reset and depress the FLD BKSP, REC BKSP, or a FLD ADV, or CHAR ADV to get to the beginning of a field.
P3	Program Display	E, U, V, X	Program is being displayed and an unacceptable key was depressed.	Reset. The only acceptable keys are: -RESET key—Displays data. -REC BKSP—Displays previous program. -REC ADV—Displays next program. -PROG SELECT—Select another program to be displayed

Code	Type of Error	Mode	Cause	Recovery Procedure
PL	Program Error	ALL	You are trying to load operator prompting in an odd level.	Reset. Load into an even level.
R1	Right Justify	ALL	You tried to use the Skip, Dup, Field Advance, or the Record Advance key while not in the first column of a Right Justify field.	Reset and either key the rest of the field or key the FLD BKSP to go to the first column. You may then depress the Skip, Dup, Field Advance, or the Record Advance key.
R2	Right Justify	ALL	You tried to use a +RJ or −RJ in a Check Digit Field (Validate or Generate), Constant field, or in program 00.	Reset and rekey the field after doing a Field Backspace.
RI	Record Insert	E, U, X	There is insufficient room in the data set for the number of records specified to be inserted.	Depress Reset and key in the correct number of records.
			OR	OR
			The number of records specified is not 01 through 99.	Reset and key in a two-digit number
RJ	Right Justify	ALL	Field has been filled and the next key depressed was not the +RJ or −RJ key.	Reset and depress the +RJ or −RJ key.
RP	Record Pool	E, U	Sector selected was greater than 26 or less than 01.	Reset and depress the REC POOL and the correct sector number.
			OR	OR
			Numeric Shift not held while keying the sector called.	Reset and repeat the function, holding NUMERIC down.
			OR	OR
			Record Pool was selected while not at the beginning of the record.	Reset. Record Backspace to position 001 of the record and continue.
			OR	OR
		V, C, S	You selected REC POOL while in a mode other than Enter, Update or Verify.	Reset and select proper mode.
			OR	OR
		E, U	Selected REC POOL while not at beginning of record.	Reset and REC BKSP. Begin REC POOL procedure.
S	Search Sequential Content	S	Search Sequential Content was initiated, but the data set is not in ascending sequential order (Numeric or Alpha or Alphanumeric).	Reset and use Search Content or do manual REC ADV to the correct record.
			OR	OR
			Record not found in a Search Sequential Content.	Reset. Record may not be in this data set; check other data sets.
				OR
				Reset. A record may not be keyed at this address since a record does not exist to match this mask.
S1	Search	S	You are in the Search mode for Disk 1 and have depressed the FUNC SEL (upper) key and a Disk 2 function (Disk 2 REC ADV, DISK 2 REC BKSP, or the DISK 2 RET TO INDEX).	Reset and depress the appropriate key.

Code	Type of Error	Mode	Cause	Recovery Procedure
S2	Search Error	S	You are doing a Disk 2 Search and depressed the REC ADV.	Reset and use the Disk 2 REC ADV.
SA	Search Address	S	Search Address contains a non-numeric character; or the zero in the third position has either been omitted or miskeyed.	Reset and key in the correct address.
			OR	OR
			The Search Address keyed in is not within the extents of the data set (cannot be address of EOD).	Reset and enter the correct address.
			OR	OR
			Search EOD depressed when BOE and EOD are the same.	Reset and select Enter to get to first record.
SD	Search Error	S	The data keyed in the Mask did not match during a Search Content or Search Sequential Content.	Reset and check the data keyed in the Search Mask and/or the data set label.
T	Field Totals	U	Incorrect program for Off-Line Field Totals	Reset and check Field Totals Program for: No period (.) or digit following the program character. Position number is greater than program length. No "N", "W", or ":" follows the position number. An invalid character follows the mask (must be **, ; : . &** characters only). Incorrect program is specified in the control program. No program character found in the first position of any program buffer.
			OR	OR
			System not in Index or Updata mode when COMPUTE FIELD TOTALS selected.	Reset and select Index or Updata mode.
TD	Field Totals	ALL	DSPL FIELD TOTALS key depressed while not at the beginning of a field.	Reset and move the cursor to the proper place.
TR	Truncation	E, U	You have tried to key either past end of program or past the record length and AUTO/REC ADV is down.	Reset and depress REC ADV key or raise AUTO/REC ADV. If all data has not been keyed, check record length.
V	Verify Error	V	You have keyed data that does not compare to the data being verified from the diskette.	Reset and rekey. After the second retry, the data will be entered to the diskette if it does not compare. The operator must key the last rekey carefully because it is the correction. This new data is reverified when the system does an Auto Field Backspace.
			OR	OR
			You are verifying an RJ field and a noncompare has occurred on the fill character.	Reset and then check program code and see that fill character is correct.

UNIT 5 KEY-TO-DISKETTE DEVICES

Code	Type of Error	Mode	Cause	Recovery Procedure
				OR
				See if the position should have been a significant character.
			OR	OR
			You depressed the +RJ or −RJ key at the beginning of a Right Justified Field that is not all zeroes or blanks.	Reset and key the correct data that should compare to the significant characters, or if there should be no significant characters in that field, do a field correct.
			OR	OR
			You depressed the +RJ or −RJ key before the entire field was verified.	Reset and correct the field.
W	Write/Read Error	ALL	Data is not being read from the disk or data cannot be written on the disk.	Reset and try again. If this does not work use another diskette. If the problem persists, call TAB Service.
				OR
				If in Enter mode, Reset and Record Backspace. The record previous to the record that received the error is the bad record and should be reentered on the next record.
	During Copy	K	Write error on Disk 1.	Record the Disk 1 address (for correcting later). Hold down the Numeric shift and press Reset to continue copying.
W1	Copy	K	Read error from Disk 2.	Record the Disk 2 address (for correcting later). Hold down the Numeric shift and press Reset to continue copying.
W2	Write/Read Error	ALL	Disk Read or Write Error.	Reset. REC BKSP, REC ADV and key the record with "W2" error again.
WP	Write Protect	X, U	Enter mode was selected with the data set protected or a change was keyed in the Update mode and REC ADV depressed.	Reset and check position 43 on the data set label to see if it is protected.
			OR	OR
		X	Entire diskette is "protected". Hole punched in the diskette indicates physical write protect—this is a diskette that should never be written on. May have programs on it.	Reset and remove the diskette. Use a different diskette.
??	System Overrun	ALL	Procedures are being used that are overloading the system.	Reset and try the same procedures again. If the "??" error condition reappears, call your TAB Service Engineer.
?2	System Not Ready	ALL	Operator depressed keys when the diskette was not loaded.	Load a diskette and depress RESET, if necessary.
NOTE: Various other "?" error codes may occur.				Reset and try the same procedure again. If the error condition reappears, call your TAB Service Engineer.

Source. TAB PRODUCTS CO., PALO ALTO, CA, COPYRIGHT © 1980.

SECTION E
OTHER DISKETTE DEVICES

The devices that have been discussed in detail in this unit act as stand-alone units using floppy disks as the recording media. They do *not* employ a microcomputer or minicomputer unit. They may however, in the case of the IBM 3741 or the TAB 701, transmit data through a data communications unit to a computer.

A Japanese company, JUKI, makes a JUKI 2041 data recorder similar to the IBM 3741 and TAB 701, and a JUKI 2042 similar to the IBM 3742 and TAB 702.

There are other data entry devices that use diskettes as a recording media. However, these devices, although they may stand alone, use minicomputers. Several data entry stations may be connected in a cluster to the minicomputer. Examples of such devices are:

1. The NORTHERN TELECOM 405 (OLD SYCOR), as the IBM 3741 and TAB 701, can stand alone, and it can transmit data to a computer. However, a minicomputer is involved. The diskette unit is different in that it can accommodate up to two or four diskettes, single- or double-sided. Double-sided means that both sides of the diskette can be written on.

2. In 1980, IBM announced the IBM 5280 Distributed Data System. This system has a diskette unit similar to the NORTHERN TELECOM 405. It also uses a minicomputer. The 5280 can be used as a stand-alone or can transmit data. This system may eventually replace the IBM 3741s and 3742s.

Programs for program control can be written in RPG or COBOL (two very common business-oriented programming languages used on large computers). A data entry operator would not be expected to write these programs unless he or she were promoted. This is why it is important for data entry students to take a programming course in RPG or COBOL if they want to advance in their careers.

It is interesting to note that the IBM 5285 and 5286 data stations used in this system can display prompting messages in foreign languages such as Spanish, Portuguese, German, French, Japanese, Danish, Swedish, Italian, and Norwegian.

3. The MOHAWK DATA SCIENCES (MDS) SERIES 21
   The Series 21 can also accommodate up to four diskettes and up to four operators. Data entry programs are written in a special language called MOBOL (Mohawk Business Oriented Language). See Figure 5.28.

4. UNIVAC UDS 2000 DATA ENTRY SYSTEM
   The UNIVAC UDS 2000 work-station consists of a keyboard, display screen, and one or two diskette units. The diskettes are one-sided, single or dual density. There is a microprocessor. The work-station may be used in a data communications environment, on-line to the host computer.

The 2000 has four modes, ENTER, VERIFY, SEARCH, and UPDATE. There are 16 program levels and programmable features such as table lookup, check digits, balance totals, and crossfooting capabilities.

Different types of keyboards may be ordered for this device. The keyboard has a lower case alpha feature (see the UNIVAC 1900 in Unit VI).

The three types of function control keys are:

FIGURE 5.28
The MDS Series 21 (Courtesy of Mohawk Sciences).

1. The field control keys used to generate, exit from, and skip over or correct fields.
2. The record control keys used to release, insert, and delete records.
3. The positioning keys used to position the cursor on the display screen.

A picture is shown in Figure 5.29.

Other equipment such as printers or tapes can be attached to all of the above systems.

Most large (host) computers that use data entered on floppy disks have diskette input/output units. The IBM 3540 diskette I/O unit (see Figure 5.30) is used on the IBM System 360 and 370. This I/O unit has a hopper that the diskette is dropped into.

For computers that do not have a diskette I/O unit, many manufacturers

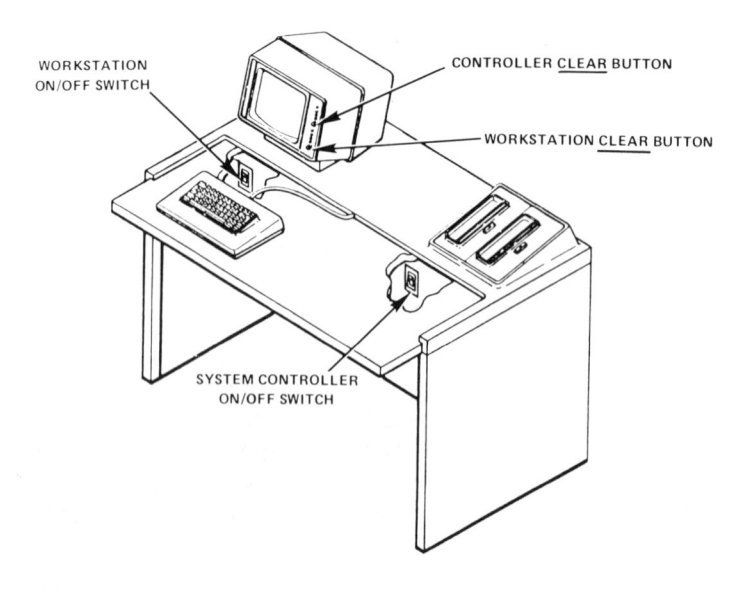

FIGURE 5.29
The UNIVAC UDS 2000 Data Entry System (Courtesy of Sperry UNIVAC).

FIGURE 5.30
The IBM 3540 Diskette I/O Unit (Courtesy of IBM Corporation).

make magnetic tape converters that copy the data from the diskette onto a magnetic tape. Then the computer can read the magnetic tape on its magnetic tape I/O unit. IBM, TAB, and JUKI all make magnetic tape converters for their diskette drives.

STUDY GUIDE

Answer these questions in your book. If asked to do so, tear out the pages and hand them to your instructor.

1. Describe these features of your diskette:

   a. Appearance _____

   _____

   b. Number of tracks = _____

   Number of sectors per track = _____

   Number of data tracks = _____

   Number of data records = _____

   c. Index arrangement

   Number of data set labels = _____

   Important items of information in each label _____

   _____

   _____

   _____

2. Give the meaning of the following acronyms:

   a. BOE _____

   b. EOE _____

UNIT 5 KEY-TO-DISKETTE DEVICES   **125**

c. EOD _____

d. CRT _____

3. State the type of information found on each line of your display screen.

   Line no. _____

   Line no. _____

   Line no. _____

   Line no. _____

   Line no. _____

   Line no. _____

   The header or data set label replaces the data lines on the screen when the machine is in _____ mode.

4. State each item of information given on the status line of your display screen (from left to right).

   Field no. _____

   Field no. _____

   Field no. _____

   Field no. _____

   Field no. _____

   Field no. _____

   Field no. _____

   Field no. _____

   Field no. _____

   Field no. _____

   Field no. _____

5. List the four parts of your keyboard and the purpose of each.

   (1) _____
   _____

   (2) _____
   _____

   (3) _____
   _____

   (4) _____
   _____

6. State the purpose of each of your device switches.

   (1) _____
   _____

   (2) _____
   _____

PART 2   DATA ENTRY EQUIPMENT

(3) _____

_____

(4) _____

_____

(5) _____

_____

7. State the purpose of the following keys:

   a. NUM SHIFT _____

   _____

   b. CHAR ADV _____

   _____

   c. CHAR BKSP _____

   _____

   d. FIELD ADV _____

   _____

   e. FIELD BKSP _____

   _____

   f. DUP _____

   _____

   g. RESET _____

   _____

   h. HEX _____

   _____

   i. PROG SEL _____

   _____

   j. RIGHT ADJ or RJ _____

   _____

   k. FUNC SEL LOWER _____

   _____

   l. FUNCT SEL UPPER _____

   _____

   m. FIELD CORR _____

   _____

If you have any other special keys list them below.

   n. _____

   _____

   o. _____

   _____

p. _____

q. _____

8. Define:

   a. Program _____

   b. Program code _____

   c. Program chaining _____

   d. Buffer _____

   e. Cursor _____

   f. Extent _____

   g. Data set _____

   h. Data set label _____

   i. Volume _____

   j. Volume label _____

   k. Disk initialization _____

   l. Prompts _____

9. State the program and field definition codes for your device in the chart below.

Function	Character Code	Field Definition
Skip numeric field		
Punch numeric field		
Duplicate numeric field		
Punch alphameric field		
Duplicate alphameric field		
Skip alphameric field		

Right adjust a numeric
field and zero fill   _____   _____
End of program   _____   _____

10. Give the reason why your screen might display the error code:

    a. **V** _____
    b. **K** _____
    c. **L** _____
    d. **M** _____
    e. **N** _____
    f. **R** _____
    g. **S** _____
    h. **6** _____

11. State two reasons why disk addresses are used.

    1. _____
    2. _____

12. Write down the disk address for track 10, sector 9 on your device. Label each part.

    _____
    _____

13. State your machine modes, the codes for each, and the use of each.

Machine Mode	**Code**	**Use**
(1) _____	_____	_____
(2) _____	_____	_____
(3) _____	_____	_____
(4) _____	_____	_____
(5) _____	_____	_____
(6) _____	_____	_____
(7) _____	_____	_____
(8) _____	_____	_____
(9) _____	_____	_____
(10) _____	_____	_____
(11) _____	_____	_____
(12) _____	_____	_____
(13) _____	_____	_____
(14) _____	_____	_____
(15) _____	_____	_____

14. Name three advantages of key-to-diskette data entry devices over buffered keypunches.

UNIT 5   KEY-TO-DISKETTE DEVICES

(1) _____

(2) _____

(3) _____

15. List at least two brands of key-to-diskette equipment other than yours.

    (1) _____

    (2) _____

16. State how the NORTHERN TELECOM 405, IBM 5280, and MOHAWK 21 devices differ from the IBM 3742.

    _____

17. List at least five special operations features available on your key-to-diskette device.

    (1) _____

    (2) _____

    (3) _____

    (4) _____

    (5) _____

18. Demonstrate to your instructor (or describe on a separate sheet of paper) how to:
    a. Get the machine in a ready status.
    b. Manually key in a record.
    c. Correct an error in a record as it is being keyed.
    d. Correct an error on the last record keyed.
    e. Return to the starting point and find the end of your data.
    f. Return to the starting point and find a specific record.
    g. Load a program from the keyboard.
    h. Load a program from a diskette.
    i. Search for a record and correct it.
    j. Delete a record.
    k. Insert or add a record.
    l. Change the data set label name.
    m. Verify two records, one with an error.
    n. Key under program control.

o. Key under program chaining control.
p. Set up a prompt, if available on your device, given a program format.
q. Design a program given a program format.

19. State why it is unwise to leave diskettes in cars.

_____

_____

UNIT 6
KEY-TO-DISK DEVICES

AFTER READING THIS UNIT YOU WILL KNOW:

When key-to-disk equipment is helpful.
What the basic parts of key-to-disk equipment are.
What two methods are used to transmit the keyed data to the main or host computer.
What types of codes may be used on magnetic tape.
What general types of keys exist on key-to-disk keyboards.
What control keys exist and the function of each.
What the meaning of the fields in the status line of your device are.
What the operational modes of your device are.
What an indexed file is.
How the key-to-disk keyboard is activated on your device.
How work is activated.
How batches are closed, interrupted, reactivated.
How batches are verified.
How records are inserted, deleted, and modified.
How chaining is done on your device.
How your device is programmed.

What the following terms mean:

ASCII	IRG
Backup	Job
Batch	KB
Batch processing	Load point
BCD	Lock code
Block	Logical record
Blocking factor	Magnetic disk
BOT marker	Magnetic tape
BPI	Manual field
Byte	Menu
Chaining	Minicomputer
Check bit	Mode
Cluster	Nine-track tape
Configuration	Odd parity
Control key	Parity bit
CRT	Password
Cursor	Peripheral device
DASD	Physical record
Data check	Polling
Data key	Program
Default value	Prompt
Density	Random access
Direct access	Response time
Disk	Search mask
Disk initialization	Sector
DMA	Sequential processing
EBCDIC	
EOT marker	Seven-track tape
Even parity	Software
Extent	Status line
External label	Tape channel
File label	Tape initialization
File protection	Tape mark
Format control	Track
Frame	Trail verify
Free form	Trailer label
Free format	Transfer rate
Function key	Uncorrectable error
Header label	Verify
Host processor	Volume
IBG	Volume label
Internal label	VTOC
Indexed file	Work termination display
Indexed set	
Invalid batch	

SECTION A
INTRODUCTION

One of the most modern types of data entry equipment is the key-to-disk (shared processor) installation. The key-to-disk equipment discussed in this unit, in contrast to that described in Unit 5, uses a *hard* disk as the storage media.

Key-to-disk equipment is helpful when:

1. There is a large volume of data.
2. There are many format (record) types for a job.
3. Test procedures can take the place of verification.

For a small volume of data and limited formats, buffered keypunches or key-to-diskette equipment may be more satisfactory.

The number of key-to-disk installations is growing rapidly. Therefore it is important that the data entry operator have some understanding of the principles and operations of these devices.

Key-to-disk equipment is made up of:

1. A minicomputer (a small computer).
2. One or more keyboards (or keystations).
3. A disk drive.
4. A magnetic tape device and/or a communications line to a central computer.

Examples of these parts are shown in Figure 6.1.

All keyboards are under the control of a minicomputer. Data is entered on the keyboard and transferred to different portions of the magnetic disk. Later this data is sent to the main computer in two ways:

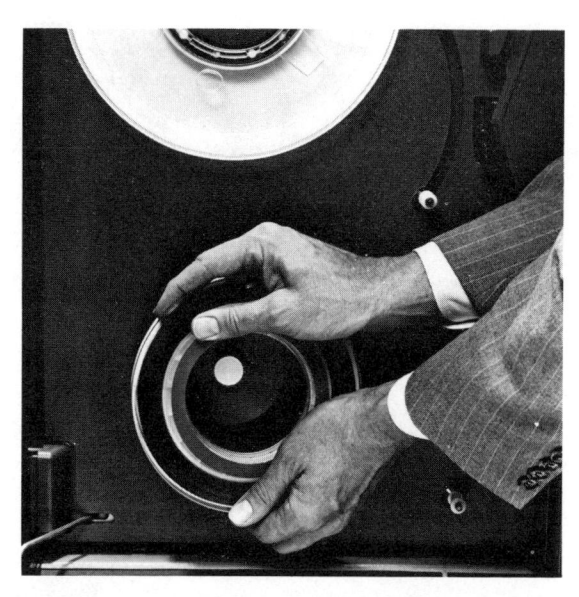

FIGURE 6.1
Components of the Sperry UNIVAC 1900/10. KEY-TO-DISK device (Courtesy of Sperry Univac).

Central control unit

Magnetic tape

Disk storage

Keystations

UNIT 6 KEY-TO-DISK DEVICES

1. By magnetic tape.
2. By a data communications link.

Figure 6.2 shows these two methods. The arrangement shown under Method 1 places the final validated data on magnetic tape. The magnetic tape is then carried or shipped to the host computer and the data is processed.

The arrangement shown in Method 2 depends on a communications unit and telephone lines used to transmit the final validated data to the host computer. Method 2 is certainly more convenient, but it is much more expensive. It also demands that the computer center have someone knowledgeable in communications as well as in data processing. Breakdowns do occur and frequently a great deal of argument goes on over whether the problem lies with the computer or with the telephone lines.

Key-to-disk configurations vary greatly from those shown in Figure 6.2. The word *configuration* means the type of devices that are used in a data entry system. Except for the minicomputer, there may be *one or more* of all of the devices shown. That is, there may be one or more tape (units), one or more keyboards, or one or more disk (units), and there might be some printers attached.

Sometimes the key-to-disk installations are ranked by the number of keyboards involved. One such ranking system is:

Type	Maximum number of Keyboards	Device Examples
Small	4 to 8	INFOREX 1303, CMC XL/40
Medium	8 to 16	NIXDORF (ENTREX) 280, FOUR PHASE IV/70, INFOREX 3300, NORTHERN TELECOMM (SYCOR) 445
Large	16 to 64	NIXDORF (ENTREX) 380/480, FOUR PHASE IV/90, CMC 1800, UNIVAC 1900/10, DATA 100, CUMMINS MULTI-MEDIA KEYSCAN

As more keystations or keyboards are attached to the minicomputer, the response time goes *up*. *Response time* is defined as the time required for a system to react to input. Typical advertisements speak of keyboards being in

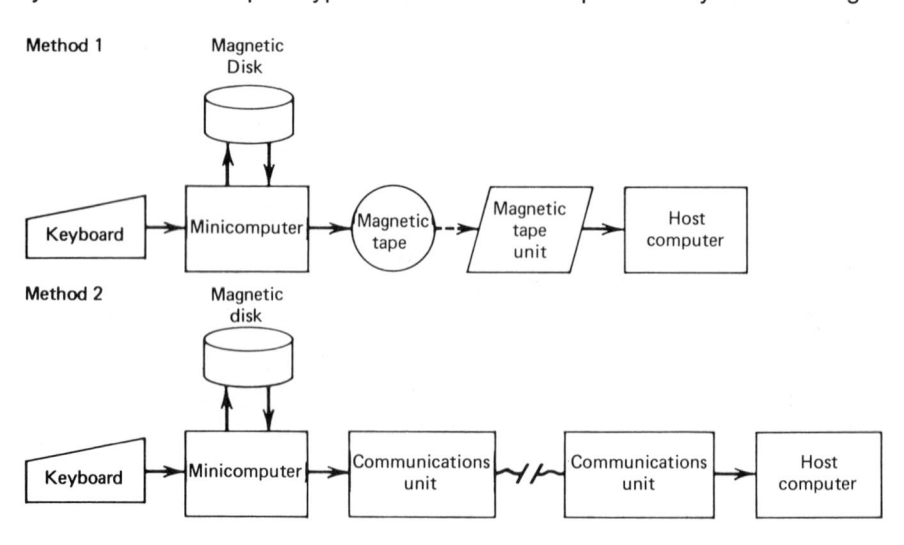

FIGURE 6.2
Key-to-disk configurations.

PART 2 DATA ENTRY EQUIPMENT

a cluster of six with a supervisor keyboard. A *cluster* is a group of similar items.

All the keyboards are under the control of the minicomputer. Data entered on the keyboard goes to various portions of the magnetic disk. Programs or instructions written for the minicomputer control the editing, validating, duplicating, skipping, and other functions. After the data has reached the disk, it can be verified. On some devices all data in a file must be completed and the file must be closed before the data can be verified. On other devices verifying can be done on the record behind the record currently being keyed. When a job is finished, it is transferred to magnetic tape if Method 1 in Figure 6.1 is used. Otherwise data is transferred over the communications link.

Although keying at the keyboards will be your main duty as a keyboard operator, it is important that you understand tape and disk concepts and the terms involved.

SECTION B
KEY-TO-DISK HARDWARE AND PROCEDURES

THE MAGNETIC TAPE

In Unit 3 the definition of a magnetic tape was given and the two types of codes used on magnetic tapes were discussed. These two codes were the six-bit *BCD* and the eight-bit *EBCDIC* code. A character can be recorded in BCD by a combination of six bits and a *parity* or *check bit* (see Figure 3.6 in Unit 3). The parallel dotted lines are called *tracks*. Therefore a BDC tape is called a *seven-track* tape.

Review the EBCDIC code examples on page 23 of Unit 3. Figure 6.3 shows an EBCDIC tape with the characters A and K. It can be seen that an EBCDIC character is recorded by a combination of eight data bits and a parity or check bit. An EBCDIC tape is said to be a *nine-track* tape.

DEFINITIONS

1. A *track* is a path on which data is recorded. A track may be horizontal as on a magnetic tape or circular as on a diskette or disk.
2. A *seven-track tape* is a tape written in the BCD code.
3. A *nine-track tape* is a tape written in the EBCDIC code.
4. A *frame* is the number of bits required to record a character on tape.
5. A *byte* is eight data bits plus one parity or check bit. (A *nibble* is four bits or one half of a byte.)
6. A *parity* (or check) *bit* is an extra bit added to a character to detect errors in reading or writing the tape.
7. *Odd parity* means that an *odd* number of bits must be on (magnetized) to record a character.

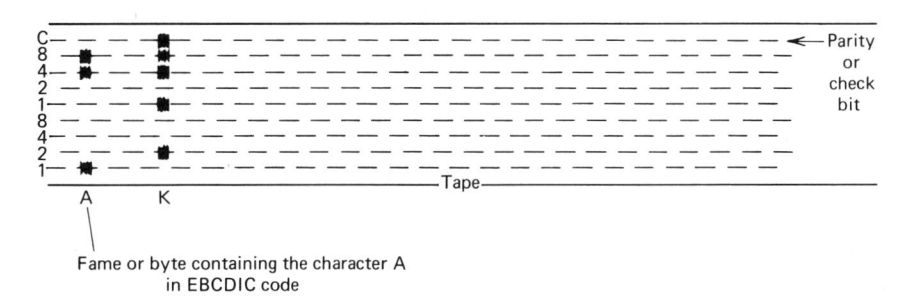

FIGURE 6.3
A Nine-track EBCDIC tape with the letters "A" and "K" written on it.

Fame or byte containing the character A in EBCDIC code

8. *Even parity* means that an *even* number of bits must be on to record a character.
9. *Density* is the number of bytes or characters written per inch (BPI).
10. *BPI* is an acronym for bytes per inch or bits per inch.

In Figure 6.3 the letter A is represented in one *byte*, and the letter K is represented in a second *byte*. The tape in Figure 6.3 is written in odd parity. This means an *odd* number of bits must always be on. The parity bit for the letter A is *off* because an odd number of bits (three) are already on. For the letter K the parity bit is turned on because without it an even number of bits are on.

Tapes may be written in different *densities*. Existing densities are 200, 556, 800, 1600, 3200, and 6200 BPI. Thirty-two-hundred BPI tapes would have 16 times more characters per inch than 200 BPI tapes. The higher the density, the more data you can get on a magnetic tape.

In Figure 6.4 examples may be seen of labeled and unlabeled tapes. The term "labeled tape" means that internal labels have been written on the tape by the use of a special computer program. Tape labels serve as a protection against accidental destruction. It is possible to accidentally write over data already recorded on tape. Tape labels also act as security. The number of people knowing the label can be limited.

MORE DEFINITIONS

11. A *volume* is the recording media available to one read/write mechanism. You may think of a volume as a single reel of magnetic tape or a single disk pack.
12. An *external label* is an adhesive paper label with an ID. It is placed on the outside of the tape or disk.
13. An *internal label* is magnetically written on the actual recording media (the tape or disk).
14. A *volume label* is an internal label that identifies the magnetic tape or disk.
15. A *header* or *file label* is an internal label at the *beginning* of a file of data on magnetic tape or disk.
16. A *trailer label* is an internal label written at the *end* of a file of data on tape or disk.
17. A *tape mark* (TM) is a special character written on magentic tape. It indicates the end of data or the end of a set of labels.
18. *Tape initialization* is the writing of an internal volume label on a magnetic tape.

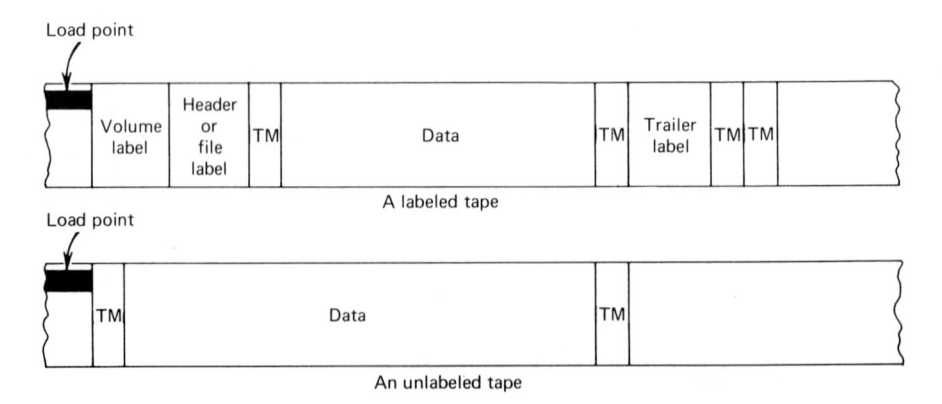

FIGURE 6.4
Tape labels.

19. A *load point marker* is a silver metallic strip, usually 12 feet or more from the front of the tape. It indicates where reading or writing may begin.
20. The *beginning of tape* (BOT) *marker* is the same thing as a load point marker.
21. The *end of tape* (EOT) or *end of reel* (EOR) *marker* is a metallic strip, usually 12 feet from the end of the tape. It indicates the last point at which data may be read or written.
22. A *tape channel* is the same as a track.
23. *Transfer rate* is the number of bytes per second that can be read. Transfer rate is quoted in KB (thousands of bytes) or inches per second.
24. *KB* means thousand bytes. Sixty KB equals 60,000 bytes per second.
25. A *data check* is an error made while reading or writing on tape or disk.

A data entry supervisor is sometimes asked to assist in data entry equipment selection. Mastering the above terms will help you to evaluate such advertisements as:

> This device has 7- or 9-track industry-compatible magnetic tape drives with speeds up to 45 inches per second. Densities of 556, 800, and 1600 BPI are available. The drives accept either 8½- or 10½-inch reels, providing up to 1200 or 2400 feet of tape respectively. All tape units have BOT and EOT sensors.

The data entry operator or supervisor may also read about blocking factors. Figure 6.5 shows examples of blocked and unblocked tapes.

MORE DEFINITIONS

26. A *logical record* is a collection of fields of data.
27. A *physical record* is one or more logical records.
28. A *block* is a physical record.
29. An *IBG* is an interblock gap, or spaces between blocks (.75 inch for 7-track tapes; .6 inch for 9-track tapes).
30. An *IRG* is an interrecord gap. This is the same as an IBG.
31. The *blocking factor* is the number of logical records per block.
32. *File protection* is a method used to protect data on a magnetic tape from accidental destruction (a file protection ring). Data on tapes is blocked for two reasons:
    a. To save storage space on the magnetic tape.
    b. To speed up I/O.

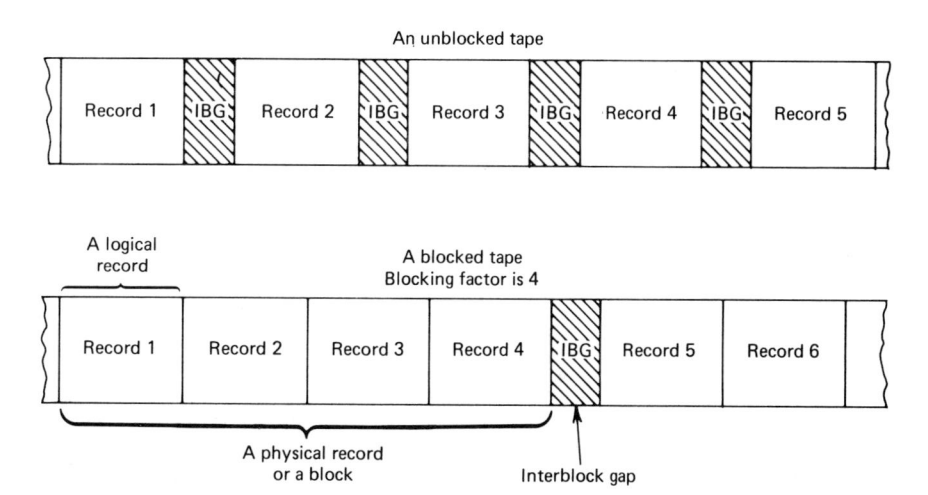

FIGURE 6.5
Blocked and unblocked tapes.

UNIT 6 KEY-TO-DISK DEVICES

Storage space on tape is saved because blocking cuts down on the number of IBGs. Thus more data can be written on the tape.

I/O is faster because tape units read in blocks. Look at Figure 6.5 again. The bottom tape, blocked four, can process four records in one read or write action. The tape in the top figure processes only one record per block. Therefore reading or writing is slower.

One then might ask, Why not use a blocking factor of 10,000 instead of 4? The blocking factor is limited by the amount of storage available in the computer. Enough main storage must be reserved to store one block of data.

Suppose we have a computer with 64,000 or 64K bytes of storage.

CASE 1   Assume an 80-character record is written on tape in 800 BPI and blocked four.

$$\text{I/O storage space} = 80 \text{ bytes (or characters)}$$
$$\times 4 = 320 \text{ bytes of storage.}$$

This is not much storage compared to 64K.

CASE 2   Assume an 80-character record in 800 BPI and blocked 10,000.

$$\text{I/O storage space} = 80 \times 10,000 = 800,000 \text{ or } 800$$
K bytes of storage.

This is larger than the storage available in the entire computer.

Therefore, the amount of main storage available limits the size of the blocking factor.

Some tape units have a *file protect* light. If this light is on, the file protection ring, a plastic ring inserted near the center of the tape, is not on the magnetic tape. Therefore, writing cannot occur. There is a saying: NO RING; NO WRITE. The file protection ring is a method of protecting data.

THE MAGNETIC DISK

The *magnetic disk* is a hard disk that revolves at high speeds. A plate has tracks as shown in Figure 6.6.

The tracks form concentric circles. The same amount of data is written on each track. This means that the density (characters per inch) is greater on the inner tracks. A read/write head moves from one track to another in much the same way a phonograph arm moves along a record.

A *track* is the area accessible to one read/write head.

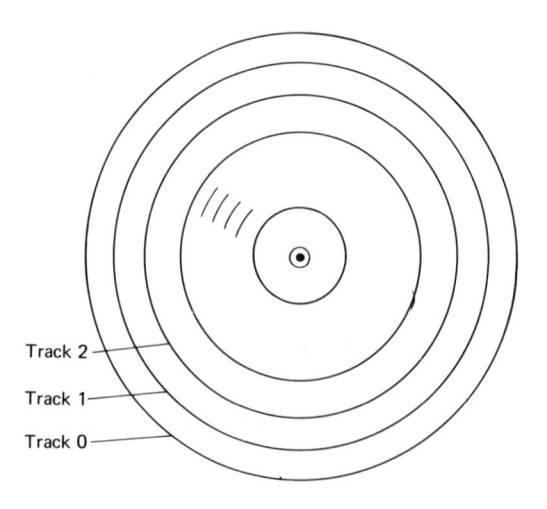

FIGURE 6.6
The magnetic disk.

Disks have a *volume label* just as tapes do. It is at the beginning of track number 0. Files of data on disk also have header and trailer labels. Records may be blocked or unblocked on disk, but there are no IBGs.

Disks read data in blocks just as magnetic tapes do. The more records in a block, the faster the unit reads. This is the only reason why records on disk are blocked.

As shown in Figure 6.1, most of the disks used in key-to-disk equipment are removable. Thus, any number of disk (packs) may be used.

OTHER DEFINITIONS

1. *VTOC* is an acronym for volume table of contents. A VTOC is a list of the batches or files of data on disk. The list is usually arranged by file name.
2. *Disk initialization* is the process of writing a volume label on a disk.
3. An *extent* is an area on the disk between some upper and lower limit. This term, used in data entry with reference to diskettes is also used when talking about hard disk packs.
4. A *sector* is a subdivision of a track. The number of characters in a sector varies with the device used.
5. *Backup* is a copy of data or programs that is kept in case the current copy is destroyed. Most centers have set times each day when copies are made.
6. *Sequential processing* is the processing of records one after the other, in the order in which they are stored or written. To obtain information in the hundredth record, the first 99 must be read.
7. *Random access* or *direct access* is a method of processing by which a record may be accessed directly without accessing the preceding records.
8. A *batch* is a group of records.
9. *Batch processing* is a method by which data is processed in large groups.
10. A *job* is a group of batches of data.
11. *DASD* is an acronym for direct access storage device. A device that will allow random access, such as a magnetic disk or drum, is a DASD.
12. A *peripheral device* is a computer I/O device such as the keyboard, printer, or magnetic tape or disk devices.
13. *DMA* is an acronym for direct memory access, a method of transferring data from one peripheral unit to another without the involvement of the CPU.

Data recorded on magnetic tape must be processed sequentially. Magnetic tapes are excellent for batch processing. They are used when a job or batch has been entered and it is necessary to transfer the batch of data to the host computer.

Magnetic disk is used for random access processing. Airlines use this type of processing to call up reservations on their *CRTs* or display screens. However, sequential processing can also be done on magnetic disk. The magnetic disk is known as a DASD. The magnetic tape is *not* a DASD, since the only type of processing possible on tape is sequential processing.

It was noted previously that sequentially organized files must be processed in the physical order in which they were written. If record number 200 is desired, the first 199 records must be processed to reach it. This is not true in an indexed file.

An *indexed file* (or *set*) has an index which is similar to the card catalog in a library. If you want to find a particular book at the library, such as *Humanized Input*, by Gilb and Weinberg, you first find the author or title in the card catalog and record the call number QA 76.7 .I55G54. Then you find the range of shelves with books marked QA 76.7. Within this bookcase the books are arranged in alphabetical and numerical order for the .I55G54 part of the call number. Therefore you locate the book without going through all the books from the call numbers beginning with A. The card catalog is an *index* which helps you zero in on a *range* (or set of shelves). Then you find the book within that range.

In indexed files there is also an index, usually in track number 0 on the disk, which is a *track index*. It tells the system the highest and lowest ID on each track. The records are arranged in sequential order by some ID. Thus a range can be narrowed to one track and then a record with a particular ID, such as a social security number, can be located.[1]

Usually when data is transferred between peripheral devices and main storage or memory the movement is controlled by the control unit in the CPU. If the transfer is made without this control, the DMA method is said to be used. DMA means *direct memory access*.

THE CENTRAL PROCESSING UNIT

In Unit 1 we learned that CPU means central processing unit. The minicomputer CPU has a memory that contains data and instructions. The CPU also has a logical unit, a control unit, and an arithmetic unit.

The success of a key-to-disk system depends on the availability of *software* or *programs*. Programs are needed to do modulus 10 or 11 checks, to do table lookups and total computations, or to copy data from disk to tape. If the manufacturer does not provide the programs, then your center must provide them. These programs are not simple program codes as used on the buffered keypunches or the key-to-diskette equipment. They are in language form, like programs used on larger computers.

The size of memory is usually quoted in bytes. For example, the size might be quoted as 64 KB or 512 KB, or 64,000 or 512,000 bytes.

As Figure 6.2 shows there is a host processor. A *host processor* is the central or main computer which does the final processing of the data keyed in by the data entry operator. This final processing produces the reports desired by the user.

THE COMMUNICATIONS CONTROLLER

Many devices using Method 2 of Figure 6.2, have a communications control unit whose transmissions are controlled by a program stored in the unit. The control unit is a link with the communications channel through which data is transferred from the computer controlling the key-to-disk devices to the host processor.

PROGRAMMING

Normal operations in key-to-disk operations are under *program* or *format control*. A *program* is a set of instructions telling the computer:

1. What type of data should be expected in each field.
2. What type of checks should be made in the field.

Examples of item 1 would be:

   a. All numeric field.

---

[1]On some large computers such a file is sometimes called an *indexed sequential file* (ISAM file). The term indexed file actually refers to *two* types of indexed files: an indexed sequential file or a virtual storage file (VSAM file). However, we will not be concerned with this technicality. We will use the term *indexed file* or *set*.

b. An alphameric field.
c. A right-justified and zero- or blank-fill field.
d. A field to be duplicated.
e. A field to be skipped and blanks or zeros inserted.

Examples of item 2 would be:

a. A check digit (see Appendix D for discussion of modulus 10 and 11).
b. Tables that specify certain values for a field.
c. Range checks that give a range within which the value entered must agree (for example, 1 to 50 for state numbers).

Unfortunately every type of key-to-disk device is programmed differently and due to the wide variety of devices available, this causes problems if a business changes key-to-disk devices. As with large computers, key-to-disk devices use different languages to communicate instructions to the device's computer.

Languages used are:

1. COBOL (an English type language).
2. RPG (Report Program Generator).
3. Special purpose languages.

The supervisor or a special data entry programmer usually writes these programs. As a data entry trainee you will not be expected to do so. If your community uses key-to-disk equipment and you wish to advance along the career path, you would be very wise to take introductory COBOL and/or RPG courses. They will make it much easier to learn a special purpose language.

Some devices are said to be able to operate under *free format* or *free form* data entry. Here one record is considered as one field. For example, on the UNIVAC 1900/10 this means:

1. The record size is 80 characters.
2. The DUP (duplicate) key causes the remainder of the record to be copied.
3. The keystation is in alpha shift.
4. The record may be released at any time and the remainder will be filled with blanks.

However, unlike the data entry equipment discussed in previous units, this format must be entered by some method. Some devices have a special command that will enter it.

Program *chaining* or *automatic program sequencing* is a method of programming a data entry device so that it switches from one program to another without the operator having to select the program manually. This feature would be used if a job involved two or more different record formats. Key-to-disk devices can be programmed to chain.

PASSWORDS Some key-to-disk systems allow *passwords* or *lock codes* to be programmed. Passwords are used to prevent operators from accessing files of data that they should not be working with. If the operator cannot furnish the correct password, the computer will not allow the operator to enter data.

VERIFYING Verifying is done as a check. It is normally done by an experienced key-to-disk operator who has not keyed the original data. On some devices a second operator can verify one record right after the first operator has entered the data, without closing the batch. This is called *trail verifying*. In key-to-disk verifying, there are two kinds of verifications:

1. *Key Verification.* Data being verified or checked is *not* displayed on the screen of some devices until after the character has been keyed from the source document by the verifying operator. It will be displayed on the screen if there is an agreement (it has been verified) or if the field is bypassed. Other devices display the sets of characters in scrambled form and unscramble them as each character is verified.

2. *Sight Verification.* The field to be verified is displayed on the screen. It can then be flagged as verified, corrected and flagged as verified, or bypassed and flagged as invalid.

There are two types of fields used in verifying.

1. Those fields programmed to be verified (they can be key or sight verified).
2. Fields flagged as invalid (they must be key verified).

Verification of a field on most key-to-disk devices may be omitted by the use of some sort of bypass key. The record and the batch are then flagged as invalid.

THE KEYBOARD

Depending on the manufacturer, each type of key-to-disk device has a different keyboard. Also, each manufacturer has different types of keyboards such as the keypunch style, keypunch/adding machine style, and the typewriter style. Each of these styles may be the EBCDIC or ASCII type. The *ASCII code* is a seven-bit code (eight with the parity bit) frequently used in data communications equipment. ASCII is an acronym for *American Standard Code for Information Interchange.*

To illustrate their differences, the EBCDIC keypunch styles for the UNIVAC 1900/10, NIXDORF 80 Series, and FOUR PHASE DATA IV keyboards are shown in Figures 6.7, 6.8, and 6.9. Each keyboard has: 1. function or control keys; and 2. data keys. These two types of keys are different colors. Some keyboards also have one color for the decimal digits and one color for the letters and special characters. Colors and their uses vary with the brand.

Control or functional keys control keyboard operations. Some control keys have two functions. When this occurs, some sort of a shift key is used to get the top label function.

Data keys are used to enter letters of the alphabet, numbers, and special characters. Although most data keys have two labels, some devices have keys with three labels. The keyboard is normally in the lower (or alpha) shift.

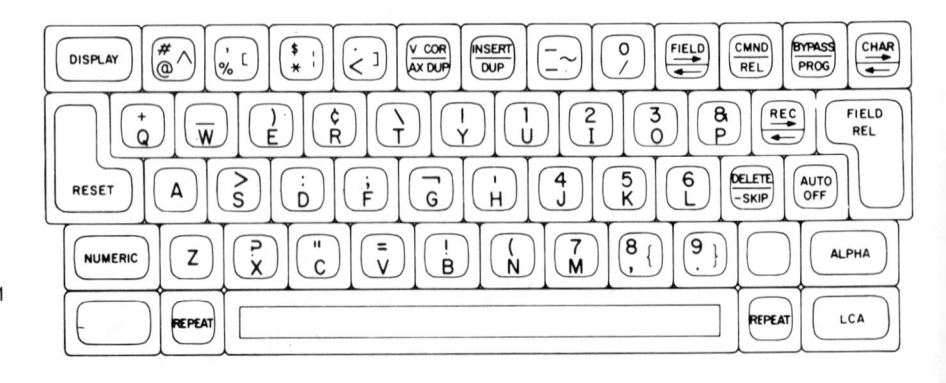

FIGURE 6.7
The SPERRY UNIVAC 1900/10 Model 3541 key station keypunch style keyboard (EBCDIC) (Courtesy of Sperry UNIVAC).

FIGURE 6.8
The NIXDORF Series 80 keypunch keyboard (Reprinted by permission of NIXDORF Corporation, Waltham, Massachusetts, USA).

If a character on the top label is desired and the field has been programmed for lower shift (alpha), the NUMERIC shift key must be held down while the appropriate key is pressed.

You should note the difference between the − (minus or hyphen) and the _ (underline), and the ' (apostrophe) and the | sign, if they exist on your keyboard.

As you read the following material, look at your keyboard or a drawing of the keyboard. Label your key in the square provided in the left margin. If you do not have this key on your device, place an X in the square provided. If the function of the key on your keyboard is somewhat different, write a description of what your key does on the lines provided.

Functional Keys

Functional or control keys have two meanings if there are two labels on the key. To obtain the upper label, a shift key must be used.

1. RESET (or CTRL or CORR RESET) key
   a. Used after errors to unlock the keyboard.
   b. Used to select the alternate meaning (upper label) for other control keys.
   c. Used to lock the shift keys.

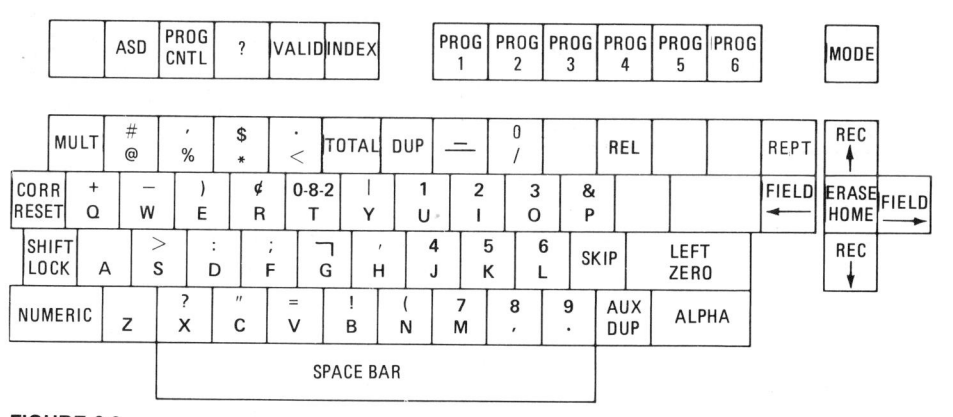

FIGURE 6.9
The FOUR PHASE DATA IV keypunch style keyboard.

UNIT 6   KEY-TO-DISK DEVICES   145

2. **REPEAT key**
   This key causes the repeating of a function. It is held down while using the data keys, and on some devices it is held down with the positioning (of the cursor) keys. This causes the action to be repeated.

3. **DISPLAY (or HELP) key**
   This key is used to display information on the screen. The type of display is determined by further keying.

4. **PROG (or PGM) key**
   The program key is used to select the program level determined by the next key pressed. On some devices the NEXT FORM key is used under program control to obtain the next program format.

5. **CMND key**
   The command key is used to begin a command or instruction to the computer's supervisor. It is used to start one of the operating modes and other operations.

6. **AUTO SKIP/DUP (or AUTO OFF or AUTO) key**
   This key is used to disable automatic skip, duplication, and generation of fields under programmed control.

Field Control Keys

Field control keys are used to generate, skip over, exit from, or correct fields.

7. **FIELD REL (ease), RIGHT ADJUST, -SKIP, or OVERSIGN keys.**
   This key is used to exit from a field or to skip over a field. All justification and fill operations are performed if any keying has taken place. However, if a negative sign is desired, the −SIGN or OVERSIGN key may be used. In the case of some devices the MINUS key must be used. The RIGHT ADJUST key performs the same function as the FIELD REL key on some devices. Normally only numeric fields are right adjusted. But it is possible to right adjust and blank fill an alpha field as follows:

   <u>L</u> <u>E</u> <u>E</u> ___ is keyed.

   Pressing the RIGHT ADJUST key gives:

   __ __ <u>L</u> <u>E</u> <u>E</u>

PART 2 DATA ENTRY EQUIPMENT

8. SKIP key

The skip key is used on some machines rather than the FIELD REL key. Usually this key places blanks in the remainder of the field unless the field has been programmed to duplicate. If blanks are not desired, on some machines the FIELD → or the FIELD ADV key can be used.

9. DUP key

The duplicate key copies characters for the current field from corresponding positions of the previous record. It is important to remember that before this key can be used, the first record must be keyed so there is something to duplicate.

Some devices have a key such as the AX DUP (or XDUP) key on the UNIVAC 1900 that causes a field to be completely generated by pressing the key only once.

10. FIELD CORR (or V CORR, CORR, or COR) key

This key is normally used in verifying. If an error has occurred, it provides the ability to correct a field by positioning the cursor at the beginning of the field. This allows the operator to rekey the field. On some devices it may also be used to correct a single character. On the NIXDORF 80 series it must be used with the FLD or RCD key to distinguish between a field and a record.

11. BYPASS (or PASS) key

This key exists on a few devices. It allows a system in the ENTER or UPDATE mode to pass over a field with unreadable or invalid data. It zero or blank fills, as programmed, and flags the data (field, record, or batch) as invalid.

Record Control Keys

These keys are used to release, insert, and delete records.

12. REL (or REL/ENTER) key

This key terminates a record without any more keying. The record is released to the system. However, if a field has been skipped and it has been programmed for a *must enter*, an error will occur on some devices.

UNIT 6   KEY-TO-DISK DEVICES

13. INS (Insert) key

The insert key is used to insert one or more records before an existing record. It cannot be used in the ENTER mode on most devices.

On a few devices this key can be used to insert one or more *characters* in a field. It shifts all the keyed characters to the right.

---

14. DEL (Delete) key

This key has different functions depending on the device. On most devices it is used to delete records. It is sometimes used to delete characters. Then it moves all characters in the field, one position to the left.

Positioning Keys

These keys cause the cursor to move forward or backward to the next keyed field. Automatic fields are skipped.

15. CHAR → (or CHAR ADV or CHR →) key

The character advance key moves the cursor forward one character.

---

16. CHAR ← (or CHAR BKSP or CHR ←) key

The character backspace key moves the cursor backward one character.

On some devices the functions 14 and 15 are combined into one key, such as $\boxed{\begin{array}{c}\text{CHAR}\\\rightarrow\\\hline\leftarrow\end{array}}$. To obtain the CHAR →, the shift key must be held down.

17. FIELD → (or FIELD ADV or FLD →) key

The field advance key moves the cursor to the first position of the next *keyed* field. Moving past the *last* keyed field is invalid.

---

18. FIELD ← (or FIELD BKSP or FLD ←) key

The field backspace key moves the cursor back to the first manual position of the field being currently keyed. If the cursor is already in the first position, the key backspaces it to the first position of the last keyed field.

On some devices the functions 16 and 17 are combined into one key, such as [FIELD →/←]. To obtain the FIELD →, the shift key must be held down.

19. REC → (or REC ADV) key
The record advance key moves to the first position of the next keyed record. Moving past the last keyed record is invalid.

20. REC ← (or REC BKSP) key
The record backspace key is used to backspace the cursor to the first position of the record being currently keyed. If the cursor is already in the first position, it moves to the first position of the previously keyed record.

On some devices functions 18 and 19 are combined into one key, such as [REC →/→]. To obtain the REC →, the shift key must be held down.

Shift Keys

The shift keys, when pressed or locked, permits the system to interpret depression of a key in an alternate way.

21. NUMERIC shift key
This shift key permits the upper character on the key to be entered.

22. ALPHA shift key
This shift key permits the lower character on the key to be entered.

23. LCA (lowercase alpha) key
Pressing or locking this key (it does not exist on all devices) is interpreted as follows:
a. If one or two characters are on the key, it will cause a lower case letter to be displayed as an upper case character with a line under it (signifying a lower case character). For example,

pressing [LCA] and [=/∨] causes ∨ to be displayed.

b. If three characters are on a key, the third character represents an ASCII character. The LCA key causes the right most character to be displayed with a line under it. For example,

pressing [LCA] and [# ∧ / @] causes ∧ to be displayed.

UNIT 6 KEY-TO-DISK DEVICES

c. If the LCA key is used with a key which has no alphabetic character or right-hand character, it acts as the ALPHA shift. This means the lower graphic symbol will be displayed.

If you have any function keys not described above, describe them in the area provided below.

24. _____

25. _____

26. _____

27. _____

28. _____

29. _____

THE DISPLAY OR VIDEO SCREEN

The current status of work being performed at the keystation is displayed differently, depending on the type of key-to-disk equipment being used. However, nearly all of these devices have the following three types of lines displayed on the screen:

1. *Status line*(s) giving information on the current work being done at the keystation.
2. *Message line*(s) giving messages to the operator.
3. *Data lines* showing prompting messages and data currently being keyed. *Prompts* are programmed messages that are displayed to indicate to the operator what data is to be keyed into a field.

On most screens the status line is displayed at the top of the screen.

However, FOUR-PHASE devices have a status line at the bottom of the screen.

Examples of video displays are shown:

1. For the UNIVAC 1900/10 in Figures 6.10 and 6.11.
2. For the NIXDORF 80 Series in Figure 6.12.
3. For the FOUR-PHASE DATA IV Series in Figure 6.13.

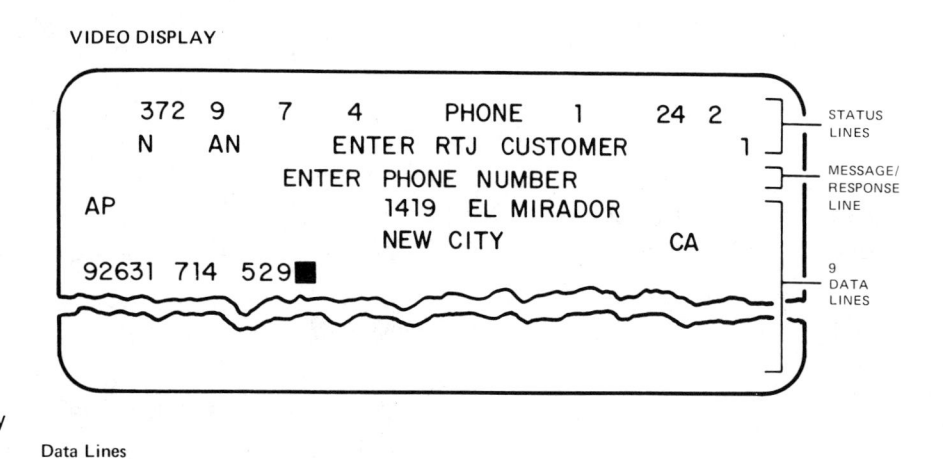

FIGURE 6.10
The Sperry UNIVAC 1900/10 3541 Keystation Video display (Courtesy of Sperry UNIVAC).

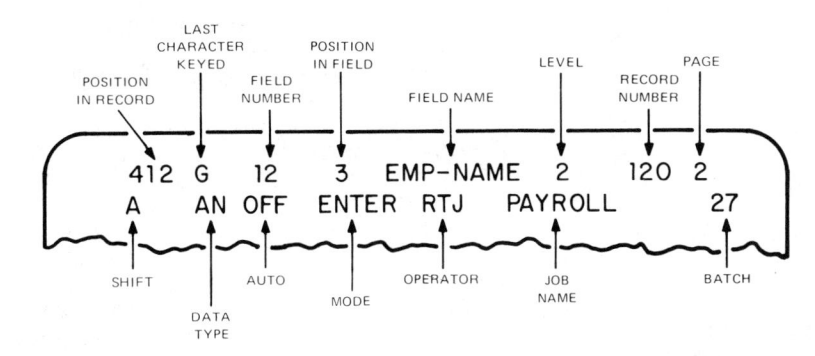

FIGURE 6.11
The Sperry UNIVAC 1900/10 3541 keystation. Status line (Courtesy of Sperry UNIVAC).

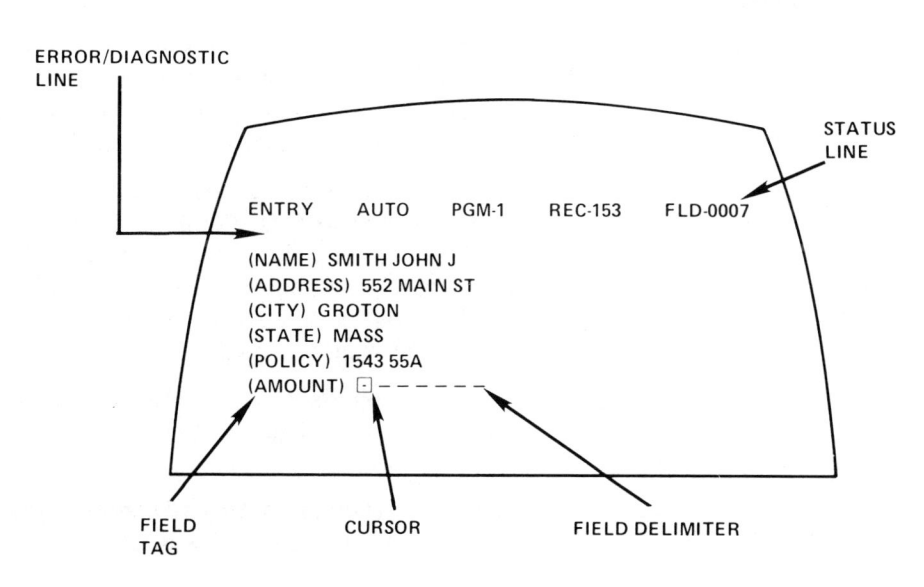

FIGURE 6.12
The NIXDORF Series 80 typical display presentation (Reprinted by permission of NIXDORF Corporation, Waltham, Massachusetts, USA).

UNIT 6 KEY-TO-DISK DEVICES   151

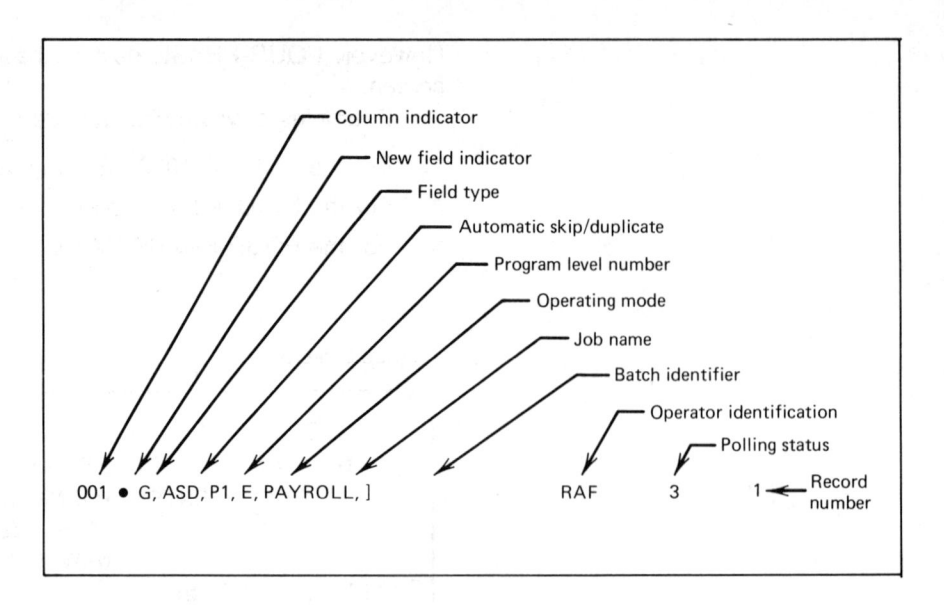

```
                                    ┌─ Column indicator
                                    │  ┌─ New field indicator
                                    │  │  ┌─ Field type
                                    │  │  │  ┌─ Automatic skip/duplicate
                                    │  │  │  │  ┌─ Program level number
                                    │  │  │  │  │  ┌─ Operating mode
                                    │  │  │  │  │  │  ┌─ Job name
                                    │  │  │  │  │  │  │  ┌─ Batch identifier
                                    │  │  │  │  │  │  │  │  ┌─ Operator identification
                                    │  │  │  │  │  │  │  │  │  ┌─ Polling status
                                    ↓  ↓  ↓  ↓  ↓  ↓  ↓  ↓  ↓  ↓  ┌─ Record number
                                   001 • G, ASD, P1, E, PAYROLL, ]   RAF   3   1 ←┘
```

FIGURE 6.13
The FOUR PHASE DATA IV status line
(Courtesy of Four-Phase Systems, Inc.)

DEFINITIONS

1. A *cursor* shows the position of the next character to be keyed. The cursor may appear as an underline or a square.

2. A *default value* is a value or option that is assumed when no specific value or option is entered. This default value or option has been programmed into the system and you can obtain it by pressing a function control key (in the case of the UNIVAC 1900, the FIELD REL key) without entering any data.

   An example of defaulting is shown in the display in Figure 6.14.

```
MODE = _____     OPERATING MODE
                   DEFAULT = ENTER
                   ENTER
                   VERIFY
                   SEARCH/MODIFY
                   UPDATE
                   FILE MGMT
                   SUPERVISOR
```

FIGURE 6.14
A UNIVAC 1900/10 Display.

3. Figure 6.14 also is an example of a menu. A *menu* is a list of options shown on a display screen. The operator may choose from these options. Figures 6.16 and 6.17 show other examples of menus.

   All the messages shown on the screen in Figure 6.14 are *prompts*. An operator who desires the ENTER mode simply presses the FIELD REL key (in the case of the UNIVAC 1900) and the *default* (ENTER) is accepted. Any other of the possible responses above must be keyed.

   When a job is terminated, there is usually a *work termination display*. Such a display gives:

1. Job identification information.
2. Batch statistics such as total records keyed, verified, and updated, and total invalid records.
3. Operator statistics such as time used, total keystrokes, keystrokes per hour, records keyed, errors, inserts, deletions, corrections, etc.

THE INSTALLATION SUPERVISOR

An installation with a key-to-disk device usually has a supervisor who is responsible for:

1. Writing programs or formats for each job.
2. Distributing work and maintaining records on work completion.
3. Monitoring operator performance.
4. Determining the time to be charged to each account.
5. Bringing the system up (turning it on) at the beginning of the day and bringing it down (turning it off) at the end of the day.
6. Performing data management activities.

The program or formats will be prepared for you by your supervisor and stored on disk. Therefore, this unit will not discuss writing program formats as the previous units have done.

SECTION C
THE UNIVAC 1900/10

The UNIVAC 1900 was rated an outstanding piece of data entry equipment by a national data entry publication.[2] The basic system consists of:

1. variable number of keystations and
2. a main cabinet containing the processor, the logical unit, the memory, the power supplies, a 7- or 10½-inch reel tape drive, a disk drive, and control and maintenance panels.

The main cabinet can contain a second tape or disk drive and optional devices can be attached such as printers, another tape unit, and another tape/disk unit. Keystations and a printer can exist at remote locations. Figure 6.2 shows some of these devices. Both methods of transferring data, shown in Figure 6.3 are available.

THE STATUS LINE AND VIDEO DISPLAY

Figure 6.10 shows the video display arrangement. The fields of the two status lines (from left to right) are as follows:

1. The keying position for the *next* character to be keyed.
2. *Last Character Keyed.* This field is blank for position 1 or if a function key is pressed.
3. *Field Number* (1 to 333). This field gives the field number into which the next character will be keyed.
4. *Position in Field* (1 to 999). This gives the position number within the *current* field for the next character to be keyed.
5. *Field Name.* This is the name of the field currently being keyed under program control. It is blank if no name was specified by the program.
6. *Program* (level) *number.* Thirty-two program levels are possible, (0 to 9, and A to Z). Although 36 level identifications are allowed, only 32 levels may be used in one program.
7. *Record Number* (1 to 65,535). The number of the record currently being

---

[2]*Data Entry Awareness Report* (Management Information Corporation), Vol. VII, No. 12 (December 1979), page 1.

keyed. The record number is changed for backspacing or forward spacing, record insertion or deletion, or releasing a record to disk.

8. *Page Number* (1 to 4). Only nine data lines can be displayed at one time. The first nine lines have a blank page number. The second nine lines would be page number 1, and so forth.

9. *Shift.* Current keyboard shift codes are shown in this field. The possible shift codes are:

A	alpha
B	numeric
a or A	lowercase alphabetic

If the shift key is pressed or locked, the programmed new shift will be displayed.

10. *Data Type.* Shows the type of data that may be entered into the current field. The data type codes are:

A	Uppercase alphabetic (capital letters)
A	Lowercase alphabetic
B	Blanks
C	COBOL character subset
H	Hexadecimal digits 0-9, A-F, (see Appendix C for explanation of the hex number system)
N	Decimal digits
S	Signed decimal digits (with + or −)
1-8	User character subset
Blank	Any character

11. *AUTO.* If ON indicates automatic skip, duplicate, or generate function.

Blank	Auto on
OFF	Auto off

12. *Mode.* The *mode* of the machine determines the operation that the machine will perform. The UNIVAC 1900 modes are:

Mode	Meaning	How Used
ENTER	Normal Entry	Use to create records in a data batch.
VERIFY	Verify	Used to compare previously entered data with that on the source document so that errors may be corrected.
SEARCH	Search/modify	Used to search a batch of data already entered and to modify any desired record under program control. This mode cannot be used for a batch that is currently active (not finished).
UPDATE	Update	Allows additional data to be keyed into each of the records of an existing batch.
FILE M	File Management	Allows the use of indexed files.

| | SUPERVISOR | Supervisor | We will not be concerned with this mode. Data entry trainees are not required to use this mode. |

13. *Operator.* Identification (entered during the work initiation command) of current operator.
14. *Job Name.* Name of current job (entered during the work initiation command).
15. *Batch.* Number (1 to 50,000) of the batch currently being keyed (entered during the work initiation command).

Message Line

The third line is the message line. Three types of messages appear here.

1. Alarm messages which describe what error has been made (example: **DATA ERROR - NOT NUMERIC**).
2. Guide messages that give special information to the operator (example: **BATCH IS IN BALANCE**).
3. Requested information (example: contents of a balance register would be displayed here if requested).

THE 1900/KEYBOARD

Figure 6.7 shows the UNIVAC 1900/10 keyboard. The power switch is on the right, bottom of the keyboard. To turn the station on, the switch should be pulled toward the operator. To turn it off, the switch should be pushed away from the operator. Brightness of the video screen characters can be adjusted by a knob in the back.

There are three audible signals given by the keystation.

1. A key click given when a key is depressed.
2. An attention tone given when the operator's attention is needed.
3. A ready tone given after a long task, such as a search, has been completed.

The keyboard has:

1. Blue control and shift keys.
2. White decimal digit keys, hyphen (minus sign key), and space bar.
3. Other gray data keys.

You should have made a list of your keys earlier in this unit. The 1900/10 keyboard is a little unusual in that there is sometimes a third character on a key. This character is called a *right-hand graphic*. The lower case alpha (LCA) key is used to select these symbols.

Before the operator starts work for the day, the supervisor must bring the system up (apply power to the system). Two situations may occur.

1. The keystation power switch is on while this process is taking place. The operator should not begin work until the following appears on the screen:

    READY - USE CMND KEY TO START WORK.

    Several other messages may be displayed before this last message.

2. The keystation power switch is turned on *after* the system has been brought up. A checkerboard pattern will appear on the screen and then a bright cursor will appear on the dark screen.

UNIT 6 KEY-TO-DISK DEVICES

WORK INITIATION

All work at the keystation must begin with the work initiation command. After the first work initiation command for the day, defaults may be used when issuing this command. A default is the value that is assumed when no information is keyed in and the FIELD REL key is pressed. The work initiation command procedure is shown in the table below.

Defaults are as follows:

Step	Default
4	EN(enter)
6	NO
8	Last job name
9	Last batch number
10	Last operator ID
11	Job name if keyed in Step 8; otherwise last program name

For all modes to select a default value, press FIELD REL. The default is automatically entered and the next entry may be made.

After the work initiation command is keyed, the first program level for the job is automatically selected.

UNIVAC 1900/10 WORK INITIATION COMMAND TABLE (H) = HOLD (R) = RELEASE

Step	Action — Perform unless OMIT appears to right under that mode.	ENTER	VERIFY	SEARCH	UPDATE	FILE M
1	Press RESET (H)					
2	Press CMND (R)					
3	(R) RESET					
4	Key in mode (as shown to the right)	EN	VE	SE	UP	FM
5	Press FIELD REL (R)			OMIT		OMIT
6	The prompt, CONTINUE(start option), will appear. Key in: NO if new batch in present mode YE(s) if batch is being continued in present mode.					
7	Press FIELD REL (R)				OMIT	OMIT
8	Key in job name and press FIELD REL (R)					
9	Key in batch no. and press FIELD REL (R)					
10	Key in operator ID and press FIELD REL (R)					
11	Key in format name and press FIELD REL (R)					
12		Enter Data	Verify Data*	Select Submode	Update Data	Enter Data

*In VERIFY if batch balance messages appear here, press the RESET key.

PART 2 DATA ENTRY EQUIPMENT

ERRORS AND GENERAL PROCEDURES

For all modes:

1. After the alarm tone and alarm message, press the RESET key to continue.
2. An *uncorrectable error* is an error in the data on the source document that has been detected by programmed checking features (such as check digits or range checks). You can program these errors to be flagged or you can bypass them in entry or verify mode. Although this error can be corrected later by the user office, there is nothing that you as an operator can do about it. For the operator, it is uncorrectable.
3. An *invalid batch* is one that contains an invalid field. You can flag this entire batch.
4. Insert and delete records in VERIFY, SEARCH, or UPDATE modes only.
5. When the system is in ENTER mode you can change a program level only in the first position of a manual field. When the system is in the VERIFY or SEARCH mode, use program selection only when beginning an insertion of a record.

Error Recovery for ENTER, UPDATE, and FILE M Modes

1. To change an incorrectly keyed character (example: keyed S rather than D):
   a. Press CHAR ← key.
   b. Key correct character.
   Alarm messages and recovery procedures are listed at the end of this section. When an alarm condition occurs:
   a. The alarm tone sounds.
   b. A checkerboard pattern appears on the screen for a half second.
   c. A message appears on the message line of the screen.
   Items 2 and 3 below cause alarm messages.
2. To correct an invalidly keyed character (example: pressed the NUMERIC and A key. Since no upper character exists, this causes an alarm condition.):
   a. Press RESET and release.
   b. Key in the correct character.
3. To correct an invalidly keyed field (examples: check digit for this field does not agree; value entered for the field is out of range; value entered for the field cannot be found in a table; and many other conditions):
   a. Press RESET and release.
   b. Press FIELD ← key if not in the first manual position of the field.
   c. Rekey the entire field.

   NOTE: In FILE M mode only the field currently being keyed may be corrected.

4. To bypass unreadable data on the source document because it cannot be read or it does not pass the validity check (example: check digit or range check):
   a. Press and hold RESET.
   b. Press and release BYPASS.
   c. Release RESET.
   d. Key in the next field.

Closing a Batch

A batch is closed when it is completely entered.

UNIT 6 KEY-TO-DISK DEVICES

Mode	Steps
ENTER	After last record is keyed: 1. Press and hold RESET. 2. Press and release CMND. 3. Release RESET. 4. Key in the letter C (for close).
VERIFY	Automatically closed after last record is verified.
UPDATE	Automatically closed when updating is finished.
SEARCH	Automatically closed when no more invalid records are found. To close before all invalid fields are corrected, follow the steps under ENTER mode.
FILE M	Follow instructions of your supervising operator.

After these steps:

1. If balance registers are being used, they will be displayed on the screen.
2. Read balance message and press RESET to continue.
3. Batch statistics will appear on the screen.
4. Press CMND or BYPASS to clear the screen.

Interrupting a Batch

Assume a batch was not completed but was written on disk and flagged as incomplete. It may be reopened at a later time (except in FILE M mode). Such a procedure might be used at the end of the day.

The steps for interrupting a batch are:

Mode	Steps
ENTER	After the last record is keyed: 1. Press and hold RESET. 2. Press and release CMND. 3. Release RESET. 4. Key in the letter I (for interrupt).
VERIFY	Follow procedure under ENTER mode.
UPDATE	Follow procedure under ENTER mode.
SEARCH	Do not interrupt.
FILE M	Not permitted.

After these steps:

1. Batch and operational statistics appear on the screen.
2. Press either CMND or BYPASS to clear the screen.

Reopening an Interrupted or Closed Batch

If you wish to reopen an interrupted or closed batch, reenter the same mode by using the work initiation command described earlier. Key in YES in response to the **CONTINUE (START OPTION)** prompt. Do not use this procedure for the SEARCH or FILE M modes.

Disabling a Batch

When you wish to take a coffee break away from the keystation or when you need to leave the keystation for a short time, disable the batch. The operator's clock stops when a batch is disabled.

The disable procedure is as follows:

Mode	Steps
ENTER	1. Press and hold RESET. 2. Press and release CMND. 3. Release RESET. 4. Key in the letter D (for disable).
VERIFY	Follow procedure under ENTER mode.
UPDATE	Follow procedure under ENTER mode.
SEARCH	Follow procedure under ENTER mode.
FILE M	Follow procedure under ENTER mode.

After these steps, the message *KEYSTATION DISABLED* will appear on the screen.

Activating a Disabled Batch

When you are ready to continue work, the keystation must be reactivated. The operator clock will be restarted when the batch is activated.

The procedure for activating a disabled batch is:

Mode	Steps
ENTER	1. Press and hold RESET. 2. Press and release CMND. 3. Release RESET. 4. Key in the letter A (for reactivate).
VERIFY	Follow procedure under ENTER mode.
UPDATE	Follow procedure under ENTER mode.
SEARCH	Follow procedure under ENTER mode.
FILE M	Follow procedure under ENTER mode.

Laboratory Exercises

Your instructor will now assign keying exercises using the information discussed above.

UPDATING The update mode is used to key additional data into records of an existing batch on disk. The cursor will be automatically positioned at the beginning of each field programmed to be updated.

To update:

1. Follow the steps in the work initiation command section described earlier.
2. Key data into the field.
3. Press FIELD REL. The cursor will be positioned at the start of the next field to be updated.
4. Repeat Steps 2 and 3 until updating has been completed.

Laboratory Exercises

Your instructor will assign update exercises.

SEARCHING AND MODIFYING

Use the SEARCH/MODIFY mode to find a selected record. Then you may change or delete the record, or insert a record before it.

The records may be searched for by:

1. The record number.
2. Invalid fields—the batch is searched sequentially for fields flagged as invalid.
3. Entire or partial contents of one or more specified fields.
4. Entire or partial contents of one or more specified fields within a record under a certain level.

Procedure

A. *Work initiation.* Key in work initiation command as described previously.

B. *Submode selection*

1. Key in the first two letters of the desired submode (default = NU). Possible choices are:
   a. CO (contents)   Specify record contents.
   b. LE (level content)   Specify contents in a record keyed under a particular level.
   c. NU (number)   Specify record number.
   d. IN (invalid field)   Records contain invalid fields.

2. Press FIELD REL and select step c, d, or e below according to the selection made above.

C. *Contents or level contents search*

1. a. For *CO option*, when **INPUT RECORD CONTENTS** prompt appears, key the *search mask*. A search mask is the field of characters, exactly as it appears in the record, that is to be searched for.
   b. For *LE option*, when **LEVEL** prompt appears, key in the program level that the record was entered under. Press FIELD REL. The prompt **INPUT RECORD CONTENTS** should appear. Key in the characters to be searched for exactly as they appear in the record.

2. To indicate the positions within a field or record that are *not* to be searched:
   a. Press and hold RESET.
   b. Press CHAR → in each position where the search is *not* to be made. Dashes will appear in these positions.
   c. Release RESET.

3. To end the search mask:
   a. Press and hold RESET.
   b. Press and release FIELD → or REC →.
   c. Release RESET.

4. Press FIELD REL.
   a. If a match occurs, the first record containing the selected search contents is displayed on the screen.

  b. If a match does *not* occur after the entire batch is searched, the message **SEARCH ARGUMENT NOT FOUND** is displayed on the screen. Pressing RESET will cause the batch to be closed.

5. If a match occurs and modification is desired, change the record.
6. To search for other records matching the current search mask (or to locate the next sequential record with the same contents in a CO search):
   a. Press and hold RESET.
   b. Press and release CMND.
   c. Release RESET.
   d. Key in the letter G (for GO AGAIN). The next record containing the selected search contents or an error message **SEARCH ARGUMENT NOT FOUND** will be displayed on the screen.
7. To change the search mask (in the CO case, from the present record through the end of the batch):
   a. Press and hold RESET.
   b. Press and release CMND.
   c. Release RESET.
   d. Key in the letter M (for new MASK). The prompt **INPUT RECORD CONTENTS** will be displayed.
8. a. for *CO option*, repeat Steps 1 to 6.
   b. For *LE option*, key in the next characters to be searched exactly as they appear in the record. Then repeat steps 2 to 6.

D. *Record number search*

1. When the prompt **NUMBER** appears, key in the number of the record to be searched for. For example, if you wish to search for the tenth record, key in 10. If more than one record is to be modified, key in the lowest record number first and then work up.
2. Press FIELD REL. The cursor will move to the beginning of the first manual keyed field in the selected record.
3. After positioning on the field to be modified (use FIELD → key), key in the correct data. Make any further modifications in the record by this method.
4. When all modifications have been made, hold down the RESET key and press the REC → key.
5. To search for another record number:
   a. Press and hold RESET.
   b. Press and release CMND.
   c. Release RESET.
   d. Key in the letter M (for new MASK).
6. Repeat Steps 1 to 4 to continue record modification in the same batch.

E. *Record containing an invalid field search.*

When IN is keyed in Part B above or Step 2 below is performed, the cursor is positioned at the beginning position of the first invalid field. If an invalid field is *not* found, the error message **SEARCH ARGUMENT NOT FOUND** is displayed. Press the RESET key to close the batch.

  If an invalid field *is* found:

1. Correct the invalid field.
2. To search for the next invalid field:

a. Press and hold RESET.
b. Press and release CMND.
c. Release RESET.
d. Key in the letter G (for GO AGAIN).
3. Repeat Step 2 to continue the invalid field search.

Laboratory Exercises

Your instructor will assign exercises using the SEARCH mode.

RECORD INSERTION

Records may *not* be inserted in ENTER or FILE M modes.

Record Insertion into a Batch

1. Position or search for the first record *past* which the insertion is to take place. For example, if a record must be inserted between records 3 and 4, position the cursor at the first keyed position of record 4.
2. Press and hold RESET.
3. Press and release INSERT.
4. Release RESET.
5. Select the program level (see program level selection section).
6. Key in the new record. The FIELD ← and REC ← keys cannot be used during this step.

Record Insertion at *END* of Batch

1. Perform the work initiation command for the ENTER mode.
2. Key in the YES option to the CONTINUE prompt.
3. Key in the new record.
4. Close the batch (press RESET and CMND keys, key in the letter C).

Record Deletion

1. Position or search for the record to be deleted.
2. Press and hold RESET.
3. Press and release DELETE.
4. Release RESET.

Records may *not* be deleted in the ENTER and FILE M modes.

PROGRAM LEVEL SELECTION

To manually select a program:

1. Move the cursor to the beginning of the selected field.
2. Press the PROG key.
3. Key in the program level (0 to 9 or A to Y).

DISPLAYS

There are four types of general registers. These registers are *programmed* and the contents may be *displayed*. The four types of general registers are:

1. Arithmetic registers, numbered A1 through A99. These registers are used to contain the results of arithmetic operators.
2. Balance registers, numbered B1 through B99. These registers are as-

signed an initial value. When the value in the register reaches zero, it is said to be in balance.

3. Character registers, numbered C1 through C99. Character registers contain only nonnumeric data and are used in character manipulations.
4. Auxiliary duplication registers, numbered D1 through D99. Auxiliary duplication registers are used to contain alphameric information which may be automatically inserted into a field by using the AX DUP key.

Displays are shown on the message line and remain there until replaced or cleared by another message.

To display the contents of a register:

1. Press DISPLAY.
2. Key in the register number (A, B, C, or D and a two-digit number, 01 through 99).

Other system displays, listed below, can be obtained by pressing DISPLAY and keying in the appropriate letter.

K   Displays the batch keying time and the number of strokes on the message line.
T   Displays current time and key-station number on the message line.
L   Displays the record currently being verified. The next key stroke blanks the screen.
R   Displays the entire page of the record.
N   Blanks out data lines.

If the display command is used, it is ended when the next character is keyed.

VERIFYING

You may omit verification of a field by using the BYPASS key, then the record and the batch are flagged as invalid. When a field is verified, the cursor moves to the next field to be verified. When the last record is verified, the VERIFY mode automatically ends.

Key Verification

To correct a keying error made while verifying: press RESET, key in the correct character, and continue. If it is an actual error in the data originally keyed, the character must be rekeyed a *second* time. The character is then considered verified, and the cursor moves on.

If more than one character is incorrect in a field, you can save time by correcting the entire field using the V COR key.

Steps for correcting an entire field are:

1. Press RESET.
2. Press and hold RESET.
3. Press V COR and release.
4. Release RESET. The cursor will return to the beginning of the field.
5. Key in the correct data.
6. Press FIELD REL if in a must release field; otherwise the release is automatic.
7. When the prompt **REKEY FIELD TO VERIFY** appears on the message line, press RESET and repeat Steps 5 and 6 (key verify).
8. The cursor will then move on to the next field to be verified.

Sight Verification

The field to be verified will be displayed. If the field is correct, press FIELD →. This flags the field as verified and moves the cursor to the beginning of the next field to be verified.

Correcting One or More Characters

1. Press and hold RESET.
2. Press CHAR → until the cursor is in the position of the incorrect character.
3. Release RESET.
4. Key in the correct character.
5. Press RESET.
6. Rekey the correct character.
7. If more incorrect characters exist, repeat Steps 1 to 6.
8. When all corrections have been made for the field, press RESET and FIELD → keys.

Correcting an Entire Field

1. Press and hold RESET.
2. Press V COR.
3. Release RESET.
4. Key in the correct field.
5. Press FIELD REL if the entire field is not keyed.
6. When the prompt **REKEY FIELD TO VERIFY** appears on the message line, press RESET.
7. Rekey the field (key verify).
8. Press RESET and FIELD → keys.

In both examples given above after the FIELD → key is pressed, the cursor is positioned at the beginning of the next field to be verified.

Laboratory Exercises

Your instructor will assign exercises to be verified.

UNIVAC 1900/10 ALARM MESSAGES AND RECOVERY

When alarm is given, read alarm message displayed on line 3 of video screen. Press RESET key. If a guide message is then displayed, perform indicated action; otherwise, refer to Alarm Messages and Recovery table. Messages are arranged in alphabetical order in the table.

Alarm Message Displayed	What Message Means	How To Recover
BATCH IS ACTIVE	Another operator is working on selected batch.	1. Press RESET key. 2. Check that job name and batch number are keyed in correctly. If it is correct, either wait for the batch to become inactive or select another batch.
BATCH IS IN BALANCE	All balance registers are equal to zero.	1. Press RESET key. 2. Note displayed batch statistics.
BATCH IS NOT FOUND	Batch number selected is not in system.	1. Press RESET key. 2. Check that job name and batch number are keyed in correctly. If it is correct, notify supervisor.
BATCH IS OUT OF BALANCE	Completed batch does not meet a requirement that has been established by the format program.	1. Press RESET key. 2. Note displayed batch statistics. Follow local operating procedures.
BATCH NUMBER RANGE ERROR	Batch number is not between 1 and 50,000.	1. Press RESET key. 2. Key in correct batch number.
BLANK NOT ALLOWED	Program does not allow blanks in field.	1. Press RESET key. 2. Key in correct data or bypass the field and notify supervisor.
CHARACTER LOST - REKEY	Last character keyed was not accepted by system.	1. Press RESET key. 2. Rekey last character.
CHARACTER TRANSMISSION ERROR-REKEY		
CHAR FWD INVALID	Illegal to use CHAR → key to move cursor beyond last character entered or verified, or beyond end of field.	1. Press RESET key. 2. Continue keying in data.
DATA ERROR - NOT ALPHA	Keyed data must be alphabetic.	1. Press RESET key. 2. Key in correct type of data or bypass the field and notify supervisor.
DATA ERROR - NOT ALPHANUMERIC	Keyed data must be alphameric.	
DATA ERROR - NOT BLANK	Keyed data must be blank.	
DATA ERROR - NOT COBOL	Keyed data must be COBOL.	
DATA ERROR - NOT HEX	Keyed data must be hexadecimal.	1. Press RESET key. 2. Key in correct type of data.
DATA ERROR - NOT LOWER CASE ALPHA	Keyed data must be lowercase alphabetic.	

UNIT 6 KEY-TO-DISK DEVICES

Alarm Message Displayed	What Message Means	How To Recover
DATA ERROR - NOT NUMERIC	Keyed data must be numeric.	
DATA ERROR - NOT PUNCTUATION	Keyed data must be punctuation.	
DATA ERROR - NOT SIGNED DECIMAL	Keyed data must be signed decimal.	
DATA ERROR - NOT USER 1 DATA ERROR - NOT USER 2 DATA ERROR - NOT USER 3 DATA ERROR - NOT USER 4 DATA ERROR - NOT USER 5 DATA ERROR - NOT USER 6 DATA ERROR - NOT USER 7 DATA ERROR - NOT USER 8 DATA ERROR - NOT USER 9 DATA ERROR - NOT USER 10	Character keyed in is not contained in data-type subset.	1. Press RESET key. 2. Key in correct character.
DISK FULL - TASK TERMINATED	DISK is full. Batch closes automatically.	Notify supervisor.
DUP KEY INVALID ON FIRST RECORD	No previous record to duplicate.	1. Press RESET key. 2. Key in data.
DUPLICATE JOB AND BATCH NUMBER	Job name and batch number just entered were entered previously.	If incorrect job name or batch number: 1. Press RESET key. 2. Key in correct job name and/or batch number. If additional records are to be entered into batch: 1. Press RESET key. 2. Press and hold RESET key. 3. Press and release BYPASS key. 4. Release RESET key. 5. Press and hold RESET key. 6. Press and release CMND key. 7. Release RESET key.
DUPLICATE JOB AND BATCH NUMBER (Continued)		8. Select mode and key in YES in response to **CONTINUE (START OPTION)** prompt. 9. Finish keying in work initiation command. 10. Enter data.
ENTER/VERIFY SEPARATION TOO SMALL	Record being verified is too near record currently being keyed.	1. Press RESET key. 2. Wait until operator working in Enter mode has completed more records.
FLD BKSP INVALID ON FIRST FIELD	Illegal to press FIELD ← key in first field of record.	1. Press RESET key. 2. Press REC ← key. 3. Press FIELD → key as often as necessary to advance to desired field.

Alarm Message Displayed	What Message Means	How To Recover
FIELD FWD INVALID	Illegal to use FIELD → key to move beyond last field entered or verified unless field is programmed for sight verification.	1. Press RESET key. 2. Key in data or key verify field.
FIELD MUST BE FULLY KEYED	All character positions of field must be keyed in.	1. Press RESET key. 2. Key in entire field or bypass field and notify supervisor.
FIELD MUST BE KEYED	All character positions of field must be keyed in.	1. Press RESET key. 2. Key in at least one character.
FORMAT ERROR (describes type)	System error has occurred.	Notify supervisor.
FORMAT NOT FOUND	Format (program) is not found in system.	1. Press RESET key. 2. Rekey program name. Be sure that name and spelling of name are correct.
ILLEGAL FILL CHAR	Character used is not allowed by program.	1. Press RESET key. 2. Press FIELD ← key. 3. Rekey field. If source data is incorrect: 1. Press RESET key. 2. Press RESET key again and hold. 3. Press and release BYPASS key. 4. Release RESET key. 5. Continue keying in next field.
INCOMPATIBLE FORMAT SELECTED	Format program just selected is not compatible with program used to enter batch.	1. Press RESET key. 2. Select correct format program.
INVALID COMMAND SELECTED	Key other than C, I, D, A, G, or M was selected after CMND key was pressed.	1. Press RESET key. 2. Press correct key.
	Record number lower than the previous number was selected in Search and Modify mode.	1. Press RESET key. 2. Key in another record number.
INVALID FIELD - CORRECT OR BYPASS	Data entered does not pass validation check.	1. Press RESET key. 2. Rekey field. If error returns: 1. Press RESET key. 2. Press RESET key again and hold. 3. Press and release BYPASS key. 4. Release RESET key.

Alarm Message Displayed	What Message Means	How To Recover
INVALID JOB NAME	Form of job name not correct: 1. Must contain 1 to 8 characters. 2. Must begin with an alphabetic. 3. Must not contain embedded blanks.	1. Press RESET key. 2. Key in correct job name.
INVALID KEY AT FIRST FIELD	Field or character backspacing invalid in first field of record.	1. Press RESET key. 2. Press REC ← key.
INVALID KEY AT MIDFIELD	Use of PROG key not valid because not at proper program-level selection point.	1. Press RESET key. 2. Press RESET key again and hold. 3. Press and release CMND key. 4. Release RESET key. 5. Rekey record, selecting new level at appropriate point.

INVALID KEYSTROKE	Character keyed is not allowed by program.	Press RESET key and then:
		1. Key in the correct character, or
		2. Bypass the field as follows:
		  (a) Press RESET key again and hold.
		  (b) Press and release BYPASS key.
		  (c) Release RESET key.
		  (d) Continue keying in next field.

INVALID LEVEL CHANGE	Level change not allowed or an incorrect level designation has been keyed.	1. Press RESET key. 2. Key the correct level or resume keying at current level. 3. Check operating instructions for job.
JOB NOT FOUND	Job name entered does not exist in system.	1. Press RESET key. 2. Check that correct operating mode is selected. 3. Rekey job name. Be sure name and spelling of name are correct.
REC BKSP INVALID IN FILE MGMT MODE	Illegal to use REC → key in File Managment mode.	1. Press RESET key. 2. Press correct key.
REC BKSP INVALID AT FIRST REC	REC → key is not allowed in the first record of the batch.	1. Press RESET key. 2. Press correct key.
REC FWD INVALID	Illegal to use REC → key to move beyond last fully keyed record.	1. Press RESET key. 2. Continue keying record.
REKEY FIELD TO VERIFY	File is programmed for key verification.	1. Press RESET key. 2. Key verify the field.
	Field must be key verified after V COR key is pressed.	

PART 2 DATA ENTRY EQUIPMENT

Alarm Message Displayed	What Message Means	How to Recover
SYSTEM ERROR #	Error in system.	Note error number and contact supervisor. Then wait for *READY-USE CMND KEY TO START WORK*. Select same batch, using work-initiation-command portion of desired mode by entering YES to *CONTINUE (START OPTION)* prompt.
TERMINAL BUSY	System is processing a previous command or performing a batch replay.	Wait until message disappears and proceed.
UNRECOVERABLE DISK ERROR-BATCH CANCELLED	Unrecoverable disk error has occurred. Batches erroneously flagged as active on disk are inaccessible.	Notify supervisor.
UNRECOVERABLE DISK ERROR-JOB CANCELLED	Unrecoverable disk error has occurred. Batches erroneously flagged as active on disk are inaccessible.	Notify supervisor.
VERIFY MISCOMPARE	Last character keyed does not match character in record.	Press RESET key and: 1. Key the correct character, or 2. Press V COR key and rekey entire field.
XDUP KEY IS INVALID	Program does not allow duplicate function in field.	1. Press RESET key. 2. Key in field data.

Source: The above material is reproduced with permission from the Sperry UNIVAC 1900/10 System Model 3541 Keystation Operator's Quick Reference Guide, UP-9101, copyright © 1978, 1979 by Sperry UNIVAC Corporation.

SECTION D
THE FOUR PHASE IV SYSTEM

The FOUR PHASE DATA IV System is found frequently in the data entry division of large industries, such as banks, insurance companies, hospitals, and government offices. For example, the Comptroller's Office of the State of Texas has a FOUR PHASE IV/90 System in the data entry division. All tax information is entered on this system using over a hundred keystations split between several CPUs. There are 14 to 20 stations per CPU. The data is stored on disk and later written on tape. Then the tape is taken to the host processor which is an AMDAHL 470 V/6.

The DATA IV exists in three versions, Versions 1, 2, and 3. Versions 2 and 3 provide up to 15 program levels, remote terminals, and other features. Version 3 has indexed file capabilities. These versions differ in memory capacity, the maximum number of terminals supported, and the I/O peripherial equipment permitted. A recent survey[3] shows the DATA IV/70 to be widely used in industry.

The System IV Versions 2 and 3 have the following properties:

System	Memory	Maximum Number of Terminals	I/O Devices		
			Card Reader	Mag Tape	Printer
40 and 50	24K to 96K	16	Yes	No	Yes
70	24K to 96K	22	Yes	Yes	Yes
90	96K to 480K	32	Yes	Yes	Yes

In addition, each system may have numerous disk drives with removable disk packs (cartridges). Typewriter or keypunch keyboards are available. The keyboards are attached to the video display unit by a 5-foot cable so placement of the two units can be adjusted to individual preference. The CRT or display screen comes in different sizes. Screens have 6, 12, or 24 possible lines and may be 48 or 81 characters in width. For all types of screens, the *bottom* line is the status line, and the next to the bottom line is the message line.

THE STATUS LINE

Figure 6.13 shows the status line arrangement for this device. Note that the third field through the eighth field are separated by commas. The status line fields (from left to right) are:

1. A three-digit *column indicator number* showing the column position of the *next* character to be keyed.

IF	Then the column Indicator Is
An edit error occurs	The column with the error
A validation error occurs	The first column of the error field

2. The *new field indicator*
   a. If a dot . appears, this indicates the next character keyed will begin a new field.
   b. This field if blank for any other position in the field.
3. The *field type*
   Field-type codes that may appear are:

Symbol	Meaning
A	Alphabetic (A to Z and blank).
G	Alphameric (any character).
H	Hexadecimal (0 to 9, A to F, see Appendix C).
I	Integer (numeric, 0 to 9 only).
L	Left-zero-fill (two types, one allows a decimal point).
N	Numeric (digits 0 to 9, special symbols or spaces).
T	Text is generated (data is stored in memory by programming and will be placed in this field).

[3]*Data Entry Awareness Report* (Management Information Corporation), Vol. VII, No. 12 (December 1979), page 13.

4. *Automatic skip/duplicate (ASD)*
    a. Blank means the automatic skip/duplicate function is OFF.
    b. Characters ASD mean the function is ON.
5. Two-character *program level number*
    a. Blank means *not* under program control.
    b. Nonblank, (P1 to P9, 10 to 15) program level, means the system is operating under program control. Look at your keyboard. There are only six program-level keys. Therefore the fifteen program levels are selected as follows:

Program Level	Keys
1	PROG 1
2	PROG 2
3	PROG 3
4	PROG 4
5	PROG 5
6	PROG 6 and the number 6
7	PROG 6 and the number 7
8	PROG 6 and the number 8
9	PROG 6 and the number 9
10	PROG 6 and the number 0
11	PROG 6 and the number 1
12	PROG 6 and the number 2
13	PROG 6 and the number 3
14	PROG 6 and the number 4
15	PROG 6 and the number 5

6. *Operating mode code* (see discussion of modes)

Code	Mode
E	ENTER
F	FIND
J	JOB STATUS
S	SHOW
V	VERIFY
X	EXIT

7. *Job name* (1 to 9 characters). This field shows the name of the current job. No spaces are allowed.
8. *Batch identifier* (1 to 6 characters). This field identifies the current batch.
    a. Version 1—numeric only.
    b. Versions 2 and 3—numbers and letters.
9. *Operator's identifier* or *ID* (3 characters). Usually this field consists of the operator's initials. However, if the keystation is idle, question marks appear in the field.
10. *Polling status* (1 digit). *Polling* means to scan remote terminals on a communications network to see if they are ready to submit data.
    a. 0 to 3 indicates NOT READY.
    b. 4 to 7 indicates READY.
    c. 2 to 6 indicates carrier is ON.
11. *Record number* (1 to 6 digits). This field shows the number of the current record in the batch.

MESSAGE LINE The message line appears on the next to last line on the screen. There are three types of messages:

1. Error messages describing error conditions (a "beep" alarm sounds), such as **CHECK DIGIT FAILED**.
2. Operator action instructions, such as **PRESS MODE KEY TO USE TERMINAL**.
3. Reports on certain conditions, such as **NO MORE RECORDS**.

MODES The *mode* of the machine determines the operation the machine will perform. The FOUR PHASE modes are:

Mode	Character	How Used
ENTER	E	Used to enter data in a record. Used to display an existing record using the REC ↑ or REC ↓ keys.
EXIT	X	Used to terminate or end data entry for the batch.
FIND	F	Used to find a record with a search mask.
VERIFY	V	Used to check data previously entered with that on the source document so that necessary corrections can be made.
SHOW	S	Used to display information on system status (for example, the number of idle screens).
JOB STATUS	J	Used to display information about batches in a specific job.
LOG/PRINT	L	Used to create a log or written history of all supervisor commands executed.
SUPERVISOR	T	Used to enter programs, or insert and delete records from index set records.

The use of the JOB STATUS, SHOW, LOG/PRINT, and SUPERVISOR modes are usually reserved for the supervising operator. Therefore, you as an operator will be concerned mainly with the ENTER, EXIT, FIND, and VERIFY modes.

It should be noted that FOUR PHASE indexed files are called *indexed sets*.

THE FOUR PHASE DATA IV KEYBOARD Figure 6.9 shows the FOUR PHASE keypunch style keyboard. The keyboard has two types of keys:

1. Control or function keys which are dark in color.
2. Data keys which are light in color.

Three peculiarities of this keyboard are:

1. There is a ? control key and a ? data key.
2. There are no CHAR ADV or BKSP keys. The FIELD → and FIELD ← keys in lower shift move one position at a time.
3. REC BKSP is REC ↑, and REC ADV is REC ↓.

Near the base of the screen, at the right, are two knobs. The knob nearest to the operator turns the unit on and off and adjusts the brightness of display characters on the screen. The knob farthest from the operator adjusts horizontal positioning of the display, much as on a TV screen.

You should have made a list of your keys earlier in this unit.

BEGINNING WORK

Before the operator starts work for the day, the supervisor must bring the system up (supply power). When the system is ready, the message **DATA IV IS READY, TYPE YOUR ID** will be displayed on the message line. The cursor will be positioned under the first question mark in the operator's ID field on the status line.

Work Initiation or Signing ON

1. Key in the three-digit ID assigned to you by your supervisor or instructor.
2. a. When the prompt **TYPE E, F, J, L, S, T, V, X, OR ?** appears on the message line, key in the code letter for the mode that you will be using. If you cannot remember what the codes mean, press the

    NUMERIC and ?/X keys. This is similar to the HELP key on other

    key-to-disk devices. (You should be using only E, F, V, and X codes or ?.)

   b. If you press an illegal key (for example W) in error, the error message **INHIBITED KEY** will blink on and off. Take the following steps.
      (1) Press CORR/RESET (stops the blinking).
      (2) Press MODE.
      (3) Key in the correct mode (E, F, V, X).

3. The prompt **TYPE JOBNAME, BATCH #** will appear. Key in the name of the job, a comma, and the batch number.
4. Press the SKIP key.
   You are now signed on.
5. If a password is required, the prompt **TYPE PASSWORD - RESTRICTED JOB** will appear. Key in the password given to you by the supervisor. The password will *not* appear on the screen.

WORK TERMINATION OR SIGNING OFF

If work is to be terminated for the day, perform the following steps:

1. Press MODE.
2. Key in the letter X (for EXIT).
3. When the following message is displayed:

    C=COMPLETE, L=LOCK, S=SIGN OFF, B=CHANGE BAT#

Type	If
C	The batch is complete or finished
S	The batch is not complete

The L or B options are reserved for your supervisor or instructor. If the C option is used, the batch cannot be accessed again except in the FIND or VERIFY modes.

The message **DATA IV IS READY, TYPE YOUR ID** will be displayed until work is started again or the power is turned off at the keystation.

UNIT 6 KEY-TO-DISK DEVICES

Work Interruption

If it is necessary to stop work for a short period of time, such as during a coffee break:

1. Press the MODE key.
2. To resume work, repeat the work initiation step.

ERRORS AND GENERAL PROCEDURES

1. To change an incorrectly keyed character (EXAMPLE: keyed 5 rather than D):
   a. Press the *unshifted* FIELD ← key.
      This moves the cursor one position at a time. If the cursor is in position 1 of a field, this moves the cursor to the last position of the preceding field.
   b. Key the correct character.
2. Changing a field with several errors may require rekeying the entire field. In this case, use the *shifted* FIELD ← key. This moves the cursor to the beginning of the current field. If the cursor is already positioned at the beginning, it moves to the beginning of the previous field (a previous field cannot be a text field).
3. The FIELD → key, *unshifted*, moves the cursor forward one character at a time. *Shifted*, it moves one field at a time where data can be entered. If used in the last record position, that record could be released, so use it with care.
4. To change the MODE, press the MODE key and the key for the appropriate mode (E, F, V, X). The mode can be changed at any time except during error conditions.
5. When errors occur:
   a. A blinking error message occurs on the message line.
   b. On some systems, a "beep" alarm goes off.
   c. The keyboard locks up.

The keyboard can be unlocked by pressing the *unshifted* CORR RESET key. Unshifted, this key acts as a RESET key. The error message will stop blinking but will remain on the screen. Alarm messages and error procedures are listed at the end of this section.

FLAGGING QUESTIONABLE FIELDS

A field is sometimes flagged when:

1. It is illegible. That is, you cannot read the data on the source document.
2. The operator is unsure of what to enter in the field. For example, the operator may be entering codes for a long activity description and is unsure if this is an appropriate code for the activity.
3. Data is to be left out of the field.

To flag a field, press the ? control key. This causes:

1. Question marks to be placed in the current and remaining positions of the field.
2. The field to be flagged as invalid. The verifier will correct the problem at a later date.

ENTERING NEW RECORDS

1. Sign on (perform work initiation) selecting the ENTER mode.
2. a. If no data exists in this batch (a new batch), the message **STARTING DATA ENTRY, NEW BATCH** will appear on the screen.

b. If data exists in this batch (not a new batch), the message **RESUME DATA ENTRY** will appear on the screen.

3. If a program is used, select the appropriate program level explained earlier under the status line section.
4. When the first prompt appears, begin entering data.
5. Overriding validation.
   Sometimes fields are programmed for check digit ranges, or matches with values in a table. If what is written on the source document is wrong, an error condition occurs. The blinking message **NOT VALID DATA** will appear on the screen. If the operator knows the correct data, the system can be forced to accept what is keyed if you:
   a. Key in the desired data.
   b. Press the unshifted CORR/RESET to stop the blinking message.
   c. Press the valid key.
      The record will be flagged to be verified later, and the cursor will move to the next field.
      Do *not* use this procedure unless your instructor or supervisor tells you to do so.

Laboratory Exercises

Your instructor will assign exercises for this section.

FINDING RECORDS FOR MODIFICATION

A record often needs to be selected (or found) to change it, delete it, or insert a record or records before it.

Finding a Record Using Entry Mode

This method allows the operator to search through a batch using the REC ↑ and REC ↓ keys. This operation is sometimes called *paging* through the batch. If it is a long batch and the record is not near the end, this procedure is not a very efficient method for finding a record. Using the FIND mode would be better.

REC ↑ means to GO BACK. REC ↓ means to GO FORWARD. To search through the batch:

1. Perform the work initiation procedure (with the ENTER mode and keying the batch name and identifier). The message **RESUME DATA ENTRY** will appear on the screen. The cursor is positioned at the *end* of the batch.
2. Press REC ↑ to move *back* through the batch to find the correct record. Each record will be displayed as you move back.

Finding a Record Using the Find Mode

1. Perform the work initiation procedure using the FIND mode. The message **TYPE SEARCH INFORMATION** will appear on the screen.
2. If a display is desired for the first record in the batch, press SKIP.
3. If a display of other records is desired, use one of two methods:
   a. Display records by record number (the ninety-ninth record would be record number 99):

      (1) Press the shifted `#/@` key to obtain #.
      (2) Key in the record number.
      (3) Press SKIP.

UNIT 6 KEY-TO-DISK DEVICES

The record should be displayed.

b. Display records by using a *search mask* (sometimes called a search argument or key):

Displaying Records Using the Search Mask

A *search mask* is a field of characters, exactly as they appear in the record, that is to be searched for. FOUR PHASE demands that a mask be entered in the form:

$$\text{nnn} \begin{Bmatrix} = \\ \neg \\ > \\ < \end{Bmatrix} *\text{MASK}*$$

Symbol	Meaning
nnn	Beginning position in the record (1 to 480)
=	Equal (default)
¬	Not equal ($\neq$)
>	Greater than
<	Less than
MASK	Actual contents of the field or mask (maximum of 42 characters) with * at the beginning and end

For example:

1. A search is to be made for a record with a social security number of 123-45-6789 beginning in position 1. The required search information would be: 1=*123456789* or 1"123456789" since = is the default case.

2. A search is to be made for all persons with ages greater than 20. The three-digit age field begins in position 50 of the record. The search information would be 50 > *020*.

To perform this type of search:

1. Key in the search information in the above form.
2. Press SKIP.

Compound search information can be entered as either AND or OR conditions on some versions of the FOUR PHASE equipment.

1. An AND condition means that *all* conditions must be true for the record to be selected. An AND is signified by a blank.
2. An OR condition means that one or more conditions must be true for the record to be selected. An OR is specified with a slash.

For example:
Position 1   Name
Position 50 Town
Search the batch for all the LEEs in MIAMI.
would give a search key of

$$1=*\text{LEE}*b50=\text{MIAMI}*$$

where b means a blank. There may be more than two conditions.
When the search is made:

If the Record Is	Then
FOUND	a. The record will appear on the screen.
	b. A **FOUND** message will appear on the screen.
NOT FOUND	a. An **END** message will appear on the screen.
	b. The record number in the status line will be set to the number of records in the batch plus one.

While the search is taking place, an * will appear on the status line in the record number field of most FOUR PHASE devices.

Once the record has been found:

1. To display records around it (regardless of the search information), press REC ↑ or REC ↓.
2. If you desire to discontinue the search, press the ALPHA key (or CTRL on the typewriter style keyboard) and the ERASE/HOME key at the same time. This turns off the search. Then REC ↑ and REC ↓ can be used.
3. To turn on the search information again, press ALPHA and ERASE/HOME at the same time.

UPDATING OR CHANGING A RECORD ALREADY RELEASED TO DISK CURRENT BATCH

1. Press REC ↑ or REC ↓ until the record is located.
2. Press shifted CORR/RESET if necessary.
3. If you must select a new program level, do so and rekey the entire record if necessary.
4. Press the DUP key to position the cursor at the beginning of the field to be changed. DUP, unshifted FIELD →, or unshifted FIELD ← move the cursor one character at a time; DUP, shifted FIELD →, or shifted FIELD ← move the cursor one field at a time. These keys do not erase the data. They position the cursor.
5. Key the desired changes.
6. Press REL to release the record to disk.

Another Batch

1. Find the record as described under the section on finding a record.
2. Do Steps 2 through 5 above.

Deleting a Record

1. Find the record to be deleted by the method described under the section on finding a record.
2. Press shifted CORR/RESET.
3. Press shifted REC.

This deletes the record and decreases the record numbers by one. You can page through the batch with REC ↑ or REC ↓ to see if the record was properly deleted.

Inserting a Record

Sometimes you must insert a record or records that have been left out. The procedure shown in Figure 6.15 is as follows:

1. Find the record that will follow the insertion by the method described in the section on finding a record.

UNIT 6   KEY-TO-DISK DEVICES

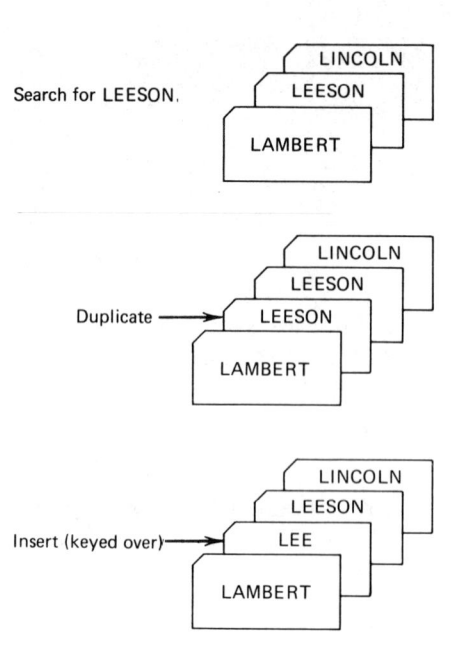

FIGURE 6.15
Record insertion.

2. Press the shifted CORR/RESET.
3. Press the shifted REC↓. This duplicates the record found, leaves the status line record number the same, but increases all following record numbers by one.
4. If the program level needs to be changed, press the shifted CORR/RESET, then press the appropriate PROG key.
5. a. If the new record to be inserted is quite different from the one duplicated:
     (1) Press the shifted ERASE/HOME to erase the screen.
     (2) Key the new record.
   b. If the new record has field that can be duplicated (from memory):
     (1) Key over all fields needing to be changed.
     (2) Use the DUP key to copy when necessary.
6. Press the SKIP key (or REL on the typewriter keyboard). The new record will be inserted and released to disk.
7. You can page through the batch with REC↑ and REC↓ to check the insertions.

Laboratory Exercises

Your instructor will assign exercises to cover this section.

VERIFYING FOUR PHASE recommends sight verification for invalid or illegible fields that were bypassed. Key verification is recommended for verifying the entire record or a portion of a record. In key verification the record is displayed, but it is scrambled (mixed up). As each field is rekeyed, the field is unscrambled if it matches or agrees.

Key Verification

1. Perform the work initiation procedure using the VERIFY (V) mode. Before keying the job name and batch ID, a prompt **TYPE S FOR SIGHT, K FOR KEY, OR R FOR RECONSTRUCT** will appear on the screen. Press MODE and the letter K.

2. After the SKIP key is pressed (and the password routine is performed if applicable), the scrambled record will appear on the screen. A prompt **VERIFY THIS RECORD** will be displayed. Key the record from the source document, starting at the location of the flashing cursor.
3. If there is an error, the prompt **VERIFY ERROR** will appear as a flashing message. In this case:
   a. Press the unshifted CORR/RESET to blank out the error message.
   b. If a single character is to be corrected, press the shifted CORR/RESET and key in the correct character.
   c. If it is necessary to correct more than one character or field, press shifted FIELD → and key the entire field.
   d. To correct the verifying operator's own error, press unshifted CORR/RESET and correct the error.
   e. Records may be inserted or deleted as described previously.
4. If you wish to unscramble the display temporarily to make sure the positioning is on the correct record or field:
   a. Press MODE and the letter S.
   b. To return to VERIFY mode and the same record and field, key R.
5. When all records are verified, the prompt **VERIFY COMPLETE. NO MORE RECORDS** will be displayed.

Sight Verification

1. Perform the work initiation procedure using the VERIFY (V) mode. Before you key in the job name and batch ID, a prompt **TYPE S FOR SIGHT, K FOR KEY, OR R FOR RECONSTRUCT** will appear on the screen. Press MODE and the letter S.
2. After the SKIP key is pressed (and the password routine is performed, if applicable), the first record in which the invalid or illegible field occurs will be displayed. Examine the record.
3. If the illegible field key (?) was used:
   a. Press the shifted CORR/RESET.
   b. Press DUP until the cursor is positioned at the beginning of the field with the question marks.
   c. Correct the data.
   d. If question marks remain in the field, delete them by using SKIP, LEFT-ZERO, or REL, depending on what was used on the original data.
4. If the field was bypassed with the VALID key:
   a. Press the shifted CORR/RESET.
   b. Press DUP until the cursor stops advancing and an error message is displayed.
   c. Press the unshifted CORR/RESET.
   d. If the field is correct, press VALID.
      If the field is incorrect, rekey the data.
5. After Steps 3 or 4, the cursor will advance to the next field. Keep pressing DUP, and repeat Steps 4 or 5.
6. To continue sight verification, use the REC ↓ key.
7. When all flagged records have been verified, the prompt **VERIFY COMPLETE. NO MORE RECORDS.** will be displayed.

Laboratory Exercises

Your instructor will assign verification exercises.

DATA IV DISPLAY MESSAGES

All the messages that you are likely to encounter as a DATA IV operator are listed here alphabetically. The probable cause of each message, and a recommended response to the message, are give in the "Description" column.

Message	Description
ALPHA A-Z ONLY	You tried to enter a nonalphabetic character in a field coded to accept only an alphabetic character. Press CORR/RESET then rekey correctly.
ALREADY IN KEY VERIFY	You attempted to enter Key Verify (K-V) mode while already in Key Verify mode. Reselect the Key option of Verify mode.
A-Z NOT ALLOWED	You tried to enter an alphabetic character in a field that is coded to accept something other than an alphabetic character. Press CORR/RESET then rekey correctly.
BAD INDEX	You keyed a number or letter to request an item that does not exist. Ensure that you are pressing INDEX at the correct point, then key the correct index number or letter.
BATCH ABORTED***FATAL ERROR	Leave the system as it is and notify your supervisor.
BATCH ACTIVE	You tried to select a batch that is being processed at another terminal, or that has been otherwise restricted. Press MODE. Make sure this is the correct batch and, if it is, notify your supervisor.
BATCH COMPLETE	The batch you tried to select has been flagged as complete. You may select this batch in Find or Verify mode only.
BATCH DOES NOT EXIST	You keyed a batch identifier for which the system has no record. Make sure this is the correct batch identifier and job name.
CAN'T BACK INTO TRAIL VERIFY	You tried to display previously entered records, which are now being trail verified. Move forward to the latest record entered and continue entering records, or exit from ENTRY mode if the job is complete.
C=COMPLETE, L=LOCK, S=SIGN OFF, B=CHANGE BAT#	These are the four options of exit mode. Choose the appropriate one as explained . . . [review, "Work Termination or Signing Off"]. Remember option B is reserved for supervisors.
CHECK DIGIT FAILED	An item of entered data failed a test to which it was subjected by check digits. Press CORR/RESET. Make sure that the source document is correct and that you have keyed correctly.
CONFIGhhXwwNOT COMPATIBLE WITH HOST	The screen size of the remote terminal is not compatible with the host's system, where hh is the height (6, 12, or 24) and ww is the width of the screen (48 or 81). Call your Four-Phase Field Engineer.
DATA IV IS READY, TYPE YOUR ID.	The system is ready for you to sign on. Key your operator identifier.
DISC IS 100% FULL	The disc on which all your records are being stored has no space remaining. Finish the record you are working on and sign off.
DISC IS 95% FULL	The disc on which all your records are being stored has very little space remaining. Press CORR/RESET and continue keying until instructed to stop by your supervisor.
DISC [RD/WR] ERROR cnnnn@d	Do not press CORR/RESET or any other key. Leave the display as it is and notify your supervisor.
EMPTY *search information*	There are no records in the batch. Press MODE. Asterisks in this and subsequent messages represent the delimiting character used when creating search information.
END *search information*	The end of the current batch was reached. Press MODE.
0 ENTER PASSWORD	Enter the password given to you by your supervisor. The password itself will not appear on the screen, but the counter will show how many characters you have entered.
ERROR *search information*	Search information following **ERROR** was improperly formed. Press MODE. Review "Selecting Records" . . . [see "Finding Records Procedures"] then key your search information properly formed.

Message	Description
EXISTING RECORD	The record displayed is not a new record. Proceed as directed.
FIELD OVERFLOW	You tried to enter more characters in a field than allowed by the program level, or you failed to release the field with SKIP or REL. After pressing CORR/RESET, press SKIP to continue to the next field.
FORCED SIGNOFF BY HOST	The host supervisor has decided to sign off your remote terminal. If the message does not clear from the screen quickly, restart your terminal by using the power-on switch.
FOUND *search information*	A record matching your search information has been found and is displayed.
HIT 'MODE' KEY AND TYPE A SINGLE LETTER	You pressed the wrong key when the system was waiting for you to key a letter to select an option, or you pressed the question-mark key. Press MODE then key the correct letter.
HOST ASSIGNMENT LOST	You did not sign on (enter your operator ID) at your remote terminal within the time specified by the host supervisor when other remote terminals were waiting for a host assignment. Press the RESET key to clear the message, then press the MODE key again.
IMPROPERLY FORMED BATCH#	The batch identifier keyed to select a batch contains an embedded blank or a character other than a letter or digit or more than six characters. Correct the identifier, then retry.
IMPROPERLY FORMED INDSET NUMBER	An invalid index set identifier was specified. The index set number must be three digits (001-999). Correct the index set identifier, then retry.
IMPROPERLY FORMED JOBNAME OR BATCH#	You keyed a jobname or batch identifier incorrectly, or you omitted the comma between the jobname and the batch identifier. Press MODE then reselect the appropriate operating mode and rekey correctly.
INHIBITED KEY	You pressed a key not allowed at this time by the system. Press CORR/RESET.
INSUFFICIENT DISC SPACE	The disc is full. Notify your supervisor.
INTEGER 0-9 ONLY	You tried to enter something other than 0-9 in a field which accepts integers only. Press CORR/RESET, then rekey, making sure you key integers only.
INSUFFICIENT MEMORY FOR INDSET OPERATION	An index set cannot be searched or an index set record cannot be selected because no system blocks are available for that operation. Notify your supervisor.
INVALID OPTION	After selecting Exit mode (X), you pressed a key other than B, C, L, or S. Press MODE, then rekey correctly.
KEY IS > ALL THOSE IN INDEX SET	The specified key field has a value greater than any key field in the index set. Ensure that you keyed the key field correctly, then retry. If this message recurs, notify your supervisor.
LOG SAYS NO SCREEN PRINT ALLOWED	An attempt was made to print a screen, but mode L has been used to disable screen printing. Notify your supervisor.
LOST KEYSTROKE- SOFT HARD	Key strokes are being entered in the system faster than they can be processed. If **LOST KEYSTROKE—SOFT** displays, press CORR/RESET, then resume keying. If **LOST KEYSTROKE—HARD** displays, leave the display as it is and notify your supervisor.
MUST ENTER	In a field where an entry is required, you pressed SKIP or tried to bypass the field. Press CORR/RESET then key the correct data in this field.
MUST FILL	You attempted to skip a must-fill field by pressing SKIP, but you pressed it at the wrong place. To skip a must-fill field, press CORR/RESET, then press SKIP at the first column of that field, otherwise key the correct data in all columns of that field.
NO FORMAT DEFINED FOR PROGRAM LEVEL	You selected a program level that is not associated with this job. Press CORR/RESET, then rekey making sure that you are selecting the correct program level.
NO FORMAT FOR PROGRAM LEVEL	A record on disc is associated with a program level that does not exist for this job. Press CORR/RESET. Leave the system as it is and notify your supervisor.

Message	Description
NO LINE ACTIVITY FOR xxx SECONDS	Communications with the host have been lost or hardware has malfunctioned. Contact the host or redial.
NO MATCH-HIT A KEY TO SEE NEXT LARGER RECORD	The key field specified in Find mode does not exist. Ensure that you are keying the key field correctly, then retry. If this message recurs, notify your supervisor.
NO MORE RECORDS	The last record on the current batch has been reached in Entry mode. Proceed as desired.
NOR RECORDS TO VERIFY	Press MODE.
NOT VALID DATA	You tried to enter data that failed a validation test. Your source document may be incorrect or you may have miskeyed. If you are certain that your source document is correct, override the validation test by using the VALID key.
OPERATOR ALREADY ACTIVE	Someone else is already signed on using your operator identifier, or you miskeyed. Ensure that you are keying the correct identifier then rekey. If this message recurs, notify your supervisor.
OPERATOR UNKNOWN	Your operator identifier has not been properly registered in the system, or you miskeyed. Ensure that you are keying the correct identifier then rekey. If this message recurs, notify your supervisor.
PRESS MODE KEY TO USE TERMINAL	The host has completed the downline load to your remote terminal, and you are now ready to press the MODE key and wait for a host assignment.
RESTARTING RECORD	You moved the cursor back to the first column in the current record. Continue keying.
RESUME DATA ENTRY	The batch you have selected already contains records. You may enter additional records.
STARTING DATA ENTRY, NEW BATCH	The batch you selected has no records in it. You may begin entering records.
TYPE A, B, C, D, S, OR ? FOR DISPLAY DESIRED	These displays are for supervisory use only. Press MODE.
TYPE COMMAND	You failed to enter a jobname and batch identifier. Press MODE then rekey correctly.
TYPE E, F, J, L, S, T, V, X, OR ?	The system is waiting for you to select one of the DATA IV operating modes. If you press the question mark data key, the complete title of each mode will display. L, S, and T are reserved for supervisors.
TYPE JOBNAME, BATCH#	The system is waiting for you to select a job and batch identifier. Key the desired jobname, a comma, the batch identifier, then press SKIP.
TYPE PASSWORD-RESTRICTED JOB	The job that you have tried to select is protected by its own password. Obtain the password from your supervisor and key it.
TYPE SEARCH INFORMATION	Key the search information you wish to use for selecting records to be displayed then press SKIP.
TYPE S FOR SIGHT, K FOR KEY, OR R FOR RECONSTRUCT	The system is now in Verify mode. Key S, K, or R for the appropriate option.
TYPE 6-9 OR 0-5 (FOR 10-15)	Key a number 6 through 9 to select a program level 6 through 9 or key a number 0 through 5 to select a program level 10 through 15.
UNASSIGNED PROGRAM LEVEL	You pressed a PROG key that is not associated with this job. Press CORR/RESET, then rekey making sure that you are pressing the correct PROG key.
VERIFY COMPLETE NO MORE RECORDS	All of the records that needed verification in the current job have been verified.
VERIFY ERROR	You keyed data that disagrees with data already in the record that you are verifying. Make sure you are keying the correct data, then follow procedures under "Verifying Existing Records" . . . .
VERIFY THIS RECORD	A record needing to be verified has been found, is displayed, and awaits your verification.

Message	Description
VERIFY THIS RECORD OUT OF BALANCE xxxxxxxxxxxx	The current record is causing an out-of-balance condition. Numbers following BALANCE are the value of the batch balance accumulator. Verify this record, and when the batch is in balance, this message will disappear.
WAITING FOR HOST ASSIGNMENT	After pressing the MODE key at your remote terminal, you are now awaiting to be assigned by the host. Be sure to sign on (enter your operator ID) as soon as this message clears from the screen, to retain your assignment
WAITING FOR TERM nn TO RELEASE INDSET iii	An index set record encountered by the program level you are using has already been exclusively accessed at another terminal. This message will automatically disappear when exclusive access is released at terminal nn. When it does, continue data entry.
0-9 OR A-F ONLY	You entered non-hexadecimal data. Press CORR/RESET then rekey the field using the allowed characters.
iii (INDSET) DISK ERROR DURING RECORD SELECTION	There is an error in data being read from disc. Leave the display as it is then notify your supervisor.

Source: The above material is reproduced with permission from the DATA IV Operators Manual, document SIV/70-12-4, copyright © 1979 by Four-Phase Systems, Inc.

SECTION E
THE NIXDORF 80 SERIES

The NIXDORF 80 Series has developed from the early ENTREX equipment. In December, 1977 ENTREX merged with NCI to form the present NIXDORF Computer Corporation. A recent study[4] shows the NIXDORF 480 to be the most widely used of the 80 Series product line. This equipment is found frequently in service bureaus and in banks.

A summary of the NIXDORF 80 Series is shown below:

System	Max. Number of Terminals	Lines/Screen	Characters/Display
280	16	7	360
380	22	7	360
480	32	10	480
480 (ADEX)	32	10/22	480/1920

All systems can include a card reader, magnetic tapes, printers, and I/O devices. All systems provide for 10 programs or formats per job. ADEX is an acronym for advanced data entry executive.

For all modes, a choice of the keypunch or typewriter style keyboards is offered, but the Model 280 will not function with mixed styles. Each keystation consists of a display screen with a rectangular cursor and a movable keyboard. The keyboard is attached to the CRT by a short cable.

THE STATUS LINE Figure 6.12 shows the status line arrangement for the 80 Series. The status line is the top line on the screen and has the following fields:

1. *The Mode of Operation.* Possible modes are: ENTRY, VERIFY, VALIDATE, UPDATE, and EXAMINE.

[4]*Data Entry Awareness Report* (Management Information Corporation), Vo. VII, No. 12 (December 1979), page 13.

2. *Automatic Function.* AUTO means the automatic functions of duplicating, skipping, emitting, incrementing, and record advancing are ON. BLANK means they are OFF.
3. *Input Format Number.* This is the program-level number being used. It is displayed as **PGM-O** to **PGM-9**.
4. *Record Count.* This is the record number displayed as **REC-nnn** where **nnn** is a three-digit number.
5. *Field Count.* This field gives the number of the field in the record at which the cursor is positioned. It is given in the form **FLD-nnnn** where **nnnn** is a four-digit number.

MESSAGE LINE

The message line appears on the second line of the screen. There are three types of messages:

1. Error messages describing error conditions such as **CHECK DIGIT ERROR**. (A high pitched tone alerts the operator.)
2. Operator action instructions such as **SELECT PGM#**.
3. Reports on certain conditions such as **BATCH OUT OF BALANCE**.

MODES

The *mode* of the machine determines the operations the machine will perform. The NIXDORF 80 Series modes are as follows:

Mode	Function
ENTRY	Used to enter data in a record.
VERIFY	Used to check data previously entered with data on the source document. Corrections are made if necessary.
VALIDATE	Used to create batch balances and perform range checks and value table lookups when data has been loaded from tape rather then keyed. This mode is rarely used.
UPDATE	Allows the operator to update or change data.
EXAMINE	Used to visually examine records in a batch. This is a protected mode.

THE NIXDORF 80 SERIES KEYBOARD

Figure 6.8 shows the NIXDORF 80 Series keypunch style keyboard. The keyboard has two types of keys.

1. Control or function keys. These are red and black in color.
2. Data keys: the numeric keys are white, and the remaining keys blue.

The home keys (where the fingers rest in the beginning position) have deeper finger-depression surfaces for easy location. The REL (release) key is slightly higher than the other keys to make it easier to locate.

To turn on the keystation power rotate the knob on the lower right side of the CRT clockwise. This knob also adjusts the volume of the error tone.

You may adjust the brightness of the screen by rotating the knob on the lower left side of the CRT.

You should have made a list of the keys on your keyboard earlier in this unit.

BEGINNING WORK

Before the operator starts work for the day, the supervisor must bring the system up (supply power). When the system is ready, the **OPERATOR HELP LIST** shown in Figure 6.16 is shown on the screen.

FIGURE 6.16
Operator help list display.

```
                    OPERATOR HELP LIST
        A   START STANDARD JOB      F   UPDATE A BATCH
        B   START A BATCH           G   VALIDATE A BATCH
        C   RESUME A BATCH
        D   VERIFY A BATCH          I   OPERATOR LOG-IN
        E   EXAMINE A BATCH         J   SUPERVISOR MODE
                       SELECTION ☐
```

If the terminal is turned off during the day and then turned back on, follow the work initiation steps.

Work Initiation or Signing ON

After the power to the keystation is turned on by the POWER ON switch:

1. Press the HELP key to display the OPERATOR HELP LIST. Figure 6.16 shows how it will appear.
2. Key in the letter I for OPERATOR LOG-IN.
3. The prompt **ENTER OPERATOR ID** _____ will appear. Key in the operator identification (ID) that has been assigned to you (one to four characters).
4. Press the REL key. The OPERATOR HELP LIST will be redisplayed on the screen.

Starting a Job

1. Press the HELP key.
2. Key in the appropriate code: A, B, C, D, E, F, G. (You will not be using the SUPERVISOR mode.)
3. If the prompt **NO OPERATOR LOGGED IN** appears, perform the work initiation.
4. Enter the STANDARD JOB NAME (up to seven characters).
5. Enter the BATCH NAME (up to ten characters).
6. Press the REL key.

Starting a Job or Batch

Case	Action
1. Job or batch	Press the HELP key.
2. Start a job	a. Key the letter A. b. When the prompt appears, enter standard job name (up to 8 characters). c. Enter the batch name (up to 10 characters). d. Press the REL key.
3. Start a batch	a. Key the letter B. b. When the prompt appears, enter the batch name (up to 10 characters). c. Press the REL key. d. Enter the format names and desired linkage as given to you by your instructor or supervisor. e. With the 380/480, enter the batch and record end edit names to you by your instructor or supervisor.

Terminating a Batch

1. Press the HELP key. Figure 6.17 shows the BATCH HELP LIST that will be displayed.
2. Press the letter A (for terminate).
3. If the BATCH LOG needs to be displayed:
   a. Press the REL key.
   b. Key the letter A (for DISPLAY BATCH LOG).
   c. Press the REL key.

Interrupting a Batch

Interrupting a batch is identical to terminating a batch except that batch balancing is not performed. To interrupt a batch:

1. Press the HELP key. FIGURE 6.17 shows the BATCH HELP LIST that will be displayed.
2. Key the letter B (for INTERRUPT).
3. Press the REL key.

Resuming a Batch

1. Press the HELP key. FIGURE 6.17 shows the BATCH HELP LIST that will be displayed.
2. Press the letter C (for DISPLAY A BATCH)
3. When the prompt **BATCH NAME** is displayed, enter the batch name.
4. When the REL key is depressed, the operator resumes work and keys the next record.

ERRORS AND GENERAL PROCEDURES

1.

To Backspace	Action
One character	Depress the ← key.
Several characters	Hold down the ← key.
By fields	Hold down the FLD key and depress the ← key once for each field to be backspaced.
By records	Hold down the RCD key and depress the ← key once for each record to be backspaced.

Note that when the RCD ← key is used, the AUTO functions are automatically turned OFF and should be activated again.

```
                                        SEARCH OPERATIONS
        A   TERMINATE                G   ERROR FLAG
        B   INTERRUPT                H   RECORD NUMBER
        C   DISPLAY BATCH LOG        I   FIELD CONTENT
        D   DISPLAY BATCH PAGE       J   CHAR SEQUENCE
        E   RETURN TO DATA           K   REPEAT
        F   FLAG ERROR
                          SELECTION □
```

FIGURE 6.17
Batch help list display.

PART 2   DATA ENTRY EQUIPMENT

2.

To Space Forward	Action
One character	Depress the → key.
Several characters	Hold down the → key.
By fields	Hold down the FLD key and depress the → key once for each field to be spaced forward.
By records	Hold down the RCD key and press the → key once for each record to be bypassed.

Note that the cursor cannot be moved forward past the last character entered in a record.

3. To return to the original position after backspacing (LOCATION RETURN), press the LOC RET key. The LOC RET key returns the cursor to the end of the batch (or to the point of the last keying). The LOC RET key cannot be used in the EXAMINE mode; use the forward spacing feature instead.

4. Fields can be programmed to be TAB fields (similar to the TAB key on the typewriter). This allows a skip over several fields not always used. The FIELD RELEASE key should be used to skip over one field. The TAB procedure is:
   a. Depress the TAB key.
   b. The cursor will skip to the beginning of the next "tab" field in the record. If none exists, the cursor will stop in the last record position.

5. Errors in characters, fields, or records can be corrected.
   a. To *correct characters* (example: keyed 5 instead of D):
      (1) Position the cursor on the character to be corrected.
      (2) Press the COR (correct) key.
      (3) Key the desired character.
   b. To *correct a field or record*:
      (1) Position the cursor on the *first* character to be corrected in the field or record.
      (2) Hold down the FLD or REC key and press the COR key.
      (3) Key the desired characters.
      (4) Press the LOC RET key.

Note that using the REL or FIELD RELEASE keys will delete the remaining data in the field or record if the REL key is then depressed. Therefore, the LOC RET key should be used.

Operator Log-Out

1. Press the HELP key. Figure 6.16 shows the OPERATOR HELP LIST that will be displayed.
2. Press the letter I (for OPERATOR LOG-IN).
3. When the system requests the OPERATOR ID, press the FIELD RELEASE key.
4. When the REL key is depressed, the operator is logged out, and the OPERATOR HELP LIST will be displayed.

Entering Data

1. Perform the work initiation or sign on procedures if necessary.
2. Perform the starting-a-job procedure.

3. Select the appropriate program level if necessary. Normally the program will be automatically selected. To select a program manually, hold down the PGM key and key in the program number.
4. When the first prompt appears, begin keying the data.
5. *Validation errors* may occur. Examples of validation errors would be a check digit is wrong or data keyed in is out of range. Also, the wrong type of data might be keyed in for a programmed field (*example*: programmed numeric and an X is keyed in).

Error Recovery

Three things happen when a validation error occurs:

1. An error tone alerts the operator.
2. An error message appears on the message line of the screen.
3. An error light appears in the upper left-hand corner of the keyboard.

The recovery procedure is:

1. Press the RESET key.
2. Position the cursor on the character or first position of the field to be corrected.
3. Rekey the character or field.
4. Press the LOC RET or REL key remembering that REL will blank out what remains in the field.

Bypassing a Field

If the source document data is in error—the correction information is not known or you cannot read the data, you can bypass the field and flag it as in error. The field can be corrected later.

The BYPASS procedure is as follows:

1. Press the RESET key.
2. Hold down the RCD key and press the letter E.

The last position of the field is flagged (#) and the cursor is released to the first position of the next field.

If a character in a field is illegible or missing, and you wish to flag that particular character; press the RCD key and the letter F.

Laboratory Exercises

Your instructor will assign exercises using the above sections.

FINDING RECORDS FOR MODIFICATION

One often needs to select or find a record to change it, delete it, or insert a record or records before it. Searches can be made in any mode.

The BATCH HELP LIST in Figure 6.17, shows that there are five types of search operations:

1. Search for the next flagged field (G search operation).
2. Search by record number (search for the fifth record, for example). This is an H operation.
3. Search for a record with a particular field content. This is the I search operation. The search key cannot cross a field boundary.
4. Search by a sequential character sequence. This is the J search operation. This sequence can cross a field boundary.

5. Repeat the previous search (K search operation.)

To perform a search:

1. If necessary, perform the work initiation or sign-on procedure.
2. Perform the starting-a-job procedure, if necessary.
3. Press the HELP key to display the BATCH HELP LIST.
4. Key in the particular types of search operation you desire (G, H, I, J, K).
5. Search operation steps:

Type	Action
G ERROR FLAG	a. Position the cursor on the first or next error flag in the batch. b. After correction, continue by pressing the letter G.[5]
H RECORD NO. (operates backwards and forwards	a. Key in the number of the desired record. b. Press FIELD RELEASE key. The search will begin with the record number changing during the search.
I FIELD CONTENT (operates in forward direction only)	a. Key in the search field using * for all nonsignificant positions and terminate with $\neq$. For example, for all phone numbers with area code 817, the search field or key would be 817 *******$\neq$. The $\neq$ is the shifted T. b. Press the FIELD RELEASE key. c. Press the REL key. The search will begin.
J CHARACTER SEQUENCE (operates in forward direction only)	a. Key in the sequential character sequence using * in nonsignificant positions. The string may be part or all of a field. b. Press the FIELD RELEASE key. c. Press the REL key. The search will begin.
R REPEAT	Hold down the RCD key and key the letter R if not using the BATCH HELP LIST. (This is the same as depressing the HELP key and keying the letter K.)

[5]To search for flags without the BATCH HELP LIST, RCD and the letter S can be used.

Updating or Correcting a Record—All Modes

1. Search to the desired record.
2. To correct a character use the GENERAL PROCEDURES FOR CORRECTING ERRORS previously described.
3. To insert a character:
   a. Place the cursor at the desired position for character insertion.
   b. Depress the INS key.
   c. Depress the COR key unless in ENTRY mode.
   d. Key in the character to be inserted. The system shifts all characters after the insertion to the right.

UNIT 6   KEY-TO-DISK DEVICES

4. To delete a character:
   a. Place the cursor at the position of the character you desire to delete.
   b. Depress the DEL key.
   c. The character will be deleted and all other characters will be shifted to the left.

Inserting a Record—All Modes

1. Search for the record that will *follow* the insertion.
2. Hold down the RCD key and press the INS key. The message **SELECT PGM #** will be displayed on the screen.
3. Hold down the PGM key and key the program number for the record to be inserted. This causes a blank record to be inserted.
4. Key in the data for the new record.

Deleting a Record

1. Search for the record to be deleted.
2. Hold down the RCD key and press the DEL key.

Laboratory Exercises

Your intructor will assign exercises in finding, adding, deleting, and changing records.

VERIFYING

The three most commonly used verify modes on the NIXDORF 80 Series and the mode codes are:

1. K—KEY VERIFY
   The cursor stops on the field to be rekeyed. If the data being entered does not agree with what has been keyed, the error tone sounds and processing stops.
2. S—SCAN OR SKIP VERIFY
   The cursor passes over a field unless it is flagged as in error. The error field is displayed with the cursor positioned on the error flag. Any characters can then be keyed. If the FIELD RELEASE key is pressed, the field is bypassed.
3. C—CONDITIONAL VERIFY
   The method of verification is used on fields which are batch balanced. If the batch is out of balance, then the C mode works as if key verification were taking place. The corrected balance must be keyed. If the batch is in balance, then the system functions as in scan verification.

Note that if batch balancing or scan verifying is taking place, then trail verifying is not possible.

The steps necessary to key verify are:

1. Press the HELP key. The OPERATOR HELP LIST will be displayed.
2. Key the letter D (for VERIFY A BATCH).
3. When the prompt BATCH NAME appears, enter the batch name (up to 10 characters).
4. If the field is programmed to be verified:
   (a) If it is correct, the value in the field will be displayed and the cursor will skip over the field.
   (b) If it is not correct, the cursor will stop on the field and an error message **VERIFY COMPARE ERROR** will be displayed.

5. If the field is incorrect, and there is a verify error:
   (a) Depress the RESET key.
   (b) Depress the COR key and key the correct value. This corrects only one character.
   (c) To correct the entire field, hold down the FLD key and depress the COR key. Then rekey the entire field.
6. When the entire batch has been verified, the message **END OF DATA** will be displayed.
7. Press the RESET key.
8. Press the HELP key which will cause the BATCH HELP LIST shown in Figure 6.17 to be displayed.
9. Key the letter A (for terminate job).

NIXDORF 80 SERIES GLOSSARY OF OPERATOR ERROR MESSAGES

The following operator error messages are generated by the 80 Series System:

ACTIVE VALUE TABLE An attempt has been made to use or modify a batch that has been assigned as a value table.

ASCENDENCY ERROR Data keyed in this field is either not equal to or less than the corresponding field of the previous record.

ATTEMPT TO MODIFY 'IN PROCESS' ENTRY This message is displayed when trying to access a batch while it is being accessed by the supervisor.

BATCH ALREADY ACTIVE IN ENTRY An attempt is being made to start a batch that has already been started in Entry Mode.

BATCH NAME PROTECTION ERROR This batch name does not conform to the Batch Name Protection "security" option under standard job control.

BATCH OUT OF BALANCE The detail fields totaled in the accumulator do not zero balance with the batch total field.

BATCH SORT FILE UNABLE TO RESUME An attempt is being made to access a sorted file.

CHECK DIGIT ERROR A number has been entered that does not agree with the check digit algorithm described in the input format, or a check digit algorithm has been assigned but not defined.

DISK 98% FULL The User portion of disk is about to be filled to capacity (PLEASE TAKE ACTION).

DISK 99% FULL Same as DISK 98% FULL.

DISK IS FULL The User portion of disk is completely filled. STOP ALL OPERATIONS. The only corrective action is to cold-start the most recent system save, and rekey all records since that time. [Your supervisor will do this.]

END OF DATA The operator has attempted to position the cursor beyond the last position of keyed data in a batch. Position cursor at last data character and continue keying.

FIELD BOUNDARY EXCEEDED, HIT FIELD REL This field has been specified with a boundary check and the operator has exceeded the number of characters allowed in the field.

FIELD COMPLETION MANDATORY The field has been defined as a must-complete field and the operator has attempted to field release without entering data in all positions.

FIELD ENTRY MANDATORY At least the first character must be entered in this field.

FIELD TOO SHORT TO DUP An attempt is being made to duplicate a field from the prior record that is shorter than the corresponding field in the current record.

HIT REL TO PROCEED; OTHERWISE HIT HELP Depressing the REL key will allow continued operation. Depressing HELP will stop the operation, and the last HELP list displayed by the system will be redisplayed.

ID ALREADY LOGGED IN The operator is currently logged in at another terminal. Either log out of previous terminal or check with supervisor.

INCORRECT PGM LINKAGE Displayed when starting a batch and entering format linkage to a non-existent PGM number.

INPUT AND BATCH RECORDS NOT EQUAL The system attempts to insert data from an Indexed Value Table into the current data field. However, the value table field requires too many character positions to fit into the current field and, consequently, the rightmost character positions are deleted.

INVALID KEYSTROKE The operator has depressed a function key while keying in a data field.

INVALID OVERSIGN SEQUENCE The numeric character to be oversigned has been depressed before the oversign key. Key oversign first, followed by the numeric character.

KEYBOARD OVERFLOW This is usually a temporary situation resulting from tags being too long, value tables being too long, or the use of too many auto fuctions. Depress RESET, and continue keying—if situation persists, notify supervisor.

KEYSTATION ERROR—NOTIFY SUPERVISOR The supervisor should attempt to document the operations being performed at that terminal (including standard job and batch name) and submit documentation and the system save to the local Customer Support Representative as soon as possible.

NAME ALREADY EXISTS OR IS INVALID The batch or library name being entered is an existing name or has been entered incorrectly.

NAME NOT FOUND IN LIBRARY The format or batch name keyed is not an existing entry in the Library. Check spelling and rekey.

NO CORRESPONDING FIELD Occurs when trying to duplicate or increment from a field nonexistent in the previous record. Also occurs when the system attempts a value table lookup using the Indexed Value Table feature and cannot find data corresponding to the data that has been keyed.

NO DATA IN BATCH An "empty" batch has been entered and terminated. This error message occurs when this "empty" batch is examined, verified, or resumed.

NO INPUT FORMATS SPECIFIED Standard job or batch operations are being attempted and no formats have been specified.

NON-EXISTENT PGM SELECTED The operator has attempted to request a program that is not defined in the standard job or batch linkages.

NON-NUMERIC CHARACTER REQUIRED The field being keyed has been defined as an alpha-only field, and the operator has attempted to enter a 0 through 9 or oversign.

NO OPERATOR LOGGED IN The operator has not logged in at this terminal; either have operator log-in or hit RESET and RELEASE to continue operation.

NO PREVIOUS RECORD Occurs in the first record of a batch when an auto dup option is used. Depress the AUTO key and key this data.

NUMERIC CHARACTER REQUIRED The field being keyed has been defined as a numeric-only field, and the operator has attempted to enter a character other than a 0 through 9, an oversign, or a numeric-only exception.

PGM SELECTION ONLY AT END OF DATA The cursor must be positioned at the end of data in the current record. To select a new program level, depress the LOC RET key and try again.

RANGE CHECK ERROR The data keyed does not agree with the range check boundaries defined for this field.

SELECT PGM # System requires the input program level number before keying record insertion. Hold down PGM key and select PGM number.

UNABLE TO INSERT Occurs when two operators are in the same batch and one operator attempts to insert a record. The batch should be interrupted to allow the record insert function to be performed.

VALUE TABLE ERROR A value has been keyed that does not agree with a value in the value table associated with that field.

VERIFY COMPARE ERROR The data keyed by the verify operator does not match the data keyed by the entry operator. Verify operator should attempt to enter the character again or correct the character.

Source: Reprinted by permission of NIXDORF Computer Corporation, Waltham, Massachusetts, U.S.A. The above material is reproduced with permission from the *NIXDORF Operator Quick-Reference Guide*, the "80 Series," Order Number SU-6801, copyright © January 1978 by NIXDORF COMPUTER.

SECTION F
ADDITIONAL TYPES OF EQUIPMENT

Other types of key-to-disk equipment that are used widely in industry are:

1. DATA 100 KEYBATCH now produced by NORTHERN TELECOM as a Model 74.
2. INFOREX models 1301, 1302, and 1303.
3. CMC models 3, 5, 12, and 20 now produced by PERTEC Computer Corporation (PCC).

There are many other key-to-disk manufacturers such as: CONSOLIDATED COMPUTER KEY EDIT, CUMMINS–ALLISON, GCS, GTE, HONEYWELL, IBM, LOCKHEED, LOGIC, MOHAWK, and RAYTHEON.

IBM usually has very good equipment, but its IBM 3790 system has problems despite recent improvements. Some of the problems are:

1. The system must be connected to an IBM 370 computer with virtual storage. Thus, one is limited to using it with a particular type of host computer.
2. Data transmission may slow down response time on the display station.
3. The cost with necessary attachments is high in comparison to the costs of other products.

IBM introduced the IBM Series/1 in 1976, but it also has problems in that it must be purchased. Also the diskette backup is not very satisfactory.

INFOREX equipment has been very popular in the past. INFOREX was one of the first key-to-disk equipment manufacturers. Recently they have introduced two new models, the INFOREX 3100 and 3200. The 3100 model is designed for data entry at a centralized location, whereas the 3200 may also be used for decentralized data entry.

PERTEC Computer Corporation has produced some popular CMC systems. The first of their series were the 3, 4, 7, and 9s. They next introduced the XL40 which can be used for distributed data entry. This model has indexed file capabilities, disk and tape units, up to 16 keystations, 32 possible program levels, and a COBOL-type programming language. It also will accommodate card-reader and printer I/O devices and has data communication possibilities.

PERTEC's 1800 model is designed for high production data entry. It can accommodate up to 64 keystations. It can be programmed with a COBOL-type language (called KOBOL) or RPGII and can deal with indexed files. It also will accommodate disk or tape, printers, and card reader I/O devices and has data communications capabilities.

CUMMINS-ALLISON has a family of distributed processing key/disk systems. The 2400 and 3400 support up to 8 keystations, the 4400 supports up to 24 keystations, and the 5400 supports up to 32 stations. This system uses a special programming language.

NORTHERN TELECOM purchased SYCOR's data entry equipment. NORTHERN TELECOM is a Canadian based firm. Their MODEL 74 key/disk can have up to 16 keystations. With a second processor up to 16 more keystations can be added. Printers, card readers, and tapes can be attached.

SUMMARY

In summary, key-to-disk equipment has the following advantages:

1. It is one of the fastest types of keying device with productivity increasing from 25 percent to 50 percent.
2. Several keyboards can share disk, tape, and printer units thus conserving costs on peripherial equipment.
3. Trail verifying is often possible.
4. The minicomputer increases the variety of edit and validate programs possible.
5. Card handling and storage can be eliminated.
6. It operates very quietly.
7. It is good for high volume jobs and jobs that require a great deal of editing.

Disadvantages of key-to-disk equipment are:

1. The expense is higher than with card data entry equipment and stand-alone key-to-diskette equipment.
2. Failure of the minicomputer causes all the keystations to be out of operation.

3. There are some problems involved in data communication transmission of data, but many of these are being solved.
4. It is poor for low volume and modest editing requirements.
5. It is much more difficult to program than the buffered keypunches and key-to-diskette equipment.

STUDY GUIDE

Answer these questions in your book. If asked to do so, tear out the pages and hand them to your instructor. If you do not have a key-to-disk system, answer the questions using the system identified by your instructor. The system will be referred to as "your device."

1. List two conditions under which key-to-disk equipment would be helpful in a data entry department.

    (1) _____

    (2) _____

2. List four basic parts of key-to-disk equipment.

    (1) _____

    (2) _____

    (3) _____

    (4) _____

3. List two methods of transmitting keyed data from key-to-disk devices to the host computer.

    (1) _____

    (2) _____

4. List two types of codes used on magnetic tape.

    (1) _____

    (2) _____

5. Give the meaning of the following acronyms:

    (1) TM _____

    (2) BOT _____

    (3) EOT _____

    (4) DASD _____

    (5) BPI _____

    (6) KB _____

    (7) VTOC _____

    (8) BCD _____

(9) DMA _____

(10) EBCDIC _____

(11) ASCII _____

(12) CRT _____

(13) IBG _____

(14) IRG _____

6. List the names of the key or keys on your key-to-disk keyboard (or that selected by your instructor) that perform the following functions:

_____ (1) Unlocks the keyboard after an error.

_____ (2) Causes an action to be repeated.

_____ (3) Used to select the program level.

_____ (4) Used to display information or a menu on the screen.

_____ (5) Used to begin a command.

_____ (6) Used to return the cursor to the beginning of a field.

_____ (7) Used to copy information from a previous record.

_____ (8) Used to key in the character N.

_____ (9) Used to erase the character N just keyed.

_____ (10) Used to delete a record.

_____ (11) Used in programmed numeric shift to key the letter N.

_____ (12) Used to insert a record.

_____ (13) Used to move the cursor from field 1 to field 3 of a keyed record.

_____ (14) Used to move the cursor from character position 1 to character position 3 of a keyed record.

_____ (15) Used to return the cursor to the beginning of a record.

_____ (16) Used to pass over and flag an invalid data field.

_____ (17) Used in verifying to correct an entire field.

_____ (18) Used in a name field to move the cursor to the next keyed field when the name is shorter than the field length.

_____ (19) Used in an amount field (zero-filled) to move the cursor to the next keyed field when the significant digits are less than the field length.

7. List two types of verification.

(1) _____

(2) _____

8. Match the following:
   (Only one answer is necessary and a letter may be reused.)

   ____ (1) The first label on a disk
   ____ (2) 1600 BPI
   ____ (3) Marks the end of a file of data
   ____ (4) Point where writing may begin on a tape
   ____ (5) An example of EBCDIC code
   ____ (6) Transfer rate
   ____ (7) Writing a volume label on a tape or disk
   ____ (8) Byte
   ____ (9) To check the correctness of data by rekeying
   ____ (10) Shows the next position to be keyed
   ____ (11) A case of odd parity
   ____ (12) An example of BCD code
   ____ (13) An example of even parity
   ____ (14) An example of a frame
   ____ (15) A blank space on tape between records
   ____ (16) A list of the files of data on a tape or disk
   ____ (17) The **A** key on the keyboard
   ____ (18) The DUP key on the keyboard
   ____ (19) A tape written in EBCDIC
   ____ (20) An internal label
   ____ (21) Tape channel
   ____ (22) Subdivided into sectors
   ____ (23) Block
   ____ (24) A group of records
   ____ (25) Software
   ____ (26) Processor for key-to-disk output
   ____ (27) A set of instructions to a computer
   ____ (28) Options listed on a display screen

   a. EOT Marker
   b. Density
   c. 0 1100 0010 or the character B.
   d. Prompt
   e. Nibble
   f. Default value
   g. 1 11 0001 or the character A
   h. Load point
   i. Mode
   j. 60 KB
   k. Job
   l. VTOC
   m. IBG
   n. Function key
   o. Data key
   p. Nine-track tape
   q. Volume label
   r. Sequential processing
   s. Header label
   t. Trailer label
   u. Track
   v. Initialization
   w. Data check
   x. Logical record
   y. Status line
   z. Cursor
   aa. Physical record
   bb. Batch
   cc. Program
   dd. Menu
   ee. Host computer
   ff. Minicomputer
   gg. Verify

9. Define:

   (1) An invalid batch _____
   _____
   _____

   (2) An uncorrectable error _____
   _____
   _____

   (3) Batch balancing _____
   _____
   _____

   (4) Trail verifying _____
   _____
   _____

10. Imagine that you have attempted to key the letter A in a programmed numeric field. List the things that happen on your device and explain how you recover.

    (1) _____
    (2) _____
    (3) _____
    Recovering actions: _____
    _____

11. List the steps necessary on your device to close a batch in ENTRY mode.

    (1) _____
    (2) _____
    (3) _____
    (4) _____

12. Imagine that a batch has not been completed and it is time to go home for the day. List the steps necessary to stop work on your device.

    (1) _____
    (2) _____
    (3) _____
    (4) _____

13. Name the modes on your device that should be used for the following operations:

    _____ (1) Keying in records for the first time.
    _____ (2) Checking the accuracy of the original keying.
    _____ (3) Inserting a record.

UNIT 6 KEY-TO-DISK DEVICES

_____ (4) Keying additional data into records already on disk.

_____ (5) Deleting a record.

14. List the steps necessary to turn on the keystation and initiate or start a keying job. The name of the job is PAYROLL.

   (1) _____
   (2) _____
   (3) _____
   (4) _____
   (5) _____
   (6) _____
   (7) _____
   (8) _____
   (9) _____

15. List three methods of protecting data on tape or disk from accidental destruction or to prevent access by unauthorized personnel.

   (1) _____
   (2) _____
   (3) _____

UNIT 7
TERMINALS

AFTER READING THIS UNIT YOU WILL KNOW:

What the advantages of using terminals are.
What the disadvantages of using terminals are.
What applications are frequently used on terminals.
What the external features and indicators of your terminal are.
What the function keys on your terminal are.
How data is entered on your terminal.
What the cursor positioning keys on your terminal are.
How data is corrected.
How characters are added and deleted.

What the following terms mean:

CRT
Cursor
Cursor wrap
Data keys
Dumb terminal
Formatted display
Function keys
Input field
Intelligent terminal
Light pen
Prompt
Protected data
RJE
Smart terminal
Terminal
Unformatted display
Wand

SECTION A
INTRODUCTION

In Unit 6, on key-to-disk devices, it was seen that with the use of a shared processor or minicomputer much more editing and validation of data was possible before the data was sent to the host computer for final processing. Data could be transmitted (1) through the use of magnetic tape or (2) through data communications.

Therefore the question arises: Why not send the data directly to the host computer as it is being keyed and have the host computer do the editing and checking? This can be done by the use of interactive remote terminals. A *terminal* is simply an I/O device for the computer. Data may be entered or received through it. Most terminals have a keyboard and a display screen.

There are three disadvantages to this method:

1. If the host computer is "down" (not operating properly and in need of repair), no data may be entered.
2. By using the host computer to do the editing and validation, computer time is being used that could be devoted to other types of processing.

3. Host computer time is much more expensive than rental or lease of other data entry devices, even key-to-disk devices.
4. Studies have shown that productivity (keystrokes per hour) is lower on terminals than on other types of data entry devices.[1]

However, despite these disadvantages, terminals are being widely used to enter data and computer programs directly to the host computer.

There are a tremendous number of terminal manufacturers. Terminals are also called *CRTs* (Cathode Ray Tubes) or *RJEs* (Remote Job Entry). Terminals are classified in one of three ways:

1. *Dumb terminals* are terminals that cannot be programmed or instructed. All they can do is send and receive data to and from the host computer.
2. *Smart terminals* can be programmed by the manufacturer to meet the special needs of the user.
3. *Intelligent terminals* can be programmed by the user.

Dumb terminals are the cheapest with prices less than $1000. Intelligent terminals are the most expensive with prices often over $25,000. Intelligent terminals are found more frequently in interactive situations such as departments dealing with order entry and material control.

Terminals can be used in many ways. A company can have:

1. One or more than one terminal on the site of the host computer, on-line.
2. A data communications network with terminals on-line to the host computer using phone lines.
3. A distributed data processing operation where terminals may be connected to a minicomputer and may also report to a host computer through data communications. (This was discussed in the key-to-disk unit.)

The interactive remote terminal has four components:

1. A keyboard located at a distance from the host computer.
2. A data communications line to transfer the data between the terminal and the host computer.
3. The host computer which receives and processes the data.
4. A CRT (in the old days a typewriter) located with the keyboard which receives output from the host computer.

A fifth element, a printer at the remote site, is often provided to print hard copies or printed reports.

The keyboards, as with the key-to-disk devices, may be keypunch or typewriter styles. Normally data is entered by the keyboard. However, on some terminals such as the IBM 3278 Display Station, shown in Figure 7.1, data may be entered by the use of a *light pen*. The pen is used to select an entry in a list of items displayed on the screen. This unit will not be concerned with this type of data entry.

Some manufacturers, such as MSI Data Corporation, specialize in portable data terminals. These are battery powered terminals and are used for special applications. They are not much larger than hand-held calculators and can easily be moved around.

Data may also be entered on some terminals by the use of a *wand*. A wand is a hand-held device that reads magnetically encoded information on labels, cards, badges, and similar material.

[1]DATAPRO 1977 User Survey, Report No. 70D-010-71, User Ratings of Key Entry Equipment, Table 3.

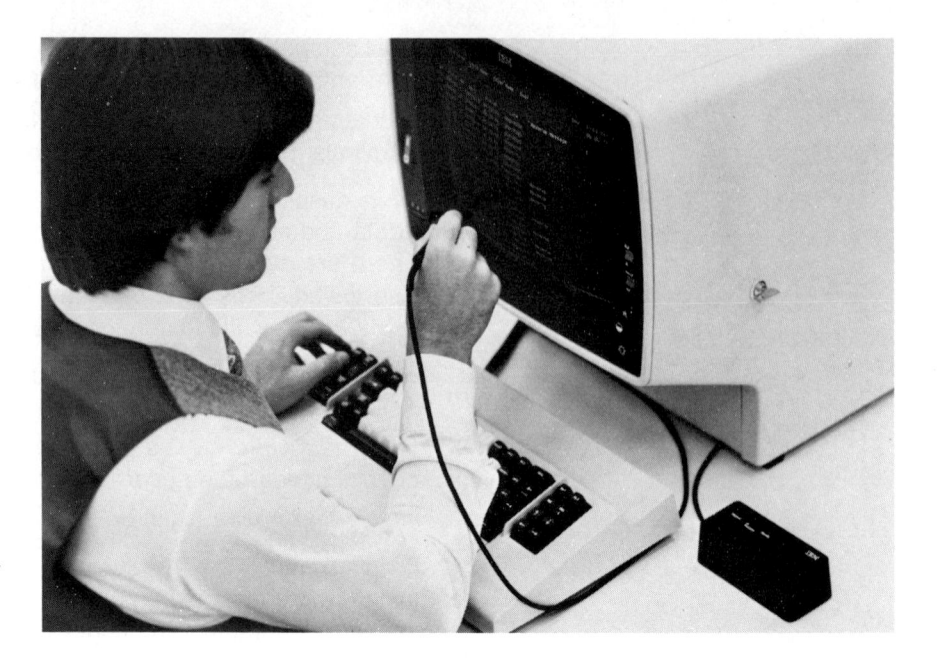

FIGURE 7.1
The IBM 3278 display station with selector light pen, magnetic slot reader, and security keylock features (Courtesy of IBM Corporation).

Terminals are used for many applications, such as:

1. *Data entry* or entering data.
2. *Inquiry*—the process of obtaining information. Updating may follow.
3. *Interactive computer/program development.* This is used for program development, and testing and updating files of data at remote terminals.
4. *Computer operator's console.* This is used to give directions to the host computer.

This unit will mainly be concerned with the first application above, data entry.

SECTION B
THE IBM 3270
INFORMATION DISPLAY SYSTEM

The IBM 3270 display stations (terminals) include models having display screen sizes varying from 480 to 3440 characters per screen. This unit is concerned with the 3270 display stations used for data entry. These are the 3275 and the 3277 display stations. There are three basic types, shown in Figure 7.2. Although screen sizes differ, the operations are similar. There are four types of keyboards available:

1. the typewriter keyboard.
2. the data entry keyboard.
3. the data entry-keypunch keyboard.
4. the operator console keyboard.

This unit will deal with the data entry-keypunch style keyboard shown in Figure 7.3.

The IBM 3275 keystation controls and indicators are shown in Figure 7.4. There are 8 lights. The labels and the functions of these lights depend upon the model.

PART 2 DATA ENTRY EQUIPMENT

FIGURE 7.2
The IBM 3275 and 3277 display stations (Courtesy of IBM Corporation).

UNIT 7 TERMINALS

FIGURE 7.2 *(Continued)*

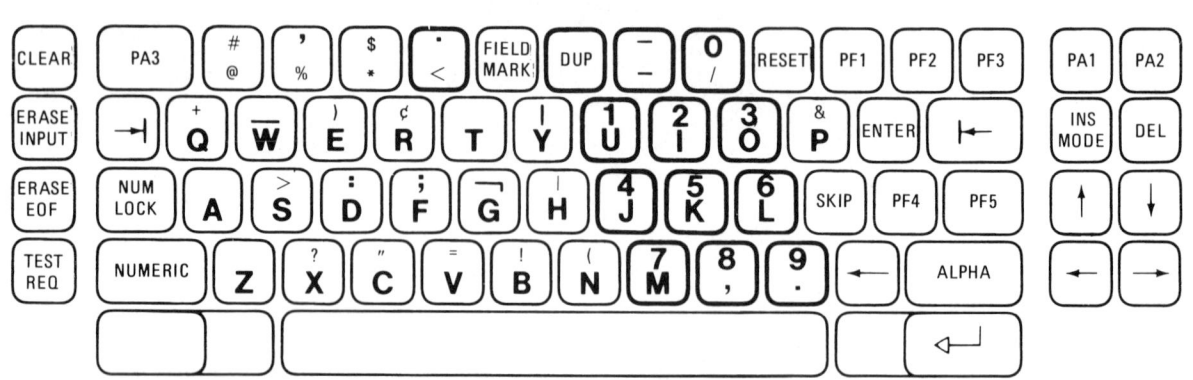

FIGURE 7.3
The IBM 3275 and 3277 data entry keypunch keyboard (Courtesy of IBM Corporation).

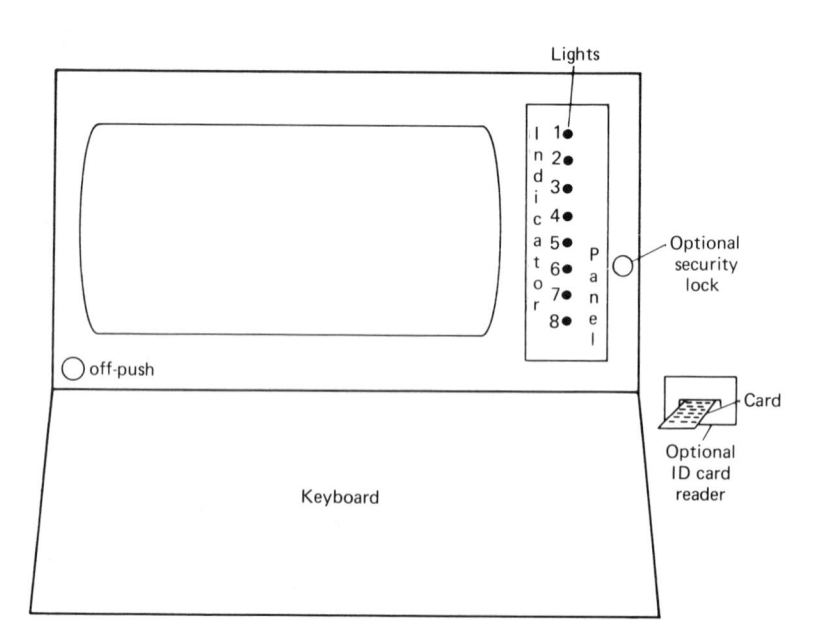

FIGURE 7.4
IBM 3275 controls and indicators.

204 PART 2 DATA ENTRY EQUIPMENT

An analysis of the indicator panel in regard to the model is shown in the table below.

Indicator		Available on		Function
Light Number	Panel Label	Model 1 & 2	Model 11 & 12	(If on)
1	SYSTEM READY	X	X	Ready to communicate with the host computer.
2	SYNC SEARCH	X		Ready for selection by the host computer.
2	FLAG DETECT		X	Beginning or end of communications detected.
3	SELECTED	X		Station *has been* selected by the host computer.
3	CU ACTIVE		X	Station is communicating with the host computer.
4	SYSTEM AVAILABLE	X	X	If on the operator may interrupt and enter data. (The program in the host computer is running.)
5	INSERT MODE	X	X	Turns on when the INS MODE key is pressed. When on, characters may be inserted into existing data shown on the screen, forcing all data to the right to be shifted. Turned off by pressing the RESET key.
6	INPUT INHIBITED	X	X	Keyboard is disabled. The keys go down, but nothing happens. Usually this is caused by trying to enter data in a field programmed to be protected. Press the reset key to turn off the light.
7	TRANSMIT	X	X	Station is transmitting to the host computer via telephone lines.
8	STATUS	X	X	Station is providing the host computer with status (usually error status).

UNIT 7 TERMINALS

STATION TURN ON PROCEDURE

Control	Action
POWER	Pull out the OFF-PUSH switch.
SECURITY LOCK	If the security lock feature is part of your terminal, you must insert and turn the security key clockwise before you pull out the OFF-PUSH switch.
BRIGHTNESS	The brightness of the characters on the screen can be adjusted by turning the outer knob of the OFF-PUSH switch. (Clockwise makes it brighter.)
CONTRAST	This is an option that makes certain characters on the screen darker than others. If this option exists on a terminal, it is controlled by an inner knob on the PUSH-OFF switch.
ALARM	If your display station has the audible alarm feature, its loudness is controlled by a knob under the removable front cover. This alarm sounds if you have keyed the next to the last character on a line on the screen. Your instructor or supervisor will help you adjust this alarm if you have this feature.

When the system is ready, a short horizontal bar will appear in the upper left-hand portion of the screen. The sign-on procedure will be different for each computer center. Your instructor will tell you about your sign-on procedure.

DEFINITIONS

1. In a *formatted display* the fields to be keyed or displayed are divided and displayed with prompts. A *prompt* is defined in number 6 below.
2. In an *unformatted screen* the data shown on the screen is not divided into fields.
3. The *cursor* on the 3270 display station is indicated by an underline character. It marks the position of the *next* character to be entered.
4. *Cursor wrap* occurs when the cursor:
    a. In forward spacing → reaches the end of the line on the screen and reappears at the left on the next line down.
    b. In backspacing ← reaches the beginning of the line and reappears at the end of the next line above.
    c. In moving up ↑ jumps from one line to another.
    d. In moving down ↓ jumps from one line to another.

    In these cases the cursor can be considered as moving around behind the screen in a circle or *wrapping around* the screen, thus the term *cursor wrap*.
5. An *input field* is an area in a record in which the operator may key data. The computer has been programmed or instructed to receive the data keyed in.
6. A *prompt* is a programmed message that appears on the screen to assist the operator in keying.
    Example:

LAST NAME _

↑ Prompt   ↑ Input field where data is to be keyed.

IBM in terminal work calls these prompts *protected data.*

THE 3275 AND 3277 DATA ENTRY - KEYPUNCH STYLE KEYBOARD

Figure 7.3 shows the 3275 and the 3277 Data entry-keyboard style keyboard. Three other possible styles for the keyboard are available. You should note the difference between the − (minus or hyphen) and the __ (underline), and the ' (apostrophe) and the | sign.

The keyboard consists of:

1. *Data keys,* used for entering data (numbers, letters, or special characters).
2. *Function keys,* used to cause certain functions or controlling actions to take place.

The data keys, except for the letter "A" and the letter "Z", (see Figure 7.3) have two characters per key. Normally the machine is in alpha or lower shift which causes the characters at the bottom of the key to be entered. To obtain a character at the top of the key (upper shift), use the NUMERIC shift key. However, if the computer has been programmed or instructed to expect numeric data for a field and you want a letter, then you must use the ALPHA shift key to get the system into lower shift.

The function keys are as follows:

1. *NUMERIC SHIFT KEY* `NUMERIC`
   Use this key to obtain the numeric shift or the character at the top of the key.

2. *ALPHA SHIFT KEY* `ALPHA`
   Use this key under programmed numeric shift to obtain a character in lower shift (on the bottom of the data key).

3. *NUM LOCK KEY* `NUM LOCK`
   Use this key to lock the machine into numeric shift. The machine remains in numeric shift until the key is pressed again.

4. *CURSOR CONTROL KEYS*
   These keys position the cursor on the screen. The functions of these keys are:

   a. *THE NEW LINE KEY* ↵
      This key moves the cursor forward to the first *input* character location on the next line on the screen. If the line is unformatted, the cursor moves to the first position on that line. If the key is held down, the cursor movement will be repeated.

   b. *THE* `SKIP` *KEY AND THE TAB KEY* →|
      These keys each cause the cursor to move to the first character of the first input field to the right.
      For example, if FRY is keyed into a 13 position field, one of these keys would be used to move to the next input field. Continuing to hold these keys down causes the action to be repeated. Note that if the screen is unformatted, use of these keys causes the cursor to return to the first position of line 1.

   c. *THE BACK TAB KEY* |←
      This key moves the cursor back to the first character in an input field. If the cursor is already in the first position, use of the key will move

the cursor back to the first position of the preceding input field. If the screen in unformatted, use of the key will move the cursor back to the first position on line 1 of the screen. Continuing to hold this key down causes the action to be repeated.

d. THE VERTICAL POSITIONING KEYS ↑ ↓

These keys cause the cursor to be moved one line up ↑ or one line down ↓ . Holding the key down causes the action to be repeated. Cursor wrap can occur.

e. THE LEFT HORIZONTAL POSITIONING KEY ← AND THE BACK-SPACE KEY ←

These keys cause the cursor to be moved back *one character* at a time. The backspace key is found on the top row. Holding these keys down causes the action to be repeated. If the cursor moves off the screen to the left, a cursor wrap occurs. That is, the cursor will reappear one line higher on the right side of the screen.

f. THE RIGHT HORIZONTAL POSITIONING KEY →

This key moves the cursor to the right or forward one character at a time. Holding the key down causes the action to be repeated. Cursor wrap can occur. That is, if the cursor moves off the screen to the left, it will reappear one line lower on the left side of the screen.

REVIEW ON CURSOR POSITIONING KEYS

1. The skip, new line, and tab keys SKIP ↵ →| all advance the cursor to the first position of an input field, with the field being on the next line for the new line key.

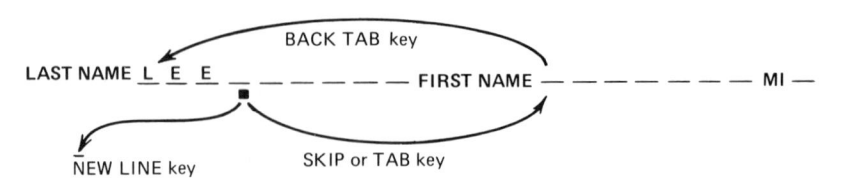

```
                    BACK TAB key
LAST NAME L E E _____ FIRST NAME ─ ─ ─ ─ ─ ─ MI ─
         NEW LINE key    SKIP or TAB key
```

FIGURE 7.5

2. *The BACK TAB key* |← *moves the cursor back* one field, positioning the cursor in the first position of the field.

3. *The vertical positioning keys* ↑ ↓
move the cursor up or down on the screen, one line at a time.
NOTE: The keys in (1) to (3) above are field and line positioning keys.

4. *The left horizontal positioning keys* (← at right on the bottom row) or the backspace key (← at right on top row) cause the cursor to be moved back, or to the left, one character at a time.

5. *SCREEN CLEARING KEYS*

a. THE CLEAR KEY CLEAR

This key causes *all characters* on the screen to be erased or blanked out. Prompts will also be erased. The action is as follows:
(1) The screen is erased.
(2) The cursor is positioned at the beginning of line 1.
(3) The INPUT INHIBITED indicator goes on. For information on how this indicator is turned off, ask your supervisor or refer to the job instructions given you.

b. *THE ERASE INPUT KEY* `ERASE INPUT`

This key erases or blanks out *all* the data displayed on the screen *in input fields*, but it does *not* erase the prompts. The cursor will move to position 1 of the first input field on the screen, and in the case of an unformatted screen, the cursor is positioned at the beginning of line 1.

c. *THE ERASE EOF KEY* `ERASE EOF`

This key erases or blanks out all characters in the input field from the cursor to the end of the field. The cursor does *not* move. Here EOF is used to mean *end of field*.

6. *THE TEST REQ KEY* `TEST REQ`

The function of this key is determined by the programming done for the station. It may be used for:
a. Making a Request For Test (RFT).
b. Logging on or off of a Teleprocessing Online Test Executive Program (TOLTEP). Your instructor or supervisor will tell you if you are to use this key.

7. *THE RESET KEY* `RESET`

This key is used to reset the INSERT MODE and INPUT INHIBITED indicators when the display station is *not sending* data. If the desired reset does not occur because the display station is sending data, press it again.

8. *THE DUPLICATE KEY* `DUP`

The key is used to duplicate or copy data such as a date (as programmed) into a field. Your job instructions will tell you when this key is to be used. When this key is pressed:
a. An asterisk * is placed in the cursor position.
b. The cursor advances to the first position of the next input field.

9. *THE FIELD MARK KEY* `FIELD MARK`

This key is used with unformatted display to mark the end of a field. It causes a semicolon (;) to be displayed on the screen.

10. *THE INSERT MODE* `INS MODE`

This key allows a character or characters to be inserted between characters which have already been keyed in an input field. The number of characters that you can insert is one less than the number of blanks remaining in that field. If an attempt is made to insert more characters than this, the INPUT INHIBITED indicator will turn on and the keyboard will be disabled.

When a character is inserted, the cursor should be placed on the character *before* which the insertion is to take place. After the character or characters are inserted, all characters to the right are moved over to the right.

11. *THE DELETE KEY* `DEL`

This key is used to delete or erase the character in the cursor position. All characters on the right are moved to the left so no blank is left.

UNIT 7 TERMINALS

12. *THE ENTER KEY* `ENTER`
    This key is used to tell the computer all data has been entered or keyed for a record and the information is ready to be sent to the host computer. The INPUT INHIBITED indicator comes on while the data is being sent to the host computer.

13. *THE PROGRAM ACCESS KEYS* `PA1` `PA2` `PA3`
    These keys provide a method of communicating with the program. The job instruction sheet or documentation will tell you if you are to use these keys. While these keys are in operation, the INPUT INHIBITED indicator comes on.

14. *THE PROGRAM FUNCTION KEYS* `PF1` `PF2` `PF3` `PF4` `PF5`
    Application programs define what happens when these keys are used. The job instruction sheet will tell you if you are to use these keys.

ENTERING DATA

1. Perform the station turn-on procedure as described earlier.
2. Sign-on for the job as instructed in your job instruction write-up or as instructed by your supervisor.
3. When the computer acknowledges your station by a go-ahead message, it will be necessary to confirm receipt of this message to the computer. Sometimes this is done with the program access keys. The job instructions will tell you what to do.
4. Begin keying data into the required input fields. In many places the fields into which data should be keyed will be of higher intensity on the screen and the characters will stand out.

ERROR CORRECTION

1. If a character has been keyed incorrectly, position the cursor at the incorrect character. Then rekey.

   Example: KAMSAS should be KANS<u>A</u>S and the cursor is positioned on the S.

   a. Position the cursor on the letter M by use of the proper cursor positioning key (in this case the `←` key).
   b. Key the letter N.
   c. Press the `SKIP` or `→|` key to get to the next field (in this case).

2. If a character has been left out of a field:
   a. Position the cursor on the character *before* which the insertion is to take place.
   b. Press the `INS MODE` key. (This will cause the INSERT MODE indicator to turn on.)
   c. Key in the character or characters to be inserted.
   d. Press the `RESET` key. (This will turn the INSERT MODE indicator off and return the station to normal mode.)
   e. Move the cursor to the point needed to continue entering data.

   Example: KASAS has been keyed when it should be KANSAS.
   a. Position the cursor on the first letter S.
   b. Press the `INS MODE` key.

        c. Key the letter N.

        d. Press the `RESET` key.

        e. Move the cursor to the next field.

3. If a character needs to be deleted:

    a. Position the cursor on the character to be deleted.

    b. Press the `DEL` key.

    All characters to the right of the deleted character will move one space to the left.

    Example: KANNSAS has been keyed and it should be KANSAS.

    a. Position the cursor on the first N.

    b. Press the `DEL` key.

    c. Position the cursor at the beginning of the next field.

4. If an entire field needs to be rekeyed from some point because incorrect keys were used.

    a. Position the cursor at the first incorrect character.

    b. Press the `ERASE EOF` key.

    c. Rekey the remainder of the field.

    Example: COLPTSFS has been keyed and it should be COLORADO.

    a. Position the cursor on the P.

    b. Press the `ERASE EOF` key.

    c. Rekey the letters ORADO.

5. If you have made an operational error such as:

    a. Keying the letter A in numeric shift (no upper shift exists).

    b. Keying letters in a field programmed numeric.

    c. Keying data into a protected field.

    d. Keying more data than a field can hold. (The INPUT INHIBITED indicator will come on and data can no longer be entered).

    Then in all these cases press the RESET key and make the necessary corrections.

6. Procedural errors are usually called to your attention by a message on the screen. The message usually tells you what to do.

7. When you have keyed an entire record, inspect it to be sure that it is correct. Then press the ENTER key. The INPUT INHIBITED indicator will come on and stay on until the host computer has accepted the record. The data that was keyed in will disappear, but the prompts will remain for the next record.

Laboratory Exercises

Your instructor will assign exercises.

PROGRAMMING   When terminals are used for data entry, the programming or instructions are not normally done by the data entry operator. Job instruction sheets will normally be provided with each job.

VERIFYING   Verifying is normally done visually on terminals before the data is transferred to the host computer.

SECTION C
OTHER TERMINAL DEVICES

Information can enter or leave a communications network through a terminal. Unfortunately, there is no standard design of terminal. There are *many* terminal manufacturers, many of whom are foreign. They produce one or more of the three types of terminals: dumb, smart, and intelligent.

Some examples of companies who produce all three types are:

ADDS	HARRIS	PERKIN-ELMER
BUNKER RAMD	HEWLETT-PACKARD	RAMTEK
BURROUGHS		SIEMANS CORPORATION (WEST GERMANY)
CONTROL DATA	HITACHI (JAPAN)	
DACOLL ENGINEERING (ENGLAND)	IBM	SYSTEMATICS GENERAL CORPORATION
DATAMEDIA	ICL	TERMINAL DATA
DIGI-LOG SYSTEMS	INFORMER	VIDEO DATA SYSTEMS
DIGITAL	NCR	VOLKER-CRAIG (CANADA)

Each of these terminals has a different keyboard arrangement. Compare the UNIVAC UTS 4000 terminal keyboard shown in Figure 7.6 with the IBM keyboard in Figure 7.3. However, as you can see, the functional keys are of the same general nature.

STUDY GUIDE

Answer these questions in your book. If asked to do so, tear out the pages and hand them to your instructor.

In completing the study guide questions, if you do not have a terminal, answer the questions using the system identified by your instructor. The system will be referred to as "your device."

FIGURE 7.6
The UNIVAC UTS 4000 terminal keyboard (Courtesy of Sperry UNIVAC).

1. List the controls and indicators on your CRT and give the function of each.

   (1) _____

   (2) _____

   (3) _____

   (4) _____

   (5) _____

   (6) _____

   (7) _____

   (8) _____

   (9) _____

   (10) _____

   (11) _____

   (12) _____

2. List the steps necessary on your terminal to ready the station for signing on.

   (1) _____
   (2) _____
   (3) _____
   (4) _____
   (5) _____
   (6) _____
   (7) _____
   (8) _____

3. List the cursor positioning keys on your keyboard and give the purpose of each.

UNIT 7 TERMINALS

Keys

(1)

(2)

(3)

(4)

(5)

(6)

(7)

(8)

(9)

☐ (10) _____

4. List the other function keys on your keyboard and give the purpose of each.

Keys

☐ (1) _____

☐ (2) _____

☐ (3) _____

☐ (4) _____

☐ (5) _____

☐ (6) _____

☐ (7) _____

UNIT 7 TERMINALS

(8) _____

(9) _____

(10) _____

(11) _____

(12) _____

(13) _____

(14) _____

(15) _____

(16) _____

5. List the steps for:
   a. Backspacing and rekeying a character in a field.

(1) _____
(2) _____
(3) _____
(4) _____

b. Backspacing to the third position in a field and rekeying the remainder of the field.

(1) _____
(2) _____
(3) _____
(4) _____
(5) _____

c. Inserting a character.

(1) _____
(2) _____
(3) _____
(4) _____
(5) _____

d. Deleting a character.

(1) _____
(2) _____
(3) _____

e. Sending a record that has been completely keyed to the host computer.

(1) _____
(2) _____

6. Define:

(1) Prompt _____
_____

(2) Cursor wrap _____
_____

(3) Formatted display _____
_____

(4) Dumb terminal _____
_____

(5) Smart terminal _____
_____

(6) Intelligent terminal _____
_____

7. Give the meaning of the following acronyms:

   (1) CRT _____

   (2) RJE _____

8. List two advantages of terminals connected to the host computer.

   (1) _____
   _____

   (2) _____
   _____

PART 3

Future Applications

AFTER READING THIS UNIT YOU WILL KNOW:

What word processing is.

What the similarities and differences between word processing and data entry are

What storage media is used in word processors.

What types of printers are used with word processors.

What types of word processing equipment are available.

Why a knowledge of word processing is important to data entry operators.

What the following terms mean:

Blind terminal   Text edit
Stand-alone   WP

UNIT 8
WORD PROCESSING AND DATA ENTRY

INTRODUCTION Before considering the future of data entry, word processing should be examined. As a data entry operator you may be working with word processing operators. Your company computer might be used for word processing as well as data entry work, regardless of the size of the computer.

Word processing has been defined as the automation of document production. It really began with the desire to produce identical documents except for personalized headings and salutations (Dear Ms. Jones, etc.). This required some sort of storage from which the document could be recalled. Word processors also have:

1. An *input device*, the keyboard.
2. A *processing device* with a memory capability.
3. An *output device* that prints the document.
4. A *display screen*.

Figure 8.1 shows an example of a word processing keyboard and display screen.

Storage media now commonly being used are:

1. *Magnetic tape* in the form of cassettes, reels, or cartridges.
2. *Magnetic cards* which are index-sized cards each with a magnetic strip across it. They will hold up to 19 lines.
3. *Floppy disks or diskettes.* Word processors as well as data entry devices use single or dual diskettes. Dual diskettes may have information recorded on both sides.
4. *Bubble memory.* This is memory made up of magnetic fields in a

FIGURE 8.1
The MICOM 2001 Word Processing System keyboard and display screen.

semiconductor used for storing data. When viewed under a powerful microscope, the fields appear to move along like bubbles.

Just as with computers, the diskettes, tapes, and magnetic cards can be used as I/O.

The most common printing mechanisms (listed from the lowest to highest speeds) are:

1. An element called a *ball* or a *selectric element.*

2. A *daisy print wheel* which looks like a daisy with characters at the end of each petal. Other daisy-type print wheels frequently referred to are the *QUME* print wheel and the DIABLO/ITEL print wheel.

3. The *ink jet* which consists of drops of fast drying ink sprayed onto paper through certain holes in a print head to form characters. Ink jet printers are practically noiseless.

Types of word processing equipment available are:

1. *THE ELECTRONIC TYPEWRITER*
   These devices are the least expensive type of word processing equipment. It can store up to five pages in memory, thus permitting short documents to be recorded and later revised. It is possible to connect two or more of these up to a communications line.

   Examples of these devices are the CONTITRONIX D-11, the IBM 75, and the QYX INTELLIGENT TYPEWRITERS.

2. *STAND-ALONE TEXT EDITING EQUIPMENT*
   In these devices information is stored on cards, magnetic tape, or floppy disks. *Stand-alone* means the same as it does in data entry: not connected to the computer.

   The term *text edit* means to manipulate text or information. The manipulations may simply be the making of additions and deletions to text. However, more sophisticated text editing provides for right-margin justification with words being hyphenated. Full-line justification spaces all words in a line so that it ends evenly, flush right. Most modern word processors provide full text editing capabilities.

There are two main types of stand-alone word processors.

a. Word processors with *blind terminals* consist of a keyboard and a printer but no display screen. Their use is declining as other systems become less expensive. Examples are the ADLER SE-2000, the ROYAL SE-6000, and the SAVIN 950 VERITEXT.

b. Word processors with *display screens.* These devices consist of a CRT screen, a keyboard, and a printer. A copy is not made on the printer until the material displayed on the screen has been determined to be correct. Display word processors are more expensive than the blind terminals. Examples are the LANIER NO PROBLEM LC, the IBM OS 6/452, and the LEXITRON VIDEO TYPE 1201, the 1202, and the 1303.

3. *SHARED LOGIC SYSTEMS*

Shared logic devices are similar to key-to-disk equipment. Information is entered from multiple keyboards, processed, and recorded on disk or diskette. The information may later be transferred to tape or sent over a communications line. Examples are the WANG Information System 130 and the 140, the WANG WP25, the A.B. DICK MAGNA SL.

RECENT EQUIPMENT DEVELOPMENTS

A recently developed word processing system, the IBM Display Writer System, can:

1. Check spelling of 50,000 words using its electronic dictionary (the user may add 500 words to this list).
2. Communicate with other office equipment over ordinary phone lines.
3. Divide the text into lines and pages and create justified text with all lines of equal length.

This system offers a choice of three printers and two diskette units. It has a display unit and a keyboard, and no programming is necessary.

Recently, companies such as FOUR PHASE have developed software word-processing packages for their key-to-disk equipment. Their equipment can also be used for word processing, thus saving the expense of buying other stand-alone word processing equipment which may cost from $6000 to $15,000 per unit. Keyboard differences are solved by having keys engraved on the top for word processing and in the front for data entry.

SOFTWARE

Small computer systems also have word-processing software capabilities. IBM's 32, 34, and 38 all have word-processing packages or programs. Many microcomputers such as the TRS-80 now have word-processing capabilities. Other micros with word processing capabilities are the Commodore PET versions 2 and 3; the HEATH H8, WH8, H88, and H89; the HEWLETT-PACKARD 85s; the NORTH STAR HORIZON, and the OHIO SCIENTIFIC CHALLENGER II SERIES. These software packages range in price from $65,000 for large computers down to less than $50 for microcomputers.

The IBM System/32 computer has a software package called the IBM WP/32. It allows the handling of large documents with speed and economy. Blocks of text can be typed and stored in the computer. Then they can be selected and included in several different documents. Additions and deletions are easily made by locating line numbers. Page numbering is automatic.

The IBM System/34 has a software package called WORDPOWER produced by Professional Computer Resources, Inc. The IBM 5251 display station is used to prepare the text. The package supports mass mail letter-

FIGURE 8.2
A Microcomputer with word processing capabilities.

writing along with mailing-label-making capabilities. As many as 10 lines of text can be inserted at one time.

Software packages for different units now include:

1. *List/Merge Functions.* These functions are used for repetitive letters and documents produced from names, addresses, and paragraphs stored in separate files.
2. *Forms Generation.* The operator can define fields or areas in which text may be entered. The Burrough's RIII System 340 allows a form to be generated on the display screen, then stored on a diskette for later use.
3. *Sort, Search, and Replace Routines.* Lists of information can be sorted or arranged alphabetically or numerically in ascending or descending order. The search/replace feature allows the operator to search for each occurrence of a string of characters. The string of characters could be a word or phrase. The machine will stop each time it finds this string of characters. A replacement can then be keyed in. Examples of this type of equipment are the CPT 8000, Lanier No Problem, MICOM 2001, and the NBI 3000.
4. *Math Functions.* Some word processing users need to total rows and columns. Sometimes they need arithmetic operations to be performed and the result to be placed at a particular place in the report. Programming will allow a formula to be created. It will even stop the machine and allow the operator to insert a new number where needed. Such abilities are provided for by Burroughs, CPT, Lanier, Micom, Wang, and AM Jacquard.
5. *BASIC Programming.* A few text-editing machines allow the operator to write programs in a language called BASIC. This is a computer language which is much more complex than the WP programming discussed previously. BASIC is an Acronym for *B*eginner's *A*ll *P*urpose *S*ymbolic *I*nstruction *C*ode. The average WP operator probably will not be required

to use this language. But the language does permit very sophisticated word processing applications. LEXITRON and MICOM offer BASIC capabilities.

Word processing can be done on a time-sharing basis over communications lines. This often causes problems that are beyond the scope of this textbook. However it can be noted here that word processors not only record and transmit text, but they communicate formatting information and other special codes. If the codes of two systems in communication differ, problems arise. Some of the problems can be overcome with the use of smart (programmable) word processors, but not if the word processing commands are different structurally. Time-sharing methods are very expensive and their use could be justified only on a high volume or 24-hour need to transmit documents.

COMPARISON OF DATA ENTRY AND WORD PROCESSING

Aspects of data entry and word processing can be compared as follows:

Data Entry	Word Processing
1. Work is generally batch oriented.	1. Random selection is needed.
2. Most keying is numeric.	2. Most keying is alpha.
3. Keyboard has less keys.	3. Keyboard has more keys.
4. Each job demands some type of programming. The program may be done or it may be done with a programming language.	4. Very little programming. Equipment is usually pre-programmed (programming is done by the manufacturer).
5. Display screen may be larger.	5. Display screen may be limited to 6 to 8 lines of text.
6. Printer may not be necessary.	6. High quality printer needed, impact type.

In summary both word processing equipment and data entry equipment are shop and user oriented. Both types are made up of input and output equipment and a processor. However the display equipment and keyboard may be somewhat different.

Data entry work is usually batch oriented. Most keying is numeric. Word processing work is done on a more random basis and is usually alphabetic. On modern sophisticated data entry equipment it is much more difficult to make procedure changes and handle new jobs than it is in word processing. This is because programs must be written for each job. Therefore much more lead time or planning time is needed in data entry work than in word processing work.

In the future, data entry operators may share equipment with word processing operators. It is even possible that data entry operators might be required to do some of both types of work. Therefore data entry operators should be aware of word processing developments.

STUDY GUIDE

Answer these questions in your book. If told to do so, tear out the pages and hand them in to your instructor.

1. List the three main parts of a word processor and a fourth part that most modern units have.

    (1) _____

(2) _____
(3) _____
(4) _____

2. List five types of word processors.

(1) _____
(2) _____
(3) _____
(4) _____
(5) _____

3. List three types of printers used in word processing.

(1) _____
(2) _____
(3) _____

4. List four types of storage media used in word processing.

(1) _____
(2) _____
(3) _____
(4) _____

5. Name four similarities between data entry and word processing.

(1) _____
(2) _____
(3) _____
(4) _____

6. Name four differences between data entry and word processing.

(1) _____
(2) _____
(3) _____
(4) _____

7. Define "word processing."

_____
_____
_____

8. State why a data entry operator should be informed about word processing developments.

_____
_____
_____
_____

9. Define "text-edit."

10. Name five applications possible with word processing programming features.

   (1) _____

   (2) _____

   (3) _____

   (4) _____

   (5) _____

AFTER READING THIS UNIT YOU WILL KNOW:

What equipment trends are.
How OCR is involved in data entry.
What some of the newer data entry devices are.
What some of the problems are with the newer data entry devices.
What the new verification policies are.
Why security is so important.
What the three EDP controls are.
How on-line data entry is controlled in regard to security.
What your responsibilities in data privacy are.
What your continuing education attitude should be.

What the following terms mean:

Backup
Centralized data entry
Data security
Decentralized or distributed data entry
Equipment security
Log
OBR
OCR
OMR
Password
POS
Voice input

UNIT 9
THE FUTURE

The IBM 3270 Information Display System (Courtesy of IBM Corporation).

INTRODUCTION

A simple data entry device, the keypunch, has evolved into the key-to-disk system. This system can also be operated as a small business computer. There is a trend in many businesses toward on-line data entry terminals. Thus data entry, data processing, and data communications are all closely connected.

In many shops data entry is no longer considered a dead-end profession. Data entry personnel may progress up the career path in operations and programming on small business computers used for data entry. An introduction to computers course and an introductory programming course will be of help if you wish to go up the career path.

Formerly data entry activities were *centralized* in one location. With the introduction of the small business computer and on-line terminals, data entry activities have been distributed or "dispersed" to multiple locations. Thus *decentralized* or *distributed data entry* has become common. The terminals used may be dumb, smart, or intelligent. As with other data entry devices, they all have keyboards.

The new equipment has a screen to display the data being keyed. Prompts or messages are also displayed to assist the operator in keying. These new systems also have sophisticated error checks and editing capabilities.

Studies show that the use of card data entry devices is declining.[1] However such devices are still used in small centers because the equipment is so cheap. Card records in low volume situations are easy to manipulate, inspect, and change. However in high volume applications even buffered keypunches are too slow.

Although key-to-disk equipment is more expensive, keying production has been shown to increase by 25 percent to 50 percent. In addition many more error and validation checks can be made. The operations are quiet and card handling and storage is eliminated.

Equipment trends are toward key-to-disk equipment and on-line terminals.

[1]*Data Entry Awareness Report* (Management Information Corporation), Vol. VIII, No. 12, (December 1980), p. 15.

NEW DATA ENTRY METHODS

1. *Optical Readers.* These devices capture data from the original form without any keying. They may read:
   a. Printed characters (optical character reader or *OCR*).
   b. Pencil marks (optical mark readers or *OMR*).
   c. Special bar codes (optical bar code reader or *OBR*).
   They will all read alphameric data.

   These devices were originally used in high volume work but were not satisfactory because they lacked error controls and validation techniques. Recently, optical readers have been combined with key-to-disk equipment in what is called a mixed media system. Figure 9.1 shows an example. The scanned data is written on tape. Rejects that cannot be read are flagged for later keyed corrections.

2. *Voice Data Entry.* Voice input devices use the human voice as input. With these devices a person's voice is converted to digital form or *voice input*. It is then matched with sample voices that were previously recorded and are stored in the device's memory.

   Two kinds of voice data systems are:
   a. The *speaker dependent system* in which the system matches the voice with previously recorded voice.
   b. The *speaker independent system* in which the system matches a voice with a pattern made up of many voices.

   The speaker independent system has poorer recognition results. Most of these systems only recognize isolated words, and the vocabulary ranges from 16 to 900 expressions.

3. *Portable Key Devices.* Portable data recorders are inexpensive and can be hand-carried. They now weigh less then 15 pounds, including the carrying case. These devices are manually operated, recording data on punched cards, paper tapes, magnetic tapes, or cassettes. Sometimes data is transmitted over phone lines to the host computer.

   These devices are often used in data entry at field locations. Examples are inventory control and maintenance reporting. They can be taken into unusual places where data entry equipment cannot normally be taken. They have the disadvantage that data editing or validation is limited.

4. *Point-of-Sale (POS) Systems.* POS systems are used in large, high-

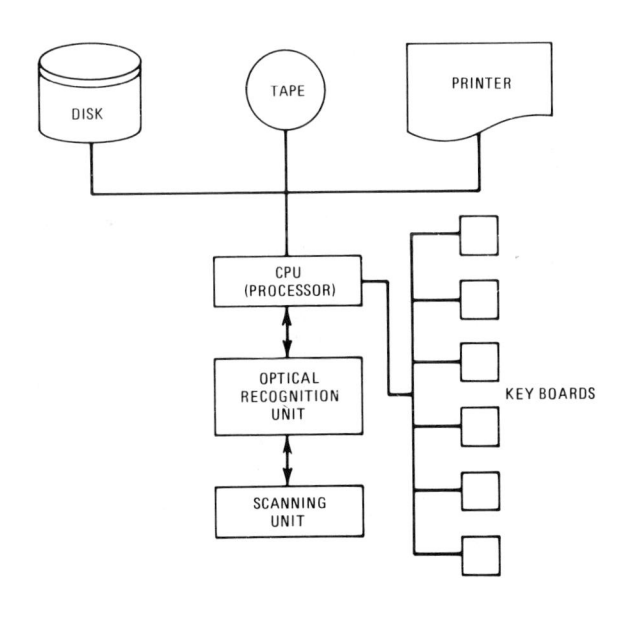

FIGURE 9.1
Mixed media system.

volume retail businesses such as large Sears or Montgomery Wards, or grocery stores. Inventory data is collected very quickly with this type of equipment. But these systems are very expensive. Input data may be keyed or read by hand-held devices.

VERIFICATION

Recent data entry developments have shown a change in verification philosophies. Today key verifying is used only when having *exact* data is essential.

When is having exact data considered unessential? An example might be the case of a mass advertising mailing. A person's name is keyed I A LEE rather than I H LEE. As long as the remainder of the mailing label is keyed correctly, the advertisement will arrive at the correct place. This situation might be considered acceptable, and thus verifying is not necessary.

In high-volume data entry, key verification slows down production. Therefore on many jobs certain selected fields are verified. These fields may be key verified or sight verified on CRTs.

Limited verification is encouraged by many key-to-disk equipment manufacturers. This is because computer programs may be written to prevent the transfer of records flagged in error. Thus no error records will be written on magnetic tape or transmitted through data communications to the host computer.

SECURITY AND CONTROL

DEFINITIONS

1. *Data Security.* The protection of data from unauthorized access.
2. *Equipment Security.* The protection of equipment from use or damage by unauthorized persons.

Computer centers must protect the equipment and data they process because of the possibilities of:

1. *Sabotage.* An outside person actually physically attacks the equipment.
2. *Theft.* Programs and data can be stolen and sold to competitors.
3. *Fraud.* For example, personnel in the center actually alter procedures of programs so that money may be transferred to their account or a relative or friend's account.
4. *Accidental Destruction.* Data can be destroyed or accidentally overwritten. This may occur because the operator mounted the wrong tape or disk. Data may also be ruined by an improperly operating I/O unit. In the case of disk drives, data can be ruined by *head crashes.* The read/write heads may not be positioned properly. This causes the metal heads to dig into the plastic disk, ruining the data on that track.
5. *Disaster.* Fires, floods, tornados, hurricanes may occur at any time.

EDP controls must also be set up to see that the data sent to a center is processed:

1. Completely.
2. Accurately.
3. On a timely basis.

Formerly when data entry was centralized a data control group could, to a large extent, see that data was processed under the above controls. Also entry or access to a center could be restricted to offer more security. But with the introduction of on-line terminals, security and data controls are becoming much more difficult. As has been seen, the accuracy and completeness of data can be controlled in key-to-disk and on-line terminals by programming edit and validation checks. However these systems *also* permit an individual to look at data and alter or change it.

Because of these problems you may find yourself working under the following conditions:

1. Terminals will be placed in areas restricted from the general public.
2. Terminals that you use may have a lock and key system. They cannot be turned on unless the operator has the proper key. This system is often used in airline terminals where the general public is always surrounding the terminals.
3. You may have a *password* assigned to you to key in before you can start a job. You will be requested to not disclose this password to anyone. The password may be changed periodically.
4. If you are an experienced operator, you may be requested to verify. In this case you might have a higher level password that allows you to change data.
5. *Logs* or a written record may be kept on the use of your terminal. Then if there are repeated log-in errors or unusual activities on your terminal, the management will check to see what is going on. (For example in the case of repeated log-in errors, someone might be experimenting to find a password.)
6. You may be asked to never leave your work or machines unattended.
7. Data in the form of cards, tapes, and diskettes will be locked up in fire resistant cabinets with copies kept at remote locations. *Backup* or copies will be regularly updated.
8. If you key a job, you will not verify it.
9. You may need a badge or identification card to get to your work station.

All of these policies and rules should not distress or upset you. These are the signs of a well-run computer center with good security policies.

Good data controls require that all data, such as that on tape, diskette, or disk, be:

1. Clearly labeled externally.
2. Labeled internally as discussed in the key-to-disk unit.
3. Controlled by a librarian.

PRIVACY

There are two concepts involved in data privacy, one which you can control and one only management can control.

Recently the privacy of computerized data has been a much discussed subject. Suggestions that have been made for management in connection with data privacy are:

1. There should be a valid reason for collecting information or data. The only acceptable reason for collecting a piece of data should be that this data is necessary for conducting an institution's business. For example a public supported college would not normally require a student to give information on his or her religion or drinking habits.
2. An individual should have control over the disclosure of personal information. For example a magazine should not have the right to give or sell your address to another publication without your permission.

3. A person should have the right to obtain a copy of the computer information being collected on him or her. This person should also have the right to have incorrect information changed or deleted.

Many of the above suggestions are now being considered by the federal and state governments. Laws regarding privacy have been and are being passed. You should make your views known to your federal, state, and local representatives.

But *you* also have privacy responsibilities just as your doctor or nurse does. You expect your personal medical problems to be kept private. You would not approve of your doctor telling all of your friends about your medical problems. In the same way, you should never discuss data involved in your work with outsiders. Data is a private matter and should not be revealed or discussed. You have ethical responsibilities in privacy just as doctors, nurses, counselors, and ministers do. *Remember this in your future work!*

CONCLUSION

In conclusion data entry:

1. Is now a career.
2. Is in demand.
3. Has many career advancement possibilities.
4. Requires that you continue your education.

Encourage your supervisors and employers to:

1. Subscribe to current data entry publications and let you read them.
2. Allow you to attend data entry conferences and seminars and to take more data processing courses. In addition talk to the instructors in your local community/junior colleges and vocational institutes about available publications and courses that you might find there.

You are in an important profession and have many exciting opportunities ahead.

STUDY GUIDE

Answer these questions in your book. If told to do so, tear out the pages and hand them in to your instructor.

1. Answer true or false by circling the correct answer.

    T or F (1) The use of card data entry equipment is increasing.

    T or F (2) The use of key-to-disk data entry equipment is increasing.

    T or F (3) The use of optical readers in connection with other data entry equipment (mixed media) is increasing.

    T or F (4) Key verification is a modern development.

    T or F (5) Manufacturers currently recommend key verification of all data recorded.

    T or F (6) Data entry is now a dead-end profession.

    T or F (7) You as an operator have no responsibilities in data privacy.

2. Give the meaning of the following acronyms:

    (1) OCR _____

(2) OMR _____

(3) OBR _____

(4) POS _____

3. Answer the following questions:
   a. Why should EDP controls be set up? To see that data is processed:

   (1) _____

   (2) _____

   (3) _____

   b. List three ways in which security can be achieved with on-line terminals:

   (1) _____
   _____

   (2) _____
   _____

   (3) _____
   _____

   c. Define:

   (1) Password _____
   _____
   _____

   (2) Backup _____
   _____
   _____

   (3) Log _____
   _____

   d. What is the operator's responsibility in data privacy?
   _____
   _____
   _____

PART 4

Laboratory Exercises

If you do not have keypunches or key-to-diskette equipment, your instructor will tell you if your are to prepare programs for Section C.

The exercises should be keyed. Record lengths are 80 positions.

Your instructor will tell you if the exercises should be verified and what type of verification should be used.

SECTION A
NUMERIC KEYING EXERCISES

JOB NAMES:
NUM01 THROUGH NUM10

Prepare a program for numeric keying unless your instructor tells you otherwise. One line of figures is equal to one record. Do *not* space between groups of figures as you key. The groups are separated to make keying easier.

Exercise 1 (NUM01)

*1	5	9	13	17	21	25	29	33	37	41	45	49	53	57	61	65	69	73	77
1471	4711	7741	4741	4477	4117	4171	1714	7711	4411	7744	4777	4111	1414	1717	4744	1177	7171	4441	1471
2582	2288	5588	5858	2852	8582	8822	8252	2258	8522	2558	2588	8528	2258	8555	8528	5522	2255	8528	5828
0369	3096	3006	9003	0943	9043	3409	9944	0094	9944	3009	9933	3366	3609	3660	9663	9630	9360	9306	6639
1231	3221	1133	1321	1122	1133	3131	2121	1313	1212	3322	3311	3312	1233	3311	2233	1231	2313	1231	1232
4564	5645	5664	4665	6445	6554	5664	5646	4655	5644	4665	5646	4644	4544	5646	5664	6546	6556	4656	6655
7889	7987	7788	7878	7979	9797	7799	9977	9898	9797	9879	9878	9988	7897	7898	7899	8798	8797	8799	9878
1926	1692	1669	2699	2962	9966	9261	2619	6192	9922	6611	6161	9191	9292	9269	9629	2299	6692	2996	9969
7589	8957	8995	8557	8775	8585	8787	8978	9878	9877	9977	8899	8987	7798	8989	7878	7979	9857	5789	7859
7517	7351	7153	7952	7195	7313	7179	7593	7359	7937	7951	7193	7795	7571	7151	7517	7379	7935	7139	7397
9571	9537	9137	9135	9357	9730	9759	9731	9557	9735	9153	9735	9713	9137	9177	9537	9313	9971	9373	9975

Exercise 2 (NUM02)

*1	5	9	13	17	21	25	29	33	37	41	45	49	53	57	61	65	69	73	77
2763	2725	2795	2711	2765	2742	2728	2706	2794	2737	2779	2750	2718	2784	2722	2734	2710	2759	2790	2754
7284	7296	7265	7221	7215	7209	7243	7279	7259	7218	7227	7231	7207	7254	7299	7210	7283	7248	7235	7297
2715	2738	2716	2701	2769	2798	2749	2775	2751	2770	2791	2736	2781	2792	2766	2733	2722	2740	2780	2787
7278	7238	7222	7211	7230	7242	7228	7212	7298	7275	7223	7288	7263	7246	7202	7237	7291	7280	7224	7245
2731	2704	2713	2746	2757	2724	2799	2773	2764	2732	2720	2778	2717	2785	2743	2774	2723	2755	2705	2783
7200	7289	7217	7274	7258	7261	7282	7260	7205	7292	7239	7272	7238	7244	7216	7287	7252	7269	7232	7296
2727	2719	2707	2782	2762	2735	2796	2745	2786	2721	2792	2730	2709	2747	2758	2713	2729	2748	2739	2760
7220	7208	7219	7241	7294	7226	7255	7290	7271	7213	7268	7203	7251	7262	7276	7243	7257	7285	7267	7249
2767	2714	2708	2752	2771	2741	2788	2726	2768	2793	2756	2700	2761	2797	2744	2753	2777	2703	2776	2789
7202	7236	7247	7229	7273	7256	7240	7214	7286	7264	7277	7281	7253	7270	7206	7266	7250	7225	7293	7233

*KEYING POSITION

Exercise 3 (NUM03)

*1	5	9	13	17	21	25	29	33	37	41	45	49	53	57	61	65	69	73	77
6438	6467	6489	6414	6422	6472	6498	6454	6443	6401	6433	6428	6469	6441	6482	6419	6406	6474	6424	6491
4600	4613	4661	4690	4666	4639	4657	4623	4604	4687	4694	4653	4678	4644	4616	4627	4651	4632	4609	4684
6415	6462	6449	6407	6426	6476	6420	6492	6431	6481	6447	6411	6463	6429	6471	6496	6448	6456	6402	6488
4655	4646	4635	4610	4668	4699	4673	4686	4612	4650	4625	4693	4680	4675	4659	4618	4637	4605	4658	4670
6497	6445	6460	6421	6434	6485	6403	6442	6477	6495	6436	6440	6417	6452	6479	6430	6422	6408	6483	6464
4688	4602	4656	4648	4671	4696	4629	4663	4611	4647	4681	4631	4692	4620	4676	4649	4626	4607	4662	4615
6484	6409	6432	6451	6427	6416	6444	6478	6494	6453	6487	6466	6404	6457	6423	6461	6439	6490	6413	6400
4624	4691	4674	4619	4606	4641	4682	4669	4633	4601	4628	4643	4698	4654	4672	4614	4622	4667	4689	4638
6470	6458	6473	6488	6468	6410	6435	6446	6455	6412	6450	6425	6480	6493	6475	6459	6418	6437	6405	6486
4664	4683	4608	4622	4630	4679	4652	4640	4617	4636	4645	4621	4634	4685	4603	4642	4677	4660	4695	4697

Exercise 4 (NUM04)

*1	5	9	13	17	21	25	29	33	37	41	45	49	53	57	61	65	69	73	77
8502	8536	8547	8529	8573	8556	8540	8514	8586	8564	8577	8581	8553	8570	8506	8566	8550	8525	8593	8533
5889	5876	5803	5877	5853	5844	5897	5861	5800	5856	5893	5868	5826	5888	5841	5871	5852	5808	5814	5867
8549	8567	8585	8557	8534	8576	8526	8551	8503	8568	8513	8571	8590	8555	8562	8594	8541	8519	8508	8520
5827	5819	5807	5882	5862	5835	5896	5845	5886	5821	5892	5830	5809	5847	5858	5813	5829	5848	5839	5860
8500	8589	8517	8574	8558	8561	8582	8560	8505	8592	8539	8572	8538	8544	8516	8587	8552	8564	8532	8595
5831	5804	5812	5846	5857	5827	5899	5873	5864	5832	5820	5878	5817	5885	5843	5874	5823	5855	5805	5883
8545	8524	8580	8591	8537	8504	8546	8563	8588	8523	8598	8512	8575	8528	8542	8530	8511	8522	8501	8579
5880	5840	5822	5833	5866	5802	5881	5836	5891	5870	5851	5875	5849	5887	5898	5869	5801	5816	5838	5815
8531	8527	8507	8554	8599	8510	8583	8548	8535	8597	8584	8596	8565	8521	8515	8509	8543	8579	8559	8518
5879	5850	5818	5884	5872	5834	5810	5859	5890	5854	5863	5825	5895	5811	5865	5842	5828	5806	5894	5837

Exercise 5 (NUM05)

*1	5	9	13	17	21	25	29	33	37	41	45	49	53	57	61	65	69	73	77
9333	9328	9369	9341	9382	9319	9306	9374	9324	9391	9301	9343	9354	9398	9372	9322	9314	9389	9367	9338
3987	3904	3923	3957	3939	3966	3990	3961	3913	3900	3994	3916	3944	3978	3953	3909	3984	3932	3951	3927
9311	9396	9347	9356	9388	9302	9358	9363	9329	9371	9326	9349	9362	9315	9331	9307	9392	9376	9320	9381
3935	3910	3999	3955	3946	3973	3968	3986	3912	3950	3905	3993	3980	3975	3959	3918	3937	3958	3970	3925
9377	9342	9395	9303	9321	9334	9360	9385	9348	9345	9330	9322	9308	9383	9336	9340	9317	9352	9379	9364
3907	3981	3976	3949	3926	3915	3931	3992	3920	3962	3911	3947	3996	3929	3963	3971	3956	3948	3902	3988
9316	9378	9351	9327	9384	9332	9309	9353	9387	9344	9323	9300	9339	9361	9357	9394	9313	9366	9304	9390
3922	3914	3967	3998	3989	3938	3928	3943	3901	3954	3933	9382	3924	3991	3906	3941	3972	3919	3974	3969
9380	9325	9346	9350	9312	9335	9358	9375	9350	9318	9359	9337	9305	9386	9399	9368	9310	9373	9393	9355
3964	3908	3952	3922	3995	3940	3917	3985	3936	3942	3983	3977	3934	3960	3945	3921	3903	3997	3930	3979

*KEYING POSITION

Exercise 6 (NUM06)

*1	5	9	13	17	21	25	29	33	37	41	45	49	53	57	61	65	69	73	77
8282	8299	8273	8239	8262	8248	8220	8206	8225	8241	8213	8209	8261	8254	8298	8236	8212	8250	8286	8277
2821	2844	2830	2865	2887	2814	2835	2879	2859	2894	2801	2890	2885	2872	2805	2868	2840	2826	2817	2853
8264	8231	8207	8224	8255	8292	8270	8245	8218	2860	8227	8289	8295	8247	8203	8252	8288	8276	8232	8211
2834	2808	2851	2829	2810	2863	2875	2842	2881	2823	2884	2838	2897	2846	2893	2858	2871	2802	2867	2816
8291	8278	8256	8249	8237	8283	8269	8215	8204	8228	8233	8200	8222	8296	8243	8257	8219	8274	8280	8260
2880	2819	2874	2866	2822	2896	2843	2857	2815	2804	2828	2833	2800	2837	2883	2869	2849	2856	2878	2891
8234	8208	8251	8229	8263	8210	8275	8242	8251	8223	8297	8284	8238	8216	8267	8202	8271	8258	8293	8246
2832	2876	2888	2852	2803	2811	2847	2895	2889	2829	2860	2818	2845	2870	2892	2855	2827	2807	2831	2864
8253	8217	8226	8240	8268	8205	8272	8285	8290	8201	8294	8259	8279	8235	8214	8287	8265	8230	8244	8221
2877	2886	2850	2812	2836	2898	2854	2861	2809	2813	2841	2825	2806	2820	2848	2862	2839	2873	2899	2882

Exercise 7 (NUM07)

*1	5	9	13	17	21	25	29	33	37	41	45	49	53	57	61	65	69	73	77
2613	2654	2698	2661	2650	2686	2609	2624	2636	2612	2660	2677	2645	2670	2655	2692	2631	2664	2618	2607
6240	6217	6226	6290	6272	6253	6205	6241	6206	6225	6248	6285	6268	6220	6201	6282	6273	6239	6299	6262
2649	2656	2691	2678	2611	2632	2676	2688	2652	2647	2695	2603	2627	2689	2637	2604	2628	2615	2669	2683
6259	6287	6265	6214	6281	6223	6230	6244	6275	6234	6221	6242	6258	6263	6210	6229	6251	6208	6235	6294
2633	2642	2600	2657	2619	2696	2623	2643	2622	2674	2680	2634	2666	2608	2651	2663	2610	2675	2681	2629
6284	6297	6216	6202	6267	6258	6238	6271	6246	6293	6219	6274	6289	6266	6257	6213	6204	6296	6243	6222
2638	2667	2616	2646	2697	2602	2671	2658	2693	2672	2685	2640	2668	2690	2605	2626	2617	2654	2684	2601
6269	6283	6237	6220	6228	6233	6281	6249	6223	6278	6256	6291	6229	6275	6210	6263	6251	6234	6208	6242
2628	2606	2625	2641	2648	2662	2639	2673	2699	2682	2621	2665	2630	2614	2687	2659	2635	2679	2644	2694
6294	6208	6259	6234	6221	6265	6279	6244	6210	6275	6226	6230	6287	6214	6251	6229	6263	6217	6223	6235

Exercise 8 (NUM08)

*1	5	9	13	17	21	25	29	33	37	41	45	49	53	57	61	65	69	73	77
5113	5109	5161	5154	5198	5136	5150	5186	5177	5131	5164	5124	5107	5155	5192	5170	5145	5160	5118	5112
1541	1525	1506	1548	1520	1562	1599	1539	1573	1582	1501	1585	1565	1505	1553	1572	1590	1526	1517	1540
5103	5127	5189	5195	5147	5152	5188	5176	5132	5111	5178	5191	5156	5149	5137	5183	5169	5115	5128	5104
1559	1587	1544	1530	1521	1565	1514	1594	1535	1508	1551	1529	1510	1563	1559	1542	1581	1523	1534	1575
5100	5133	5196	5143	5157	5122	5119	5174	5180	5166	5134	5108	5151	5129	5163	5110	5175	5142	5181	5123
1584	1594	1516	1502	1538	1567	1571	1558	1593	1546	1580	1519	1574	1566	1522	1596	1543	1557	1515	1504
5197	5184	5138	5116	5167	5102	5171	5158	5193	5146	5190	5185	5172	5105	5140	5168	5126	5117	5153	5101
1533	1528	1500	1537	1583	1569	1556	1578	1510	1549	1581	1529	1575	1591	1508	1523	1551	1534	1563	1549
5194	5159	5135	5179	5114	5187	5165	5130	5144	5121	5182	5199	5173	5139	5162	5148	5128	5106	5125	5141
1559	1534	1594	1508	1544	1521	1510	1575	1530	1565	1587	1514	1551	1529	1563	1535	1579	1526	1517	1553

*KEYING POSITION

Exercise 9 (NUM09)

*1	5	9	13	17	21	25	29	33	37	41	45	49	53	57	61	65	69	73	77
1369	0969	6169	5469	9869	3669	5069	8669	1269	7769	5369	2669	4069	6869	0569	7269	8569	9069	0169	1769
1896	9796	1696	3896	7196	0296	6796	8496	9396	5896	4696	2496	0796	7096	9296	3196	4596	6496	5596	6096
2769	8969	9569	0369	5269	8869	7669	3269	1169	4769	0869	3469	5169	2969	1069	7569	2369	4269	6369	8169
9996	7396	6296	4896	3996	2596	0696	2096	9496	6596	8296	4196	7996	2196	3596	1496	8796	3096	5996	4496
3369	0069	3769	8369	6969	4969	5669	7869	9169	2869	8069	6669	7469	1969	9669	4369	5769	1569	2269	0469
6196	5496	3696	7296	1396	0996	9896	8596	1796	9096	0196	5096	8696	7796	5396	2696	4096	6896	0596	1296
9769	1669	3869	8469	6769	0269	7169	5869	9369	4669	3169	0769	2469	9269	7069	4569	6469	5569	6069	1869
2296	1596	0496	9696	6996	7496	6696	8096	8396	3796	1996	5796	4396	2896	7896	9196	5696	4996	3396	0096
9469	7969	3569	1469	8769	3069	5969	4469	2169	6569	8269	9969	7369	6269	4869	3969	4169	2569	0669	2069
2396	7596	0896	1196	8196	6396	4296	7696	9596	5196	8896	1096	2996	3496	0396	4796	8996	2796	3296	5296

Exercise 10 (NUM10)

*1	5	9	13	17	21	25	29	33	37	41	45	49	53	57	61	65	69	73	77
2934	0234	3634	7334	7634	4034	4734	8134	7034	6634	1434	8634	6434	7734	5334	0634	5034	2534	9334	3334
7643	8943	9743	7743	6143	2643	5343	4443	0343	7143	8843	6843	9343	0043	5643	1443	6743	4143	5243	0843
6734	5134	8534	6834	1334	4934	5734	3434	7634	0834	9034	6234	5534	0334	2034	7134	2634	9434	4134	1934
9643	8243	6243	2143	4543	3543	0743	1943	2743	4743	5843	8643	9243	1343	3043	6043	0943	3943	4843	2943
9534	3234	6434	7234	3934	9234	0534	6034	8234	6134	5834	7434	1734	8934	0034	3834	4434	1634	8734	5234
7343	5743	6443	9943	2743	1243	4643	3143	0443	3243	8343	2043	7843	1743	8543	4343	7443	2343	5543	0543
4534	2434	8034	9134	3734	0434	4634	6334	8834	2334	9834	1234	7534	2834	4234	3034	1134	2234	0134	7834
5143	7543	4943	8743	9843	6943	0143	1643	3843	1543	8043	4043	2243	3343	6643	0243	3643	9143	7043	8143
9734	3534	4834	8334	1034	9934	5434	0734	2734	3134	1834	7934	4334	0934	1534	6534	5934	9634	8434	2134
0643	2843	4243	6543	1143	9543	2543	7943	6343	9443	3743	5443	9043	5943	1043	3443	7243	8443	1843	2043

*KEYING POSITION

SECTION B
ALPHABETIC KEYING EXERCISES

**JOB NAMES:
ALPHA01 THROUGH
ALPHA10**

Each line is a record. Skip one space between each column. If there are less than 80 characters, advance to the next record after keying the last character.

EXERCISES

241

Exercise 1 (ALPHA01)

DELETE CODE	DISPLAY SCREEN	DISK	CATALOG	ALPHAMERIC	BCD CODE
ENVIRONMENT	MULTIPROCESSING	MULTIPROGRAMMING	DISKETTE	BLOCK	ASCII
DEFAULT	EQUIVALENCE	INTEGER	BATCH PROCESSING	DATA SET	DATA CONTROL
OVERFLOW	DENSITY	VERTICAL	BYTE	CONSOLE	COMPUTER
ZERO PUNCH	INTERLOCK	BINARY NUMBER	EXPONENT	SOFTWARE	TAPE MARK
WORK AREA	HORIZONTAL	RECORD ADVANCE	FLOPPY DISK	SMART TERMINAL	DUMB TERMINAL
SUBROUTINE	PROGRAM DRUM	BASIC	INPUT	TIME SHARING	WORD PROCESSING
MULTIPLEXOR	BACKSPACE	CASSETTE	EBCDIC CODE	FUNCTIONAL KEYS	INTERPRET
BASE ADDRESS	CARTRIDGE	EXECUTION	RJE	REMOTE JOB ENTRY	HEXADECIMAL
CARRIER	EXPLICIT ADDRESS	FLOATING POINT	PORT	POS	PARITY
FLOWCHART	FORMS	IMMEDIATE DATA	MODEM	OCR	MICR
IPL	INTERACTIVE	DISTRIBUTIVE PROCESSING	LEFT ZERO	MEMORY	RIGHT JUSTIFY

Exercise 2 (ALPHA02)

ABEND	ADDRESS	BOOTSTRAP	SEEK	SIGNAL	SUPERVISOR
TWELVE PUNCH	QUEUE	TAG	SELECTOR	SIX BIT CODE	TERMINAL JOB
INTERRUPT	INVERTED FILE	PICTURE	ALPHANUMERIC	SECONDARY STORAGE	WEIGHT
ERASABLE STORAGE	EQUIVALENT	VOICE UNIT	CHECK BIT	SATELLITE COMPUTER	PERFORMANCE
DATA PROCESSING	CONDITION NAME	CRT	GROUP INDICATE	SCAN	SIMULTANEOUS
VERB	VOID ITEM	DASD	HALF DUPLEX	ALTERNATE TRACK	ANALOG COMPUTER
PHYSICAL RECORD	PERIPHERAL	RANDOM NUMBER	HOME RECORD	CHARACTER	RECOGNITION
OBJECT COMPUTER	OFFLINE	ACCESS TIME	EIGHT BIT CODE	HASP	HEADER LABEL
WAIT STATE	WIRE PRINTER	ERROR LOCK	SYNONYM	SOURCE LANGUAGE	JOGGLE
TELECOMMUNICATIONS	TABLE LOOKUP	ONLINE	CENTRALIZED	JOB INSTRUCTION	CHECK WORD
BOOLEAN OPERATION	BOOK	WORD	DEMONSTRATE	PERMEATION	DOCUMENTATION
PHASE	MODULE	PROGRAM CONTROL	DOCUMENT	DATA ATTRIBUTE	TRANSMITTAL FORM

Exercise 3 (ALPHA03)

ARRAY	WORD LENGTH	SOURCE DOCUMENT	ACCEPT	ACCOUNTING MACHINE	ACCURACY
NSI	VERIFIER	FONTS	SEPARATE	SEQUENTIAL	MNEMONIC
CURSOR	QTAM	CLOSED SHOP	LOAD POINT	OP CODE	EXTENT
QUERY	COBOL	TRACE	ASSIGN	DISK LABEL	TAPE LABEL
EXCLUSIVE OR	ACCELERATION TIME	WORK FILE	COLLECTION	COLLEGE	DISK ADDRESS
VALIDATION	IOCS	EVENT	SOCIETY	INTERNATIONAL	PROMOTE
PARTITION	RADIX	FORTRAN	TOP NOTCH	SOCIOLOGY	UNABRIDGED
OPERAND	EXCEPTION	ACCUMULATOR	USEFUL	ACATE	MOODY
WORKMARK	ESD	INTERRECORD GAP	TEMPLE	CORSICANA	WEATHERFORD
TOGGLE	PARITY BIT	VTAM	ORCHARD	HARTFORD	UNIVERSITY
TIME SHARING	OPERATING SYSTEM	PARAMETER	MASSACHUSETTS	REMOVABLE	CHIP
COMBINED FILE	TRACK	OPTION	WHEEL	FUSE	SYMBOL

Exercise 4 (ALPHA04)

BUSY MODE	SEPARATE	HEXIDECIMAL	VOCABULARY	BLIND TERMINAL	CPU
ANSI	ANDING	AUTO FEED	PUNCHING STATION	SECURITY	DATA CELL
CLUSTER	COMPILE	FACTOR	READING STATION	ARCHITECTURE	GATE
DATA BANK	DUPLEX	DATA LINK	ENTER MODE	COLLATING SEQUENCE	STACKER
QUOTIENT	MULTIPLIER	APL	APPLICATION	DATA DIVISION	JECL
MULTIPLICAND	FACTOR	CORE STORAGE	CORNER CUT	EFFECTIVE ADDRESS	KEYBOARD
FILE DESCRIPTION	AUTO SKIP	EDIT MODE	DATA ITEM	INTERRECORD GAP	MAINTENANCE
HOST PROCESSOR	OEM	DIRECT ACCESS	FILL CHARACTER	HOPPER	DIVIDEND
DATA RECORDER	PACKET	PACKED DECIMAL	FOREGROUND	JOB CONTROL	PASSWORD
REGISTER	REALTIME	RECEIVE MODE	GANG PUNCH	MASTER FILE	DIAGRAM
PARAGRAPH	ROM	RECORD NAME	REEL	OPERATOR CONSOLE	STATISTICAL
READ HEAD	ROS	FILE NAME	ROUND OFF	EJECT	PANEL

Exercise 5 (ALPHA05)

DECOLLATE	DECREMENT	DATA BASE	SECTOR	SIGNIFICANT DIGIT	COLUMN
FULL DUPLEX	JCL	CYCLE	TERMINAL	MINICOMPUTER	STATUS
HORIZONTAL FEED	LOOPING	PROCEDURE	IDENTIFICATION	THRASING	OPTICAL
IMPACT PRINTER	MONITOR	VOLUME	PRIVATE LIBRARY	DATA ENTRY	ACOUSTIC
ERROR RESET	NONNUMERIC	ELEVEN PUNCH	DATA CARD	PRIVILEGED INSTRUCTION	N CAROLINA
SKIP KEY	OFFSET	OVER PUNCH	CROSS FOOT	COUNTER	AUSTIN
READ CHECK	PACK	ZERO FILL	VIRTUAL STORAGE	VALIDITY CHECK	MINIMUM
MVS	PLATEN	WRAP AROUND	EMULATE	ELEMENTARY ITEM	MAXIMUM
SWITCH	CORPORATION	TEXT EDITOR	FORMATTED RECORD	BTAM	ABBREVIATION
AUTOMATIC	KEYPUNCH	MODE	BUFFER	WORKING STORAGE	ODESSA
SUBSIDIARY	ILLINOIS	SEARCH	ZERO SUPPRESS	OVERWRITE	MIDLAND
BUSINESS	MAINE	HARDWARE	WPM	ZONE PUNCH	VAN HORN

Exercise 6 (ALPHA06)

COM	ABNORMAL	ABSTRACT	RPG	HOLLERITH CODE	FIELD
MICROCOMPUTER	ALABAMA	THESIS	BAR PRINTER	BACKGROUND	CHARACTER SET
MCGREGOR	TEXAS	SWEETWATER	SYNCHRONOUS	SYMBOL	BACKUP
MISSISSIPPI	COLORADO CITY	OREGON	WRITE ENABLE	TELETYPEWRITER	SWAP
LOUISIANA	MISSOURI	WYOMING	OBJECT CODE	WAND	TAPE UNIT
WAXAHACHIE	GOVENOR	MEXIA	VTOC	ZERO OUT	OPEN SHOP
ABILENE	MINIMIZE	GEORGIA	END USER	EOB	EOD
STATIONARY	COMPLIANCE	NEBRASKA	DATA FLOW	DATA TRANSFER	DEBUG
STERLING	BIG SPRING	COUNTY	PAGING	VSAM	VOLATILITY
PECOS	VAN ZANDT	EOR	OVERLAY	PAPER TAPE	PAGE PRINTER
EL PASO	POST	EOT	ZAP	OUTPUT	NETWORK
ITAN	SAN ANGELO	TM	CHANNEL	CHAINING	CHECK DIGIT

Exercise 7 (ALPHA07)

CHECK POINT	ACTIVE PROGRAM	WEST GERMANY	IRELAND	ADDROUT FILE	ARITHMETIC UNIT
BIT	SHAMROCK	ENGLAND	GREECE	WHEELER	POCKET
STORAGE CONTROL	DENMARK	EXERCISE	INDIA	SUPPLEMENTAL	MAIN LINE SWITCH
TELEX	CUBA	ACTUAL KEY	ADDEND	PROOF READ	COMMAND ERROR
ON DEMAND	WEST	WOOD	TERRACE	FRANCE	FIELD BACKSPACE
PARALLEL	CALCULATION	TURNPIKE	HIGHWAY	MCLENNAN	FIELD SEPARATOR
ENCODE	LEVER	RIBBON	EQUIPMENT	TRAVIS	SEARCH EOD
DECODE	KEYTAPE	INSCRIBER	QUESTION	QUERIES	RETURN TO INDEX
VARIABLE	STARWHEEL	AMARILLO	GRAPHICS	MAIN FRAME	FUNCTION SELECT
ZOOMING	AUXILIARY	LABORATORY	DIRECTORY	CONVERSION	PROGRAM LOAD
WATS	FIELD DEFINITION	NOTCH	PROGRAMMER	MODEM	SEARCH CONTENT
FILE	BLANK COLUMN	APPLICATION	RELIABILITY	UPDATE	LABEL

Exercise 8 (ALPHA08)

ARRAY	BURROUGHS	PUNCHED CARD	CREDIT	VALIDATE	EFFICIENCY
PLOTTER	CDC	CURSOR WRAP	ASYNCHRONOUS	AUTO DUP KEY	ATTRIBUTE
RESET KEY	NCR	POLLING	POST	BATCH NUMBER	INDEXED SET
STATUS LINE	ASSEMBLE	ATTENTION KEY	VALUE	XEROX	TEXT FIELD
SEARCH MODE	IBM	SCREEN STATUS	COMMERCIAL	INVALID BATCH	MANUAL FIELD
LOG OFF	HONEYWELL	DETAIL RECORD	INDEXED FILE	SEARCH MASK	DAISY WHEEL
MISMATCH	DEC	FIELD ADVANCE	TEXT EDIT	LIGHT PEN	WAND
SCANNING	DATAPOINT	SELECT PROGRAM	MAGNETIC CARD	BUBBLE MEMORY	CHAINING
TAB	DATA GENERAL	DISPLAY PROGRAM	FORMATTED DISPLAY	PROGRAM SEQUENCING	DATA KEY
NONVERIFY	WANG	FIELD TOTAL	MEDIA	DEFAULT VALUE	ATTENUATOR
DELETE RECORD	RADIO SHACK	LOG ON	AUXILIARY	BURST MODE	BUS
DEBIT	TAB	SURVEY	BUG	AVAILABILITY	OCTAL

Exercise 9 (ALPHA09)

CICS	CHARACTERISTIC	MOHAWK	GCS	COLOR	PROCESSING
PASSWORD	SINGER	DATA ACTION	GTE	MICROFILM	PANEL
LOCK CODE	SIMILARITY	TALLY	OLIVETTI	EXIT	TABLES
AUTOMATIC	RESUME	CONSOLIDATED COMPUTER	SCAN DATA	PICTURE	SECURITY
WP	IMPLEMENTATION	CUMMINS ALLISON	SCAN OPTICS	CANCEL	SENSE
QUME PRINTER	TEXAS INSTRUMENTS	FOUR PHASE	WESTINGHOUSE	CODING	DIGITAL
TERMINAL	CONTROL DATA	LOCKHEED	GENESIS ONE	CYLINDER	GARBAGE
DATA SET	SPERRY UNIVAC	NIXDORF	MEMOREX	FOREGROUND	IMPERATIVE
FUNCTION KEY	DECISION DATA	CMC	HARRIS	TEMPLATE	EVALUATION
AUDIO	PRIME COMPUTER	NORTHERN TELECOM	SYCOR	SUBPROGRAM	PRIORITY
MINICOMPUTER	HEWLETT PACKARD	DATAPOINT	SCAN DATA	HEADING	DECIMAL
KEYSTATION	SOUTHWEST TECHNICAL PRODUCTS		TRIVEX	REPRODUCER	ANALYST

Exercise 10 (ALPHA10)

STAFF	FUNCTIONAL	ACCOUNT	MILEPOST	IMPENDING	SUBROUTINE
METHODS	SPECIFICATIONS	RECOMMEND	COMPANY	MANUFACTURE	EXTERNAL
STRATEGY	BUDGET	THEORY	CORPORATION	GOVERN	INTERNAL
ATTEMPTS	PLANNINGS	INDECISIVE	SEMESTER	POTENTIAL	LIBRARIES
ALTERNATIVE	SEQUENCES	COMPETENT	FINANCIAL	MASTER	UTILITY
EXTENSIVE	MEASURE	ABILITY	SCHOOLS	INTERPERSONAL	INDICATOR
DIRECT	EDUCATION	CRISIS	SUPERVISOR	ASCENDING	RESULTING
POLICIES	ELIMINATE	CLARIFY	BOSS	DESCENDING	IDENTIFYING
ASSUMPTIONS	MANAGEMENT	ROUTINE	EMPLOYER	SCHEMATIC	RESULTANT
RESULTS	MAXIMUM	TYPES	EMPLOYEE	JOB DESCRIPTION	SPECIFICATION
ALTERNATIVE	MINIMUM	CAUSE	RECREATION	DUTIES	DESCRIPTION
INFEXIBLE	COMPRISE	FORECAST	TECHNIQUE	QUALIFICATIONS	EXTENSION

SECTION C
KEYING EXERCISES UNDER PROGRAM CONTROL

For the following exercises:

1. Prepare a program format.
2. Prepare prompts if possible.
3. Get your program(s) approved by your instructor.
4. Key the program(s) and load them.
5. Use standard abbreviations (see Appendix B).
6. Do not key special characters (periods, dashes, commas, dollar signs, # signs) unless you are instructed to do so.
7. Unless otherwise instructed:
   a. Numeric fields should be right justified and zero filled.
   b. Alphameric fields should be left justified and blank filled.
   c. Any missing numeric fields should be zero filled and missing alphameric fields should be blank filled.
8. The word "street" or its abbreviation should *not* be keyed.
9. In the case of route and box numbers, leave the house number blank.
10. In an alphameric field that is mostly numeric, program it numeric. Then if a letter appears in one or two columns only of that field, program those columns alpha shift.

Exercise 1

1. Prepare a program format for the following:

   a. **Columns**

1	Record code, letter A
2–13	First name
14	Middle initial
15–28	Last name
29–33	House number (right justify and zero fill)
34–48	Street name or route or box numbers
49–52	Apartment number or letter (left justify and blank fill)
53–65	City name
66–67	State abbreviation
68–72	Zip code number

   b. Prepare prompts if possible.

2. Get your program approved by your instructor, key it, and load it.
3. Key the following data:

JOB NAME: ADDR01

Name	Address	City	State	Zip
Jane Zeigler	1219 St. Charles Ave.	New Orleans	LA	70140
Jackye Clay	P.O. Box 844	Gainesville	TX	76240
David Creasey	645 Plantation Dr.	Honolulu	HI	96818
Andrew Barkan	566 Londonberry Rd.	Atlanta	GA	30327
Laura T. Haines	300 Brook Dr. Apt. #27	College Sta	TX	77840
Beth Auda	123 Orenda Circle	Westfield	NJ	07090
Julie Buck	888 Rolling Pass	Glenwood	IL	60025
Terry Brown	7034 Sage Terrace	Ft. Worth	TX	76109
Christopher Beykirch	206 Skyline Dr.	Sedalia	MO	65301
Becca Springsteen	3795 Thunder Rd.	Asbury Park	NJ	08403
Clarence Clemmons	511 82nd St.	Blauvelt	NJ	11209
Tad Armstrong	109 N. 62nd	Waco	TX	76710
Louis P. Boudreaux	708 Summit Ridge	Franklin	LA	70535
Kathy Courts	5048 Fawnwood Ct.	Broken Arrow	OK	74012
Barry Brooks	1054 Fairmont #4B	Dallas	TX	75219
Laurie J. Johnson	P.O. Box 97	Montverde	FL	32756
James Dover	4347 Merrywood Dr.	Birmingham	AL	35207
Jaime B. Garza	P.O. Box 104	Crosbyton	TX	79322
Doug Gray	P.O. Box 2107	Spartanburg	SC	29309
Gretchen Hein	5356 Southern Ave.	San Angelo	TX	76901
Robert A. Hatter	P.O. Box 44	Nacona	TX	76255
Jon Landau	2122 10th Ave. #12A	Brooklyn	NY	11219
Cindy Heller	3215 Dauphine	Northbrook	IL	60022
Carolyn Frye	64 Lone Tree Rd.	New Caanan	CT	06840
Clifton C. Lyon	14122 Cedar Ln.	Houston	TX	77057
Marc Centrone	10806 Mt. Mesabi	Devon	PA	19333

JOB NAME: ADDR02

Felicia Park	Harvard Univ.	Cambridge	MA 02138
Susan Roberts	520 Yates	Lubbock	TX 79409
Audrey K. Roden	4215 Justin NW	Albuquerque	NM 87114
Keith Tidmore	Rt. 2 Box 49B	Bolivar	TN 38008
Nick Buckingham	1220 Rhiannon	Silver Spgs	MD 20906
Steve Rodgers	5505 Zeta Blvd.	Rockwall	TX 75087
Tami Townsend	7402 Whispering Oaks	Austin	TX 78745
Steve Smetak	613 Rose St. #7	Lexington	KY 40508
Duncan D. Brown	666 Wild Ave.	Portland	OR 97222
Beth Floor	10025 Brookside Ln.	Omaha	NE 68124
Susan Streck	1712 Wishingwell	Overland Park	KS 66213
Ronald Woods	1001 Rollingstone Ln.	Las Vegas	NV 89106
Anna Maria Thompson	1744 W. Aztec	Flagstaff	AZ 86001
Katherine A. Todd	3608 Lee Shore	Tampa	FL 33609
William Nelson	Rt. 1 Box 30F	Abbott	TX 76711
Allen Miller, III	3299 Bosque Blvd.	Waco	TX 76707
Neil J. Younger	48 Harvest Rd.	Cinnamon	SD 57105
Bradley Maxwell	830 Vineyard Ct.	Toledo	OH 43607
Tom Peters	220 Moselle Pl.	Grosse Point	MI 48236
Charlotte L. Davis	358 Elmwood	Braintree	MA 02184
Peter Gabriel	23 Heather Hill Ln.	Colorado Spgs	CO 80901
Susan Land	1917 Ash Crescent	Minneapolis	MN 55426
Tanya K. Irving	348 Flamingo Way	Highland Park	IL 60035
Suzanne Dinger	5307 Lamp Post Ln.	Richardson	TX 75080

JOB NAME: SAVINGS

Exercise 2   Savings Checks

Record Position	Information
1	Record Code (letter S)
2–7	Date, numeric
8–15	Amount, numeric (nnnnnn∧nn)
16–25	Account number (numeric)—first two digits are bank number
26–27	Deposit or debit code (41, 45, 51, or 57) 41 and 45 = deposit 51 and 57 = debit

REMEMBER

Right justify and zero fill numeric fields. Do not key any special characters.

```
                        SAVINGS CHECK                              ①
                              Pampa, Texas,  8/14      19 80
PAY TO MYSELF OR BEARER
  One Thousand and no/100 ─────────── Dollars, $ 1000.00
THE COMMUNITY NATIONAL BANK OF PAMPA
      PAMPA, TEXAS              J. R. Jones
                                Signature of Depositor
                              Account Number      Code
                              0 4 8 3 2 1 0 4 8 9   4 1
```

```
                        SAVINGS CHECK                              ②
                              Pampa, Texas,  8/15      19 80
PAY TO MYSELF OR BEARER
  One hundred and fifty and no/100 ─────── Dollars, $ 150.00
THE COMMUNITY NATIONAL BANK OF PAMPA
      PAMPA, TEXAS              T. H. Thortenberry
                                Signature of Depositor
                              Account Number      Code
                              0 4 4 6 1 3 2 8 6 2   4 5
```

```
                        SAVINGS CHECK                              ③
                              Pampa, Texas,  8/15      19 80
PAY TO MYSELF OR BEARER
  Fifty and 50/100 ─────────────── Dollars, $ 50.50
THE COMMUNITY NATIONAL BANK OF PAMPA
      PAMPA, TEXAS              J H. Lee
                                Signature of Depositor
                              Account Number      Code
                              0 4 2 1 3 8 5 6 2 1   5 1
```

EXERCISES

Savings Check 4

SAVINGS CHECK

Pampa, Texas, 8/15 19 80

PAY TO MYSELF OR BEARER

Sixty five and 24/100 ———— Dollars, $65.24

THE COMMUNITY NATIONAL BANK OF PAMPA

PAMPA, TEXAS

J. Rodney Lee
Signature of Depositor

Account Number: 0468314248 Code: 21

Savings Check 5

SAVINGS CHECK

Pampa, Texas, 8/16 19 80

PAY TO MYSELF OR BEARER

Seventy five and no/100 ———— Dollars, $75.00

THE COMMUNITY NATIONAL BANK OF PAMPA

PAMPA, TEXAS

E. L. Biggerstaff
Signature of Depositor

Account Number: 0481324692 Code: 57

Savings Check 6

SAVINGS CHECK

Pampa, Texas, 8/16 19 80

PAY TO MYSELF OR BEARER

Twenty five and no/100 ———— Dollars, $25.00

THE COMMUNITY NATIONAL BANK OF PAMPA

PAMPA, TEXAS

Hazel Martin
Signature of Depositor

Account Number: 042138524 8 Code: 41

SAVINGS CHECK ⑦

Pampa, Texas, 8/25 19 80

PAY TO MYSELF OR BEARER

Thirty six and 50/100 —————————— Dollars, $ 36 50

THE COMMUNITY NATIONAL BANK OF PAMPA
PAMPA, TEXAS

Mary Brewer
Signature of Depositor

Account Number | Code
0 4 2 1 6 4 2 8 3 2 | 5 1

SAVINGS CHECK ⑧

Pampa, Texas, 8/25 19 80

PAY TO MYSELF OR BEARER

Forty and no/100 —————————— Dollars, $ 40 00

THE COMMUNITY NATIONAL BANK OF PAMPA
PAMPA, TEXAS

Jackie Talbert
Signature of Depositor

Account Number | Code
0 4 3 3 3 4 4 2 8 2 | 5 7

SAVINGS CHECK ⑨

Pampa, Texas, 8/26 19 80

PAY TO MYSELF OR BEARER

Forty five and 10/100 —————————— Dollars, $ 45 10

THE COMMUNITY NATIONAL BANK OF PAMPA
PAMPA, TEXAS

John Rasor
Signature of Depositor

Account Number | Code
0 4 1 1 1 2 2 2 4 5 | 4 1

EXERCISES

SAVINGS CHECK ⑩

Pampa, Texas, 8/26 19 80

PAY TO MYSELF OR BEARER

Nine hundred and no/100 —————— Dollars, $ 900.00

THE COMMUNITY NATIONAL BANK OF PAMPA

PAMPA, TEXAS

Clyde Koehne
Signature of Depositor

Account Number: 0446821388 Code: 45

SAVINGS CHECK ⑪

Pampa, Texas, 8/27 19 80

PAY TO MYSELF OR BEARER

Ninety five and 36/100 —————— Dollars, $ 95.36

THE COMMUNITY NATIONAL BANK OF PAMPA

PAMPA, TEXAS

Ann Garrett
Signature of Depositor

Account Number: 0414683128 Code: 45

SAVINGS CHECK ⑫

Pampa, Texas, 8/29 19 80

PAY TO MYSELF OR BEARER

Five hundred and no/100 —————— Dollars, $ 500.00

THE COMMUNITY NATIONAL BANK OF PAMPA

PAMPA, TEXAS

Rosemary Taylor
Signature of Depositor

Account Number: 04883312 Code: 57

PART 4 LABORATORY EXERCISES

SAVINGS CHECK (13)

Pampa, Texas, 8/30 19 80

PAY TO MYSELF OR BEARER

Four hundred fifty and no/100 ———— Dollars, $ 450.00

THE COMMUNITY NATIONAL BANK OF PAMPA
PAMPA, TEXAS

Joan Culverhouse
Signature of Depositor

Account Number: 048821342 1   Code: 51

SAVINGS CHECK (14)

Pampa, Texas, 8/30 19 80

PAY TO MYSELF OR BEARER

Three hundred twenty and no/100 ———— Dollars, $ 325.00

THE COMMUNITY NATIONAL BANK OF PAMPA
PAMPA, TEXAS

Margaret Cole
Signature of Depositor

Account Number: 049213854 2   Code: 51

SAVINGS CHECK (15)

Pampa, Texas, 9/1 19 80

PAY TO MYSELF OR BEARER

One hundred seventy five and no/100 ———— Dollars, $ 175.00

THE COMMUNITY NATIONAL BANK OF PAMPA
PAMPA, TEXAS

Joe Spacek
Signature of Depositor

Account Number: 04892135 68   Code: 45

EXERCISES

SAVINGS CHECK (16)

Pampa, Texas, 9/1 19 80

PAY TO MYSELF OR BEARER

Two hundred and no/100 —————— Dollars, $ 200.00

THE COMMUNITY NATIONAL BANK OF PAMPA

PAMPA, TEXAS

Betty Plog
Signature of Depositor

Account Number: 0 4 9 9 9 2 0 8 4 2   Code: 4 1

SAVINGS CHECK (17)

Pampa, Texas, 9/1 19 80

PAY TO MYSELF OR BEARER

Seventy five and no/100 —————— Dollars, $ 75.00

THE COMMUNITY NATIONAL BANK OF PAMPA

PAMPA, TEXAS

Ila Post
Signature of Depositor

Account Number: 0 4 8 6 1 3 2 8 4 2   Code: 5 1

SAVINGS CHECK (18)

Pampa, Texas, 9/2 19 80

PAY TO MYSELF OR BEARER

Eighty five and 45/100 —————— Dollars, $ 85.45

THE COMMUNITY NATIONAL BANK OF PAMPA

PAMPA, TEXAS

Mary Brown
Signature of Depositor

Account Number: 0 4 9 9 8 1 3 1 2 4   Code: 4 1

Check 19

SAVINGS CHECK

Pampa, Texas, 9/3 1980

PAY TO MYSELF OR BEARER

One hundred thirty and no/100 ———— Dollars, $130.00

THE COMMUNITY NATIONAL BANK OF PAMPA
PAMPA, TEXAS

B. W. Chessor
Signature of Depositor

Account Number: 0 4 3 2 4 6 1 3 8 4   Code: 5 7

Check 20

SAVINGS CHECK

Pampa, Texas, 9/4 1980

PAY TO MYSELF OR BEARER

Forty and 20/100 ———— Dollars, $40.20

THE COMMUNITY NATIONAL BANK OF PAMPA
PAMPA, TEXAS

Margaret Harbaugh
Signature of Depositor

Account Number: 0 4 6 6 4 2 1 3 8 5   Code: 5 1

Check 21

SAVINGS CHECK

Pampa, Texas, 9/5 1980

PAY TO MYSELF OR BEARER

Sixty six and no/100 ———— Dollars, $66.00

THE COMMUNITY NATIONAL BANK OF PAMPA
PAMPA, TEXAS

Dr. Bill Rhode
Signature of Depositor

Account Number: 0 4 6 8 3 1 2 4 9 8   Code: 4 5

EXERCISES

```
                                SAVINGS CHECK                                (22)

                                  Pampa, Texas,   9/6        19 80
PAY TO MYSELF OR BEARER
 Seven hundred twenty five and no/100 ——————— Dollars, $ 725 00
THE COMMUNITY NATIONAL BANK OF PAMPA
        PAMPA, TEXAS                    Jean Revercomb
                                        Signature of Depositor

                                   Account Number      Code
                                   0 4 8 2 1 3 6 9 6 8    4 1
```

```
                                SAVINGS CHECK                                (23)

                                  Pampa, Texas,   9/7        19 80
PAY TO MYSELF OR BEARER
 Eight hundred and no/100 ————————————— Dollars, $ 800 00
THE COMMUNITY NATIONAL BANK OF PAMPA
        PAMPA, TEXAS                    Lauri Johnson
                                        Signature of Depositor

                                   Account Number      Code
                                   0 4 9 6 8 3 4 2 1 8    5 1
```

```
                                SAVINGS CHECK                                (24)

                                  Pampa, Texas,   9/8        19 80
PAY TO MYSELF OR BEARER
 Thirty five and no/100 —————————————— Dollars, $ 35 00
THE COMMUNITY NATIONAL BANK OF PAMPA
        PAMPA, TEXAS                    Ralph Lee
                                        Signature of Depositor

                                   Account Number      Code
                                   0 4 8 3 1 4 2 8 1 3    5 7
```

SAVINGS CHECK (25)

Pampa, Texas, 9/9 19 80

PAY TO MYSELF OR BEARER

Twenty and no/100 —————————————— Dollars, $20.00

THE COMMUNITY NATIONAL BANK OF PAMPA
PAMPA, TEXAS

Bob Lord
Signature of Depositor

Account Number: 0466831242   Code: 41

SAVINGS CHECK (26)

Pampa, Texas, 9/10 19 80

PAY TO MYSELF OR BEARER

Forty five and no/100 —————————————— Dollars, $45.00

THE COMMUNITY NATIONAL BANK OF PAMPA
PAMPA, TEXAS

James Pippen
Signature of Depositor

Account Number: 0438214682   Code: 41

SAVINGS CHECK (27)

Pampa, Texas, 9/10 19 80

PAY TO MYSELF OR BEARER

Seventy and no/100 —————————————— Dollars, $70.00

THE COMMUNITY NATIONAL BANK OF PAMPA
PAMPA, TEXAS

James Richards
Signature of Depositor

Account Number: 0438216986   Code: 41

EXERCISES

SAVINGS CHECK (28)

Pampa, Texas, 9/25 19 80

PAY TO MYSELF OR BEARER

Three hundred forty five and no/100 —————— Dollars, $345.00

THE COMMUNITY NATIONAL BANK OF PAMPA
PAMPA, TEXAS

David Parker
Signature of Depositor

Account Number: 046321444 Code: 51

SAVINGS CHECK (29)

Pampa, Texas, 9/25 19 80

PAY TO MYSELF OR BEARER

Six hundred ten and no/100 —————— Dollars, $610.00

THE COMMUNITY NATIONAL BANK OF PAMPA
PAMPA, TEXAS

Jeannete McGinnes
Signature of Depositor

Account Number: 0481346912 Code: 51

SAVINGS CHECK (30)

Pampa, Texas, 9/25 19 80

PAY TO MYSELF OR BEARER

Fifty five and 60/100 —————— Dollars, $55.60

THE COMMUNITY NATIONAL BANK OF PAMPA
PAMPA, TEXAS

Curtis Lee
Signature of Depositor

Account Number: 049186321 Code: 57

JOB NAME: DRIVERS

Exercise 3 Driver's License Records

Record Position	Information
1–7	License number, numeric
8	Type of license, numeric
9–35	Name of person (first name, middle initial, last name)
36	Purge code (alphameric or blank)

Left justify and blank fill alphameric fields. Right justify and zero fill numeric fields. Leave one space before and after the middle initial.

License Number	License Type	Name	Purge Code
001 5219	1	CLARENCE BISHOP	L
001 8422	1	ROBERT W CANTRILL	F
003 1845	2	LESTER M HAWTHORNE	E
026 2249	3	RECTOR CORREA	
173 8819	1	MICHAEL R ROE	F
478 4355	3	TIMOTHY G BIDPATH	
529 3449	1	DANIEL M RODRIGUEZ	
546 8542	2	JOHN R BOEDEKER	E
570 6875	1	DAVE M POINDEXTER	
610 5217	1	GLENN E EGELSTON	L
615 6145	1	MARIA J CENTANO	
615 9170	1	PAUL K MCCLURKIN	
617 3647	1	JAMES R WISNER II	
671 4457	1	BILLY D HALFIN	E
692 6583	2	LEONARDO ANTOMAS JR	
700 9896	1	ANTONIO SANMIGUEL	
704 8120	1	ALLEN D SIMONS JR	
712 9430	3	ALFRED G ALEJANDRO	
713 6004	2	ANNE R SIMMONS	F
717 9622	1	VICTORIA JENSON	E

JOB NAME: PAYROLL

Exercise 4 Payroll

Record Position	Information
1–2	Week number
3–9	Employee number, alphameric
10–11	Tax class, numeric
12–19	Year-to-date gross pay, nnnnnn₋nn
20–25	Year-to-date FIT, nnnn₋nn
26–30	Quarterly FICA, nnn₋nn
31–37	Gross pay, nnnnn₋nn

Right justify and zero fill all fields. Do not key any special characters.

EXERCISES

Week Number	Employee Number	Tax Class	YTD Gross	YTD FIT	QTR FICA	Gross Pay
1	7885396	0	125.00	22.50	6.00	125.00
2	7885921	1	170.00	38.88	9.30	85.00
1	7895645	99	1,285.00	.00	61.68	1,285.00
1	7923186	20	2,000.00	313.20	96.00	2,000.00
4	8004213	4	8,200.00	842.64	195.00	400.00
5	A000010	5	8,300.01	578.30	195.00	500.00
6	A000011	6	7,800.00	657.96	118.20	400.00
7	A000012	6	7,900.00	675.96	118.20	500.00
14	A000013	6	7,900.00	675.96	19.20	500.00
27	A000017	6	7,900.00	675.96	19.20	500.00
40	A000020	6	7,900.00	675.00	19.20	500.00
42	A000021	6	7,800.00	925.96	164.00	3,000.00
3	A000022	2	600.00	179.28	28.52	200.00
5	A000023	0	1,125.00	231.30	44.83	225.00
6	A000024	1	390.00	65.52	14.43	65.00
7	A000025	2	525.00	70.56	16.03	75.00
8	A000028	3	760.00	90.72	20.80	95.00
10	A000030	0	1,090.00	376.20	77.99	190.00
11	A000040	2	1,705.00	298.64	58.57	155.00
12	A000041	4	780.00	30.42	59.57	65.00

JOB NAME: LONGDIST

Exercise 5   Long Distance Records

Record Position	Information
1	Record code (letter L)
2-7	Date, numeric
8-12	Total amount, numeric nnn.nn
13-17	Client number, numeric
18-21	Matter number, numeric
22-31	Phone number called, area code and seven digit phone number, numeric
32-42	Billing number
43-45	Time in minutes, numeric
46-48	Attorney number, numeric (in BY at the bottom of the form)

Right justify and zero fill numeric fields. Left justify and blank fill alphameric fields. Do not key special characters.

LONG DISTANCE ①	LONG DISTANCE ②
Date: March 23, 1980 Total Amt. $10.91	Date: 5/2/80 Total Amt. $4.48
CHARGE:	CHARGE:
Client: Arlington Electronics	Client: TCU Cleaners
Client Number: 07979	Client Number: 09731
Matter: Environmental Law	Matter: Co. vs Saxton Ins. Agency
Matter Number: 0224	Matter Number: 0444
Party Called: Scott Blair (Name)	Party Called: Andrew Bradshaw (Name)
Fayetteville, AR. 501 442-8369 (Place) (A.C.) (No. Called)	Seattle, WA. 206 546-3824 (Place) (A.C.) (No. Called)
Calling Attorney: Irene Schmidt	Calling Attorney: Rob Westbrook
024-6267-352 N (Special Billing No.)	018-0354-294 S (Special Billing No.)
31 Min. $10.70 $ (Time) (Charges) (Tax)	11 Min. $4.48 $.09 (Time) (Charges) (Tax)
Call not completed:	Call not completed:
Remarks: Line 1	Remarks:
Call placed by: VC/283	Call placed by: Andrea Cox/100

EXERCISES

LONG DISTANCE — ③

Date: 2/6/80 Total Amt. $2.15

CHARGE:
Client: Dr. Ralph Norman
Client Number: 06442
Matter: IRS Audit
Matter Number: 1209
Party Called: Lea Norman
(Name)

Thousand Oaks Ca.   408   252-4874
(Place)   (A.C.)   (No. Called)

Calling Attorney: JBD

054-0294-312 P
(Special Billing No.)

3 Min. $2.10 $.05
(Time)   (Charges)   (Tax)

Call not completed: _____
Remarks: Operator-assisted

Called placed by: R.L./010

LONG DISTANCE — ④

Date: 5/2/80 Total Amt. $1.68

CHARGE:
Client: TCU Cleaners
Client Number: 09731
Matter: Co. vs Saxton Ins. Agency
Matter Number: 0728
Party Called: Andrew Bradshaw
(Name)

Aledo, Tx.   817   441-9225
(Place)   (A.C.)   (No. Called)

Calling Attorney: WRS

469-3742-217 G
(Special Billing No.)

3 Min. $1.68 $.05
(Time)   (Charges)   (Tax)

Call not completed: _____
Remarks:

Call placed by: R.L./010

LONG DISTANCE (5)

Date 6/13/79 Total Amt. $ 4 72
CHARGE:
  Client: J. C. Rungren
  Client Number: 04932
  Matter: Rungren vs TRA
  Matter Number: 0382
  Party Called: Mervin Rife
  _____(Name)

Little Rock   501   663-5731
(Place)   (A.C.) (No. Called)

Calling Attorney RAL
    038-2734-918 T
    (Special Billing No.)

 5   Min. $ 4.64 $ .08
(Time)   (Charges) (Tax)

Call not completed: _____
Remarks: Line 7

      Called placed by: VC/283

LONG DISTANCE (6)

Date 4/19/80 Total Amt. $ 4.68
CHARGE:
  Client: Tri-Cor, Inc.
  Client Number: 05614
  Matter: Labor Dispute
  Matter Number: 0103
  Party Called: Robert C. Philips
  _____(Name)

Dallas   214   358-5630
(Place) (A.C.)   (No. Called)

Calling Attorney: Nick L. Barkley
    063-0888-218 R
    (Special Billing No.)

 13 Min. $ 4.59 $ .09
(Time)   (Charges) (Tax)

Call not completed: _____
Remarks:

      Call placed by: Joan Roberts/642

EXERCISES

LONG DISTANCE ⑦

Date: 8-14-80 Total Amt. $ 1.83
CHARGE:
  Client: Suzanne Dinger
  Client Number: _____
  Matter: Personal
  Matter Number: _____
Party Called: _____
  (Name)

Pampa, Tx.   806   413-8210
(Place)   (A.C.) (No. Called)

Calling Attorney: Lee
061-8304-913 N
(Special Billing No.)

3 Min. $ 1.80 $ .03
(Time)   (Charges) (Tax)

Call not completed: _____
Remarks:

Called placed by: Suzanne Dinger/812

LONG DISTANCE ⑧

Date: Aug. 16, 1980 Total Amt. $ 11.26
CHARGE:
  Client: Hillside Lakes
  Client Number: 01145
  Matter: Real Estate Litigation
  Matter Number: 0954
Party Called: Mrs. Julie Buck
  (Name)

Chicago   312   924-7072
(Place)   (A.C.) (No. Called)

Calling Attorney: Warren Bridges
086-2566-701 H
(Special Billing No.)

32 Min. $ 11.04 $ .22
(Time)   (Charges) (Tax)

Call not completed: _____
Remarks: Line 4

Call placed by: MWB/001

LONG DISTANCE ⑨

Date: September 21, 1980 Total Amt. $ 7.10
CHARGE:
Client: Central Texas Chemical
Client Number: 07714
Matter: Patent
Matter Number: 0309
Party Called: Dr. M.R. Breedlove (Name)

Austin, Texas / 512 / 472-6289
(Place) (A.C.) (No. Called)

Calling Attorney: Dan Fletz
098-2015-119 B (Special Billing No.)

29 Min. / $ 6.96 / $ .13
(Time) (Charges) (Tax)

Call not completed: ___
Remarks: Evening Rates

Called placed by: LS/682

LONG DISTANCE ⑩

Date: 5-21-80 Total Amt. $ 4.60
CHARGE:
Client: San Antonio Hardware Co.
Client Number: 09631
Matter: Copyright
Matter Number: 0883
Party Called: William Strickland (Name)

Atlanta, Georgia / 404 / 926-7410
(Place) (A.C.) (No. Called)

Calling Attorney: Dan Fletz
098-2015-119 B (Special Billing No.)

7 Min. / $ 4.51 / $ .09
(Time) (Charges) (Tax)

Call not completed: ___
Remarks:

Call placed by: LS/682

LONG DISTANCE ⑪

Date: 7-7-80 Total Amt. $ 15.42
CHARGE:
  Client: Duncan Oil Co.
  Client Number: 05252
  Matter: Anti trust litigation
  Matter Number: 0421
  Party Called: Christopher Lee
               (Name)

Houston   713   622-5648
(Place)   (A.C.) (No. Called)

Calling Attorney: Andrea Johnston
044-0976-231 H
(Special Billing No.)

42 Min. $ 15.12 $ .30
(Time)   (Charges)   (Tax)

Call not completed: _____
Remarks: Line 11

Called placed by: RL/010

LONG DISTANCE ⑫

Date: July 7, 1980 Total Amt. $ 11.57
CHARGE:
  Client: Around-the-World Tours
  Client Number: 02281
  Matter: ATW Tours vs Aviana Airlines
  Matter Number: 0430
  Party Called: Zachary Swan
               (Name)

Indianapolis   317   545-5647
(Place)   (A.C.)   (No. Called)

Calling Attorney: Durk Holby
021-0728-327 F
(Special Billing No.)

24 Min. $ 11.34 $ .23
(Time)   (Charges)   (Tax)

Call not completed: _____
Remarks: Operator-assisted

Call placed by: Liz/684

(13) LONG DISTANCE

Date: May 10, 1980 Total Amt. $ 6.77
CHARGE:
Client: Grubbs Dalstin
Client Number: 03379
Matter: Merger
Matter Number: 0851
Party Called: Allen Covington (Name)

Baltimore   301   342-5394
(Place)   (A.C.)   (No. Called)

Calling Attorney: Durk Holbey
021-0728-327F
(Special Billing No.)

18 Min. $ 6.64 $ .13
(Time)   (Charges)   (Tax)

Call not completed: ___
Remarks:
Called placed by: Liz/684

(14) LONG DISTANCE

Date: August 16, 1980 Total Amt. $ 20.19
CHARGE:
Client: Gordon Sims & Sons
Client Number: 03774
Matter: Sims vs Jennifer Bailey
Matter Number: 0505
Party Called: Andrew R. Travis (Name)

San Diego, Ca.   714   283-0160
(Place)   (A.C.)   (No. Called)

Calling Attorney: WRS
469-3742-217G
(Special Billing No.)

52 Min. $ 19.79 $ .40
(Time)   (Charges)   (Tax)

Call not completed: ___
Remarks: Operator-assisted Line 2
Call placed by: R.L./010

EXERCISES

LONG DISTANCE (15)

Date: Oct. 3, 1980   Total Amt. $ 13.59

CHARGE:
Client: Tina S. Morrison
Client Number: 02090
Matter: Guardianship
Matter Number: 0133
Party Called: Colleen Watson
              (Name)

Abilene, Tx.   915   677-4588
(Place)   (A.C.)   (No. Called)

Calling Attorney: T. C. Kline

596-2463-722D
(Special Billing No.)

37 Min. $ 13.32 $ .27
(Time)   (Charges) (Tax)

Call not completed: _____
Remarks: Operator-assisted Line 6

Called placed by: TCK/901

LONG DISTANCE (16)

Date: 4-2-80   Total Amt. $ 7.63

CHARGE:
Client: Bennett Pest Control
Client Number: 07639
Matter: Bankruptcy
Matter Number: 0950
Party Called: C. L. Rickey
              (Name)

Galveston, Tx.   713   744-2883
(Place)   (A.C.)   (No. Called)

Calling Attorney: FKP

438-1245-688D
(Special Billing No.)

22 Min. $ 7.48 $ .15
(Time)   (Charges) (Tax)

Call not completed: _____
Remarks:

Call placed by: R.L./010

LONG DISTANCE ⑰	LONG DISTANCE ⑱
Date: Jan. 17, 1980 Total Amt. $16.16	Date: 7/28/80 Total Amt. $15.39
CHARGE:	CHARGE:
Client: City of Sherman, Ill.	Client: Mr. & Mrs. Louis McDonald
Client Number: 04411	Client Number: 09281
Matter: Urban Renewal	Matter: Estate Plan & Wills
Matter Number: 0391	Matter Number: 0133
Party Called: K. B. King (Name)	Party Called: Jerry Smith (Name)
Chicago 312 924-6130 (Place) (A.C.) (No. Called)	Washington, D.C. 202 521-8761 (Place) (A.C.) (No. Called)
Calling Attorney: PSD	Calling Attorney: AA
099-0633-817 F (Special Billing No.)	072-0391-219 R (Special Billing No.)
44 Min. $15.84 $ .32 (Time) (Charges) (Tax)	20 Min. $15.09 $ .30 (Time) (Charges) (Tax)
Call not completed:	Call not completed:
Remarks:	Remarks:
Called placed by: PSD/902	Call placed by: SLR/903

EXERCISES

Form 19

LONG DISTANCE

Date: November 18, 1980   Total Amt. $ 5.55

CHARGE:
- Client: Office
- Client Number: 06512
- Matter: Income Tax
- Matter Number: 0421
- Party Called: Meyer Supply Co. (Name)

Ft. Worth, Tx.   817   244-1222
(Place)   (A.C.)   (No. Called)

Calling Attorney: R. L. Biggerstaff

061-8304-913 N
(Special Billing No.)

17 Min. $ 5.44 $ .11
(Time)   (Charges)   (Tax)

Call not completed: _____

Remarks: Direct Dial Line 9

Call placed by: Mary Cross/900

Form 20

LONG DISTANCE

Date: June 29, 1980   Total Amt. $?

CHARGE:
- Client: Office
- Client Number: 68314
- Matter: Divorce
- Matter Number: 0342
- Party Called: Frank Dunlop (Name)

Austin   512   451-7602
(Place)   (A.C.)   (No. Called)

Calling Attorney: Biggerstaff

061-8304-913 N
(Special Billing No.)

Approx. 4 Min. $? $?
(Time)   (Charges)   (Tax)

Call not completed: _____

Remarks: Direct Dial line 9

Call placed by: Mary Cross/900

JOB NAME: COPIER   Exercise 6   IBM Copier II Charge

Record Position	Information
1	Record code (letter X)
2-7	Date, numeric
8-12	Amount, numeric nnn$_\wedge$nn
13-17	Client number, numeric
18-21	Matter number, numeric
22	Office Charge (0 = no or blank; 1 = yes or √)
23-25	Attorney number, numeric (in BY at the bottom of the form)

Right justify and zero fill numeric fields. Left justify and blank fill alphameric fields. Do not key special characters.

```
IBM COPIER II CHARGE   ①

        Date  4-2-80

TOTAL COPIES   11

AMOUNT          $ 2.20

CHARGE
    Client  Bennet Pest Control
    Client No.  07639
    Matter  Bankruptcy
    Matter No.  0950
CHARGE OFFICE EXPENSE _____
        By  FKP/RL/010
            Lawyer/Non-lawyer
```

```
IBM COPIER II CHARGE   ②

        Date  3-10-80

TOTAL COPIES   4

AMOUNT          $ .80

CHARGE
    Client  Barrett-Howell III
    Client No.  02981
    Matter  Will
    Matter No.  0563
CHARGE OFFICE EXPENSE _____
        By  DH/RL/001
            Lawyer/Non-lawyer
```

```
IBM COPIER II CHARGE   ③

        Date  5-15-80

TOTAL COPIES   7

AMOUNT          $ 1.40

CHARGE
    Client  TMPA
    Client No.  07779
    Matter  Closing
    Matter No.  0217
CHARGE OFFICE EXPENSE _____
        By  TT/RL/005
            Lawyer/Non-lawyer
```

```
IBM COPIER II CHARGE   ④

        Date  4-3-80

TOTAL COPIES   5

AMOUNT          $ 1.00

CHARGE
    Client  Fowler Home
    Client No.  06148
    Matter  Endowment
    Matter No.  0307
CHARGE OFFICE EXPENSE _____
        By  JC/RL/006
            Lawyer/Non-lawyer
```

EXERCISES

```
IBM COPIER II CHARGE  ⑤
           Date  10-12-79
TOTAL COPIES     10
AMOUNT           $ 2.00
CHARGE
   Client  Burton Oil Co.
   Client No.  05263
   Matter  General
   Matter No.  0317
CHARGE OFFICE EXPENSE _____
         By  TT / RL / 005
             Lawyer/Non-lawyer
```

```
IBM COPIER II CHARGE  ⑥
           Date  6-13-80
TOTAL COPIES  _____
AMOUNT           $ _____
CHARGE
   Client  Virginia Smith
           (NEW FILE)
   Client No.  _____
   Matter  Zoning Change
   Matter No.  0431
CHARGE OFFICE EXPENSE _____
         By  PSD / RL / 011
             Lawyer/Non-lawyer
```

```
IBM COPIER II CHARGE  ⑦
           Date  8-11-80
TOTAL COPIES     1
AMOUNT           $ .20
CHARGE
   Client  NW Life Ins.
   Client No.  08474
   Matter  Pension Plan Rev.
   Matter No.  0240
CHARGE OFFICE EXPENSE _____
         By  JJ / RL / 015
             Lawyer/Non-lawyer
```

```
IBM COPIER II CHARGE  ⑧
           Date  4-9-79
TOTAL COPIES     16
AMOUNT           $ 1.74
CHARGE
   Client  Smith-Allison Bros.
   Client No.  64281
   Matter  Estate
   Matter No.  0398
CHARGE OFFICE EXPENSE  ✓
         By  CS / RL / 050
             Lawyer/Non-lawyer
```

IBM COPIER II CHARGE ⑨

Date 7/14/80

TOTAL COPIES 4

AMOUNT $.40

CHARGE
Client Curtis Formal Wear
Client No. 01238
Matter Co. vs Gary Johnson
Matter No. 0496
CHARGE OFFICE EXPENSE

By RAL/LJ/049
Lawyer/Non-lawyer

IBM COPIER II CHARGE ⑩

Date 4-3-80

TOTAL COPIES 7

AMOUNT $1.40

CHARGE
Client Fadal Jewelers, Inc.
Client No. 02885
Matter Employment Contr.
Matter No. 0339
CHARGE OFFICE EXPENSE

By DH/RL/040
Lawyer/Non-lawyer

IBM COPIER II CHARGE ⑪

Date 12/18/79

TOTAL COPIES 12

AMOUNT $1.20

CHARGE
Client Gil Horn
Client No. 06849
Matter Estate
Matter No. 0398
CHARGE OFFICE EXPENSE

By SR/LJ/035
Lawyer/Non-lawyer

IBM COPIER II CHARGE ⑫

Date 7/1/80

TOTAL COPIES 5

AMOUNT $1.00

CHARGE
Client Carl Johnson
Client No. 04522
Matter Property Settlements
Matter No. 0316
CHARGE OFFICE EXPENSE

By JLC/RL/036
Lawyer/Non-lawyer

```
IBM COPIER II CHARGE  (13)
          Date  8-13-80
TOTAL COPIES   9
AMOUNT            $ 1.80
CHARGE
   Client   Steve Dalton
   Client No.   01178
   Matter   Divorce
   Matter No.   0255
CHARGE OFFICE EXPENSE _____
          By  JLC/RL/036
              Lawyer/Non-lawyer
```

```
IBM COPIER II CHARGE  (14)
          Date  7-21-80
TOTAL COPIES   3
AMOUNT            $ .60
CHARGE
   Client   Lori Brooks
   Client No.   08335
   Matter   Child Custody
   Matter No.   0994
CHARGE OFFICE EXPENSE _____
          By  JLC/RL/036
              Lawyer/Non-lawyer
```

```
IBM COPIER II CHARGE  (15)
          Date  7-2-80
TOTAL COPIES   8
AMOUNT            $ 1.60
CHARGE
   Client   Andrew Gibb
   Client No.   04200
   Matter   Criminal
   Matter No.   0316
CHARGE OFFICE EXPENSE _____
          By  Miller/RL/030
              Lawyer/Non-lawyer
```

```
IBM COPIER II CHARGE  (16)
          Date  9-1-80
TOTAL COPIES   2
AMOUNT            $ .40
CHARGE
   Client   Murray's Bar & Grill
   Client No.   07720
   Matter   Co. vs Coors
   Matter No.   0737
CHARGE OFFICE EXPENSE _____
          By  CS/RL/050
              Lawyer/Non-lawyer
```

IBM COPIER II CHARGE ⑰
Date 4-26-80
TOTAL COPIES 12
AMOUNT $ 2.40
CHARGE
  Client Hiller & Heine
  Client No. 05922
  Matter Co. vs WWISD
  Matter No. 0708
CHARGE OFFICE EXPENSE
    By AB/RL/020
       Lawyer/Non-lawyer
	IBM COPIER II CHARGE ⑱
	Date 2-11-80
	TOTAL COPIES 1
	AMOUNT $ .20
	CHARGE
	  Client Cox Records
	  Client No. 07979
	  Matter Trust
	  Matter No. 042
	CHARGE OFFICE EXPENSE
	    By MJZ/RL/025
	       Lawyer/Non-lawyer

IBM COPIER II CHARGE ⑲
Date 3-30-80
TOTAL COPIES 3
AMOUNT $ .60
CHARGE
  Client Lane Lanching
  Client No. 02218
  Matter General
  Matter No. 0194
CHARGE OFFICE EXPENSE
    By SD/RL/026
       Lawyer/Non-lawyer
	IBM COPIER II CHARGE ⑳
	Date 1-13-80
	TOTAL COPIES 3
	AMOUNT $ .60
	CHARGE
	  Client Jones Auto Parts
	  Client No. 03077
	  Matter IRS Audit
	  Matter No. 0321
	CHARGE OFFICE EXPENSE
	    By MM/RL/027
	       Lawyer/Non-lawyer

EXERCISES

JOB NAME: POSTAGE

Exercise 7   Postage Charges

Record Position	Information
1	Record code (letter P)
2-7	Date, numeric
8-12	Amount, numeric nnn˄nn
13-17	Client number, numeric
18-21	Matter number, numeric
22-27	RRR number, numeric
28	Mail code
	1 = Additional postage
	2 = Certified mail
	3 = Special delivery
	4 = Registered mail
	5 = Express mail
	6 = Insured mail
29-31	Attorney number (in BY at the bottom of the form)

Right justify and zero fill all numeric fields. Left justify and blank fill all alphameric fields. Do not key special characters.

POSTAGE CHARGE   ①

8/18/80 $ 1.79

CLIENT: TRA

CLIENT NO.: 07208

MATTER: Dissolution

MATTER NO.: 0591

FOR: _____ ADDITIONAL POSTAGE
   ✓ CERTIFIED MAIL
   RRR NO. 369404
   _____ SPECIAL DELIVERY
   _____ REGISTERED MAIL
   _____ EXPRESS MAIL
   _____ INSURED MAIL

BY J. Roberts/642

9/78

POSTAGE CHARGE   ②

2/12/80 $ 1.40

CLIENT: Centex Ranch

CLIENT NO.: 02616

MATTER: General

MATTER NO.: 0111

FOR: _____ ADDITIONAL POSTAGE
   ✓ CERTIFIED MAIL
   RRR NO. 337401
   _____ SPECIAL DELIVERY
   _____ REGISTERED MAIL
   _____ EXPRESS MAIL
   _____ INSURED MAIL

BY RL/010

9/78

POSTAGE CHARGE ③

7/23/80 $ 1.53
CLIENT: Curry Corp.
CLIENT NO.: 01849
MATTER: Profit Sharing
MATTER NO.: 0885
FOR: ____ ADDITIONAL POSTAGE
     ✓ CERTIFIED MAIL
     RRR NO. 352219
     ____ SPECIAL DELIVERY
     ____ REGISTERED MAIL
     ____ EXPRESS MAIL
     ____ INSURED MAIL

BY VC/283

9/78

POSTAGE CHARGE ④

12/3/80 $ 1.66
CLIENT: Cameron & Associates
CLIENT NO.: 05119
MATTER: Trademark
MATTER NO.: 0927
FOR: ____ ADDITIONAL POSTAGE
     ✓ CERTIFIED MAIL
     RRR NO. 399576
     ____ SPECIAL DELIVERY
     ____ REGISTERED MAIL
     ____ EXPRESS MAIL
     ____ INSURED MAIL

BY MJZ/458

9/78

POSTAGE CHARGE ⑤

10/15/80 $ 1.92
CLIENT: Atlantic Stereo
CLIENT NO.: 07231
MATTER:
MATTER NO.: 0442
FOR: ____ ADDITIONAL POSTAGE
     ✓ CERTIFIED MAIL
     RRR NO. 374212
     ____ SPECIAL DELIVERY
     ____ REGISTERED MAIL
     ____ EXPRESS MAIL
     ____ INSURED MAIL

BY LS/682

9/78

POSTAGE CHARGE ⑥

9/1/80 $ 2.05
CLIENT: Christine M. Dowdy
CLIENT NO.: 03398
MATTER: Will
MATTER NO.: 0102
FOR: ✓ ADDITIONAL POSTAGE
     ____ CERTIFIED MAIL
     RRR NO. 360023
     ____ SPECIAL DELIVERY
     ____ REGISTERED MAIL
     ____ EXPRESS MAIL
     ____ INSURED MAIL

BY Liz/684

9/78

EXERCISES

POSTAGE CHARGE ⑦ 11/9/80 $ 1.66 CLIENT: Rejcek Salvage CLIENT NO.: 01581 MATTER: Retirement Plans MATTER NO.: 0226 FOR: ____ ADDITIONAL POSTAGE ✓ CERTIFIED MAIL RRR NO. 387411 ____ SPECIAL DELIVERY ____ REGISTERED MAIL ____ EXPRESS MAIL ____ INSURED MAIL BY RL/010 9/78	POSTAGE CHARGE ⑧ 1/2/80 $ 2.95 CLIENT: Krochne Sport. Goods CLIENT NO.: 02986 MATTER: Real Estate MATTER NO.: 0113 FOR: ✓ ADDITIONAL POSTAGE ____ CERTIFIED MAIL RRR NO. 271993 ____ SPECIAL DELIVERY ____ REGISTERED MAIL ____ EXPRESS MAIL ____ INSURED MAIL BY RL/010 9/78
POSTAGE CHARGE ⑨ 1/6/80 $ 2.45 CLIENT: Sarah Keeney CLIENT NO.: 07715 MATTER: Child Visitation MATTER NO.: 0351 FOR: ____ ADDITIONAL POSTAGE ____ CERTIFIED MAIL RRR NO. 276944 ____ SPECIAL DELIVERY ✓ REGISTERED MAIL ____ EXPRESS MAIL ____ INSURED MAIL BY RL/010 9/78	POSTAGE CHARGE ⑩ 8/19/80 $ 2.83 CLIENT: Corner Drug CLIENT NO.: 05592 MATTER: Sale of Business MATTER NO.: 0661 FOR: ____ ADDITIONAL POSTAGE ✓ CERTIFIED MAIL RRR NO. 369422 ____ SPECIAL DELIVERY ____ REGISTERED MAIL ____ EXPRESS MAIL ____ INSURED MAIL BY RL/010 9/78

```
      POSTAGE CHARGE  (11)
 9/3/80          $ 2.70
CLIENT:  Brazos Corp.
CLIENT NO.:  08173
MATTER:  Patent
MATTER NO.:  0662
FOR: ____ ADDITIONAL POSTAGE
      ✓   CERTIFIED MAIL
     RRR NO. 365534
     ____ SPECIAL DELIVERY
     ____ REGISTERED MAIL
     ____ EXPRESS MAIL
     ____ INSURED MAIL
            BY  RL/010
9/78
```

```
      POSTAGE CHARGE  (12)
 3/15/80         $ 6.65
CLIENT:  Sharon Dow
CLIENT NO.:  07714
MATTER:  Martin vs SWTP
MATTER NO.:  0298
FOR: ____ ADDITIONAL POSTAGE
     ____ CERTIFIED MAIL
     RRR NO. 304566
     ____ SPECIAL DELIVERY
      ✓   REGISTERED MAIL
     ____ EXPRESS MAIL
     ____ INSURED MAIL
            BY  RL/010
9/78
```

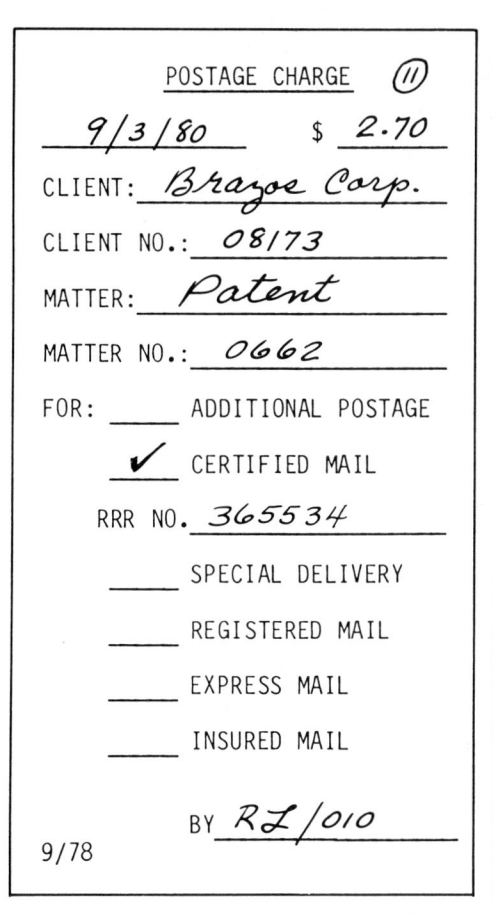

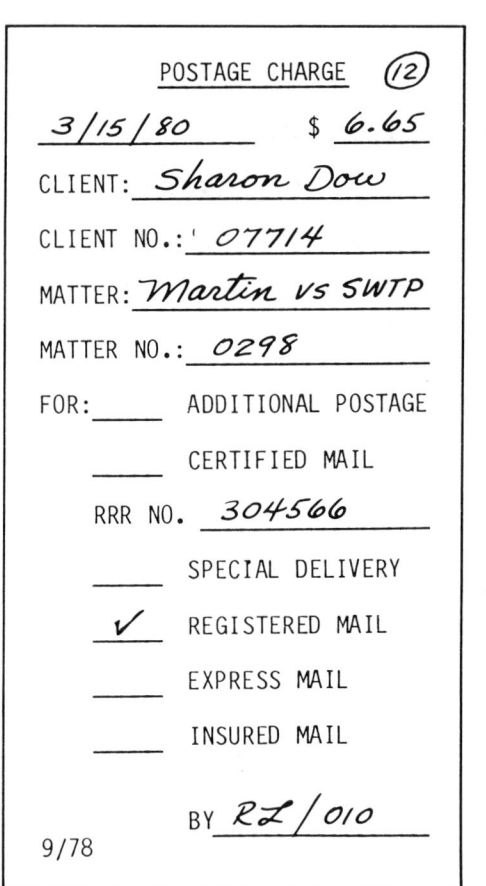

```
      POSTAGE CHARGE  (13)
 4/25/80         $ 2.57
CLIENT:  John Cole
CLIENT NO.:  03411
MATTER:  Cole vs Jones
MATTER NO.:  0699
FOR: ____ ADDITIONAL POSTAGE
      ✓   CERTIFIED MAIL
     RRR NO. 327916
     ____ SPECIAL DELIVERY
     ____ REGISTERED MAIL
     ____ EXPRESS MAIL
     ____ INSURED MAIL
            BY  RL/010
9/78
```

```
      POSTAGE CHARGE  (14)
 6/29/80         $ 3.25
CLIENT:  KXII Radio
CLIENT NO.:  07189
MATTER:  Retirement
MATTER NO.:  0333
FOR: ____ ADDITIONAL POSTAGE
     ____ CERTIFIED MAIL
     RRR NO. 343122
     ____ SPECIAL DELIVERY
     ____ REGISTERED MAIL
     ____ EXPRESS MAIL
      ✓   INSURED MAIL
            BY  RL/010
9/78
```

```
        POSTAGE CHARGE    ⑮
   5/29/80        $  2.85
CLIENT: Elsie's Jr. Shop
CLIENT NO.:  0717
MATTER:  General
MATTER NO.:  0988
FOR:  ____  ADDITIONAL POSTAGE
      ____  CERTIFIED MAIL
      RRR NO.  332549
       ✓    SPECIAL DELIVERY
      ____  REGISTERED MAIL
      ____  EXPRESS MAIL
      ____  INSURED MAIL

              BY   RL/010
9/78
```

JOB NAME: LAWFIRM

Exercise 8   Law Firm Time Records

Record Position	Information
1	Record code (letter T), duplicate
2-4	Attorney number, numeric
5-20	Attorney name
	column 5 — First initial
	column 6 — Middle initial
	columns 7 through 20 — Last name
21-26	Date, month/day/year, numeric
27-28	Task code, alphameric
29	Service code, alphameric
30-31	Department code, numeric
32-36	Client number, numeric
37-40	Matter number, numeric
41-43	Billing rate per hour (in dollars) STD = $50. If blank, fill with zeros
44	Billable code 1 = billable 0 = nonbillable
45-49	Time (in hours and quarters of an hour) nnn$_\wedge$nn

Right justify and zero fill all numeric fields. If time is 0 hours, .75 quarters, key 75 and press the LEFT ZERO or the RIGHT ADJUST key. Left justify and blank fill alphameric fields.

BIGGERSTAFF, LEE & MITCHELL

DAILY TIME REPORT

ATTORNEY NAME: L.B. JOHNSON DATE: 6/29/80
ATTORNEY NO.: 008 PAGE: 1 of 2

TASK CODES

AH	Attend Hearing	EV	Evaluate	PF	Proof
AN	Analyze	EX	Examine	PL	Pleading
AR	Arrange	IC	Interoffice Conference	PR	Prepare
BR	Brief	IT	Interrogatories	RE	Revise
CA	Court Appearance	IV	Investigation	RS	Research
CI	Conf. in Office	LI	Letter From	RV	Review
CL	Close File	LO	Letter To	RR	Receive & Review
CO	Conf. Out of Office	MO	Memo From	TC	Telephone Conf.
CR	Closing Report	MT	Memo To	TF	Telephone Call From
DO	Deposition, Oral	NT	Note To	TT	Telephone Call To
DR	Draft	NF	Note to File	TR	Trial
DT	Dictate	OF	Open File	TO	Title Opinion
DW	Deposition, Written	OL	Opinion Letter	TV	Travel
EA	Examine Abstract	PO	Process	WK	Work On

SERVICE CODES

Client
- B Banking
- C Corporate
- E Estate Planning
- D Domestic Relations
- G Utilities
- L Litigation
- P Probate
- R Real Estate
- T Taxation
- M Employee Benefits

Administrative (99999/9999)
- A Professional Activities
- F Firm non-billable
- U Recruiting
- Y Continuing Legal Education
- X Client non-billable
- N Civic
- I Charitable

DEPARTMENT CODES

Use Coding Schedule

CLIENT NAME: NEWMAN BROS., INC.   MATTER NAME: CO. VS N.E. IRON MANUFACTURES

TASK CODE	SERVICE CODE	DEPT. CODE	CLIENT NUMBER	MATTER NUMBER	STD./E RATE	N/B	TIME HRS.	QTRS.
		39	07388	0133	☒ STD.	✓ B		
LO	CLIENT FORWARDING CHECK & NOTE							.25

CLIENT NAME: ESTATE OF MARY DOE   MATTER NAME: ESTATE

TASK CODE	SERVICE CODE	DEPT. CODE	CLIENT NUMBER	MATTER NUMBER	STD./E RATE	N/B	TIME HRS.	QTRS.
	P	73	08613	0828	☒ STD.	✓ B		
PR	APPLICATION FOR PROBATE						1	—
LO	CLERK FILING APPLICATION							.25

CLIENT NAME: J.L. CUMMINS   MATTER NAME:

TASK CODE	SERVICE CODE	DEPT. CODE	CLIENT NUMBER	MATTER NUMBER	STD./E RATE	N/B	TIME HRS.	QTRS.
			12655	0109	☑ STD.	✓ B		
TF	HARRY JONES REF CAMPER							.25
TT	PAT HILL REF CAMPER							.25
TT	HARRY JONES							.25
TF	SAM THOMPSON							.25
TF	CARL HEESTROM							.25

EXERCISES

BIGGERSTAFF, LEE & MITCHELL

DAILY TIME REPORT   ATTORNEY NAME: L. B. JOHNSON   DATE: 6/29/80

ATTORNEY NO.: 008   PAGE 2 of 2

TASK CODES

AH Attend Hearing	EV Evaluate	PF Proof
AN Analyze	EX Examine	PL Pleading
AR Arrange	IC Interoffice Conference	PR Prepare
BR Brief	IT Interrogatories	RE Revise
CA Court Appearance	IV Investigation	RS Research
CI Conf. in Office	LI Letter From	RV Review
CL Close File	LO Letter To	RR Receive & Review
CO Conf. Out of Office	MO Memo From	TC Telephone Conf.
CR Closing Report	MT Memo To	TF Telephone Call From
DO Deposition, Oral	NT Note To	TT Telephone Call To
DR Draft	NF Note to File	TR Trial
DT Dictate	OF Open File	TO Title Opinion
DW Deposition, Written	OL Opinion Letter	TV Travel
EA Examine Abstract	PO Process	WK Work On

SERVICE CODES

Client
- B Banking
- C Corporate
- E Estate Planning
- D Domestic Relations
- G Utilities
- L Litigation
- P Probate
- R Real Estate
- T Taxation
- M Employee Benefits

Administrative (99999/9999)
- A Professional Activities
- F Firm non-billable
- U Recruiting
- Y Continuing Legal Education
- X Client non-billable
- N Civic
- I Charitable

DEPARTMENT CODES

Use Coding Schedule

CLIENT NAME: R.M. JONES   MATTER NAME: GENERAL

TASK CODE	SERVICE CODE	DEPT. CODE	CLIENT NUMBER	MATTER NUMBER	STD. ☒ E ___ RATE	N ___ B ✓	HRS.	QTRS.
		30	01289	0109				
TT	WHITE, REF SETTLEMENT NEGO							.25
TT	CLIENT, "	"	"	"				.50
TT	WHITE, "	"	"	"				.25

CLIENT NAME: ALASKA POWER   MATTER NAME: MOUNTAIN PEAK PLANT

TASK CODE	SERVICE CODE	DEPT. CODE	CLIENT NUMBER	MATTER NUMBER	STD. ☒ E ___ RATE	N ___ B ✓	HRS.	QTRS.
		30	06182	0166				
TF	RON HAGGER OF EDC							.25

CLIENT NAME: ___   MATTER NAME: ___

TASK CODE	SERVICE CODE	DEPT. CODE	CLIENT NUMBER	MATTER NUMBER	STD. ☐ E ___ RATE	N ✓ B ___	HRS.	QTRS.
	F		13428	0109				
TF	KASNER							.25
IC	COLE							.25

BIGGERSTAFF, LEE & MITCHELL

DAILY TIME REPORT

ATTORNEY NAME: L.B. JOHNSON
DATE: 6/30/80
ATTORNEY NO.: 008
PAGE: 1 of 1

TASK CODES

Code	Description	Code	Description	Code	Description
AH	Attend Hearing	EV	Evaluate	PF	Proof
AN	Analyze	EX	Examine	PL	Pleading
AR	Arrange	IC	Interoffice Conference	PR	Prepare
BR	Brief	IT	Interrogatories	RE	Revise
CA	Court Appearance	IV	Investigation	RS	Research
CI	Conf. in Office	LI	Letter From	RV	Review
CL	Close File	LO	Letter To	RR	Receive & Review
CO	Conf. Out of Office	MO	Memo From	TC	Telephone Conf.
CR	Closing Report	MT	Memo To	TF	Telephone Call From
DO	Deposition, Oral	NT	Note To	TT	Telephone Call To
DR	Draft	NF	Note to File	TR	Trial
DT	Dictate	OF	Open File	TO	Title Opinion
DW	Deposition, Written	OL	Opinion Letter	TV	Travel
EA	Examine Abstract	PO	Process	WK	Work On

SERVICE CODES

Client
- B Banking
- C Corporate
- E Estate Planning
- D Domestic Relations
- G Utilities
- L Litigation
- P Probate
- R Real Estate
- T Taxation
- M Employee Benefits

Administrative (99999/9999)
- A Professional Activities
- F Firm non-billable
- U Recruiting
- Y Continuing Legal Education
- X Client non-billable
- N Civic
- I Charitable

DEPARTMENT CODES

Use Coding Schedule

CLIENT NAME: J.R. CLAYTON **MATTER NAME:** NEW CLIENT

TASK CODE	SERVICE CODE	DEPT. CODE	CLIENT NUMBER	MATTER NUMBER	STD./E RATE	N/✓B	HRS.	QTRS.
		L 60	22642	0109	☒ STD.	✓		
CI	ADAMS & WILLIAMS						1	—

CLIENT NAME: RICHLAND FARMS **MATTER NAME:** IMMIGRATION MATTER

TASK CODE	SERVICE CODE	DEPT. CODE	CLIENT NUMBER	MATTER NUMBER	STD./E RATE	N/✓B	HRS.	QTRS.
		30	00942	0125	☒ STD.	✓		
IC	REF HOW TO RESPOND TO LETTER							

CLIENT NAME: ALASKA POWER **MATTER NAME:** 1980 SERIES, REVENUE BONDS

TASK CODE	SERVICE CODE	DEPT. CODE	CLIENT NUMBER	MATTER NUMBER	STD./E RATE	N/✓B	HRS.	QTRS.
		30	06171	0984	☒ STD.	✓		
RV	PURCHASE CONTRACT & OS						2	—
	WORK ON PURCHASING CONTRACT						2	.50

BIGGERSTAFF, LEE & MITCHELL

DAILY TIME REPORT

ATTORNEY NAME: R.L. LEE
ATTORNEY NO.: 009
DATE: 6/29/80
PAGE: 1 of 1

TASK CODES

AH	Attend Hearing	EV	Evaluate	PF	Proof
AN	Analyze	EX	Examine	PL	Pleading
AR	Arrange	IC	Interoffice Conference	PR	Prepare
BR	Brief	IT	Interrogatories	RE	Revise
CA	Court Appearance	IV	Investigation	RS	Research
CI	Conf. in Office	LI	Letter From	RV	Review
CL	Close File	LO	Letter To	RR	Receive & Review
CO	Conf. Out of Office	MO	Memo From	TC	Telephone Conf.
CR	Closing Report	MT	Memo To	TF	Telephone Call From
DO	Deposition, Oral	NT	Note To	TT	Telephone Call To
DR	Draft	NF	Note to File	TR	Trial
DT	Dictate	OF	Open File	TO	Title Opinion
DW	Deposition, Written	OL	Opinion Letter	TV	Travel
EA	Examine Abstract	PO	Process	WK	Work On

SERVICE CODES

Client
- B Banking
- C Corporate
- E Estate Planning
- D Domestic Relations
- G Utilities
- L Litigation
- P Probate
- R Real Estate
- T Taxation
- M Employee Benefits

Administrative (99999/9999)
- A Professional Activities
- F Firm non-billable
- U Recruiting
- Y Continuing Legal Education
- X Client non-billable
- N Civic
- I Charitable

DEPARTMENT CODES

Use Coding Schedule

CLIENT NAME: ALASKA POWER
MATTER NAME: LEAVERAGE LEASING

TASK CODE	SERVICE CODE	DEPT. CODE	CLIENT NUMBER	MATTER NUMBER	STD. / E RATE	N / ✓ B	TIME HRS.	QTRS.
		30	06171	1123	☒ STD.	✓		
RS	IN PREPARATION FOR MEETING						2	—

CLIENT NAME: L.L. PAYNE
MATTER NAME: MILLROSE RESORTS

TASK CODE	SERVICE CODE	DEPT. CODE	CLIENT NUMBER	MATTER NUMBER	STD. / E RATE	N / ✓ B	TIME HRS.	QTRS.
		30	18621	0109	☒ STD.	✓		
TF	CO PAYNE						1	—
TT	REAL ESTATE AGENT							.25
TT	ATTY. FOR ABSTRACT CO.							.25

CLIENT NAME: FIRST NATIONAL BANK
MATTER NAME: CAPITAL INFUSION

TASK CODE	SERVICE CODE	DEPT. CODE	CLIENT NUMBER	MATTER NUMBER	STD. / E RATE	N / ✓ B	TIME HRS.	QTRS.
		36	01420	1891	☒ E 50	✓		
RE	REORGANIZATION AGREEMENT						1	—

JOB NAME: **Exercise 9 Inventory**
INVENTORY

Record Position	Information
1	Delete code (blank or the letter D)
2–3	Fund code, numeric
4–9	Company ID code, numeric
10–17	Serial number, alphameric
18–43	Description, alphameric
44–46	Class code, numeric
47–49	Quantity, numeric
50–56	Unit cost (nnnnn˄nn)
57–60	Date of purchase (nn/nn), month and year, duplicate
61–71	Vendor abbreviation, alphameric
72–76	Location, alphameric
77–79	Department code, numeric
80	Record code, letter I, duplicate

1. Key the first set of data below. Use September 1981 for the date. Do not key any special characters. Right justify and zero fill all numeric fields. Left justify and blank fill all alphameric fields.

2. These records are in numerical order by company ID.
    a. For additions search for the company ID that will follow your add record. Insert the new record.
    b. For deletions search for the company ID number of the record to be deleted. Place the letter D in column 1 by pressing FUNCT SEL (lower) and DELETE REC.
    c. For changes or updates, search by company ID number. Then make the changes shown on the change forms. Any field left blank on the change form should be left as it is.

EXERCISES

INVENTORY LIST

Fund Code	Company ID	Serial Number	Description	Class Code	Qty.	Unit Cost	Vendor Abbrev.	Location	Dept. Code	Delete Code
16	168321	AB168429	BLACKBOARD	9	3	100.00	CENTEX SPLY	FO 010	12	
16	168322	AB154231	LADDER	74	1	24.95	GIBSON DISC	PP 001	83	
16	168323	AB168342	DESK, EXECUTIVE	382	1	1,000.00	HENSONS	AC 420	100	
16	168324	AB182461	TYPEWRITER, ELECTRIC	418	10	1,000.00	IBM	AS 100	234	
16	168325	CD834216	DISK PACK	502	6	73.00	MEMREX	AS 102	234	
16	168326	14836021	CHAIR, STUDENT	40	50	50.00	ABC SUPPLY	AS 104	232	
16	168327	92836066	CABINET, FILE LEGAL	189	2	683.00	ABC SUPPLY	FO 160	232	
16	168328	X8634215	BOOKCASE	188	6	418.00	ABC SUPPLY	FO 160	232	
16	168329	KA862413	DESK, TEACHER	132	2	342.00	ABC SUPPLY	LA 832	232	
16	168330	836820KB	DRINKING FOUNTAIN	142	1	850.00	ABC SUPPLY	FO 160	141	
16	168331	14832044	COAT RACK	146	1	145.23	ABC SUPPLY	FO 160	80	
16	168332	EF861234	WASTE BASKET	147	6	15.00	ABC SUPPLY	FO 040	80	
16	168400	GA823482	ADDING MACHINE, ELECTRIC	419	6	200.00	ABC SUPPLY	AS 100	234	
8	168401	16842999	BASKET BALL	984	24	20.00	B & B SPORT	HP 810	114	
8	168402	18683774	FILM PROJECTOR	685	1	542.00	VISUAL AIDS	FA 100	82	
8	168403	68342184	TABLE, FOLDING	213	1	200.00	BARNETT CO	AS 212	82	
8	168404	MX423145	RUG	181	1	150.00	HENSONS	AC 420	82	
8	168405	88683999	SCREEN, PROJECTION	686	1	45.00	VISUAL AIDS	FA 100	82	
8	168406	16453216	SMALL TOOL	683	1	26.00	HANDY DAN	PP 001	83	
8	168407	18888888	PLANER	684	1	168.00	HANDY DAN	PP 001	83	

INVENTORY ADDS AND DELETIONS

Fund Code	Company ID	Serial Number	Description	Class Code	Qty.	Unit Cost	Vendor Abbrev.	Location	Dept. Code	Delete Code
16	168333	XY128432	CAGES, ANIMAL	337	6	54.00	ALLIED RES	SB 421	68	
16	168334	XY129422	BURNERS	338	12	10.00	ALLIED RES	SB 428	68	
	168403	68342184								D
	168322	AB154231								D

PART 4 LABORATORY EXERCISES

INVENTORY CHANGE FORM

COMPANY ID `1 6 8 4 0 5`

CHANGE

- [ ] ✓ FUND CODE `☐☐`
- [ ] SERIAL NO `☐☐☐☐☐☐☐`
- [ ] DESCRIPTION `☐☐☐☐☐☐☐☐☐☐☐☐☐☐☐☐☐☐☐☐☐☐`
- [ ] CLASS CODE `☐☐☐`
- [ ] QUANTITY `☐☐☐`
- [ ] UNIT COST `☐☐☐☐☐☐`
- [ ] VENDOR `☐☐☐☐☐☐☐☐☐`
- [x] LOCATION `F A 2 0 0`
- [ ] DEPARTMENT CODE `☐☐☐`

COMPANY ID `1 6 8 3 3 4`

CHANGE

- [ ] ✓ FUND CODE `☐☐`
- [ ] SERIAL NO `☐☐☐☐☐☐☐`
- [ ] DESCRIPTION `☐☐☐☐☐☐☐☐☐☐☐☐☐☐☐☐☐☐☐☐☐☐`
- [ ] CLASS CODE `☐☐☐`
- [ ] QUANTITY `☐☐☐`
- [ ] UNIT COST `☐☐☐☐☐☐`
- [ ] VENDOR `☐☐☐☐☐☐☐☐☐`
- [x] LOCATION `5 B 4 2 2`
- [x] DEPARTMENT CODE `6 6`

INVENTORY CHANGE FORM

COMPANY ID `1 6 8 3 2 3`

CHANGE

- [✓] FUND CODE `1 4`
- [ ] SERIAL NO `☐☐☐☐☐☐☐`
- [ ] DESCRIPTION `☐☐☐☐☐☐☐☐☐☐☐☐☐☐☐☐☐☐☐☐`
- [ ] CLASS CODE `☐☐☐`
- [ ] QUANTITY `☐☐☐`
- [ ] UNIT COST `☐☐☐☐☐☐`
- [ ] VENDOR `☐☐☐☐☐☐☐☐`
- [ ] LOCATION `☐☐☐☐`
- [ ] DEPARTMENT CODE `☐☐☐`

COMPANY ID `1 6 8 3 2 9`

CHANGE

- [ ] FUND CODE `☐☐`
- [✓] SERIAL NO `K B 8 6 2 4 1 3`
- [ ] DESCRIPTION `☐☐☐☐☐☐☐☐☐☐☐☐☐☐☐☐☐☐☐☐`
- [ ] CLASS CODE `☐☐☐`
- [ ] QUANTITY `☐☐☐`
- [ ] UNIT COST `☐☐☐☐☐☐`
- [ ] VENDOR `☐☐☐☐☐☐☐☐`
- [ ] LOCATION `☐☐☐☐`
- [ ] DEPARTMENT CODE `☐☐☐`

INVENTORY CHANGE FORM

COMPANY ID `1 6 8 3 3 2`

CHANGE

- [ ] ✓ FUND CODE `☐☐`
- [ ] SERIAL NO `☐☐☐☐☐☐`
- [✓] DESCRIPTION `F I L E ␣ B A S K E T ␣ ␣ ␣ ␣ ␣ ␣ ␣ ␣ ␣`
- [ ] CLASS CODE `☐☐☐`
- [ ] QUANTITY `☐☐☐`
- [ ] UNIT COST `☐☐☐☐☐☐`
- [ ] VENDOR `☐☐☐☐☐☐☐☐`
- [ ] LOCATION `☐☐☐☐☐`
- [ ] DEPARTMENT CODE `☐☐☐`

COMPANY ID `1 6 8 4 0 4`

CHANGE

- [ ] ✓ FUND CODE `☐☐`
- [ ] SERIAL NO `☐☐☐☐☐☐`
- [ ] DESCRIPTION `☐☐☐☐☐☐☐☐☐☐☐☐☐☐☐☐`
- [ ] CLASS CODE `☐☐☐`
- [✓] QUANTITY `☐ 3 ☐`
- [ ] UNIT COST `☐☐☐☐☐☐`
- [ ] VENDOR `☐☐☐☐☐☐☐☐`
- [ ] LOCATION `☐☐☐☐☐`
- [ ] DEPARTMENT CODE `☐☐☐`

EXERCISES

JOB NAME: INSRENEW

Exercise 10 Chaining Exercise

Insurance Renewal Records

Program 1

Record Position	Information
1	1
2	0 (duplicate)
3	2 (duplicate)
4-9	Membership number (numeric)
10-15	Previous file code (alphameric)
16-18	City number (numeric)
19-41	Member name (alphameric)
42-43	Year of birth (numeric)
44-47	Expiration date (month, year), (numeric)
48	Blank
49-71	Second name (alphameric)
72-80	Social Security No. (numeric)

Program 2

Record Position	Information
1	2
2-18	Duplicate from record 1
19-43	Address (alphameric)
44-62	City (alphameric)
63-64	State abbreviation (alphameric)
65-69	Zip code (numeric)

COMPANY XYZ INSURANCE RENEWAL RECORDS

Membership No.	File Code	City No.	Member Name	Yr. of Birth	Exp. Date	Second Name	SS Number
143892	A13456	123	J R Koehne 683 S 5th San Francisco, California 94111	27	10-81	M L Koehne	342-81-4686
143893	A84216	883	J M Pickens 6831 Brannon Dr Waco, Texas 76710	30	8-81	S M Lee	361-89-4216
143894	B42813	381	M O Bremer 3135 Townsend Dallas, Texas 75241	42	9-81	M M Smith	888-61-9216
143895	C81345	666	E L Revercomb 643 Nottingham Baltimore, Maryland 21208	38	6-81	S S Revercomb	456-85-9686
143896	A68412	942	R L Post 813 Oak Santa Monica, California 90410	26	10-81	S M Post	813-22-4091
143897	B91238	888	R R Moon 1613 Curtiss Ames, Iowa 50010	40	3-81	S L Moon	238-44-9186
143898	C89423	860	M O Jones 427 Vine Colorado City, Texas 79512	45	4-82	L L Copley	884-21-9916
143899	C91823	423	R J O'Rear 1631 6th St. SE Childress, Texas 79201	44	12-81	L M Simons	641-38-9821
143900	D41238	424	L L King 831 Lake Heights Hartford, Conn 06105	48	11-81	R M Shirley	342-99-8718
143901	E68312	425	L R Clayton 1841 Lake Shore Boston, Mass 02106	50	12-81	H M Martin	168-34-9123
143902	F98341	681	A O Lee 448 Chaparral Ft. Worth, Texas 76103	55	1-82	R L Cole	388-44-9188
143999	G92458	541	A A Duncan 1842 S Hills Circle Delta, Utah 84624	56	2-82	A B Duncan	389-42-9998
144000	G93400	683	B R Jones 1800 Live Oak Kansas City, Kansas 66110	39	3-81	C L Workman	168-44-8133
144001	G94813	921	B B Lindley 14003 Main St. Louis, Missouri 63112	60	2-81	L L Jones	248-31-4911
144002	G94900	981	B M Little 1892 Brookview Chicago, Illinois 60690	65	6-81	B B Little	683-32-9188
144005	H60423	568	C C Carpenter 512 Hanover Mexia, Texas 76667	24	7-81	J C Carpenter	433-81-7765
144016	T16578	321	J D Norman Rt. 2 Roscoe, Texas 79545	04	11-81	S A Lee	561-78-9543

JOB NAME: **Exercise 11   Chaining Exercise**
INSCERT **Certificates of Insurance**

Program 1, Batch Total

Field No.	Record Position	Information
1	1–6	Date (month, day, year), numeric
2	7–9	Group policy number (account no.), RJ, numeric
3	10–17	Decreasing life (net premium), numeric
4	18–25	Level life (net premium), numeric
5	26–33	Accident and health (net premium), numeric

Program 2, Certificate information

Field No.	Record Position	Information
1	1–6	Certificate number
2	7–9	Group policy number (duplicate)
	10	Blank
3	11	Type, I or C
		I = issued now; C = cancellation
		C is used if records are stamped cancellation. If no stamp, key I.
4	12	First initial
5	13	Second initial
6	14–28	Last name (key: Jr, Sr, II, III, etc. Do not key Ms, Mr, Mrs, etc.)
7	29–31	Age, numeric
8	32	Single/joint code (S or J). If a second insured name is listed and any item in 8 is checked, key J for joint. Otherwise, key S for single.
9	33–38	Effective date of insurance, numeric
10	39–40	Term in months, numeric (convert days to months)
11	41–42	Beginning day of disability benefits (01, 07, 14, 30)
12	43	Retroactive code, R or E; R unless there is a check mark by the number of days insured.
13	44	Decreasing/level life code, D or L; determined by position of the amount of insurance (next field)
14	45–51	Amount of insurance, numeric
15	52–57	Monthly disability benefit, numeric
16	58–63	Disability premium, numeric
17	64–69	Life premium, numeric

PROGRAM ONE

```
REPORT AND REMITTANCE                ABC INSURANCE COMPANY
ACCOUNT NO. ②431                     P. O. BOX 334  WACO, TEXAS  76710
                                          ①
1. Ending date of the period covered by this report:  12      1      79
                                                   (Month) (Day)  (Year)
```

EXAMPLE

	DECREASING LIFE	LEVEL LIFE	A & H
2. Gross premiums on certificates issued............	534.01	6.56	923.74
3. Gross amount returned on cancelled certificates.	90.60		225.82
4. Net premiums..	③ 443.41	④ 6.56	⑤ 697.92
5. Less retained commission of ____ %...............			
6. Net remittance due ABC INS......................			

COMPANY *City National Bank*
CITY *Denver, Colo.*
AGENT *Jeannete McGinnes*

The enclosed $ *1147.89* is submitted in connection with the insurance written and/or cancelled as shown above.

Type of remittance:
[✓] Check   [ ] Deposit Slip

PROGRAM TWO

```
         ABC INSURANCE COMPANY   P. O. BOX 334   WACO, TEXAS  76710
                        ②                                     Certificate ①
Group Policy Number  431                                       Number 268421
```

Name of Insured Debtor
④ *John* ⑤ *Doe* ⑥ *Smith*   ⑦ Age 25   Address 1620 Main Denver, Colo.

Name of Second Insured   Age   Address

| Effective Date of Insurance ⑨ 3/26/79 | Term in Months ⑩ 6 | Expiration Date 9/20/79 | ⑧ [ ] Joint Life [ ] Spouse | [ ] Business Partner |

Disability Benefits Will Commence with *1st* Day
If insured is Disabled ⑪
for At Least *14* Days ⑫

Coverages	Amt of Ins ⑭	Monthly Dis Premium	Disability Premium	Life Premium
Decreasing Life	$ 322.86	⑮ $ 53.81	⑯ $ 5.62	⑰ $ .94
Level Life ⑬	$			

Creditor Beneficiary:
City National Bank

Second Beneficiary

I hereby certify that I am in good health and that my age as stated above is true and correct.

Insured Debtor: *John D. Smith*
Second Insured: _____

INSTRUCTIONS:
Mail this copy to ABC INSURANCE COMPANY on or about the first day of the month following the date of issue. Please be certain all sections are complete. Missing information will delay the processing of your report and may invalidate coverage.

CERTIFICATE OF INSURANCE
INSURANCE COMPANY COPY

EXAMPLE

EXERCISES

Report and Remittance

ABC INSURANCE COMPANY
P. O. BOX 334 WACO, TEXAS 76710

ACCOUNT NO. **261**

1. Ending date of the period covered by this report: **7** (Month) **31** (Day) **80** (Year)

	DECREASING LIFE	LEVEL LIFE	A & H
2. Gross premiums on certificates issued	19.70		49.37
3. Gross amount returned on cancelled certificates			
4. Net premiums	19.70		49.37
5. Less retained commission of ___%			
6. Net remittance due ABC INS			

COMPANY **Home Furniture –**
CITY **Madison, Kansas**
AGENT **Betty Smiley**

The enclosed $ **69.07** is submitted in connection with the insurance written and/or cancelled as shown above.

Type of remittance:
☑ Check   ☐ Deposit Slip

ABC INSURANCE COMPANY P. O. BOX 334 WACO, TEXAS 76710

Group Policy Number **261**
Certificate Number **684325**

Name of Insured Debtor: **L. C. Jones**   Age: **62**   Address: **Rt. 4 Burleson, Kansas**

Name of Second Insured: Age: Address:

Effective Date of Insurance: **7/9/80**   Term in Months: **18**   Expiration Date: **1/9/82**
☐ Joint Life   ☐ Spouse   ☐ Business Partner

Disability Benefits Will Commence with **1st** Day
If insured is Disabled for At Least **14** Days

Coverages / Amt of Ins
Decreasing Life $ **1045.80**
Level Life $ _____

Monthly Dis Premium: $ **58.10**
Disability Premium: $ **26.75**
Life Premium: $ **13.80**

Creditor Beneficiary: **Home Furniture**
Second Beneficiary: **E. M. Jones**

I hereby certify that I am in good health and that my age as stated above is true and correct.

Insured Debtor: **L. C. Jones**
Second Insured: _____

INSTRUCTIONS:

Mail this copy to ABC INSURANCE COMPANY on or about the first day of the month following the date of issue. Please be certain all sections are complete. Missing information will delay the processing of your report and may invalidate coverage.

CERTIFICATE OF INSURANCE
INSURANCE COMPANY COPY

```
            ABC INSURANCE COMPANY    P. O. BOX 334    WACO, TEXAS  76710
                                                      Certificate
Group Policy Number  261                              Number  684324
```

Name of Insured Debtor	Age	Address
John Harwood	27	3415 Oak Topeka, Kansas
Name of Second Insured	Age	Address

Effective Date of Insurance 7/19/80	Term in Months 6	Expiration Date 1/19/81	☐ Joint Life ☐ Spouse	☐ Business Partner

Disability Benefits Will Commence with 1st Day If insured is Disabled for At Least 14 Days	Coverages Amt of Ins Decreasing Life $ 489.60 Level Life $	Monthly Dis Premium $ 81.60	Disability Premium $ 8.52	Life Premium $ 1.43

Creditor Beneficiary: Home Furniture	Second Beneficiary Ella Harwood	I hereby certify that I am in good health and that my age as stated above is true and correct.

INSTRUCTIONS:

Insured Debtor: John Harwood

Second Insured: _____

Mail this copy to ABC INSURANCE COMPANY on or about the first day of the month following the date of issue. Please be certain all sections are complete. Missing information will delay the processing of your report and may invalidate coverage.

                    CERTIFICATE OF INSURANCE
                     INSURANCE COMPANY COPY

```
            ABC INSURANCE COMPANY    P. O. BOX 334    WACO, TEXAS  76710
                                                      Certificate
Group Policy Number  261                              Number  684325
```

Name of Insured Debtor	Age	Address
M. R. Cacy	46	812 Mitchell Kansas City, Kan.
Name of Second Insured	Age	Address

Effective Date of Insurance 7/7/80	Term in Months 18	Expiration Date 1/7/82	☐ Joint Life ☐ Spouse	☐ Business Partner

Disability Benefits Will Commence with 7th Day If insured is Disabled for At Least 14 ✓ Days	Coverages Amt of Ins Decreasing Life $ 513.72 Level Life $	Monthly Dis Premium $ 28.54	Disability Premium $ 14.10	Life Premium $ 4.47

Creditor Beneficiary: Home Furniture	Second Beneficiary E. M. Cacy	I hereby certify that I am in good health and that my age as stated above is true and correct.

INSTRUCTIONS:

Insured Debtor: M. R. Cacy

Second Insured: _____

Mail this copy to ABC INSURANCE COMPANY on or about the first day of the month following the date of issue. Please be certain all sections are complete. Missing information will delay the processing of your report and may invalidate coverage.

                    CERTIFICATE OF INSURANCE
                     INSURANCE COMPANY COPY

EXERCISES

REPORT AND REMITTANCE	ABC INSURANCE COMPANY
ACCOUNT NO. 543	P. O. BOX 334 WACO, TEXAS 76710

1. Ending date of the period covered by this report: __8__ (Month) __29__ (Day) __80__ (Year)

	DECREASING LIFE	LEVEL LIFE	A & H
2. Gross premiums on certificates issued............	285.25	32.11	
3. Gross amount returned on cancelled certificates.			
4. Net premiums......................................	285.25	32.11	
5. Less retained commission of ____%.............			
6. Net remittance due ABC INS.....................			

COMPANY _City National Bank_
CITY _Springfield, Ill._
AGENT _Ed Schwartz_

The enclosed $ 317.36 is submitted in connection with the insurance written and/or cancelled as shown above.

Type of remittance:
☑ Check   ☐ Deposit Slip

ABC INSURANCE COMPANY   P. O. BOX 334   WACO, TEXAS 76710

Group Policy Number _543_   Certificate Number _234813_

Name of Insured Debtor _Ann Garrett_   Age _50_   Address _1620 Pine Chicago, Ill._

Name of Second Insured   Age   Address

Effective Date of Insurance _8/28/80_   Term in Months _36_   Expiration Date _8/28/83_   ☐ Joint Life ☐ Spouse   ☐ Business Partner

Disability Benefits Will Commence with _1st_ Day If insured is Disabled for At Least _14_ Days

Coverages	Amt of Ins	Monthly Dis Premium	Disability Premium	Life Premium
Decreasing Life	$ 9,505.08	$	$	$ 165.39
Level Life	$			

Creditor Beneficiary: _City National Bank_
Second Beneficiary _Frances Jones_

I hereby certify that I am in good health and that my age as stated above is true and correct.

Insured Debtor: _Ann Garrett_
Second Insured: _____

INSTRUCTIONS:

Mail this copy to ABC INSURANCE COMPANY on or about the first day of the month following the date of issue. Please be certain all sections are complete. Missing information will delay the processing of your report and may invalidate coverage.

CERTIFICATE OF INSURANCE
INSURANCE COMPANY COPY

```
           ABC INSURANCE COMPANY     P. O. BOX 334      WACO, TEXAS  76710
                                                    Certificate
Group Policy Number  543                            Number  234814
```

Name of Insured Debtor A. L. Tally	Age 36	Address 1014 Cook Pampa, Tx.
Name of Second Insured	Age	Address

Effective Date of Insurance 8/27/80	Term in Months 24	Expiration Date 8/27/82	☐ Joint Life ☐ Spouse	☐ Business Partner

Disability Benefits Will Commence with 1st Day If insured is Disabled for At Least 14 Days	Coverages Amt of Ins Decreasing Life $9,406.56 Level Life $	Monthly Dis Premium $	Disability Premium $	Life Premium $ 109.12

Creditor Beneficiary: City National Bank	Second Beneficiary Joe Turner	I hereby certify that I am in good health and that my age as stated above is true and correct.

INSTRUCTIONS:

Insured Debtor: A. L. Tally

Second Insured: _____

Mail this copy to ABC INSURANCE COMPANY on or about the first day of the month following the date of issue. Please be certain all sections are complete. Missing information will delay the processing of your report and may invalidate coverage.

CERTIFICATE OF INSURANCE
INSURANCE COMPANY COPY

```
           ABC INSURANCE COMPANY     P. O. BOX 334      WACO, TEXAS  76710
                                                    Certificate
Group Policy Number  543                            Number  234815
```

Name of Insured Debtor John Charles Thomas	Age 44	Address 1513 Curtiss Ames, Iowa
Name of Second Insured	Age	Address

Effective Date of Insurance 8/25/80	Term in Months 24	Expiration Date 8/25/82	☐ Joint Life ☐ Spouse	☐ Business Partner

Disability Benefits Will Commence with 1st Day If insured is Disabled for At Least 7 Days	Coverages Amt of Ins Decreasing Life $ Level Life $ 1,540.30	Monthly Dis Premium $	Disability Premium $	Life Premium $ 32.11

Creditor Beneficiary: City National Bank	Second Beneficiary Nina Lee	I hereby certify that I am in good health and that my age as stated above is true and correct.

INSTRUCTIONS:
One Installment of $961.05 Due 8/25/81
@ $961.05 due 8/25/82

Insured Debtor: John Charles Thomas

Second Insured: _____

Mail this copy to ABC INSURANCE COMPANY on or about the first day of the month following the date of issue. Please be certain all sections are complete. Missing information will delay the processing of your report and may invalidate coverage.

CERTIFICATE OF INSURANCE
INSURANCE COMPANY COPY

EXERCISES

```
ABC INSURANCE COMPANY    P. O. BOX 334    WACO, TEXAS  76710
```

Group Policy Number 543			Certificate Number 234816
Name of Insured Debtor T.C. Williams		Age 60	Address 1810 High Rd. Oklahoma City, Okla.
Name of Second Insured		Age	Address

Effective Date of Insurance 8/25/80	Term in Months 12	Expiration Date 8/25/81	☐ Joint Life ☐ Spouse	☐ Business Partner

Disability Benefits Will Commence with 1st Day If insured is Disabled for At Least 30 Days	Coverages Decreasing Life Level Life	Amt of Ins $ 356.16 $	Monthly Dis Premium $	Disability Premium $	Life Premium $ 2.07

Creditor Beneficiary: City National Bank	Second Beneficiary Clara Williams	I hereby certify that I am in good health and that my age as stated above is true and correct.

INSTRUCTIONS:

Insured Debtor: T.C. Williams

Second Insured: _____

Mail this copy to ABC INSURANCE COMPANY on or about the first day of the month following the date of issue. Please be certain all sections are complete. Missing information will delay the processing of your report and may invalidate coverage.

CERTIFICATE OF INSURANCE
INSURANCE COMPANY COPY

```
ABC INSURANCE COMPANY    P. O. BOX 334    WACO, TEXAS  76710
```

Group Policy Number 543			Certificate Number 234817
Name of Insured Debtor Geneva Leavell		Age 32	Address 1813 Lake Heights Phoenix, Ariz.
Name of Second Insured		Age	Address

Effective Date of Insurance 8/22/80	Term in Months 6	Expiration Date 2/22/81	☐ Joint Life ☐ Spouse	☐ Business Partner

Disability Benefits Will Commence with 1st Day If insured is Disabled for At Least 30 Days	Coverages Decreasing Life Level Life	Amt of Ins $ 334.38 $	Monthly Dis Premium $	Disability Premium $	Life Premium $ .97

Creditor Beneficiary: City National Bank	Second Beneficiary Mary Lou Leavell	I hereby certify that I am in good health and that my age as stated above is true and correct.

INSTRUCTIONS:

Insured Debtor: Geneva Leavell

Second Insured: _____

Mail this copy to ABC INSURANCE COMPANY on or about the first day of the month following the date of issue. Please be certain all sections are complete. Missing information will delay the processing of your report and may invalidate coverage.

CERTIFICATE OF INSURANCE
INSURANCE COMPANY COPY

ABC INSURANCE COMPANY   P. O. BOX 334   WACO, TEXAS   76710

Group Policy Number 543

Certificate Number 234819

Name of Insured Debtor Annie May Cole	Age 38	Address 3204 Valley View Cedar Rapids, Iowa
Name of Second Insured	Age	Address

Effective Date of Insurance 8/22/80	Term in Months 9	Expiration Date 3/22/81	☐ Joint Life ☐ Spouse	☐ Business Partner

Disability Benefits Will Commence with 1st Day If insured is Disabled for At Least 14 Days	Coverages Decreasing Life Level Life	Amt of Ins $171.00 $	Monthly Dis Premium $	Disability Premium $	Life Premium $ .74

Creditor Beneficiary: City National Bank	Second Beneficiary C. L. Cole	I hereby certify that I am in good health and that my age as stated above is true and correct.

INSTRUCTIONS:

Insured Debtor: Annie May Cole

Second Insured: _____

Mail this copy to ABC INSURANCE COMPANY on or about the first day of the month following the date of issue. Please be certain all sections are complete. Missing information will delay the processing of your report and may invalidate coverage.

CERTIFICATE OF INSURANCE
INSURANCE COMPANY COPY

ABC INSURANCE COMPANY   P. O. BOX 334   WACO, TEXAS   76710

Group Policy Number 543

Certificate Number 234818

Name of Insured Debtor Lou Carl Keeney	Age 28	Address 1382 Monticello Tulsa, Okla.
Name of Second Insured	Age	Address

Effective Date of Insurance 8/22/80	Term in Months 6	Expiration Date 2/22/81	☐ Joint Life ☐ Spouse	☐ Business Partner

Disability Benefits Will Commence with 1st Day If insured is Disabled for At Least 14 Days	Coverages Decreasing Life Level Life	Amt of Ins $163.92 $	Monthly Dis Premium $	Disability Premium $	Life Premium $ .48

Creditor Beneficiary: City National Bank	Second Beneficiary Forrest Keeney	I hereby certify that I am in good health and that my age as stated above is true and correct.

INSTRUCTIONS:

Insured Debtor: Lou Carl Keeney

Second Insured: _____

Mail this copy to ABC INSURANCE COMPANY on or about the first day of the month following the date of issue. Please be certain all sections are complete. Missing information will delay the processing of your report and may invalidate coverage.

CERTIFICATE OF INSURANCE
INSURANCE COMPANY COPY

```
┌─────────────────────────────────────────────────────────────────────────┐
│        ABC INSURANCE COMPANY    P. O. BOX 334    WACO, TEXAS  76710     │
│                                                    Certificate           │
│ Group Policy Number  543                           Number  234820        │
├─────────────────────────────────────┬───────┬───────────────────────────┤
│ Name of Insured Debtor              │ Age   │ Address                   │
│   Martha Harbaugh                   │  33   │  Rt. 5  McGregor, Tx.     │
├─────────────────────────────────────┼───────┼───────────────────────────┤
│ Name of Second Insured              │ Age   │ Address                   │
├──────────────┬──────────────┬───────┴───────┼──────────────┬────────────┤
│ Effective    │ Term in      │ Expiration    │ ☐ Joint Life │ ☐ Business │
│ Date of Ins. │ Months       │ Date          │ ☐ Spouse     │   Partner  │
│   8/18/80    │   12         │   8/18/81     │              │            │
├──────────────┴──┬───────────┴───────┬───────┴──────┬───────┴──┬─────────┤
│ Disability      │ Coverages  Amt of │ Monthly Dis  │Disability│ Life    │
│ Benefits Will   │            Ins    │ Premium      │ Premium  │ Premium │
│ Commence with   │ Decreasing        │              │          │         │
│  1st Day        │ Life    $1,116.84 │ $            │ $        │ $ 6.48  │
│ If insured is   │ Level Life $      │              │          │         │
│ Disabled for    │                   │              │          │         │
│ At Least 7 Days │                   │              │          │         │
├─────────────────┴───────────────────┴──────────────┴──────────┴─────────┤
│ Creditor Beneficiary:        │ Second Beneficiary │ I hereby certify    │
│   City National Bank         │                    │ that I am in good   │
│                              │                    │ health and that my  │
│                              │                    │ age as stated above │
│                              │                    │ is true and correct.│
│ INSTRUCTIONS:                │                    │                     │
│                              │                    │ Insured Debtor:     │
│                              │                    │   Martha Harbaugh   │
│                              │                    │ Second Insured:     │
│                                                                         │
│ Mail this copy to ABC INSURANCE COMPANY on or about the first day of    │
│ the month following the date of issue. Please be certain all sections   │
│ are complete. Missing information will delay the processing of your     │
│ report and may invalidate coverage.                                     │
│                                                                         │
│                        CERTIFICATE OF INSURANCE                         │
│                         INSURANCE COMPANY COPY                          │
└─────────────────────────────────────────────────────────────────────────┘
```

```
┌─────────────────────────────────────────────────────────────────────────┐
│ REPORT AND REMITTANCE              ABC INSURANCE COMPANY                │
│ ACCOUNT NO.  105                    P. O. BOX 334  WACO, TEXAS  76710   │
│                                                                         │
│ 1. Ending date of the period covered by this report:  9    31    80    │
│                                                     (Month)(Day)(Year)  │
│                                                                         │
│                                    ┌──────────┬──────────┬──────────┐   │
│                                    │DECREASING│  LEVEL   │  A & H   │   │
│                                    │  LIFE    │  LIFE    │          │   │
│                                    ├──────────┼──────────┼──────────┤   │
│ 2. Gross premiums on certificates  │  169.96  │  26.39   │          │   │
│    issued........................  │          │          │          │   │
│ 3. Gross amount returned on        │          │          │          │   │
│    cancelled certificates.......   │          │          │          │   │
│ 4. Net premiums.................   │  169.96  │  26.39   │          │   │
│ 5. Less retained commission        │          │          │          │   │
│    of ____%....................    │          │          │          │   │
│ 6. Net remittance due ABC INS...   │          │          │          │   │
│                                    └──────────┴──────────┴──────────┘   │
│ COMPANY  American National Bank        The enclosed $ 196.35            │
│ CITY     Ft. Worth, Tx.                is submitted in connection with  │
│ AGENT    John Hennig                   the insurance written and/or     │
│                                        cancelled as shown above.        │
│                                                                         │
│                                        Type of remittance:              │
│                                          ☑         ☐                    │
│                                        Check   Deposit Slip             │
└─────────────────────────────────────────────────────────────────────────┘
```

Certificate 1

ABC INSURANCE COMPANY   P. O. BOX 334   WACO, TEXAS 76710

Group Policy Number: 105
Certificate Number: 148321

Name of Insured Debtor	Age	Address
Ronnie Biggerstaff	35	1025 N. Charles Dumas, Tx.
Name of Second Insured	Age	Address

Effective Date of Insurance	Term in Months	Expiration Date	Joint Life / Spouse	Business Partner
8/4/80	18	2/4/82	☐	☐

Disability Benefits Will Commence with 7th Day If insured is Disabled for At Least 14 ✓ Days

Coverages	Amt of Ins	Monthly Dis Premium	Disability Premium	Life Premium
Decreasing Life	$1,697.22			$14.79
Level Life	$			

Creditor Beneficiary: American National Bank
Second Beneficiary: Mrs. Ronnie Biggerstaff

I hereby certify that I am in good health and that my age as stated above is true and correct.

Insured Debtor: Ronnie Biggerstaff
Second Insured: _____

INSTRUCTIONS:
Mail this copy to ABC INSURANCE COMPANY on or about the first day of the month following the date of issue. Please be certain all sections are complete. Missing information will delay the processing of your report and may invalidate coverage.

CERTIFICATE OF INSURANCE
INSURANCE COMPANY COPY

Certificate 2

ABC INSURANCE COMPANY   P. O. BOX 334   WACO, TEXAS 76710

Group Policy Number: 105
Certificate Number: 148322

Name of Insured Debtor	Age	Address
James Leslie Carpenter	27	1816 N. 8th Mineral Wells, Tx.
Name of Second Insured	Age	Address

Effective Date of Insurance	Term in Months	Expiration Date	Joint Life / Spouse	Business Partner
9/11/80	11 plus	7/28/81	☐	☐

Disability Benefits Will Commence with 1st Day If insured is Disabled for At Least 14 Days

Coverages	Amt of Ins	Monthly Dis Premium	Disability Premium	Life Premium
Decreasing Life	$2,175.25			$12.20
Level Life	$			

Creditor Beneficiary: American National Bank
Second Beneficiary: Mrs. James Leslie Carpenter

I hereby certify that I am in good health and that my age as stated above is true and correct.

Insured Debtor: J. L. Carpenter
Second Insured: _____

INSTRUCTIONS:
Mail this copy to ABC INSURANCE COMPANY on or about the first day of the month following the date of issue. Please be certain all sections are complete. Missing information will delay the processing of your report and may invalidate coverage.

CERTIFICATE OF INSURANCE
INSURANCE COMPANY COPY

EXERCISES

```
ABC INSURANCE COMPANY    P. O. BOX 334    WACO, TEXAS  76710
```

Group Policy Number _105_   Certificate
                                                           Number _148323_

Name of Insured Debtor   Age   Address
  Malisa Jordan   _22_   _1412 Main Dallas, Tx._

Name of Second Insured   Age   Address

| Effective Date of Insurance _August 20, 1980_ | Term in Months _24_ | Expiration Date _August 27, 1982_ | ☐ Joint Life ☐ Spouse | ☐ Business Partner |

Disability Benefits Will   Coverages   Amt of Ins   Monthly Dis   Disability   Life
Commence with _1st_ Day   Premium   Premium   Premium
If insured is Disabled   Decreasing Life $ _2,768.40_
for At Least _14_ Days   Level Life $ $ $ $ _32.47_

Creditor Beneficiary: Second Beneficiary   I hereby certify that I am in good
  American National Bank   _J. R. Jordan_   health and that my age as stated
                                                              above is true and correct.
INSTRUCTIONS:
                                                              Insured Debtor: _Malisa Jordan_

                                                              Second Insured: _____

Mail this copy to ABC INSURANCE COMPANY on or about the first day of the month following the
date of issue. Please be certain all sections are complete. Missing information will delay
the processing of your report and may invalidate coverage.

                              CERTIFICATE OF INSURANCE
                              INSURANCE COMPANY COPY

```
ABC INSURANCE COMPANY    P. O. BOX 334    WACO, TEXAS  76710
```

Group Policy Number _105_   Certificate
                                                           Number _148324_

Name of Insured Debtor   Age   Address
  Wesley Martin   _54_   _832 Mockingbird Ln.   Dallas, TX._

Name of Second Insured   Age   Address

| Effective Date of Insurance _8/20/80_ | Term in Months _36_ | Expiration Date _8/30/83_ | ☐ Joint Life ☐ Spouse | ☐ Business Partner |

Disability Benefits Will   Coverages   Amt of Ins   Monthly Dis   Disability   Life
Commence with _1st_ Day   Premium   Premium   Premium
If insured is Disabled   Decreasing Life $ _6,286.32_
for At Least _7_ Days   Level Life $ $ $ $ _110.50_

Creditor Beneficiary: Second Beneficiary   I hereby certify that I am in good
  American National Bank   _Mrs. Wesley Martin_   health and that my age as stated
                                                              above is true and correct.
INSTRUCTIONS:
                                                              Insured Debtor: _Wesley Martin_

                                                              Second Insured: _____

Mail this copy to ABC INSURANCE COMPANY on or about the first day of the month following the
date of issue. Please be certain all sections are complete. Missing information will delay
the processing of your report and may invalidate coverage.

                              CERTIFICATE OF INSURANCE
                              INSURANCE COMPANY COPY

ABC INSURANCE COMPANY P. O. BOX 334 WACO, TEXAS 76710	
Group Policy Number *105*	Certificate Number *148325*

Name of Insured Debtor *Frances Koehne*	Age *41*	Address *6842 Alexander Itlay, Tx.*
Name of Second Insured	Age	Address

Effective Date of Insurance *8/13/80*	Term in Months *6 plus*	Expiration Date *3/31/81*	☐ Joint Life ☐ Spouse	☐ Business Partner

Disability Benefits Will Commence with *1ST* Day If insured is Disabled for At Least *14* Days	Coverages Decreasing Life Level Life	Amt of Ins $ $ *919.64*	Monthly Dis Premium $	Disability Premium $	Life Premium $ *6.87*

Creditor Beneficiary: *American National Bank*	Second Beneficiary *Holby Koehne*	I hereby certify that I am in good health and that my age as stated above is true and correct.
INSTRUCTIONS:		Insured Debtor: *Frances Koehne*
		Second Insured:

Mail this copy to ABC INSURANCE COMPANY on or about the first day of the month following the date of issue. Please be certain all sections are complete. Missing information will delay the processing of your report and may invalidate coverage.

CERTIFICATE OF INSURANCE
INSURANCE COMPANY COPY

ABC INSURANCE COMPANY P. O. BOX 334 WACO, TEXAS 76710	
Group Policy Number *105*	Certificate Number *148326*

Name of Insured Debtor *Hugo Rasor*	Age *64*	Address *942 Live Oak Arlington, Tx.*
Name of Second Insured	Age	Address

Effective Date of Insurance *8/22/80*	Term in Months *4*	Expiration Date *12/22/80*	☐ Joint Life ☐ Spouse	☐ Business Partner

Disability Benefits Will Commence with *1ST* Day If insured is Disabled for At Least *14* Days	Coverages Decreasing Life Level Life	Amt of Ins $ $ *260.41*	Monthly Dis Premium $	Disability Premium $	Life Premium $ *1.18*

Creditor Beneficiary: *American National Bank*	Second Beneficiary *Mrs Hugo Rasor*	I hereby certify that I am in good health and that my age as stated above is true and correct.
INSTRUCTIONS:		Insured Debtor: *Hugo Rasor*
		Second Insured:

Mail this copy to ABC INSURANCE COMPANY on or about the first day of the month following the date of issue. Please be certain all sections are complete. Missing information will delay the processing of your report and may invalidate coverage.

CERTIFICATE OF INSURANCE
INSURANCE COMPANY COPY

```
                    ABC INSURANCE COMPANY      P. O. BOX 334      WACO, TEXAS  76710
                                                                  Certificate
    Group Policy Number  105                                      Number  148327
    Name of Insured Debtor                    Age      Address
       Henry L. Rhea                           42       412 Lake Jackson  Waco, Tx.
    Name of Second Insured                    Age      Address

    Effective Date of | Term in Months | Expiration Date | ☐ Joint Life      ☐ Business
    Insurance 8/23/80 |      6         |    2/23/81      | ☐ Spouse            Partner
    Disability Benefits Will   | Coverages        Amt of Ins | Monthly Dis | Disability | Life
    Commence with  7th  Day    |                             | Premium     | Premium    | Premium
    If insured is Disabled     | Decreasing Life  $          |             |            |
    for At Least  14   Days    | Level Life       $2,694.70  | $           | $          | $ 18.34
    Creditor Beneficiary:        Second Beneficiary           I hereby certify that I am in good
    American National Bank       Mrs. Henry L. Rhea           health and that my age as stated
    INSTRUCTIONS:                                             above is true and correct.

                                                              Insured Debtor:  Henry L. Rhea
                                                              Second Insured:

    Mail this copy to ABC INSURANCE COMPANY on or about the first day of the month following the
    date of issue.  Please be certain all sections are complete.  Missing information will delay
    the processing of your report and may invalidate coverage.

                                       CERTIFICATE OF INSURANCE
                                       INSURANCE COMPANY COPY
```

JOB NAME: **Exercise 12   FORTRAN Computer Program**
FORTRN1
1. Key the entire FORTRAN program. Each line is an 80-position record.
2. Your instructor may ask you to plan a keying program. If so, note the following:

    Columns 1 to 5 are numeric (RJ and blank fill)

    Column 6 may be blank or numeric

    Columns 7 to 72 are alphameric

    Columns 73 to 80 are skipped

IBM EXERCISE 12 — FORTRAN Coding Form

GX28-7327-6 U/M 050**
Printed in U.S.A.

PROGRAM: FORTRAN LAB 1
PROGRAMMER: IVA HELEN LEE
DATE:
PUNCHING INSTRUCTIONS — GRAPHIC: Ø 0 1 I Z — PUNCH: N A N A A
PAGE 1 OF Ø
CARD ELECTRO NUMBER*

```
C     PROGRAM           FORTRAN LAB 1
C     PROGRAMMER        IVA HELEN LEE
C     INSTALLATION      MCC
C     COMPUTER          IBM SYSTEM 370
C     DATE              11/Ø1/8Ø
C     REMARKS           THIS REPORT PRINTS STUDENT AVERAGES AND THE CLASS
C                       AVERAGE.
C***------------------------------------------------------------------***
C*    FIELD NAMES USED                                                   *
C***------------------------------------------------------------------***
C             STUNO  = STUDENT NO
C             GR1    = TEST GRADE NUMBER1
C             GR2    = TEST GRADE NUMBER2
C             GR3    = TEST GRADE NUMBER3
C             STUAV  = STUDENT AVERAGE
C             CLAV   = CLASS AVERAGE
C             TOT    = TOTAL FOR STUDENT AVERAGES
C             COUNT  = TOTAL OF STUDENTS COUNTED
C***------------------------------------------------------------------***
C*    FIELD TYPES DEFINED                                                *
C***------------------------------------------------------------------***
      INTEGER STUNO,CODE,COUNT
      REAL GR1,GR2,GR3,STUAV,CLAV,TOT
C***------------------------------------------------------------------***
```

*A standard card form, IBM electro 888157, is available for punching statements from this form

**Number of forms per pad may vary slightly

```
C*   INITIALIZE COUNTERS
C***
     TOTAL = 0
     COUNT = 0
C***
C*   HEADINGS
C***
10   WRITE (3,10)                                                        ***
10   FORMAT ('1',33X,'TEST SCORES')                                      *
     WRITE (3,20)                                                        ***
20   FORMAT ('0',32X,'CLASS AVERAGE')                                    *
     WRITE (3,30)
30   FORMAT ('0',3X,'STUDENT NO.',9X,'TEST #1',9X,'TEST #2',9X,'TEST #3'
    1,9X,'AVERAGE',/)
C***
C*   INPUT FILE FORMAT
C***
40   READ (1,50,END=90) STUND,GR1,GR2,GR3,CODE                           ***
50   FORMAT (I2,F3.0,F3.0,F3.0,6PX,I1)                                   *
C***
C*   CHECK FOR INVALID CARDS
C***
     IF(CODE .EQ. 3) GO TO 70
     WRITE (3,60) STUND
```

```fortran
      60 FORMAT ('b',6X,I2,6X,'*** INVALID RECORD ***',/)
         GO TO 40
C***
C*       STUDENT AVERAGE CALCULATIONS
C***
         STUAV = (GR1+GR2+GR3)/3
C***
C*       PRINT ROUTINE
C***
         WRITE (3,80) STUNO,GR1,GR2,GR3,STUAV
      80 FORMAT ('b',6X,I2,17X,F4.0,13X,F4.0,12X,F4.0,12X,F7.2)
C***
C*       TOTAL AVERAGE AND STUDENT COUNT
C***
         TOT = TOT + STUAV
         COUNT = COUNT + 1
         GO TO 40
C***
C*       END OF JOB ROUTINE
C***
      90 CLAV = TOT / COUNT
         WRITE (3,100) CLAV
     100 FORMAT ('0',49X,'CLASS AVERAGE',11X,F8.2)
         STOP
```

FORTRAN Coding Form

PROGRAM: FORTRAN LAB1
PROGRAMMER: IVA HELEN LEE
PAGE 4 OF 4
CARD ELECTRO NUMBER: 0012
(columns 73-76): NANA

```
END
```

JOB NAME: **Exercise 13   COBOL Computer Program**
COBOL1
1. Key the entire COBOL program. Each line is an 80-position record.
2. Your instructor may ask you to plan a keying program. If so, note the following:

        Columns 1 to 6 are numeric

        Column 7 is blank or alphameric

        Columns 8 to 72 are alphameric with a subfield beginning in Column 12

        Columns 73 to 80 are skipped

EXERCISES

COBOL Coding Form

PROGRAM: COBOL 1
PROGRAMMER: IVA HELEN LEE
PAGE 1 OF 5
PUNCHING INSTRUCTIONS — GRAPHIC: 1 O Ø I Z PUNCH: N A N A

```
001010  ***
001020  IDENTIFICATION DIVISION.
001030  ***
001040  PROGRAM-ID.
001050      COBOL1.
001050  AUTHOR.
001050      IVA HELEN LEE.
001060  INSTALLATION.
001060      MCC.
001070  DATE-WRITTEN.
001070      Ø6/23/79.
001080  DATE-COMPILED.
001090  REMARKS.
001090      THIS PROGRAM PRINTS AN ADDRESS LIST.
001100  ***
001110  ENVIRONMENT DIVISION.
001120  ***
001130  CONFIGURATION SECTION.
001140  SOURCE-COMPUTER. IBM-370-135.
001150  OBJECT-COMPUTER. IBM-370-135.
001160  SPECIAL-NAMES.
001170      CØ1 IS TO-TOP-OF-PAGE.
001180  INPUT-OUTPUT SECTION.
001190  FILE-CONTROL.
```

308 PART 4 LABORATORY EXERCISES

IBM — COBOL Coding Form

GX28-1464-5 U/M 050*
Printed in U.S.A.

SYSTEM		PUNCHING INSTRUCTIONS						PAGE 2 OF 5
PROGRAM COBOL 1		GRAPHIC	I	O	ϕ	I	Z	CARD FORM # *
PROGRAMMER IVA HELEN LEE	DATE	PUNCH	N	A	N	A	A	

SEQUENCE (PAGE) (SERIAL) | CONT. | A | B | COBOL STATEMENT | IDENTIFICATION

```
ϕϕ2/ ϕ     SELECT ADDRESS-INPUT-FILE,
ϕϕ2/ ϕ         ASSIGN TO SYSϕϕ5-UR-254ϕR-S.
ϕϕ2/ ϕ     SELECT ADDRESS-OUTPUT-FILE,
ϕϕ2/ ϕ         ASSIGN TO SYSϕϕ7-UR-14ϕ3-S.
ϕϕ2/ ϕ*** ------------------------------------------------------------ ***
ϕϕ2/ ϕ DATA DIVISION.
ϕϕ2/ ϕ*** ------------------------------------------------------------ ***
ϕϕ2/ ϕ FILE SECTION.
ϕϕ2/ ϕ FD  ADDRESS-INPUT-FILE,
ϕϕ2 /ϕ     RECORD CONTAINS 8ϕ CHARACTERS,
ϕϕ2   ϕ    RECORDING MODE IS F,
ϕϕ2   ϕ    LABEL RECORDS ARE OMITTED,
ϕϕ2   ϕ    DATA RECORD IS ADDRESS-INPUT-CARD.
ϕϕ2   ϕ ϕ1 ADDRESS-INPUT-CARD.
ϕϕ2   ϕ    ϕ5  NAME-IN                     PICTURE X(25).
ϕϕ2   ϕ    ϕ5  STREET-IN                   PICTURE X(25).
ϕϕ2   ϕ    ϕ5  CITY-STATE-ZIP-IN           PICTURE X(25).
ϕϕ2   ϕ    ϕ5  FILLER                      PICTURE X(5).
ϕϕ2   ϕ
ϕϕ2 /ϕ FD  ADDRESS-OUTPUT-FILE,
```

*A standard card form, IBM Electro C61897, is available for punching source statements from this form.
Instructions for using this form are given in any IBM COBOL reference manual.
Address comments concerning this form to IBM Corporation, Programming Publications, 1271 Avenue of the Americas, New York, New York 10020.

*No. of sheets per pad may vary slightly

COBOL Coding Form

SYSTEM:
PROGRAM: COBOL 1
PROGRAMMER: IVA HELEN LEE
DATE:

PUNCHING INSTRUCTIONS — GRAPHIC: 1 Ø O I Z ; PUNCH: N N A A A
PAGE 3 **OF** 5

```
003010     RECORD CONTAINS 133 CHARACTERS,
003020     RECORDING MODE IS F,
003030     LABEL RECORDS ARE OMITTED,
003040     DATA RECORDS IS ADDRESS-PRINT-LINE.
003050 01  ADDRESS-PRINT-LINE.
003060     05  CARRIAGE-CONTROL         PICTURE X.
003070     05  NAME-OUT                 PICTURE X(25).
003080     05  FILLER                   PICTURE X(10).
003090     05  STREET-OUT               PICTURE X(25).
003100     05  FILLER                   PICTURE X(10).
003110     05  CITY-STATE-ZIP-OUT       PICTURE X(25).
003120     05  FILLER                   PICTURE X(37).
003130 WORKING-STORAGE SECTION.
003140 01  PROGRAM-INDICATORS.
003150     77  ALL-FINISHED             PICTURE XXX VALUE 'NO'.
003160***
```

```cobol
004010*  THIS MODULE IS THE MAINLINE IN THE PROGRAM. IT OPENS THE        *
004020*  FILES, READS THE INPUT FILE, AND CLOSES THE FILES. IT IS        *
004030*  ENTERED FROM THE OPERATING SYSTEM AND EXITS TO THE              *
004040*  OPERATING SYSTEM.                                               *
004050***
004060  0-MAINLINE.
004070      OPEN INPUT ADDRESS-INPUT-FILE,
004080           OUTPUT ADDRESS-OUTPUT-FILE.
004090      MOVE SPACES TO ADDRESS-PRINT-LINE.
004100      WRITE ADDRESS-PRINT-LINE BEFORE ADVANCING TO-TOP-OF-PAGE.
004110      READ ADDRESS-INPUT-FILE,
004120          AT END MOVE 'YES' TO ALL-FINISHED.
004130      PERFORM 1-PRINT-ADDRESS-PRINT-LINE
004140          UNTIL ALL-FINISHED = 'YES'.
004150      CLOSE ADDRESS-INPUT-FILE, ADDRESS-OUTPUT-FILE.
004160      STOP RUN.
004170***
004180*  THIS MODULE PRINTS THE ADDRESS LIST. IT IS ENTERED FROM AND     *
```

COBOL Coding Form

SYSTEM:
PROGRAM: COBOL 1
PROGRAMMER: IVA HELEN LEE
DATE:
PAGE 5 **OF** 5

PUNCHING INSTRUCTIONS:
GRAPHIC: 1 Ø O I Z
PUNCH: N N A A A

Sequence	Cont	A / B — COBOL Statement	Identification
ØØ51	Ø*	EXITS TO THE Ø-MAINLINE MODULE.	*
ØØ51	Ø***		***
ØØ51	Ø	1-PRINT-ADDRESS-PRINT-LINE.	
ØØ51	Ø		
ØØ51	Ø	MOVE SPACES TO ADDRESS-PRINT-LINE.	
ØØ51	Ø	MOVE NAME-IN TO NAME-OUT.	
ØØ51	Ø	MOVE CITY-STATE-ZIP-IN TO CITY-STATE-ZIP-OUT.	
ØØ51	Ø	WRITE ADDRESS-PRINT-LINE AFTER ADVANCING 1 LINES.	
ØØ51	Ø	READ ADDRESS-INPUT-FILE	
ØØ51	Ø	AT END MOVE 'YES' TO ALL-FINISHED.	

312   PART 4   LABORATORY EXERCISES

APPENDIX A
GLOSSARY OF DATA ENTRY TERMS

Access The act of obtaining data already stored.

Accumulator A counting device that retains an accumulated sum until the device is reset.

Acronym A word formed from the first letter or letters of each word in a phrase or name. Occasionally a letter is taken from the last part of the word (such as BIT for BInary digiT).

Address An identifier that tells the location of information on a diskette or disk. Usually it is a number that gives a track and sector number.

ALC The acronym for Assembly Language Coding. A programming language.

ALPHA An abbreviation for alphabetic. A letter of the alphabet.

Alphameric A contraction of alphanumeric. A term for letters of the alphabet (A to Z), digits (0 to 9), and special characters such as (, *, ?, /, etc).

ASCII Code The acronym for American Standard Code for Information Interchange. A seven-bit code (eight bits with the parity bit).

Automatic Field A field that is completed automatically and that the operator does not have to key manually. Examples: automatic skip or duplicate.

Automatic Program Sequencing See chaining.

Auxiliary Storage Device See secondary storage device.

Backup A copy of data or programs that is kept in case the current copy is destroyed.

Basic The acronym for Beginner's All-purpose Symbolic Instruction Code. A programming language.

Batch A group of records.

Batch Balancing The comparison of final totals compiled at the end of a batch with predetermined totals.

Batch Processing A processing method by which data is saved and processed in large groups.

BCD The acronym for Binary Coded Decimal. A six-bit code (seven bits with the parity bit).

Begin Field Code The letter used in some data entry program methods to mark the beginning of a data field. It defines the shift and the type of field.

Binary The base-2 number system. A binary digit is a 0 or 1.

BIT The acronym for BInary DigiT.

Blank Fill To leave unused positions in a field blank.

Blind Terminal A word processor with no display screen.

Block A physical record. Also, to write data on a magnetic tape so that there is more than one logical record per block.

Blocking Factor The number of logical records per block.

BOE The acronym for Beginning Of Extent. The address at which the data for a job begins.

BOT Marker Beginning Of Tape marker. A silver reflector or metallic strip indicating where reading or writing may begin. (On 2400-foot tapes the reflector is 12 feet from the beginning of the tape.)

BPI The acronym for Bytes Per Inch. (Also bits per inch.)

Bubble Memory Memory made up of magnetic fields in a semiconductor used for storing data. When viewed under a powerful microscope, the fields appear to move along like bubbles.

Buffer A memory area where data or instructions can be stored.

Byte Eight data bits plus one parity or check bit.

Centralized Data Entry The placement of data entry equipment in one central location.

Chaining A method of programming a data entry device in which program level changes are done automatically without the operator having to select a new program level manually.

Character A letter, a digit, or a special character. Any symbol.

Character Set The numbers, letters, and special characters available on a particular device.

Check Bit An extra bit added to a code to detect errors in reading or writing by the I/O unit.

Check Digit A digit in a field that provides information about other digits (used in error checks).

Cluster A group of similar items.

COBOL The acronym for COmmon Business Oriented Language. A programming language used in business work.

Column A vertical line or the vertical punching positions on a card.

COM The acronym for Computer Output Microfilm. Computer output is recorded on film.

Command Code See Begin Field Code.

Computer A device that can solve problems and manipulate data.

Configuration The type of devices that are used in a data entry system.

Console The part of a device that the human operator uses to communicate with the system.

Constant Data stored in a memory buffer area and later recalled and placed in specified positions of the data being keyed.

Continuation Character See Continue Field Code.

Continue Field Code In some data entry program methods, the characters that follow the Begin Field Code. They indicate the program shift for the remainder of the field.

Controller A device that supervises certain types of activities. Its operations are controlled by a program stored and executed in the unit. It is in itself a small computer. A communications controller would supervise communications activities. An I/O controller would supervise I/O activities.

Control Key See Function Key.

Control Punch An 11 punch or 12 punch in a numeric field that can never be negative. This punch usually has some special meaning.

CPU The acronym for Central Processing Unit. The part of the computer that contains the logical unit, the arithmetic unit, the control unit, and in some cases memory.

CRT The acronym for Cathode Ray Tube. A video screen or display device for displaying data and other information. The device uses a cathode ray tube, hence the name.

Cursor A marker character on the display screen that shows the position of the next character to be keyed.

Cursor Wrap A condition in which the cursor reaches the end of a line on a display screen and reappears on the line below or above, depending on the motion of the cursor (forward or backward).

Daisy Wheel A print wheel that looks like a daisy with characters at the end of each petal.

DASD An acronym for Direct Access Storage Device. A device that will allow random or direct access, such as the magnetic disk or drum.

Data A formalized representation of facts suitable for processing by people or by automatic means.

Data Check An error has been detected in reading or writing by the I/O unit.

Data Communications The movement of data in coded form by means of an electrical transmission system such as telephone lines.

Data Control The procedures necessary in data processing to ensure that data is processed completely, accurately, and on a timely basis.

Data Entry Device Equipment which will convert source data in human-readable form into a code that can be understood by the computer.

Data Key A key on the data entry keyboard that is used to enter letters of the alphabet, numbers, and special characters.

Data Privacy (a) The right of the individual to control the distribution of information concerning the individual. (b) The obligation of data processing personnel to *not* disclose information or data to outsiders.

Data Processing Operations performed on data to achieve a desired objective.

Data Security The protection of data from unauthorized access.

Data Set A group of records for a particular job.

Data Set Label An internal label identifying the data in a data set.

Data Validation The examination of data for correctness in regard to ranges (upper and lower limits), check digits, or presence in a table.

Decentralized Data Entry The placement of data entry equipment at many locations with each place doing its own data entry.

Decode To convert data from a coded form into human-readable form.

Default Value A value or option that is assumed when no specific value or option is entered.

Density The number of bytes or characters written per inch on recording media.

Digit Punch The area on a punched card reserved to represent digits.

Direct Access A processing method by which a record may be accessed without having to process the preceding records. Also called random access.

Disc Another spelling for disk.

Disk See magnetic disk.

Diskette A flexible magnetic disk on which data may be recorded in magnetized form. Sometimes called a floppy disk.

Disk Initialization The process of writing an internal volume label on a magnetic disk.

Distributed Data Entry See decentralized data entry.

DMA The acronym for direct memory access. A method of

transferring data from one peripheral unit to another without the involvement of the CPU.

DP The acronym for Data Processing.

Dumb Terminal A terminal that cannot be programmed or instructed.

Duplicate To make an exact copy of data.

EBCDIC The acronym for Extended Binary Coded Decimal Interchange Code. An eight-bit code (nine bits with the parity bit).

Editing To check the correctness of data. Second meaning: To insert special characters and blank characters to make numbers more readable on output.

EDP The acronym for Electronic Data Processing. The processing of data mainly by electronic digital computers.

Encode To convert data in a human-readable form into a code that the computer can understand.

EOD The acronym for End Of Data. The last address plus one at which data has actually been keyed.

EOE The acronym for End Of Extent. The last address at which data for a job may be keyed.

EOT Marker End Of Tape Marker. A metallic strip indicating the last place where data may be read or written on magnetic tape. (For 2400-foot tapes it is usually 12 feet from the end of the tape.)

Equipment Security The protection of equipment from use or damage by unauthorized persons.

Even Parity When a character is recorded, an even number of bits must be on, or magnetized.

Extent An area on disk or diskette between some upper and lower limit where data may be read or written.

External Label A paper adhesive label with an ID that is placed on the outside of a magnetic tape, disk, or diskette.

Field A collection of characters that have some meaning.

Field Continuation Code See continue field code.

Field Definition Character See begin field code.

File A collection of records.

File Label An internal label written at the beginning of a file of data on magnetic tape or disk.

File Protection A method used to protect data on a magnetic tape from accidental destruction. This is done by removing a plastic ring from the center of the back of the tape.

Flippy disk A diskette that may have data written on both sides.

Floppy disk See diskette.

Format Control The operation of a data entry device under program control.

Formatted Display Fields to be keyed are divided and displayed on a screen with prompts.

FORTRAN The acronym for FORmula TRANslator. A programming language used in scientific and mathematical work.

Frame The number of bits required to record a character on tape.

Free Form See free format.

Free Format One record is considered as one field.

Function Key Sometimes called a control key. A key on the data entry keyboard that is used to control keyboard operations.

GIGO An acronym for Garbage In—Garbage Out.

Hard Copy A printed copy in human-readable form from an output device.

Hardware Physical equipment or machinery.

Hash Total The arithmetic total of the numbers in a specific field.

Header label See file label.

Hex An abbreviation for hexadecimal.

Hexadecimal The base-16 number system. Hexadecimal digits are 0 through 9, A through F.

High Order Position The left-most position of a field.

Host Processor The central or main computer which does the *final* processing of the data that the data entry operator keys.

IBG An acronym for InterBlock Gap. Blank space left between blocks of data on magnetic tape (.75 inch for 7-track tapes; .6 inch for 9-track tapes.)

Indexed File A file that is created with an index allowing the file to be accessed randomly.

Indexed Set See indexed file.

Input Data transferred from an input device (such as a card reader or terminal) to the memory of the computer.

Input Field In terminal terminology an area in a record in which the operator may key data.

Intelligent Terminal A terminal that can be programmed by the user.

Internal Label A label written on the actual recording media (tape or disk).

Interpret To print on a punched card what has already been punched.

Invalid Batch A batch that contains an invalid field, that is a field that has been flagged as invalid.

I/O The acronym for Input/Output.

IRG The acronym for InterRecord Gap. See IBG.

Job A group of batches of data.

KB The acronym for thousand bytes. Actually in terms of IBM storage capacity, 2 to the tenth power or 1024.

Key Verification The data being verified is not displayed on the screen until there is an agreement or the field is bypassed. Some devices display the characters in scrambled form and they are unscrambled as they are verified.

LCA An acronym for lowercase alpha.

Left Justify To begin keying of data in a field in the left-most or high-order position.

Left Zero To fill in the left-most nonsignificant digits of a numerical field with zeros.

Light Pen A light sensitive pen with which an operator can identify a portion of a displayed message on a screen. This pen can act as an input device.

Load Point See BOT marker.

Lock Code See password.

Log A written record of computer or terminal activities.

Logical Record A collection of fields of data.

Low-Order Position The right-most position of a field.

Machine Status The state of a data entry device at a given time. Example: ready, not ready, waiting.

Magnetic Card A card that has been magnetically coated. Data can be recorded on it.

Magnetic Disk A flat circular plate on which data can be recorded in a magnetized form.

Magnetic Tape A tape on which data may be recorded in magnetized form.

Main Storage The memory of a computer, sometimes called internal storage. Data and instructions can be fetched faster from this type of storage.

Manual Field A field that must be manually keyed. It is not automatically processed.

Menu Options listed on a display screen for the operator to choose from.

Minicomputer A computer that is more expensive than the small personal computers. It is not as expensive as the host computers.

Mode The mode of a data entry device determines the type of operation that will be performed.

Modem The acronym for MOdulator-DEModulator. A device that acts as an interface between a communications line and a data processing device.

Modulus 10 A data validation method that will detect simple transposition errors (reversing digits) in keying.

Modulus 11 A data validation method that will detect both single and double transposition errors (reversing digits) in keying.

Network A system of computer systems that are connected. Terminals are used for communications.

Nibble Four bites or a half of a byte.

Nine-Track Tape A magnetic tape on which data is written in the EBCDIC code.

OBR The acronym for Optical Bar code Reader. A device that reads special bar codes.

OCR The acronym for Optical Character Recognition. Characters are printed in such a way that they can be read by machines as well as humans.

Octal The base-8 number system. Octal digits consist of 0 through 7.

Odd Parity When a character is recorded, an odd number of bits must be on, or magnetized.

Off-line Not connected to the computer.

OMR The acronym for Optical Mark Reader. A device that reads pencil marks.

On-line Connected to the computer.

Optical Bar Code A data entry device that senses bar codes on a form and interprets this code as a character.

Optical Scanning The use of a light to examine patterns.

Output Data transferred from the memory of the computer to some storage or output device (such as a printer).

Overwrite The recording of data on a medium such that it destroys any data that was previously stored there.

Paging Through a Batch Finding a record in a batch by using the record advance or backspace keys.

Parity Bit See check bit.

Password A special security code that is usually keyed to allow access to a file.

Peripheral Device A computer I/O device such as a keyboard, printer, magnetic tape device, or magnetic disk device.

Physical Record One or more logical records.

PL/1 The acronym for Programming Language One. A programming language used in both business and scientific applications.

Polling Checking the terminals in a network to see if they have any data to transmit.

Port An access point for data entry or exit.

Portable Data Recorder A data entry device that may be hand-carried.

Privacy See data privacy.

Program A set of instructions to the computer. A set of instructions for a data entry device.

Program Code Codes for a program that define the automatic operations of a data entry device.

Program Level See program number.

Program Number The number indicating the program storage area that you are currently using.

Program Sequencing See chaining.

Prompt A programmed message that appears on the display screen to assist the operator.

Protected Data In IBM terminal terminology, a prompt is protected data. That is it is an area in which data cannot be keyed.

Qume Printer A daisy-wheel-type printer. See daisy wheel.

Random Access See direct access.

Record See logical record.

Record Format A plan of how fields of data will appear in a record.

Record Pooling An area on a diskette or disk in which records may be stored in order to be later recalled and inserted into data being keyed.

Recording Media The material upon which data is recorded. Examples are cards, diskettes, disks, or tapes.

Response Time The time required for a system to react to input.

Right-Hand Graphic A third character on keys of some data entry keyboards.

Right Justify The last character of data in a field is keyed in the right-most position, or low order position.

RJE The acronym for Remote Job Entry. The submission of jobs through terminals to the host computer.

Row A horizontal line or the horizontal punching positions on a card.

RPG II The acronym for Report Program Generator, Version II. A programming language used in business applications.

Search To examine a set of items (records or data in a table) for a certain property that has been described to the data entry device.

Search Mask A property (or information) that is being looked for in the search of a group of items.

Secondary Storage Device Storage other than main storage in which data may be kept when the computer is turned off. Examples are diskettes, tapes, and disks.

Sector A subdivision of a track. The number of characters in a sector varies with the device used.

Security See data security and equipment security.

Sequential Processing The processing of records one after the other in the order in which they were written.

Seven-Track Tape A magnetic tape on which data is written in the BCD code.

Sight Verification The field to be verified is displayed on the screen. It is then verified, corrected, or flagged.

Smart Terminal A terminal that is programmed by the manufacturer to meet the special needs of the user.

Soft Copy Output from an output device that is not in printed form. Output on a video screen or audible output.

Software A computer program. Instructions to the computer.

Source Document An original document on which data was first recorded.

Status Line A line on the display screen giving information on the current work being done at the keystation.

Statistics The collection, organization, and interpretation of numerical data.

Tape See magnetic tape.

Tape Channel See track.

Tape Initialization The process of writing an internal volume label on a magnetic tape.

Tape Mark A special character written on magnetic tape to indicate the end of data or the end of a set of labels.

Terminal An I/O device, usually equipped with a keyboard and a display device, through which data may be entered or received.

Text Edit To manipulate text or information. The manipulations may be additions, insertions, or margin justifications.

TM The acronym for Tape Mark. See tape mark.

Track A path on which data is written on a recording medium. On magnetic tape, they are parallel lines; on magnetic disk or diskettes they are concentric circles.

Trail Verify A verifying process in which the verifying operator verifies one record behind the keying operator. The batch has not been closed in this process.

Trailer Label An internal label written at the end of a file of data on magnetic tape or disk.

Transfer Rate The number of bytes or characters per second that can be read. Transfer rate is quoted in KB or inches per second.

Uncorrectable Error An error that the operator is not able to correct at the time it is detected. (The correct data is not known at that time.)

Unformatted Display The opposite of formatted display. Fields of data to be keyed are not displayed on a screen with prompts.

Update To key additional data into a selected record of an existing batch.

Verify To check the correctness of data.

Voice Input An input device that uses the human voice as input.

Volume The recording media available to one read/write

mechanism. (A magnetic tape, magnetic disk, or diskette may be thought of as a volume for our purposes).

Volume Label   An internal label that identifies the magnetic tape, disk, or diskette.

VTOC   The acronym for Volume Table Of Contents. A list of the batches or files of data on a disk or tape. The list is usually printed in some order, for example by the file names.

Wand   A hand-held device that reads magnetically encoded information on labels, cards, badges, and similar material.

Word Processing   The automation of document production.

Work Termination Display   Information on the display screen given when a job is terminated.

WP   The acronym for Word Processing.

Zero Balancing   See batch balancing.

Zero Fill   To fill the unused positions of a numeric field with leading zeros.

Zone Punch   In the Hollerith card, a punch in the upper three rows of the card (a zero, 11 or 12 punch).

APPENDIX B
STANDARD ABBREVIATIONS

ADDRESS ABBREVIATIONS AS SPECIFIED BY THE U.S. POST OFFICE

The abbreviations listed here may be used in addresses on mail. By using the city-state abbreviations, it is possible to enter city, state, and zip code on the last line of address within a maximum of 22 positions: 13 positions for city, 1 space between city and state, 2 positions for state, 1 space between state and zip code, and 5 positions for zip code.

Two-Letter State and Territory Abbreviations

Alabama	AL	Montana	MT
Alaska	AK	Nebraska	NE
Arizona	AZ	Nevada	NV
Arkansas	AR	New Hampshire	NH
American Somoa	AS	New Jersey	NJ
California	CA	New Mexico	NM
Canal Zone	CZ	New York	NY
Colorado	CO	North Carolina	NC
Connecticut	CT	North Dakota	ND
Delaware	DE	Northern Mariana Islands	CM
District of Columbia	DC	Ohio	OH
Florida	FL	Oklahoma	OK
Georgia	GA	Oregon	OR
Guam	GU	Pennsylvania	PA
Hawaii	HI	Puerto Rico	PR
Idaho	ID	Rhode Island	RI
Illinois	IL	South Carolina	SC
Indiana	IN	South Dakota	SD
Iowa	IA	Tennessee	TN
Kansas	KS	Trust Territories	TT
Kentucky	KY	Texas	TX
Louisiana	LA	Utah	UT
Maine	ME	Vermont	VT
Maryland	MD	Virginia	VA
Massachusetts	MA	Virgin Islands	VI
Michigan	MI	Washington	WA
Minnesota	MN	West Virginia	WV
Mississippi	MS	Wisconsin	WI
Missouri	MO	Wyoming	WY

Street Designators and Frequently Used Place Names

Academy	ACAD	Creek	CRK
Air Force Base	AFB	Crescent	CRES
Agency	AGNCY	Crossing	XING
Airport	ARPRT	Dale	DL
Alley	ALY	Dam	DM
Annex	ANX	Depot	DPO
Arcade	ARC	Divide	DV
Arsenal	ARSL	Drive	DR
Avenue	AVE	East	E
Bayou	BYU	Estates	EST
Beach	BCH	Expressway	EXPY
Bend	BND	Extended	EXT
Big	BG	Extension	EXT
Black	BLK	Fall	FL
Boulevard	BLVD	Falls	FLS
Bluff	BLF	Farms	FRMS
Bottom	BTM	Ferry	FRY
Branch	BR	Field	FLD
Bridge	BRG	Fields	FLDS
Brook	BRK	Flats	FLT
Burg	BG	Ford	FRD
Bypass	BYP	Forest	FRST
Camp	CP	Forge	FRG
Canyon	CYN	Fork	FRK
Cape	CPE	Forks	FRKS
Causeway	CSWY	Fort	FT
Center	CTR	Fountain	FTN
Central	CTL	Freeway	FWY
Church	CHR	Furnace	FURN
Churches	CHRS	Gardens	GDNS
Circle	CIR	Gateway	GTWY
City	CY	Glen	GLN
Clear	CLR	Grand	GRND
Cliffs	CLFS	Great	GR
Club	CLB	Green	GRN
College	CLG	Ground	GRD
Common	CMM	Grove	GRV
Corner	COR	Harbor	HBR
Corners	CORS	Haven	HVN
Course	CRSE	Heights	HTS
Court	CT	High	HI
Courts	CTS	Highlands	HGLDS
Cove	CV	Highway	HWY

Hill	HL	Park	PARK
Hollow	HOLW	Parkway	PKY
Hot	H	Pass	PASS
House	HSE	Path	PATH
Inlet	INLT	Pike	PIKE
Institute	INST	Pillar	PLR
Island	IS	Pines	PNES
Islands	IS	Place	PL
Isle	IS	Plain	PLN
Junction	JCT	Plains	PLNS
Key	KY	Plaza	PLZ
Knolls	KNLS	Port	PRT
Landing	LNDG	Point	PT
Lake	LK	Prairie	PR
Lakes	LKS	Radial	RADL
Lane	LN	Ranch	RNCH
Light	LGT	Ranches	RNCHS
Little	LTL	Rapids	RPDS
Loaf	LF	Resort	RESRT
Locks	LCKS	Rest	RST
Lodge	LDG	Ridge	RDG
Loop	LOOP	River	RIV
Lower	LWR	Road	RD
Mall	MALL	Rock	RK
Manor	MNR	Row	ROW
Meadows	MDWS	Run	RUN
Meeting	MTG	Rural	R
Memorial	MLM	Saint	ST
Middle	MDL	Sainte	ST
Mile	MLE	San	SN
Mill	ML	Santa	SN
Mills	MLS	Santo	SN
Mines	MNS	School	SCH
Mission	MSN	Seminary	SMNRY
Mound	MND	Shoal	SHL
Mount	MT	Shoals	SHLS
Mountain	MTN	Shode	SHD
National	NAT	Shore	SHR
Naval Air Station	NAS	Shores	SHRS
Neck	NCK	Siding	SDG
New	NW	South	S
North	N	Space Flight Center	SFC
Orchard	ORCH	Speedway	SPDWY
Oval	OVAL	Spring	SPG
Palms	PLMS	Springs	SPGS

Spur	SPUR	Tunnel	TUNL
Square	SQ	Turnpike	TPKE
State	ST	Upper	UPR
Station	STA	Union	UN
Street	ST	University	UNIV
Stream	STRM	Valley	VLY
Sulphur	SLPHR	Viaduct	VIA
Summit	SMT	View	VW
Tannery	TNRY	Village	VLG
Tavern	TVRN	Ville	VL
Terminal	TERM	Vista	VIS
Terrace	TER	Walk	WALK
Ton	TN	Water	WTR
Tower	TWR	Way	WAY
Town	TWN	Wells	WLS
Trace	TRCE	West	W
Track	TRAK	White	WHT
Trail	TRL	Works	WKS
Trailer	TRLR	Yards	YDS

APPENDIX C

THE HEXADECIMAL AND OCTAL NUMBER SYSTEMS

In Unit 3 it was pointed out that a four-digit number 1111 in base-2 or binary means 15 in our base 10.

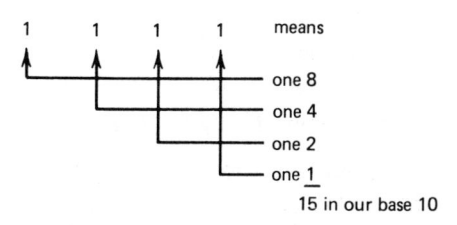

```
1   1   1   1   means
            one 8
        one 4
    one 2
one 1
15 in our base 10
```

These digits are called the 8421 bits or digits.

In our number system (base 10) there are 10 digits, 0 through 9. That is, the highest digit is one less than the base 10. By the same reasoning in the hexadecimal number system or base 16, there would be 16 digits with the highest digit 1 less than 16.

Now look at the following chart of the possible combinations of four BITS or binary digits and their relationship to our base-10 and base-16 number systems.

Base 2	Base 10	Base 16 (hex)
0001	1	1
0010	2	2
0011	3	3
0100	4	4
0101	5	5
0110	6	6
0111	7	7
1000	8	8
1001	9	9
1010	10	A
1011	11	B
1100	12	C
1101	13	D
1110	14	E
1111	15	F

Note the following facts:

APPENDIX C

1. The base-10 number can be calculated from the place position of the bits. In binary the number 1010 is:

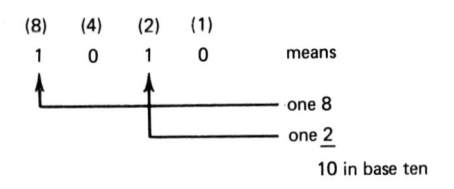

```
(8)  (4)  (2)  (1)
 1    0    1    0     means
 ↑         ↑
 |         |————— one 8
 |—————————————— one 2
                       10 in base ten
```

2. It can also be seen that with four bits there are 16 ($2^4 = 2 \times 2 \times 2 \times 2 = 16$) possible combinations which corresponds to base 16.

3. After our digit 9 in base 16, six more digits are needed. These digits must be one character. Therefore, someone chose to use:

   A for our 10
   B for our 11
   C for our 12
   D for our 13
   E for our 14
   F for our 15

   Therefore the base-16 10 is really our 16.

It certainly does seem strange to see letters in a number! But computer console messages are sometimes displayed in hex; and in a special print-out of memory called a dump, numbers sometimes appear in hex.

However, the only time one may encounter this system is with the HEX key on some data entry devices.

These numbers can be converted to our base-10 system or vice versa. The number 111 in base 16 would mean:

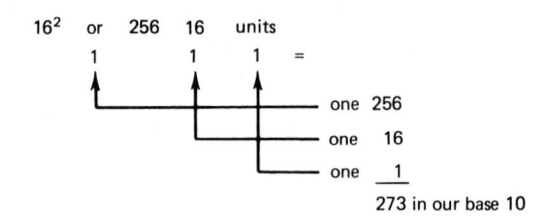

```
16²  or  256    16    units
 1          1    1    =
 ↑          ↑    ↑
 |          |    |——— one  256
 |          |———————— one   16
 |———————————————————— one    1
                              273 in our base 10
```

Conversions can be made between base 10 and base 16 as follows:
Convert 183_{10} to base 16 (hex).

```
16 | 183
16 |  11    R    7         ↑
       0    R    11    B
```

So $183_{10} = B7_{16}$. This is called the remainder method.

Proof:

$B7_{16} = B \times 16 = 11 \times 16 = 176$
$\phantom{B7_{16} = B} 1 \times 7 = \underline{7}$
$\phantom{B7_{16} = B \times 16 = 11 \times 16 = } 183$ (base 10)

Another Example:

APPENDIX C

Convert 592_{10} to base 16.

```
16 | 592
16 |  37   R   0    ↑
16 |   2   R   5
         0   R   2
```

So $592_{10} = 250_{16}$

Proof:

$$250_{16} = 2 \times 16^2 = 2 \times 256 = 512$$
$$5 \times 16 = 80 = 80$$
$$1 \times 0 = 0 = 0$$
$$\overline{592_{16}}$$

BASE EIGHT OR OCTAL   On some computers the binary digits are grouped in threes rather than in fours, giving a base-8 number ($2^3 = 2 \times 2 \times 2 = 8$). If work is done on a base-8 (octal) computer, the same reasoning exists. The only digits available would be 0 to 7 (one less than the base).

Base 2 (4 2 1 digits)	Base 10	Base 8 (Octal)
0 0 1	1	1
0 1 0	2	2
0 1 1	3	3
1 0 0	4	4
1 0 1	5	5
1 1 0	6	6
1 1 1	7	7

Conversion can be made between base 10 and base 8 as follows:
Convert 183_{10} to base 8.

```
8 | 183
8 |  22   R   7    ↑
8 |   2   R   6
        0   R   2
```

So $183_{10} = 267_8$

Proof:

$$267_8 = 2 \times 8^2 = 2 \times 64 = 128$$
$$6 \times 8 = 48 = 48$$
$$7 = 7$$
$$\overline{183 \text{ base 10}}$$

APPENDIX D
METHODS OF DATA VALIDATION

1. *The self-checking number.* A code number with a calculated digit called a *check digit* is added to the field to catch substitution errors. A substitution error means keying the wrong digit; for example, you key a 5 instead of a 6.

    An example of a check digit for the number 6021 is as follows: sum the digits, $6 + 0 + 2 + 1 = 9$. The check digit is 9. Therefore, you use an ID number of 60219. Then if the sum of the first four digits is not equal to the last digit, there is an error. The problem with check digits is that they do not catch transposition errors. That is, if the number had been keyed 60129, the reversal of the 1 and 2 would not be caught. Modulus methods catch transposition errors.

2. *Modulus 10 method.* The modulus 10 method will catch simple transposition errors but it will not catch double transposition errors.

EXAMPLE for 6021

   a. Multiply the units position and every second position by 2.
   b. Add the products of these multiplications and the alternate digits that were not multiplied by 2.
   c. Subtract the sum from the next highest number ending in 0. This difference is the check digit.

   For the number 6021

$$1 \times 2 = 2$$
$$0 \times 2 = 0$$
$$2$$
$$\underline{6}$$
$$10$$

   $10 - 10 = 0$ The check digit is 0.

The number 60210 would be used.

Then if the number 60120 were keyed, the following check would be made:

$$2 \times 2 = 4$$
$$0 \times 2 = 0$$
$$1$$
$$\underline{6}$$
$$11$$

$$20 - 11 = 9$$

9 does not check with the check digit 0. Therefore there is an error. Modulus 10 will not catch double transposition errors all of the time. If the transposed errors are multiplied by the same weight, the erroneous number still checks.

3. *Modulus 11 check.* The modulus 11 check will catch double transposition errors. In fact, it will catch 97% of all substitution, transposition, and double transposition errors. The disadvantage of the Modulus 11 method is that the check digit may be 10, in which case an X is used for the check digit. (If it is 11, 0 is used.) If one must have an all numeric number, then one must resort to Modulus 10. In this case double transpositions will not be detected. Or cases giving an X check digit could be eliminated (but this cannot always be done). Authors differ on the maximum weights used. The assignment of the limit seems arbitrary.

EXAMPLE 6021

a. Weights are assigned from left to right increasingly by one to the maximum assumed. If the weight exceeds the maximum, start at 2 again. Add the products.

$$\begin{aligned} 1 \times 2 &= 2 \\ 2 \times 3 &= 6 \\ 0 \times 4 &= 0 \\ 6 \times 5 &= \underline{30} \\ &38 \end{aligned}$$

b. Divide the sum by 11 and obtain the remainder.

$$11 \overline{\smash{)}38} \quad\text{3 with remainder of 5}$$

c. Subtract the remainder from 11. This is the check digit. Six is the check digit ($11 - 5 = 6$). Therefore the number 60216 would be used.

In data entry your device does all of this for you. An error condition occurs if there is no match with what you key.

APPENDIX E
THE 96 COLUMN CARD CODE

Character Set and Punch Combinations

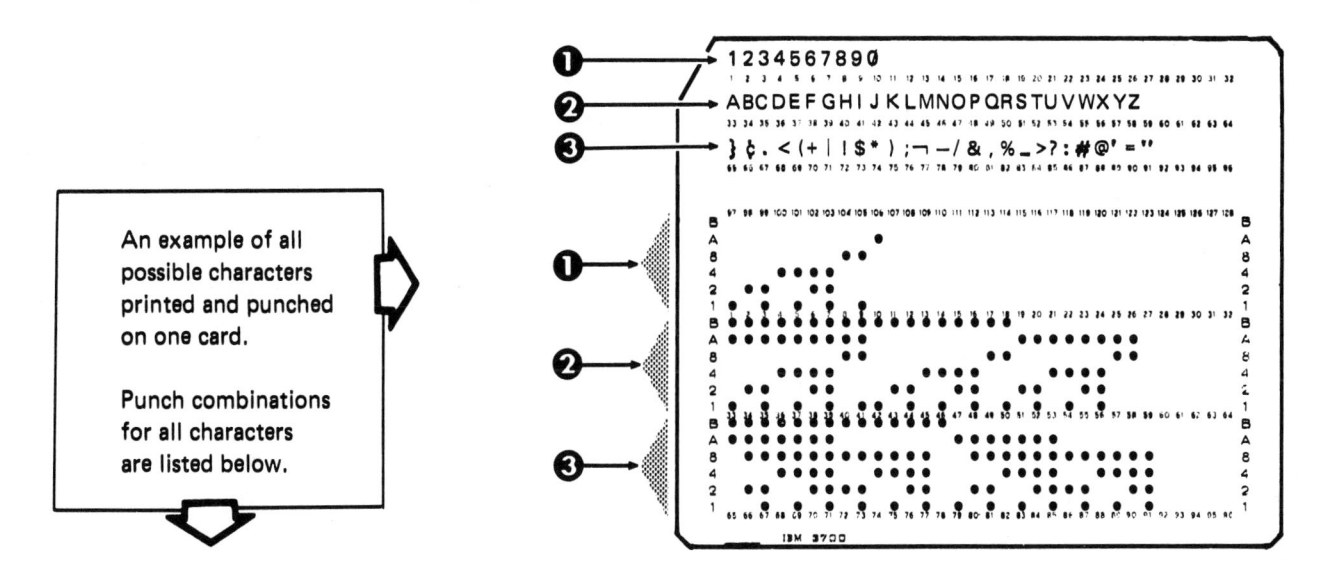

An example of all possible characters printed and punched on one card.

Punch combinations for all characters are listed below.

❶ NUMERIC CHARACTERS

Zone Punches		1	2	3	4	5	6	7	8	9	0
	B										
	A										A
Digit Punches	8								8	8	
	4				4	4	4	4			
	2		2	2			2	2			
	1	1		1		1		1		1	

Note: Any character can be punched into any column of any tier.

APPENDIX E
IBM System three 96-column card codes used on the IBM 5496 Data Recorder (Courtesy IBM Corporation).

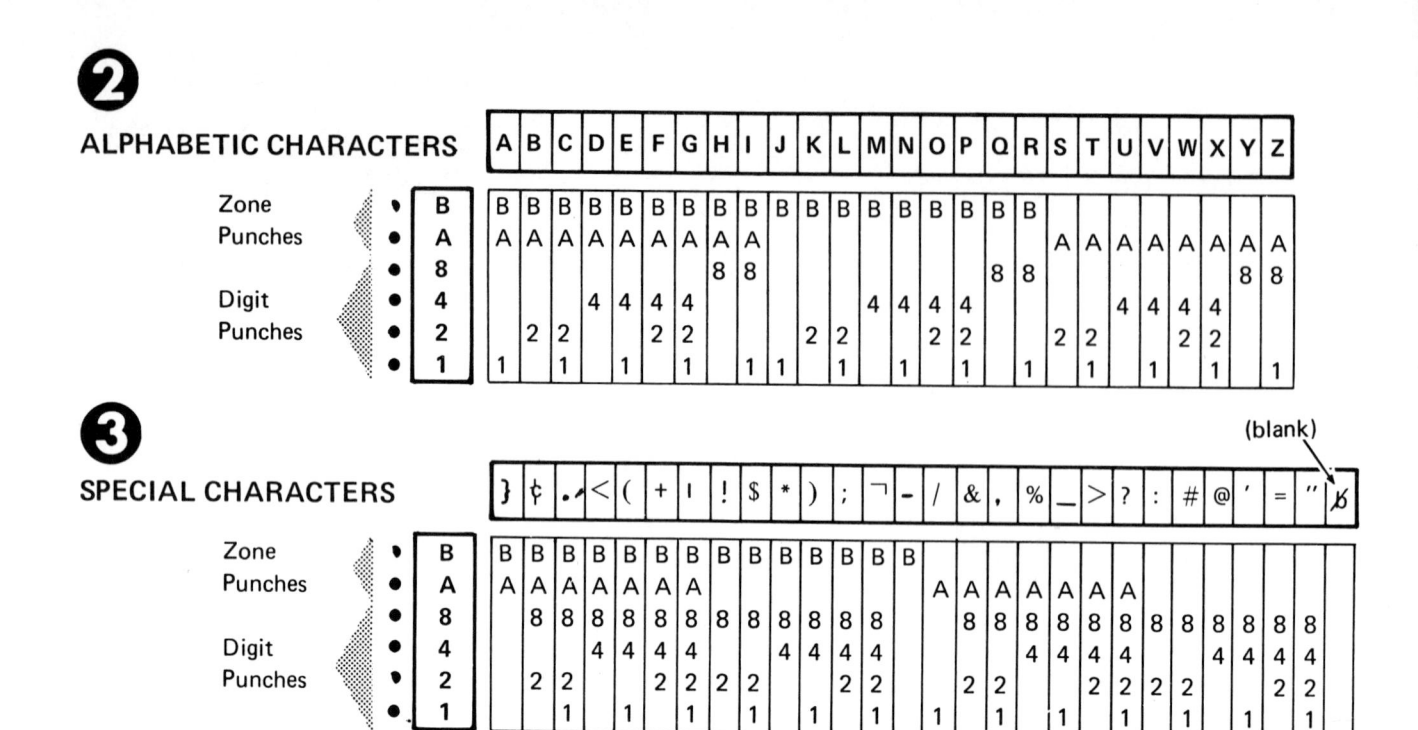

❷ ALPHABETIC CHARACTERS

Character	A	B	C	D	E	F	G	H	I	J	K	L	M	N	O	P	Q	R	S	T	U	V	W	X	Y	Z
Zone Punches B	B	B	B	B	B	B	B	B	B	B	B	B	B	B	B	B	B	B								
A	A	A	A	A	A	A	A	A	A										A	A	A	A	A	A	A	A
8								8	8							8	8									
Digit Punches 4				4	4	4	4				4	4	4			4	4	4		4	4	4	4			
2		2	2		2	2		2			2	2		2		2	2		2		2	2		2	2	
1	1		1		1		1		1	1	1		1		1	1		1	1		1		1	1		1

❸ SPECIAL CHARACTERS

Character	}	¢	.	<	(	+	|	!	$	*	)	;	¬	-	/	&	,	%	_	>	?	:	#	@	'	=	"	(blank)
Zone Punches B	B	B	B	B	B	B	B	B	B	B	B	B																
A		A	A	A	A	A	A	A	A	A	A	A				A	A	A	A	A								
8	8		8		8			8		8		8	8				8	8		8	8	8	8	8			8	
Digit Punches 4				4	4					4	4					4		4		4	4			4			4	
2		2		2		2			2	2		2			2	2		2		2		2		2		2	2	
1			1		1		1	1	1		1	1	1		1		1		1		1	1	1		1		1	

APPENDIX E *(Continued)*

APPENDIX F
EMPLOYMENT PREPARATION

OBTAINING DATA ENTRY JOB LEADS

The first step in obtaining a data entry job is to find out what job openings exist. Possible sources, in order of the possible value to you, are:

1. *Your Data Entry Instructor.* Your instructor is a good source of job information since employers frequently contact the instructors. If your work has been good, your instructor will usually be glad to recommend you and tell you about openings.
2. *Your College Placement Office.* If your institution has a placement office, you should contact this office and fill out their forms. Employers frequently contact these offices. Some firms visit campuses at certain times of the year to recruit employees.
3. *Intern and Co-op programs.* If your institution has an intern or cooperative program, by all means participate in it. If you do good work while interning, companies will often hire you.
4. *Newspapers.* Look at the newspapers' classified ads and visit companies that are advertising data entry positions. Do not waste time on blind ads (no company name, only a box number given) or ads telling you to call a phone number.

The above sources are free. It is also possible to contact a job employment agency. Some companies search through these agencies for employees on a "fee paid" basis. That is, if you accept the job, the company pays the agency a fee for finding you. Be very careful about dealing with an employment agency on any other basis. Use it as a last resort since they will charge you a fee, usually a percentage of your salary for a certain period of time.

PREPARING FOR THE JOB INTERVIEW

You should *prepare* for a job interview. Things that you may do in preparation are:

1. Do some research on the firm that you are applying to. Find out what type of work they do. Be prepared to ask a couple of questions using this information.
2. Think of five or six things that you want the employer to know about you. Be prepared to tell these things to the employer.
3. Think of five or six things that you can do for the employer. Be prepared *to sell yourself*.
    a. If you don't have any work experience say:
    "I do not have any work experience, but 'this is what I can do for you. . . '." Possible approaches are:

            (1) I am a hard worker.
            (2) I get along well with people.
            (3) I am dependable and will not miss work or be late.
            (4) I am interested in banking (or ---), and that is why I am applying here.
        b. If you are an older person who is going back into the job market, possible approaches are:
            (1) I am settled here in the community and will not be moving off.
            (2) My children are grown, and you can depend on me to be at my work station faithfully.
            (3) Also some of the remarks in (3) above would apply to you.
4. Be prepared to answer some of the following questions:
    a. What do you feel that you can do for our company?
    b. What are your strengths?
    c. What are your weaknesses?
    d. What are your goals (or ambitions) for the future?
    e. Why should we hire you?
    f. Have you ever been fired?
    g. Why did you decide to apply for a job with this company?
    h. Do you work well under pressure?
    i. What kind of a person are you?
    j. If you are changing jobs:
        (1) Why did you leave your last job?
        (2) What did you think of your last boss?
    k. What questions do you want to ask me? (The interviewer is asking you if you have any questions.)

    Interviewers may ask you personal questions on politics, religion, number of children, child care plans, etc. This is no longer an accepted practice. Questions of this type should not be asked and certainly not unless they are asked of both sexes. If these questions are asked and you really want the job, be extremely careful about your answer. You can respond in a general way and ask a question of the interviewer, thus trying to change the subject.

5. Take another copy of your résumé (discussed later) with you in case the interviewer has lost the first copy of your résumé.

6. Choose the clothes that you will wear carefully. Do *not* wear blue jeans. Women should wear a dress or a skirted suit. A conservative pants suit might be acceptable in some places, but a dress is more acceptable. The style and colors should be conservative. Do *not* chew gum or smoke during the interview.

CHANGING JOBS

If you become dissatisfied with a job, do not quit. First:

1. Find another job.
2. Give two weeks' notice.
3. Give future advancement on the job as your reason for leaving.

Never just walk out on a job no matter how angry you get. This will cause difficulty in getting future jobs. Even if you do not give this employer as a reference, personnel at the firm where you are applying will probably contact the employer.

If you are changing jobs, be prepared to answer questions about why you have left past jobs. Future employers will usually react favorably to reasons such as advancement or better salaries. They will react unfavorably to criticism of past bosses or fellow employees.

APPLYING FOR A JOB
1. Prepare a résumé to give to the firm. (See the résumé section below.)
2. Make a list of references to give. Choose persons who you feel will give you a *good* reference and *ask* the person's permission to give them as a reference. Possible references might be:
   a. Teachers.
   b. Past employers.
   c. Pastors, priests, or rabbis.
   d. Any business person that has known you for a long period of time.
3. Be prepared to be tested. Tests vary. You may encounter one or more of the following situations:
   a. No tests are given. Recommendations and the interview are the principal considerations.
   b. Time tests on a data entry device or a typewriter are given.
   c. Clerical tests are given.
   d. Psychological tests are given. This is very rare.
4. Be prepared for the questions mentioned earlier.

THE RÉSUMÉ A résumé or summary of your personal information and job experience needs to be prepared. An example of a résumé is shown below.

MS. REBECCA BREMER
3207 Clifton
Waco, TX 76710
(817) 772-6883

SUMMARY OF EXPERIENCE AND QUALIFICATIONS

I. *Work Experience*

There are two possible approaches to this section: specific information or a description of areas of accomplishment. The latter choice might be better for you if you do not have much job experience. Examples of both approaches are given below.

Specific Information Approach

A. 1980–81   Lee, Biggerstaff, and Mitchell
             1401 Washington
             Waco, TX 76703

   Position: Output clerk for law firm. Checked computer output and stored it for users. Distributed output to users.

   Reported to: Ms. Jane Mille, Office Supervisor.

B. 1978–80   Campus Records
             1608 Campus Dr.
             Waco, TX 76703

   Position: Salesperson. Waited on customers, operated cash register. Also did some bookkeeping and stock ordering.

   Reported to: Mr. James Robbins.

C. 1977–78   Kolache Kitchen
             1800 Colcord
             Waco, TX 76708

   Position: Bakery salesperson. Waited on customers, operated cash register.

   Reported to: Ms. Mary Schmidt.

Accomplishment Approach

A. Data Control: Responsible for organizing, checking, and distribution of computer output for a law firm.

B. Office Skills: Acquired typing and filing skills in local records firm while doing stock ordering. Also acquired bookkeeping skills. Enabled the records firm to catch up on a backlog of stock ordering.

C. Sales: Worked in local bakery and records store as sales person. Learned how to meet the public and influence sales.

II. *Education*
    A. Presently attending McLennan Community College (MCC), Waco, TX as a data processing major.
        a) Data processing courses completed:
           Data Entry
           Introduction to Computers
           Data Processing Operations
        b) Currently taking RPGII Programming.
    B. High school diploma, McLean High School, Waco, TX, 1979.

III. *Personal*
    A. Born November 11, 1960 in Waco, TX.
    B. Single.
    C. Honorary Societies
       National Honor Society, Sr. year, McLean High.
       Edward Literary Society, Sr. year, McLean High.
    D. Organizational Memberships
       McLennan Community College DPMA Club, 1979 to present.
    E. Special Activities
       1. McLean High School Yearbook Editor, 1979.
       2. McLean High School Student Council Member, 1979.
       3. McLean High School Tennis Team, 1978-80.
       4. American Diabetes Association, president of youth division, Heart-of-Texas Unit, 1978-79, Board of Directors, 1977-80.
       5. Heart-of-Texas Campfire Girls, 1975-80.
       6. Christian Youth Fellowship, First Christian Church, Waco.

WHAT TO DO IF YOU ARE REJECTED

If you are rejected on your first few job applications, do not be discouraged. You are gaining valuable job-interview experience, and the next application may be just the one for you. Keep looking. Be sure to get your teacher and the college or institution to help you.

APPENDIX G
JOB DESCRIPTIONS

The following job descriptions are for a large computer center. Smaller centers may not have lead or senior operators and data control and librarian work might be done by data entry operators.

Data Processing Operations Manager
Directs computer operations, data entry, and operational controls such as data control and scheduling. Normally reports to the computer center manager or director.

Lead Computer Operator
Has some supervisory duties. Checks, makes assignments to, instructs, and directs other computer operators and may have some large scale computer console operations duties. Normally reports to the data processing operations manager.

Senior Computer Operator
Performs computer console operations under the supervision of the lead computer operator. Maintains operating, maintenance, and production records.

Computer Operator
Operates peripheral equipment such as printers, tape, disk, and diskette drives, card readers, and punches. May operate the console under the direction of the senior computer operator.

Computer Operator Trainee
Usually assists the computer operator in operating the peripheral equipment.

Magnetic Media Librarian
Keeps records and assigns magnetic tapes, disks, and diskettes for specific jobs.

Data Control Clerk
Prepares jobs for processing by preparing job control, prepares batch totals, prepares documentation when needed for processing, audits and distributes output. In large centers there will be a data control supervisor reporting to the data processing operations manager.

Scheduler
Schedules work and may do some of the data control work.

Data Entry Supervisor
Directs and assigns the activities of the data entry section. Normally reports to the data processing operations manager.

Lead Data Entry Operator
Trains new employees, instructs operators, may act as a verifier.

Data Entry Operator
Operates data entry equipment under some supervision. Does some verifying.

Data Entry Operator Trainee
Operates data entry equipment under close supervision.

Word Processing Supervisor
Supervises the operation of word processing operations.

Word Processing Operator
Operates word processing equipment under supervision.

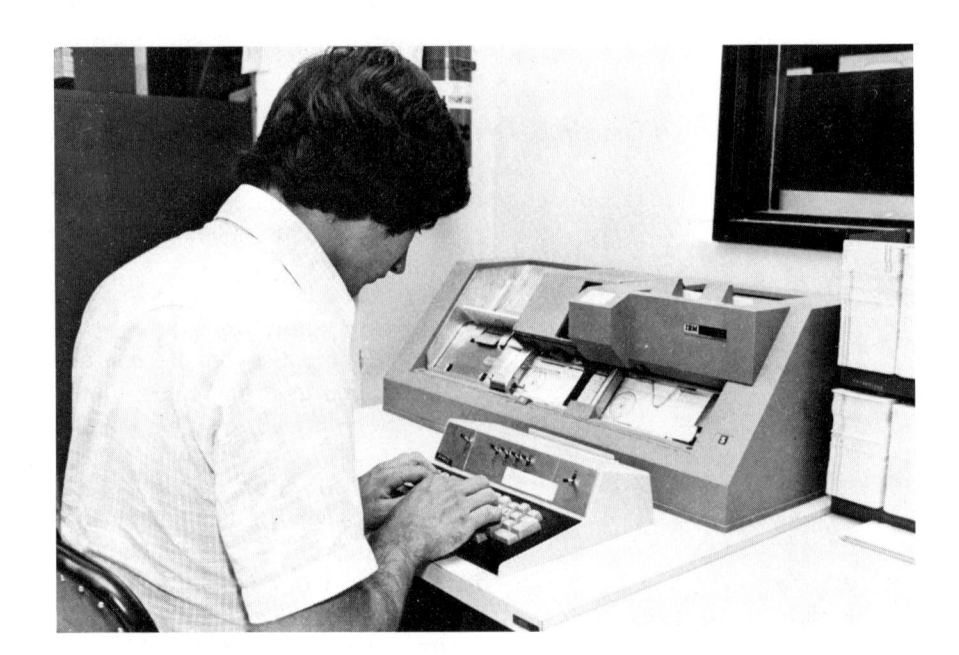

APPENDIX H

THE IBM 029 UNBUFFERED KEYPUNCH

The use of the IBM 029 is disappearing in industry because:

1. The device operates very slowly.
2. Once an error is made it cannot be corrected before the character is punched because the IBM 029 has no data memory or buffer area.
3. Verification requires a separate device, the IBM 059.

However, these devices are very cheap. Institutions that still have card input for computers retain these devices. Many colleges keep this equipment for student use.

If your institution uses this equipment, you will need to study the information in this appendix.

EXTERNAL FEATURES

The external features of the IBM 029 are shown in Figure H-1.

1. The four positions in the card path are:
   (1) *The Card Hopper.* The station where blank cards are placed, 9 edge down, face forward.

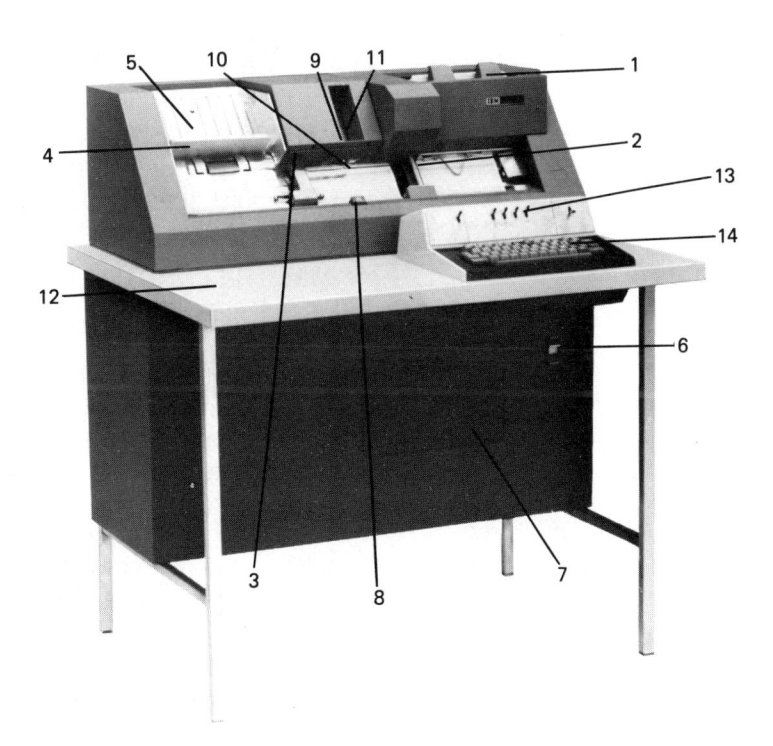

FIGURE H-1
The IBM 029 unbuffered keypunch (Courtesy of IBM Corporation).

(2) *The Punching Station.* Where punching takes place.
(3) *The Reading Station.* Where cards are read if being duplicated.
(4) *The Card Stacker.* Where punched cards are deposited.

2. Other features are (see numbers in Figure H-1):

(5) *Card Scale.* The stacker has a card scale by which one may estimate the number of cards that have been keyed. The card scale has a switch that locks the keyboard when the stacker is full.

(6) *Main-Line Switch.* When this switch is turned on, the machine is ready for operation.

(7) *Chip Box.* This box holds the paper chips punched out of the card. One must empty the chip box when it is full. Fuses can be found near the chip box.

(8) *Backspace Key.* If you use the space bar past the card column desired, use the backspace key to return to the proper column. However, it does no good to backspace if an incorrect character has already been punched in the card.

(9) *Program Unit.* The IBM 029 has no memory or buffer area. However, two programs may be initiated by the use of a program card placed on the program drum. This unit has eight starwheels which when lowered read the codes punched on the program card placed on the program drum. When the starwheels are lowered, the machine is said to be under *program control*. If the starwheels are not lowered, the machine is said to be operated *manually*. The advantage of operating under program control is that certain actions such as skipping or duplicating (copying) can be done at faster speeds. Switches on the keyboard console (13) are used in operations under program control.

(10) *Program Lever.* When the program lever is turned to the left, the starwheels are lowered to read the punches on the program card. The program drum should *never* be removed when the starwheels are in a lowered position. Such an action causes the starwheels to be stripped off. The starwheels then fall down into the machine. They must be found and replaced. Replacing the starwheels is a very tiresome and tedious operation.

(11) *Column Indicator.* This indicator is located at the bottom or base of the program drum holder. The indicator shows the *next* column in which a punch will occur.

(12) *Reading Board.* This surface is used to hold source documents.

(13) THE FUNCTIONAL CONTROL SWITCHES
These switches are shown in Figure H-2.
   a. AUTO SKIP/DUP Switch. When this switch is on and the machine is under program control, automatic skipping and duplicating take place.
   b. The PROG SEL Switch. The setting of this switch determines if the machine is operating under the control of program 1 or program 2.
   c. The AUTO FEED Switch. When this switch is on, it causes another card to be automatically fed when column 80 is keyed or the release key is pressed.
   d. The PRINT Switch. When this switch is on, it causes printing on the card of the characters keyed.
   e. The LZ PRINT Switch. When this switch is on and operation is

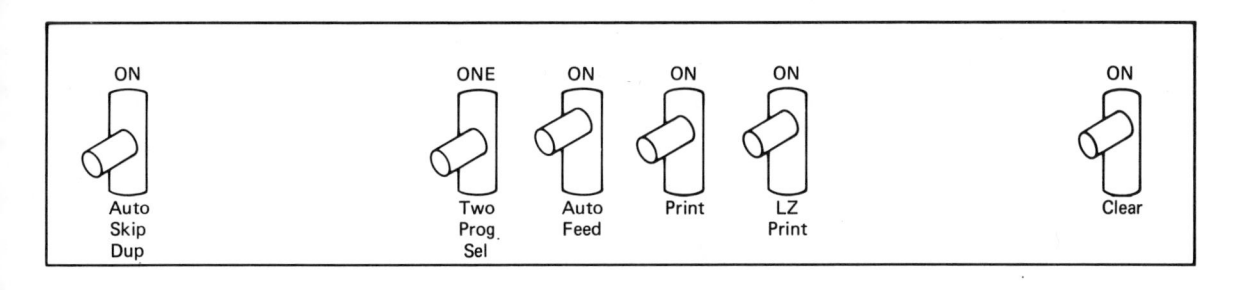

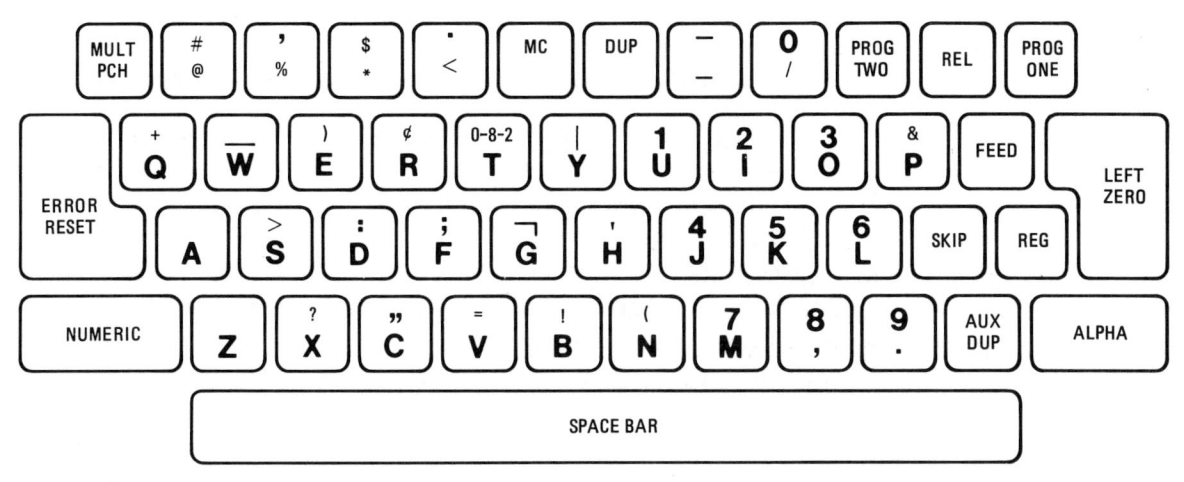

FIGURE H-2
The IBM 029 keyboard and console.

under program control, left zeros are automatically inserted when the left zero key is pressed.

f. The CLEAR Switch. When this switch is pushed upward to the ON position, all cards are cleared from the card path and placed in the stacker. This switch does not need to be held in the ON position. Simply pushing it up causes the cards to be cleared.

3. KEYBOARD CONTROLS

The keyboard contains two types of keys: *data keys* and *function keys*. Data keys cause the entering of data. The blue, or function keys, cause certain functions or controlling actions to take place.

If *not* under program control, pressing a data key (keys with numbers, letter, or special characters) will cause the character on the bottom of the key to be punched. If you desire the top character, hold down the numeric key when you press the key for the top character.

You should note the difference between the − (minus or hyphen) and the __ (underline), and the ' (apostrophe) and the | sign if they exist on your keyboard. The keyboard shown in Figure H-2 is a 64-character keyboard. A 48-character keyboard also exists. This keyboard has fewer special characters.

FUNCTION KEYS

The IBM 029 function keys are:

1. **FEED KEY**

   If keying, this key feeds in two cards if depressed twice. The first card is positioned against the punch unit, and the second card is prepositioned.

APPENDIX H

2. REG KEY
The register key causes any card inserted manually or preregistered to be positioned against the punch unit. A second card is not fed from the hopper.

3. REL KEY
This key is used to release the card to the next station in the card path. If keying under program control, any auto dup fields are automatically duplicated at the punch station.

4. SKIP KEY
   a. In program mode, this key skips to the next field.
   b. In manual mode, this key causes a single space.

5. DUP KEY
   a. In programmed mode, one depression causes an entire field to be duplicated.
   b. In manual mode, duplication occurs one column at a time until the key is released.
      In both cases information is copied from the reading station into the card at the punching station.

6. AUX DUP KEY
See the special features section below for an explanation of this key.

7. MC or MASTER CARD KEY
See the special features section below for an explanation of this key.

8. MULT PCH KEY
Using the multiple punch key places the keyboard in numeric shift and allows the operator to key several punches into one column. This allows keying a combination that is not one of the standard characters.

9. ALPHA SHIFT KEY
When depressed this key places a programmed numeric shift keyboard into an alpha shift (lowercase).

10. NUMERIC SHIFT KEY
When depressed this key places an alpha shift keyboard into numeric shift (upper case).

11. ERROR RESET KEY
When depressed this key unlocks the keyboard. See the section below on reasons for a locked keyboard.

12. LEFT ZERO KEY
In programmed mode, depressing this key causes the correct number of leading zeros to automatically be inserted in a field without actually keying the leading zeros.

13. PROG ONE and PROG TWO KEYS
In programmed mode these keys allow the operator to shift from one program to the other by pressing the appropriate key.

OPERATING PROCEDURES

Manual Keying

1. Place cards in the hopper and turn the main-line switch on.
2. Set console switches as follows: AUTO SKIP/DUP to ON, AUTO FEED to ON, PRINT to ON. The setting of the remaining switches can be in any position.
3. Press the FEED key until two cards are fed in.
4. Key the information on the card.

5. If there are *not* 80 characters to be keyed, press the REL key after keying the last character. This causes the card to be released to the next station and positions the next card at the punching station.

Error Corrections

Error Detected While Keying the Card

1. Press the REL key. This causes the error card to be released to the reading station, and a blank card to be registered at the punching station.
2. Press the DUP key until the column indicator is positioned on the column with the error.
3. Key the correction and finish keying the card record.
4. When the error card is released to the stacker, remove it immediately.

Error Detected at a Later Date

1. Insert the error card at the reading station. Insert it in the two notches and under the plastic guides. Push the card all the way to the left until it hits the reading station. Then push the card slightly to the right. The right-hand side of the card will not be flat in the card bed, but it will be flat after it is registered and goes through the reading station.
2. Insert a blank card manually at the punching station, under the metal guides. Push the card to the left until it hits the punching station. Then push it back slightly to the right making sure that the right edge is under the card pusher.
3. Depress the REG key.
4. Press the DUP key until the error column is reached. Rekey the columns in error and duplicate the remaining columns.
5. Throw away the error card and replace it with the corrected card.

Laboratory Work

Your instructor will now give you some exercises to key manually.

PROGRAMS

The IBM 029 is instructed by using a program card with programming codes punched in it. Each field in the program card has:

1. A punched code which describes the function needed.
2. A field definition code showing for how many columns this action is to take place.

The chart below shows the functions necessary for the laboratory exercises in this text:

Function	Character Code	Field Definition
Skip	− (11 punch)	& (12 punch)
Punch numeric	b (blank)	&
Duplicate numeric	0 (zero)	&
Punch alphameric	1	A (12 + 1)
Duplicate alphameric	/	A
8 column, left-zero field	2	&
7 column, left-zero field	3	&

APPENDIX H

Function	Character Code	Field Definition
6 column, left-zero field	2, 3	&
5 column, left-zero field	1, 2	&
4 column, left-zero field	1, 3	&
3 column, left-zero field	1, 2, 3	&

Example to Illustrate Operations Procedures

A program card is to be planned for the following data:

Columns 1–6	Duplicate numeric date
Columns 7–11	Duplicate alphameric course abbreviation
Columns 12–20	Punch social security number
Columns 21–33	Punch last name
Columns 34–45	Punch first name
Column 46	Punch middle initial
Columns 47–52	Punch amount of tuition and fees (left zero) nnnn$_\wedge$nn
Columns 53–80	Blank

A record layout with the planned codes is shown below in Figure H-3. Punch this program card. It should appear as shown in Figure H-3.

KEYING UNDER PROGRAM CONTROL

Preparation

1. Mount the program card on the program drum. Your instructor will show you how to:
   a. Hold the drum with the handle at the bottom.
   b. Insert the program card so that the 80 column goes into the clamping strip and the 9 edge fits tightly against the rim of the drum.
   c. Turn the handle to the center.
   d. Wrap the card around the drum.
   e. Insert the card under the toothed edge.
   h. Turn the handle as far to the right as it will go.
2. Insert the drum on the spindle in the program unit so that the aligning pin falls into its hole. The drum should fit tightly with no gap between it and the column indicator.
3. Close the program unit cover.
4. Set all console switches up except the clear switch.
5. Then if any fields are to be duplicated, the AUTO SKIP DUP switch should be left off for the first card. Otherwise the keyboard will lock up because there is nothing in the read station to duplicate.
6. Turn the program control lever to the left.

Keying the First Card Under Program Control

1. Press the feed key until two cards are fed.
2. Key in the current date. You do not need to hold down the NUMERIC shift key since this field has been programmed numeric. This field is being keyed in the first card so that there will be something to duplicate in the other cards.
3. Key in the course abbreviation and number. Use DP310 holding down the numeric key for the 310 because this field was programmed al-

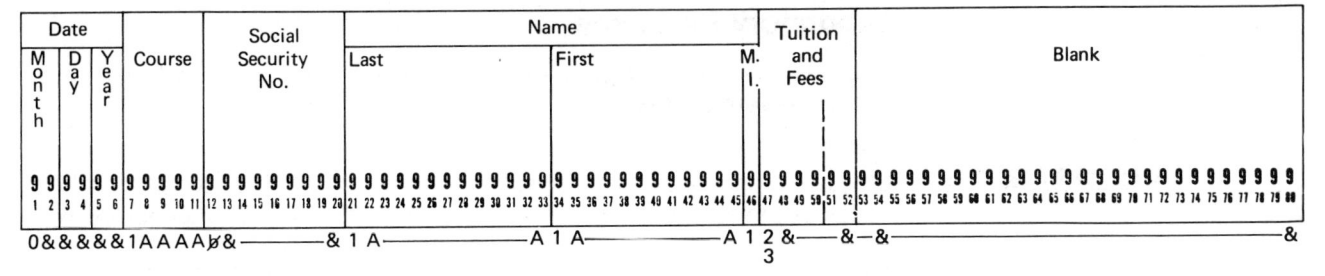

FIGURE H-3
Record layout and program codes.

phameric. This field is also being keyed in the first card so that there will be something to duplicate in the other cards.

4. Key in your social security number (you need not hold down the numeric shift key).
5. Key in your last name. If you do not use the entire field, depress the SKIP key.
6. Key in your first name. If you do not use the entire field, depress the SKIP key.
7. Key in your middle initial. If you have none, press the SKIP key.
8. Assume your tuition is $110.16. Key in 11016 and press the LEFT ZERO key. This inserts leading zeros without your having to determine how many should be keyed in.
9. Press the REL key.
10. Turn on the AUTO SKIP DUP switch.

Now try keying the next two records. Note that the first two fields are automatically duplicated from the first card. The column indicator should have moved to column 12. You are now positioned for the third field, the social security number.

SS#	Name	Tuition
123-45-6754	Lee, Iva H	150.00
675-88-9766	Harbaugh, Maggie	34.67

Note that skipping and duplicating are now fully automatic. If you have a long job and need to start again manually, just place the last card that you keyed at the reading station and feed in two blank cards. Then you will have the fields to duplicate again.

If a negative number is being keyed, when the units position is keyed the MULT PCH key may be used with the minus key and the digit. For example, for a −123, the units position would be keyed by holding the MULT PCH key and keying a − and a 3. The same result would occur if an L were keyed since an 11 punch and a 3 punch give the letter L.

NOTE: There are two keys for the comma and period to be used depending on whether you are in the NUMERIC or ALPHA shift.

It is very important that the program drum *never* be removed with the starwheels in a lowered position (that is, with the program lever turned to the left). Before removing the program drum, the program lever should be turned to the right to raise the starwheels. As stated previously, such an action often strips off the starwheels. They fall down into the machine. If this happens, the top of the machine must be removed. The tiny starwheels must then be found and tediously replaced with pliers.

APPENDIX H

Laboratory Exercises

Your instructor will assign some exercises from the textbook to be keyed under program control.

PROGRAM TWO Only two program levels are possible on the IBM 029. The program level-two codes use rows 4 through 9 of the program card. The codes are as follows:

Function	Character Code	Field Definition
Skip	5	4
Punch numeric	b (blank)	4
Duplicate numeric	6	4
Punch alphameric	7	4,7
Duplicate alphameric	6,7	4,7
8 column, left-zero field	8	4
7 column, left-zero field	9	4
6 column, left-zero field	8,9	4
5 column, left-zero field	7,8	4
4 column, left-zero field	7,9	4
3 column, left-zero field	7,8,9	4

To key under program level-two, the PROG SEL switch much be set on TWO, or the PROG TWO key must be pressed.

REASONS AND CORRECTIVE PROCEDURES FOR KEYBOARD LOCKUPS

The following conditions can cause the keyboard to lock:

1. In a field programmed numeric or while holding the numeric shift key, the A or Z key is pressed. Action: Press the ERROR RESET key.
2. Under programmed numeric control, a blank column is duplicated. Action: Press the ERROR RESET key or the ALPHA shift key.
3. A card is not registered at the punching station. Action: Press the REG or FEED key.
4. The REG key is pressed when a card is already registered. Action: Press the ERROR RESET key.
5. The machine is turned off while a card is still registered in the card bed. Action: Use the CLEAR switch.
6. The stacker is full. Action: Remove the cards from the stacker.
7. Under programmed control with the AUTO SKIP DUP switch on, no card is in the reading unit or the card is blank. Action: Turn off the automatic switches, press the ERROR RESET key, and clear the cards from the card bed.

MAINTENANCE AND USUAL CONDITIONS

1. You may be required to change the printer ribbon. Your reference manual will give directions for this operation.
2. You may wish to dust or wipe off the keyboard. Use a soft damp cloth, but never spray cleaning solutions or water on the machine. Consume no food or drinks at the keyboard.
3. Empty the chip box periodically.
4. *Card Jams.* If the card is jammed in the card bed,
    a. If the jam is in the hopper, remove the cover of the hopper. Pull the handle underneath it forward and remove the card.

b. If the jam is under the punch unit:
   (1) Open the cover to the program unit and hold down the pressure roll release lever. Gently pull out the card.
   (2) If the card will not move, hold down the MULT PCH key. Key the &, -, and 0 through 9. Then hold down the pressure roll release lever and try pulling the card out.
   (3) If a card tears leaving pieces under the punch unit, hold down the metal guides at the bottom of the punch position and press the REG key; hold down the MULT PCH key; key the &, -, and 0-9; then try to push the bits of paper out from under the punch dies with a piece of a card.
   (4) As a last resort, use the card saw as described in the unit on the IBM 129.

SPECIAL FEATURES

The IBM 029 has several special features available which cost extra money. They are described in detail in the 029 reference manual. A summary of these features follows.

1. AUXILIARY DUPLICATION, CARD INSERTION, AND INTERSPERSED GANGPUNCHING FEATURES
   a. The auxiliary duplication feature involves another, separate drum unit on the back of the machine. A master card can be mounted on the drum. By pressing the AUX DUP key, data can be duplicated from the master card into the same columns of the card currently being keyed.
   b. With the card insertion feature a prepunched master duplicating card can be inserted manually into the read station by use of a special INSERT switch and the MC function key.
   c. The interspersed gangpunching feature allows recognition of a master card by the upper left or right corner cut. (Detail cards have the opposite cut.) Punching occurs from master to detail card and detail to detail card.
2. HIGH SPEED SKIPPING
   This feature allows special programming for faster skipping.
3. VARIABLE LENGTH CARD FEED
   This feature allows the use of cards with 51, 60, 66, or 80 columns.
4. Larger Reading Board
   The board is extended at the left adding about 12 inches.
5. Self-Checking and Modulus 10 and 11 Features
   These features provide a method of validating certain fields when they are being keyed. The methods are explained in Appendix D.

VERIFYING

Verifying is not possible on the IBM 029. It must be done on a separate machine, the IBM 059 verifier.

SUMMARY

The IBM 029 is an older data entry device that is unbuffered. That is, it has no data storage area which allows corrections before the data is punched. Its main disadvantages in comparison with other data entry equipment are:

1. It is slow.
2. Mistakes cannot be corrected by backspacing and rekeying.
3. Only two program levels are possible.
4. It is not possible to both key and verify on the same machine.
5. It has a very limited number of special features.

APPENDIX H

STUDY GUIDE ON THE IBM 029 KEYPUNCH

Answer these questions in your book. If told to do so, tear out the pages and hand them in to your instructor.

1. List the external features of the IBM 029 keypunch, giving the purpose of each feature.

   (1) _____

   (2) _____

   (3) _____

   (4) _____

   (5) _____

   (6) _____

   (7) _____

   (8) _____

   (9) _____

   (10) _____

   (11) _____

   (12) _____

   (13) _____

   (14) _____

2. List each special switch and give the purpose of each.

   (1) _____

(2) _____

(3) _____

(4) _____

(5) _____

(6) _____

3. List each function key on your keyboard that you have used in exercises on this unit. Give the purpose of each.

(1) _____

(2) _____

(3) _____

(4) _____

(5) _____

(6) _____

(7) _____

(8) _____

(9) _____

(10) _____

(11) _____

4. Define:

(1) Duplicate _____

(2) Program _____

(3) Program code _____
_____

(4) Left zero _____
_____

5. State the program and field definition codes for program level-one:

Operation	Program Code	Field Definition Code
a. Punching alphanumeric	_____	_____
b. Duplicating alphameric	_____	_____
c. Punching numeric	_____	_____
d. Duplicating numeric	_____	_____
e. Skipping	_____	_____
f. 8 column, left-zero	_____	_____
g. 7 column, left-zero	_____	_____
h. 6 column, left-zero	_____	_____
i. 5 column, left-zero	_____	_____
j. 4 column, left-zero	_____	_____
k. 3 column, left-zero	_____	_____

6. List the conditions under which the keyboard might lock up and state the corrective actions necessary.

(1) _____
_____

(2) _____
_____

(3) _____
_____

(4) _____
_____

(5) _____
_____

(6) _____
_____

(7) _____
_____

7. Describe on a separate sheet of paper or demonstrate to your instructor how to:
   a. Prepare the machine for operation.
   b. Manually key a record.
   c. Correct an error in a record.
   d. Design and prepare a program card.
   e. Mount the program card on the program drum.
   f. Key a record under program control.

  g. Change the printing ribbon if required.
  h. Clean your machine.
  i. Use any special features that your instructor may designate.

8. List five disadvantages of the IBM 029.

 (1) _____

 (2) _____

 (3) _____

 (4) _____

 (5) _____

9. List any special features that your machine may have.

INDEX

A.B. Dick Magna SL, 224
Abilities needed, 11
Access, 313
Accumulate feature, 51
Accumulator, 313
Acoustical covers, 59
Acronym, 4, 313
Activating a disabled batch, 159
Additional program buffers, 100
Address, 313
Address abbreviations (as specified by U.S. Post Office), 319
ADDS terminals, 212
Adler SE-2000, 224
ALC (Assembly Language Coding), 313
Alpha, 313
Alphabetic keying exercises, 241–244
Alphanumeric (alphameric), 28, 313
Ampersand or 12 punch, 28
Arithmetic registers, 162–163
ASCII Code (American National Standard Code for Information Interchange), 24, 144, 313
Automatic field, 313
Automatic keying, 39, 74
Automatic program sequencing, 115, 142. See also Chaining
Auxiliary duplication registers, 163
Auxiliary storage device, 6, 317

Backup, 141, 233, 313
Balance registers, 162–163
Ball or selectric element, 223
BASIC (Beginner's All Purpose Symbolic Instruction Code), 225, 313
Basic data exchange, 72
Batch, 141, 157–159, 313
Batch balancing, 313
Batch processing, 11–12, 141, 313
BCD (binary coded decimal), 19, 313
BCD tape, 137, 317
Begin field code, 313
Binary, 313
BIT (binary digit), 19–20, 313
Blank fill, 28, 313
Blind terminal, 224, 313
Block, 139, 313
Blocking factor, 139, 313
BOE (beginning of extent), 73, 313

BOT (beginning of tape) marker, 139, 313
BPI (bytes per inch), 138, 313
Bubble memory, 222–223, 313
Buffer, 73–74, 313
Buffered keypunch, 22–23, 37–68
　IBM 129 data recorder, 40–51
　IBM 5496 data recorder, 61–63
　introduction to, 38–40
　study guide, 64–68
　TAB 501 Punch/Verifier, 63–64
　UNIVAC 1710, 51–60
　UNIVAC 1810, 60–61
Bunker Ramo terminals, 212
Burroughs terminals, 212
Byte, 137, 313

Card hopper, 39, 40
Card I/O attachment, 51
Card release button, 41
Card stacker, 39, 41
Centralized data, 230
Centralized data entry, 11–12, 313
Chaining, 59, 99, 115, 142, 143, 313. See also Automatic program sequencing
Character, 17, 313
Character registers, 163
Character set, 313
Check bit, 137, 313. See also Parity bit
Check digit, 313
Chip box, 41
Cluster, 137, 313
CMC models 3, 5, 12, and 20 key-to-disk equipment, 192–193
COBOL (common business-oriented language), 123, 314
Column, 17, 314
Column 81 verification punching, 59
Column indicator, 40
COM (computer output microfilm), 314
Combination punch/read unit, 41
Command code, 313
Computer operators, duties of, 7
Computers and computer centers, 3–8, 314
　comparison of human being and, 5
　meaning of, 4–5, 6
　organization of, 6–7
　study guide, 7–8
　types of data processing, 4

Configuration, 136, 314
Console, 314
Consolidated Computer Key Edit key-to-disk equipment, 192–193
Constant, 314
Continuation character, 314
Continue field code, 314
Contitronix D-11, 223
Control Data terminals, 212
Control key, see Function key
Control punch, 28, 314
Controller, 314
CPU (Central Processing Unit), 3, 6, 314
CRT (Cathode Ray Tube), 73, 141, 201, 314
Cummins-Allison key-to-disk equipment 192–193
Current record buffer or storage, 73
Cursor, 76, 152, 162, 206, 314
Cursor wrap, 206, 314

Dacoll Engineering terminals, 212
Daisy wheel, 223, 314
DASD (direct access storage device), 141, 314
Data, 314
Data check, 139, 314
Data communications, 314
Data control, 314
Data entry:
　Computers and computer centers, 3–8, 314
　equipment, 35–218
　future applications, 219–236
　glossary of terms, 313–318
　hexadecimal and octal number systems, 323–325
　history of, 15–33
　introduction to, 1–33
　laboratory exercises, 237–312
　meaning of, 4, 5
　operations, 9–13
　standard abbreviations, 319–322
Data entry device, 10, 314
Data Entry Management Association (DEMA), 11
Data entry operator, duties of, 10
Data entry personnel, duties of, 7
DATA IV System, 169–183

beginning work, 173
display messages, 180-183
entering new records, 174-175
errors and general procedures, 174
finding records for modification, 175-177
flagging questionable fields, 174
keyboard, 172-173
message line, 172
properties, 170
status line, 170-171
updating or changing a record already released to disk current batch, 177-178
verifying, 178-179
work interruption, 174
work termination or signing off, 173-174
Data key, 39, 42-43, 73, 144-145, 207, 314
Data line, 150
DATA 100 KEYBATCH key-to-disk equipment, 192-193
Data privacy, 233-234, 314
Data processing, 4, 5, 314
Data security, 232, 314
Data set, 72, 314
Data set label, 73, 83-86, 109-110, 314
Data validation, 11-12, 314
  methods of, 327-328
Datamedia terminals, 212
Decentralized or distributed data entry, 11-12, 230, 314
Decode, 7, 314
Default value, 152, 314
Delete record, 85, 109
DEMA (Data Entry Management Association), 11
Density, 138, 314
Digi-Log Systems terminals, 212
Digit punch, 17, 314
Digital terminals, 212
Direct access, 74, 141, 314
Disabling a batch, 159
Disk, 140-141, 316
Disk address, 74
Disk copy, 99
Disk initialization, 73, 100, 141, 314
Disk unit, 73
Diskettes, 70-73, 314
  advantages of, 71
  handling of, 71
  internal characteristics, 72
  loading a program at a later time, 95
  storing and loading programs on, 94-95
  storing program with data, 94-95
Display screen, 222, 224
Display unit or CRT, 73, 141, 201, 314
Distributed or decentralized data entry, 11-12, 230, 314
DMA (direct memory access), 141, 142, 314-315
DP (data processing), 315
Drive spindle hole, 70
Dumb terminal, 201, 315
Duplicate, 41, 315

EBCDIC (Extended Binary Coded Decimal Interchange Code), 23, 137, 315
Editing, 315
EDP (electronic data processing), 315
Eject unit, 41
Employment preparation, 331-334
  applying for the job, 333
  changing jobs, 332
  how to prepare, 331-332
  obtaining leads, 331
  rejection (what to do), 334
  resume, 333-334
Encode, 7, 315
EOD (end of data), 73, 315
EOE (end of extent), 73, 315
EOR (end of reel) marker, 139
EOT (end of tape) marker, 139, 315
Equipment, 35-218
  buffered keypunches, 22-23, 37-68
  history of, 22-25
  key-to-disk devices, 133-198
  key-to-diskette devices, 71-131
  terminals, 201-218
  unbuffered keypunches, 337-347
Equipment security, 315
Error codes, alarm messages, and recovery procedures:
  FOUR PHASE IV, 180-183
  IBM 3742, 101
  NIXDORF 80, 191-192
  TAB 702, 115-122
  UNIVAC 1900/10, 165-169
Even parity, 138, 315
Extent, 73, 315
External label, 138, 315

Field, 25, 47, 315
Field continuation code, 314
Field definition character, 313
Field width, 27
File, 25, 315
File label, 138, 315
FILE M mode, 157
File protection, 139, 140, 315
Flippy disk, 70, 315
Floppy disk, 70, 222, 315
Format control, 142, 315
Formatted display, 206, 315
FORTRAN (formula translator), 315
FOUR PHASE, 169-183
  beginning work, 173
  display messages, 180-183
  entering new records, 174-175
  errors and general procedures, 174
  finding records for modification, 175-177
  flagging questionable fields, 174
  keyboard, 172-173
  message line, 172
  properties, 170
  status line, 152, 170-171
  updating or changing a record already released to disk current batch, 177-178
  perifying, 178-179
  work interruption, 174
  work termination or signing off, 173-174

Frame, 137, 315
Free format or free form data entry, 143, 315
Function key, 39, 42-43, 73, 144, 145-146, 207, 315
Function select key, 73
Future applications, 219-236
  introduction to, 230
  new data entry methods, 231-232
  privacy, 233-234
  security and control, 232-233
  study guide, 234-235
  trends, 229-236
  verification, 232
  word processing and data entry, 221-228

GCS key-to-disk equipment, 192-193
GIGO (Garbage In—Garbage Out), 10, 315
Glossary of terms, 313-318
GTE key-to-disk equipment, 192-193

Hard copy, 75, 315
Hard disk, 134
Hardware, 315
Harris terminals, 212
Hash total, 315
Head crashes, 232
Head slot, 70
Header or file label, 138, 315
Heath H8, WH8, H88, and H89, 224
Hewlett-Packard 85s, 224
Hewlett-Packard terminals, 212
Hexadecimal (hex), 315, 324, 325
High order position, 27, 315
Hitachi terminals, 212
Hold buffer or storage, 74
Hollerith, Dr. Herman, 16
Hollerith punched card, 16-19
Honeywell key-to-disk equipment, 192-193
Host processor, 142, 315

IBG (interblock gap), 139, 315
IBM card, 16-19
IBM key-to-disk equipment, 192-193
IBM OS 6/452, 224
IBM System/32 computer, 224
IBM System/34, 224-225
IBM terminals, 212
IBM 029 unbuffered keypunch, 22, 337-349
  error corrections, 341
  example to illustrate operations procedure, 342
  external features, 337-339
  function keys, 339-340
  keying under program control, 342-343
  maintenance and usual conditions, 344-345
  manual keying, 340-341
  program level-two codes, 344
  programs, 341-342
  reasons and corrective procedures for keyboard lockups, 344
  special features, 345
  study guide, 346-349
  verifying, 345

IBM 75, 223
IBM 129 data recorder, 40-51
　card path for, 41
　DATA READ procedure, 44
　error corrections, 44
　example to illustrate operations
　　procedures, 45-46
　function keys, 43-44
　keyboard console, 41-42
　keyboard controls, 42-44
　keying under program control, 46-47
　loading a program, 45-46
　main features, 40
　maintenance and unusual conditions,
　　50-51
　manual punching (program level 0), 44
　operating features, 41
　operator procedures, 44-45
　programs, 45
　punching out a program, 48
　special features, 51
　special function keys, 47
　verifying, 48-50
IBM 3270 Information Display System,
　202-211
　entering data, 210
　error correction, 210-211
　review on cursor positioning keys,
　　208-210
　station turn on procedure, 206-207
　3275 and 3277 data entry-keypunch
　　style keyboard, 207-208
　verifying, 211
IBM 3278 display station, 202
IBM 3540 Diskette I/O Unit, 124, 125
IBM 3741, 75, 123
IBM 3742, 75-101, 123
　to begin (operating procedure), 80
　chaining, 99
　compared to TAB 702, 102
　data set label, 83-84
　disk copy operations, 96
　display screen, 76
　dual data station, 75-76
　error recovery, 101
　errors, 82
　example to illustrate programmed
　　operations procedure, 90-91
　function select keys, 79-80
　index track or track zero, 82-86
　keyboard, 76-80
　keying under program control (program
　　has been loaded), 93-94
　loading a program from diskette at a
　　later time, 95
　loading a program from the key-
　　board, 92
　maintenance and unusual condi-
　　tions, 100
　manual keying, 86-90
　modifying or changing data set label
　　information, 84-85
　operating features, 76-82
　program code chart, 91
　programs, 90
　searching for records, 95
　second data set label creation

　　procedure, 85-86
　special features available for, 99-100
　special functions keys, 78-79
　status line, 80-82
　storing and loading programs on a
　　diskette, 94-95
　switches, 77
　verifying, 96-99
　verifying errors or mismatches, 97-99
IBM 5280 Distributed Data System, 123.
　See also Instructor's Guide, 96
IBM 5285, 123
IBM 5286, 123
IBM 5496 Data Recorder, 61-63
ICL terminals, 212
Index, 142
Indexed file (or set), 141-142, 315
Indexed sequential file (ISAM) file, 142
Index hole, 70
Index track or track zero, 72, 82-83, 109
INFOREX 1301, 1302, and 1303
　key-to-disk equipment, 192-193
INFOREX 3100 and 3200, 193
Informer terminals, 212
Ink jet, 223
Input device, 3, 6, 222, 315
Input field, 206, 315
Intelligent terminal, 201, 315
Internal label, 138, 315
Interpret, 50, 60, 315
Interrupting a batch, 158
Interspersed master card, 59
Invalid batch, 157, 315
I/O (Input/Output), 5, 315
IRG (interrecord gap), 139, 315

Job (group of batches of data), 141, 315
Job descriptions, list of, 335-336
Job prospects, 10-11
JUKI 2041 data recorder, 123
JUKI 2042, 123

KB, 139, 315-316
Keyboard, 40, 73
Keyboard console, 40, 41
Key-to-disk devices, 133-198
　additional types of equipment, 192-193
　communications controller, 142
　control processing unit, 142
　display or video screen, 150-152
　equipment, 134-135
　field control keys, 146-147
　FOUR PHASE DATA IV System,
　　169-183
　functional keys, 144, 145-146
　hardware and procedures, 137-153
　installation supervisor, 153
　introduction to, 134-137
　keyboard, 144-150
　magnetic tape, 137-140
　NIXDORF 80 Series, 183-192
　passwords, 143
　positioning keys, 148-149
　programming, 142-143
　ranking system, 136
　record control keys, 147-148
　shift keys, 149-150

　study guide, 194-198
　UNIVAC 1900/10, 153-169
　verifying, 143-144
Key-to-diskette devices, 71-131
　addresses, 74
　advantages of, 71
　care and handling of, 71
　definitions, 72-73
　device characteristics, 73-74
　diskettes, 70-73
　IBM 3741, 75
　IBM 3742, 75-101
　internal characteristics, 72, 73-74
　other devices, 123-125
　study guide, 125-131
　TAB 702, 102-122
Keypunches, 22, 337-347
Key verification, 144, 316

Labeled and unlabeled tapes, 138
Laboratory exercises, 237-312
　alphabetic keying, 241-244
　keying under program control, 244-312
　numeric keying, 238-241
Lanier No Problem LC, 224
LCA (lowercase alpha), 316
Left justified, 28, 316
Left-zero (or right-adjust), 47, 316
Lexitron Video Type 1201, 1202, and 1303,
　224
Light pen, 201, 316
Load point marker, 139, 313
Lock codes, 143, 233, 316
Lockheed key-to-disk equipment, 192-193
Log, 233, 316
LOGIC key-to-disk equipment, 192-193
Logical record, 25, 139, 316
Logical unit, 4
Low order position, 27, 316

Machine status, 316
Magnetic card, 222, 316
Magnetic disk, 140-141, 316
Magnetic tape, 137-140, 222, 316
Main storage, 4, 316
Mainline switch, 40
Manager, duties of, 6-7
Manual field, 316
Manual keying, 39, 53, 74, 86-90, 110
Media, 16
Menu, 152, 316
Message line, 150, 155, 184
MICOM 2001 Word Processing
　System, 222
Minicomputer, 201, 316
Mismatch, 97
Mode, 75, 102-103, 123, 154, 157, 172,
　183, 184, 316
Modem (modulator-demodulator), 316
Modulus 10 or 11, 59, 316, 327-328
Mohawk Data Sciences (MDS) Series 21,
　123, 124
Mohawk key-to-disk equipment, 192-193
Mohawk 6415 data recorder, 24
Multi-card layouts, 25

NCR terminals, 212

Network, 316
Nibble, 137, 316
Nine-track tape, 137, 316
96 column card code, 329–330
96 column punched card, 19–22
NIXDORF 80 Series, 151, 183–192
  beginning work, 184–186
  bypassing a field, 188
  deleting a record, 190
  entering data, 187–188
  error recovery, 188
  errors and general procedures, 186–188
  finding records for modification, 188–190
  glossary of operator error messages, 191–192
  inserting a record—all modes, 190
  interrupting a batch, 186
  keyboard, 184
  message line, 184
  modes, 184
  operator log-out, 187
  resuming a batch, 186
  starting a job, 185
  status line, 183–184
  terminating a batch, 186
  updating or correcting a record—all modes, 189–190
  verifying, 190–191
  work initiation or signing ON, 185
Northern Telecom 405 (Old Sycor), 123
North Star Horizon, 224
Numeric fields, 28–29
Numeric keying exercises, 238–241

OBR (optical bar code reader), 231, 316
OCR (optical character reader), 231, 316
Octal, 316, 325
Odd parity, 137, 316
Off-line, 11–12, 316
Off-line field totals, 100
Ohio Scientific Challenger II Series, 224
OMR (optical mark reader), 231, 316
On-line, 11–12, 316
Operating switches, 73
Operational controls personnel, duties of, 7
Operations, 9–13
  abilities needed, 11
  duties of the operator, 10
  job prospects, 10–11
  study guide, 12–13
  work environment, 11–12
Optical bar code, 231, 316
Optical readers, 231, 316
Optical scanning, 316
Output device, 4–5, 6, 222, 316
Overwrite, 316

Paging, 175, 316
Parity bit, 137, 313. See also Check bit
Password, 143, 233, 316
Peripheral device, 141, 316
Peripheral equipment, 10
Perkin-Elmer terminals, 212
Permanent diskette label, 70
Physical record, 139, 316

PL/1 (Programming Language One), 316
Polling, 316
Port, 316
Portable data recorder, 316
Portable key devices, 231
POS (point-of-sale) systems, 231–232
Previous record buffer or storage, 74
Privacy, see Data privacy
Processing in batches, 11–12
Processing device, 222
Production counters, 59
Production statistics, 51
Program, 39, 74, 142–143, 316
Program buffers or storage, 74
Program code, 45, 131–132, 316
Program control, 39, 74
  keying exercises under, 244–312
Program level, 317
Program number, 317
Program sequencing, see Chaining
Programmer, duties of, 6–7
Prompt, 74, 104, 150, 152, 206, 317
Prompting program, 112–114
Proof keyboard, 100
Protected data, 207, 317

Qume printer, 137
QYX Intelligent Typewriter, 223

Ramtek terminals, 212
Random access or direct access, 74, 141, 314
Range, 142
Raytheon key-to-disk equipment, 192–193
Record, 25, 139, 316
Record design, 25–29
Record format, 10, 317
Record insert, 100
Record pooling, 108, 317
Recording media, 10, 317
Registers, 162–163
Response time, 136, 317
Right-hand graphic, 155, 317
Right justified, 27, 317
RJE (remote job entry), 201, 317
Row, 17, 317
Royal SE-6000, 224
RPG II (Report Program Generator, Version II), 123, 317

Savin 950 Veritext, 225
Scientific data processing, 4
Search, 317
Search on content, 99
Search mask, 160, 176, 317
Secondary storage device, 6, 317
Sector, 72, 141, 317
Security, 232, 314
Selectric or ball element, 223
Self-checking number, 99
Self-checking number device, 51. See also Modulus 10 or 11
Sequential processing, 141, 317
Seven-track tape, 137, 317
Siemans Corporation terminals, 212
Sight verification, 144, 317

Smart terminal, 201, 317
Soft copy, 317
Software, 142, 224–226, 317
Source data, 22
Source document, 10, 317
Speaker dependent system, 231
Speaker independent system, 231
Stacker stop switch, 41
Stand-alone, 223
Standard abbreviations:
  list of, 319–322
  state and territory (U.S. Post Office), 319
  street designators and frequently used place names, 320–322
Statistics, 51, 317
Status line, 76, 104, 150, 317
  FOUR PHASE, 170–171
  IBM 3742, 80–82
  NIXDORF 80 Series, 183–184
  TAB 702, 104
  UNIVAC 1900, 153–155
Storage or hold buffer, 74
Systematics General Corporation terminals, 212
Systems analyst, duties of, 6–7

TAB 501 punch/verifier, 63–64
TAB 701, 123
TAB 702 data entry device, 102–122
  chaining, 115
  compared to IBM 3742, 102
  data entry device, 102–103
  data keys, 105–106
  data set label, 104
  disk copy operations, 114
  display screen, 103–104
  error codes and recovery procedures, 115–122
  errors, 108–109
  example to illustrate programmed operations procedure, 111–114
  index track or track zero, 109
  keyboard, 105–108
  keying under program control (program has been loaded), 114
  loading a program from the keyboard, 113–114
  manual keying, 110
  modifying or changing a data set label, 109
  power-on information, 105
  programs, 110–111
  prompting program, 112–113
  searching for records, 114
  second data set label creation procedure, 110
  special function keys, 107
  status line, 104
  storing and loading programs on a diskette, 114
  switches, 106–107
  unloading a diskette, 105
  verifying, 114
Tape, see Magnetic tape
Tape channel, see Track
Tape initialization, 138, 317

Tape label, 138
Tape mark, 317
Temporary adhesive label, 70
Terminal, 317
Terminal Data terminals, 212
Terminals, 201–218
   defined, 200
   IBM 3270 Information Display System, 202–211
   introduction to, 200–202
   other terminal devices, 212
   study guide, 212–218
Text edit, 223, 317
TM (tape mark), 138, 317
Track index, 142
Track or track zero, 72, 82–83, 109, 137, 139, 140, 317
Trail verifying, 144, 317
Trailer label, 138, 317
Transfer rate, 139, 317

Uncorrectable error, 157, 317
Unformatted display, 206, 317
Unique field, 89
Unit record (one record) machines, 25
UNIVAC 1710, 51–60
   advantages of VIP over IBM 129, 52–53
   error corrections, 55
   example to illustrate operations procedures, 56–57
   interpreting, 60
   keyboard, 52
   keying under program control, 57
   load data procedure, 55
   maintenance and unusual conditions, 58–59
   manual keying, 53
   manual keying procedure, 55
   program load procedure, 56–57
   programs, 55–56
   special features, 59–60
   special function keys, 54–55
   special lights, 53–54
   verifying, 57–58
UNIVAC 1810, 60–61
UNIVAC 1900/10, 153–169
   activating a disabled batch, 159
   alarm messages and recovery, 165–169
   closing a batch, 157–158
   displays, 162–163
   error recovery for ENTER, UPDATE, and FILE M modes, 157
   errors and general procedures, 157–159
   interrupting a batch, 158
   keyboard, 155
   key verification, 163–164
   message line, 155
   program level selection, 162
   record insertion, 162
   reopening an interrupted or closed batch, 158
   searching and modifying, 160–162
   sight verification, 164
   status line and video display, 153–155
   updating, 159
   verifying, 163–164
   work initiation, 156
UNIVAC 1900/10 key-to-disk device, 135
UNIVAC 1900/10 Model 3541 key station keypunch style keyboard, 144, 151
UNIVAC UDS 2000 data entry system, 123–124
Unlabeled and labeled tapes, 138
Update, 317

Variable length cards, 51, 59
Variable record length from 1 to 128, 100
Verify, defined, 317
Verifying, 10
   FOUR PHASE, 178–179

IBM 029, 345
IBM 129, 48–50
IBM 3270, 211
IBM 3742, 97–99
   key-to-disk devices, 143–144
   NIXDORF 80 Series, 190–191
   TAB 702, 114
   UNIVAC 1710, 57–58
   UNIVAC 1900, 163–164
Video Data Systems terminals, 212
Virtual storage file (VSAM file), 142
Voice data entry, 231
Voice input, 231, 317
Volker-Craig terminals, 212
Volume, 73, 138, 317–318
Volume label, 73, 138, 141, 318
VTOC (volume table of contents), 141, 318

Wand, 201, 318
WANG Information Systems 130 and 140, 224
WANG WP25, 224
Work environment, 11–12
Word processing and data entry, 221–228, 318
   comparison of, 226
   introduction to, 222–224
   recent equipment developments, 224
   software, 224–226
   study guide, 226–228
Work termination display, 152, 318
WP, see Word processing and data entry
Wrapping around, 206

Zero balancing, 318
Zero filled, 27, 318
ZIP codes, 27
Zone punch, 17, 318